Praise for

THE DEATH AND LIFE OF THE GREAT AMERICAN SCHOOL SYSTEM

segment of professionals who are recognizing that while well-intentioned, NCLB was and remains the wrong path." —*Teacher Librarian*

"Readable, engaging and well referenced . . . This book is garnering considerable attention from the entire political spectrum. Ravitch provides us with fair warning of failed market-based reforms Canadian educational policy makers would be foolish not to heed. Ravitch's book is a worthy read. I highly recommend it for all concerned with public education in Canada." —*Our Schools, Our Selves*

"A devastating critique of the school assessment/accountability movement, with meticulous thoroughness. . . . In the body of *The Death and Life of the Great American School System*, Ravitch meticulously records, analyzes and evaluates the impact of the accountability movement's attempts at 'school reform.' . . . Ravitch seeks for an enriched, vital, and productive school experience that equips students to become effective citizens, capable of high-level work and leadership in civic organizations . . . a valuable, accessible and important contribution to the criticism and analysis of the present trends in American education." —Joel Shatzky, *Jewish Currents*

"This may well be the most important book on education published this year . . . a book hard to put down . . . [an] indispensable book." —*Voice of Reason*

"If you are truly interested in how education can be improved, read *The Death and Life of the Great American School System*." —*Vallejo Times Herald*

"The book functions as an intellectual memoir, explaining her journey and the larger history of the educational reform movement. . . . Ravitch paints a sobering picture of the current mess." —*World Magazine*

"Should be required reading for politicians who are about to destroy public education in New Jersey, and newspaper editors as well." —*The Star-Ledger*

"[A] masterly new book . . . Ravitch has found her new métier as the great critic of new-capitalist school reform in our second Gilded Age." —*The Nation*

"Ravitch combines a compelling mea culpa with clear analysis to demolish each and every assumption behind what passes for school reform today . . . there is something extremely rewarding about reading this book . . . you should read Diane Ravitch's book—right away. It is well written, it is relentless, and because it's penned by a once-leading voice behind the policies the book itself criticizes, it is extremely valuable." —*International Socialist Review*

"An urgent warning of impending danger. With the nation's educational system at greater risk than ever, it should be required reading for every school administrator and school board member in the United States." —Roger Bortz, ScienceShelf.com

"A sincere mea culpa. Admirably, she tells us that she took John Maynard Keynes' advice: 'When the facts change, I change my mind.'" —*Social Education*

"This is a rich book and a deep topic. . . . Ravitch is deeply worried, troubled even, by the market-based reforms and high-stakes testing that are dominating education today. . . . All this is not new to opponents of No Child Left Behind and the Obama administration's Race to the Top efforts. But in Ravitch's retelling there is a melancholy that is rich. Here is a fierce advocate now wise and sad for the fight and the time lost." —*Brooklyn Rail*

"A sobering narrative by a former advocate of choice and market-inspired educational reforms who had the courage to change her mind." —*Science*

"Ravitch urges us to rethink such tests as a part of public education. Further, she calls for school curriculum to improve. Ravitch wants school time for students to study art, history, literature and science. We ignore her at their—and our—peril." —*Sacramento News & Review*

"With the nation's educational system at even greater risk than it was in 1983, Ravitch's powerful warning should be required reading for every school administrator and school board member in the United States." —*Dallas Morning News*

"A must-read for anyone concerned about the current condition of American pre-college public education." —*Silver City Sun-News*

"With the nation's educational system at even greater risk than it was in 1983, Ravitch's powerful warning should be required reading for every school administrator and school-board member." —*Seattle Times*

"Ravitch is a talented writer who makes complex cultural and political entanglements easy for the lay reader to follow." —*New York Journal of Books*

"The eminent historian Diane Ravitch considers, as so many others have, how to mend the nation's rickety education apparatus. But *Death and Life* cannot be filed away as just another volume on the endless shelf of broken-schools literature, for it also marks a major authorial about-face." —*Commentary* magazine

"Perhaps most important (because practically no one else has dared), Ravitch analyzes the imperious role played by the super-sized private funders of school reform—the Eli and Edythe Broad Foundation, the Walton Family Foundation, and especially the Bill & Melinda Gates Foundation. *Death and Life* serves as a guide—comprehensive, well documented, and disturbing—to the transformation of public education in America today." —*Dissent*

"*The Death and Life of the Great American School System* leaves virtually no educational icon unscathed. . . . Ravitch concludes her terrific and timely book with a plea that the best way to enhance education is to rescue the curriculum from the culture wars, set rigorous statewide or national standards for content, and improve the conditions in which teachers work and students learn." —*WBUR.org*

"Ravitch's hopeful vision is of a national curriculum—she's had enough of fly-by-night methods and unchallenging requirements. She's impatient with education that is not personally transformative. She believes there is experience and knowledge of art, literature, history, science, and math that every public school graduate should have." —*Christian Science Monitor*

"The book intelligently and readably addresses today's education controversies, using a combination of anecdotes, case studies, and statistics. . . . It's a must-read for education policymakers at all levels of government." —*National Review*

"I hope in this review I have convinced you of the importance and the power of this book. It is yet another book about which I can say that anyone concerned about public schools should read—or in this case, devour. It is that good, that rich, that important." —*DailyKos*

THE DEATH AND LIFE OF THE GREAT

AMERICAN
SCHOOL SYSTEM

Also by Diane Ravitch

AUTHOR

Edspeak: A Glossary of Education Terms, Phrases, Buzzwords, and Jargon
*The Language Police: How Pressure Groups Restrict What Students
    Learn*
Left Back: A Century of Failed School Reforms
National Standards in American Education: A Citizen's Guide
*The Schools We Deserve: Reflections on the Educational Crisis of Our
    Times*
The Troubled Crusade: American Education, 1945–1980
The Revisionists Revised: A Critique of the Radical Attack on the Schools
The Great School Wars: New York City, 1805–1973

COAUTHOR

*What Do Our 17-Year-Olds Know? A Report on the First National
    Assessment of History and Literature*

EDITOR

*Debating the Future of American Education: Do We Need National
    Standards and Assessments?*
The American Reader
Brookings Papers on Education Policy

COEDITOR

The English Reader
Kid Stuff: Marketing Sex and Violence to America's Children
Making Good Citizens: Education and Civil Society
City Schools: Lessons from New York
New Schools for a New Century: The Redesign of Urban Education
Learning from the Past: What History Teaches Us about School Reform
The Democracy Reader
Challenges to the Humanities
Educating an Urban People: The New York City Experience
*Against Mediocrity: Improving the Teaching of the Humanities in
    America's High Schools*
*The School and the City: Community Studies in the History of American
    Education*

THE DEATH AND LIFE OF THE GREAT

AMERICAN
SCHOOL SYSTEM

How Testing and Choice
Are Undermining Education

REVISED AND EXPANDED EDITION

DIANE RAVITCH

BASIC BOOKS

A Member of the Perseus Books Group

New York

Books published by Basic Books are available at special discounts for bulk purchases
in the United States by corporations, institutions, and other organizations. For more
information, please contact the Special Markets Department at the Perseus Books
Group, 2300 Chestnut Street, Suite 200, Philadelphia, PA 19103, or call
(800) 810-4145, ext. 5000, or e-mail special.markets@perseusbooks.com.

Designed by Pauline Brown

The Library of Congress has catalogued the hardcover as follows:

Ravitch, Diane.
The death and life of the great American school system : how testing and choice are
undermining education / Diane Ravitch.
    p. cm.
Includes bibliographical references and index.
ISBN 978-0-465-01491-0 (alk. paper)
1. Public schools—United States. 2. Educational accountability—United States.
3. Educational tests and measurements—United States. 4. School choice—United
States. I. Title.
LA217.2.R38 2009
379.1—dc22
                              2009050406

ISBN: 978-0-465-02557-2 (paperback)
ISBN: 978-0-465-02821-4 (e-book)

10 9 8 7 6

*This book is dedicated
with love to my grandchildren
Nico Zev
Aidan Thor
Elijah Lev*

Contents

Acknowledgments

I HAVE BEEN FORTUNATE in having the help of many readers who offered their comments as the book evolved. Individual chapters, and in some cases, the entire book, were read by Samuel Abrams, Linda Darling-Hammond, Matthew Di Carlo, Michael J. Feuer, Leonie Haimson, E. D. Hirsch Jr., Rita Kramer, Henry Levin, Jeffrey Mirel, Aaron Pallas, Linda Perlstein, Robert Pondiscio, Michael Ravitch, Sarah Reckhow, Richard Rothstein, Robert Shepherd, Lorraine Skeen, Sol Stern, and Andrew Wolf. Jordan Segall and Jennifer Jennings assisted me in interpreting demographic data. Of course, none of these individuals is responsible in any way for my conclusions or errors.

In pursuing information, I was helped by many people, including Anthony Alvarado, Elizabeth Arons, Jennifer Bell-Ellwanger, Kenneth J. Bernstein, Alan Bersin, Andrew Beveridge, Jonathan Burman, Sheila Byrd, David Cantor, Kathleen Cashin, Carl Cohn, John de Beck, Carmen Fariña, David Ferrero, Eric Hanushek, Jeffrey Henig, Frederick Hess, Sam Houston, Dan Katzir, Richard Kessler, Mitz Lee, Robert Linn, Tom Loveless, Karen Hawley Miles, Howard Nelson, Michael Petrilli, Margaret Raymond, Bella Rosenberg, Anthony Shorris, Jacques Steinberg, Nancy Van Meter, Robin Whitlow, Joe Williams, Frances O'Neill Zimmerman, and Camille Zombro.

Barbara Bartholomew was my interlocutor in San Diego, hauling me to appointments, helping me digest what I learned, and generally keeping me on task as I interviewed teachers, administrators, and district officials.

I was fortunate to have Diana Senechal as research assistant and editor in the final stages of revising the manuscript. She made sure that every word was just right, every footnote was accurate, every URL worked, the grammar and usage were correct, and the language flowed as it was supposed to. I can never thank her enough for the time that she enthusiastically invested in this book, other than to acknowledge it here.

For supporting my research, I thank the William E. Simon Foundation and the Achelis-Bodman Foundation.

I am thankful for the friendship of inspiring mentors, past and present, including Jeanne S. Chall, Lawrence A. Cremin, E. D. Hirsch Jr., Sandra Priest Rose, and Albert Shanker.

My deepest gratitude goes to my friend, colleague, and partner, Mary Butz, who encouraged me as I wrote this book. I have been informed by her practical wisdom and experience, based on her thirty-five years in the classroom as a teacher, principal, and mentor to other principals. She enabled me to see the many challenges that educators face daily and to understand how difficult it is to open a new school and how important it is to create a positive and caring school culture.

I thank my energetic literary agent, Lynn Chu of Writers Representatives, who believed in this project from the beginning. John Sherer, publisher of Basic Books, has been an enthusiastic supporter of the book, for which I am grateful. Many thanks to Meredith Smith, Antoinette Smith, and Kärstin Painter of Basic Books for their careful review of the manuscript, and to Lynn Goldberg and Angela Hayes of Goldberg-McDuffie, who were steadfast allies. And I am grateful to Tim Sullivan, my editor at Basic Books, who quickly understood the book and suggested the title of my dreams. We both agreed that the title is a fitting homage to Jane Jacobs, whose book *The Death and Life of Great American Cities* helped to create a renaissance in the nation's cities. Since I live the life that she wrote about, in a wonderful urban neighborhood saved by historic preservation, I love the idea of associating my book with hers, most especially with the hope that American education in general and urban education in particular might also experience a renaissance.

DIANE RAVITCH
BROOKLYN, NEW YORK

CHAPTER ONE

What I Learned About School Reform

In the fall of 2007, I reluctantly decided to have my office repainted. It was inconvenient. I work at home, on the top floor of a nineteenth-century brownstone in Brooklyn. Not only did I have to stop working for three weeks, but I had the additional burden of packing up and removing everything in my office. I had to relocate fifty boxes of books and files to other rooms in the house until the painting job was complete.

After the patching, plastering, and painting was done, I began unpacking twenty years of papers and books, discarding those I no longer wanted, and placing articles into scrapbooks. You may wonder what all this mundane stuff has to do with my life in the education field. I found that the chore of reorganizing the artifacts of my professional life was pleasantly ruminative. It had a tonic effect, because it allowed me to reflect on the changes in my views over the years.

At the very time that I was packing up my books and belongings, I was going through an intellectual crisis. I was aware that I had undergone a wrenching transformation in my perspective on school reform. Where once I had been hopeful, even enthusiastic, about the potential benefits of testing, accountability, choice, and markets, I now found myself experiencing profound doubts about these same ideas. I was trying to sort through the evidence about what was working and what was not. I was trying to understand why

I was increasingly skeptical about these reforms, reforms that I had supported enthusiastically. I was trying to see my way through the blinding assumptions of ideology and politics, including my own.

I kept asking myself why I was losing confidence in these reforms. My answer: I have a right to change my mind. Fair enough. But why, I kept wondering, why had I changed my mind? What was the compelling evidence that prompted me to reevaluate the policies I had endorsed many times over the previous decade? Why did I now doubt ideas I once had advocated?

The short answer is that my views changed as I saw how these ideas were working out in reality. The long answer is what will follow in the rest of this book. When someone chastised John Maynard Keynes for reversing himself about a particular economic policy he had previously endorsed, he replied, "When the facts change, I change my mind. What do you do, sir?"[1] This comment may or may not be apocryphal, but I admire the thought behind it. It is the mark of a sentient human being to learn from experience, to pay close attention to how theories work out when put into practice.

What should we think of someone who never admits error, never entertains doubt but adheres unflinchingly to the same ideas all his life, regardless of new evidence? Doubt and skepticism are signs of rationality. When we are too certain of our opinions, we run the risk of ignoring any evidence that conflicts with our views. It is doubt that shows we are still thinking, still willing to reexamine hardened beliefs when confronted with new facts and new evidence.

The task of sorting my articles gave me the opportunity to review what I had written at different times, beginning in the mid-1960s. As I flipped from article to article, I kept asking myself, how far had I strayed from where I started? Was it like me to shuffle off ideas like an ill-fitting coat? As I read and skimmed and remembered, I began to see two themes at the center of what I have been writing for more than four decades. One constant has been my skepticism about pedagogical fads, enthusiasms, and movements. The other has been a deep belief in the value of a rich, coherent school curriculum, especially in history and literature, both of which are so frequently ignored, trivialized, or politicized.[2]

Over the years, I have consistently warned against the lure of "the royal road to learning," the notion that some savant or organization has found an easy solution to the problems of American education. As a historian of education, I have often studied the rise and fall of grand ideas that were promoted as the sure cure for whatever ills were afflicting our schools and students. In 1907, William Chandler Bagley complained about the "fads and reforms that sweep through the educational system at periodic intervals." A few years later, William Henry Maxwell, the esteemed superintendent of schools in New York City, heaped scorn on educational theorists who promoted their panaceas to gullible teachers; one, he said, insisted that "vertical penmanship" was the answer to all problems; another maintained that recess was a "relic of barbarism." Still others wanted to ban spelling and grammar to make school more fun.[3] I have tried to show in my work the persistence of our national infatuation with fads, movements, and reforms, which invariably distract us from the steadiness of purpose needed to improve our schools.

In our own day, policymakers and business leaders have eagerly enlisted in a movement launched by free-market advocates, with the support of major foundations. Many educators have their doubts about the slogans and cure-alls of our time, but they are required to follow the mandates of federal law (such as No Child Left Behind) despite their doubts.

School reformers sometimes resemble the characters in Dr. Seuss's *Solla Sollew,* who are always searching for that mythical land "where they never have troubles, at least very few." Or like Dumbo, they are convinced they could fly if only they had a magic feather. In my writings, I have consistently warned that, in education, there are no shortcuts, no utopias, and no silver bullets. For certain, there are no magic feathers that enable elephants to fly.

As I flipped through the yellowing pages in my scrapbooks, I started to understand the recent redirection of my thinking, my growing doubt regarding popular proposals for choice and accountability. Once again, I realized, I was turning skeptical in response to panaceas and miracle cures. The only difference was that in this case, I too had fallen for the latest panaceas and miracle cures; I too had drunk deeply of the elixir that promised a quick fix to intractable problems. I too had jumped aboard a bandwagon, one festooned with banners celebrating the power of accountability, incentives, and markets. I too was captivated by these ideas. They promised to end bureaucracy, to ensure that poor children were not neglected, to empower poor parents, to enable poor children to escape failing schools, and to close the achievement gap between rich and poor, black and white. Testing would shine a spotlight on low-performing schools, and choice would create opportunities for poor kids to leave for better schools. All of this seemed to make sense, but there was little empirical evidence, just promise and hope. I wanted to share the promise and the hope. I wanted to believe that choice and accountability would produce great results. But over time, I was persuaded by accumulating evidence that the latest reforms were not likely to live up to their promise. The more I saw, the more I lost the faith.

It seemed, therefore, that it would be instructive to take a fresh look at the reform strategies that are now so prominent in American education and to review the evidence of their effectiveness. This book is my opportunity to explain what I have learned about school reform and also to suggest, with (I hope) a certain degree of modesty and full acknowledgment of my own frailties and errors, what is needed to move American education in the right direction.

THE FIRST ARTICLE I EVER WROTE about education was published in a small (and now defunct) education journal called the *Urban Review* in 1968. Its title—"Programs, Placebos, Panaceas"—signaled what turned out to be a constant preoccupation for me, the conflict between promise and reality, between utopian hopes and knotty problems. I reviewed short-term compensatory education programs—that is, short-term interventions to help kids who were far behind—and concluded that "only sustained quality education makes a difference." My second article, titled "Foundations: Playing God in the Ghetto" (1969), discussed the Ford Foundation's role in the protracted controversy over decentralization and community control that led to months of turmoil in the public schools of New York City.[4] This question—the extent to which it is appropriate for a mega-rich foundation to take charge of reforming public schools, even though it is accountable to no one and elected by no one—will be treated in this book. The issue is especially important today, because some of the nation's largest foundations are promoting school reforms based on principles drawn from the corporate sector, without considering whether they are appropriate for educational institutions.

In the late 1960s, the issue of decentralization versus centralization turned into a heated battle. Newspapers featured daily stories about community groups demanding decentralization of the schools and blaming teachers and administrators for the school system's lack of success with minority children. Many school reformers then assumed that African American and Hispanic parents and local community leaders, not professional educators, knew best what their children needed.

As the clamor to decentralize the school system grew, I became curious about why the system had been centralized in the first place. I spent many days in the New-York Historical Society library studying the history of the city's school system; the last such history had been published in 1905. I discovered that the system had been decentralized in the nineteenth century. The school reformers of the 1890s demanded centralization as an antidote to low-performing schools and advocated control by professionals as the cure for the incompetence and corruption of local school boards. As I read, I was struck by the ironic contrast between the reformers' demands in the 1890s for centralization and the reformers' demands in the 1960s for decentralization. The earlier group consisted mainly of social elites, the latter of parents and activists who wanted local control of the schools.

So intrigued was I by the contrast between past and present that I determined to write a history of the New York City public schools, which became *The Great School Wars: New York City, 1805–1973*.[5] This was quite a challenge for someone who had graduated from the Houston public schools and—at that time—had no advanced degrees in history or education. As I was completing the book, I earned a doctorate from Columbia University in the history of American education, and the book became my dissertation. While writing and pursuing my graduate studies, I worked under the tutelage of Lawrence Cremin, the greatest historian of American education of his era.

In the mid-1970s, Cremin persuaded me to write a critique of a group of leftist historians who attacked the underpinnings of public schooling. They called themselves revisionists, because they set themselves the goal of demolishing what they saw as a widespread myth about the benevolent purposes and democratic accomplishments of public education. The authors, all of them professors at various universities, treated the public schools scornfully as institutions devised by elites to oppress the poor. This point of view was so contrary to my own understanding of the liberating role of public education—not only in my own life but also in the life of the nation—that I felt compelled to refute it.

The resulting book was called *The Revisionists Revised: A Critique of the Radical Attack on the Schools*.[6] In that book, I defended the democratic, civic purposes of public schooling. I argued that the public schools had not been devised by scheming capitalists to impose "social control" on an unwilling proletariat or to reproduce social inequality; the schools were never an instrument of cultural repression, as the radical critics claimed. Instead, I held, they are a primary mechanism through which a democratic society gives its citizens the opportunity to attain literacy and social mobility. Opportunity leaves much to individuals; it is not a guarantee of certain success. The schools cannot solve all our social problems, nor are they perfect. But in a democratic society, they are necessary and valuable for individuals and for the commonweal.

My next book was a history of national education policy from 1945 to 1980, an era notable for major court decisions and federal legislation. In *The Troubled Crusade: American Education, 1945–1980*, I analyzed the many fascinating controversies associated with McCarthyism, progressive education, the civil rights movement, bilingual education, the women's movement, and other social and political upheavals.[7]

While writing *The Troubled Crusade*, I became increasingly interested in issues related to the quality of the curriculum. I began studying the history of pedagogy, curriculum, and standards, especially the teaching of literature and history and the representation of our culture in schools. In 1987, I coauthored a book with my friend Chester E. (Checker) Finn Jr. called *What Do Our 17-Year-Olds Know?* which reported on the first federal test of history and literature. We lamented what seemed to be a loss of cultural memory, a position that hit a public nerve but was scorned in the academic world, which was then caught up in postmodernism and a revolt against "the canon." Our view was that you can't reject the canon if you have no knowledge of it.[8]

In 1985, California State Superintendent Bill Honig invited me to help write a new history curriculum for the state. Over a two-year period, I worked closely with teachers and scholars to draft a curriculum framework that integrated history with literature, geography, the arts, social sciences, and humanities. With this framework, California would become the first state to require all students to study three years of world history and three years of U.S. history, with a substantial infusion of history and biography in the elementary grades. The framework was adopted by the State Board of Education in 1987 and remains in place to this day with only minor revisions to update it. Over the past two decades, the state of California replaced its reading curriculum, its mathematics curriculum, and its science curriculum, but the history curriculum—touching on some of the most sensitive and controversial topics and events in American and world history—endured.[9]

I had not, to this point in my life, given much thought to issues of choice, markets, or accountability.

Then something unexpected happened: I received a telephone call in the spring of 1991 from President George H. W. Bush's newly appointed education secretary, Lamar Alexander. Alexander, a moderate Republican, had been governor of Tennessee. The secretary invited me to come to Washington to chat with him and his deputy David Kearns, who had recently been the chief executive officer of Xerox. We met for lunch at the elegant Hay-Adams Hotel, near the White House. We talked about curriculum and standards (Secretary Alexander later joked that I talked and he listened), and at the end of lunch he asked me to join the department as assistant secretary in charge of the Office of Educational Research and Improvement and as his counselor.

I went home to Brooklyn to think about it. I was a registered Democrat, always had been, and had never dreamed of working in a government job, let alone a Republican administration. I had no desire to leave Brooklyn or to abandon my life as a scholar. And yet I was intrigued by the thought of working in the federal government. Surely education was a nonpartisan issue, or so I then imagined. I decided that this would be a wonderful opportunity to perform public service, learn about federal politics, and do something totally different. I said yes, was confirmed by the Senate, moved to Washington, and spent the next eighteen months as assistant secretary and counselor to the secretary in the U.S. Department of Education.

During my time at the department, I took the lead on issues having to do with curriculum and standards. The federal government is prohibited by law from imposing any curriculum on states or school districts. Nonetheless, my agency used its very small allotment of discretionary funds (about $10 million) to make grants to consortia of educators to develop "voluntary national standards" in every academic subject. Our assumption was that so long as the standards were developed by independent professional groups and were voluntary, we were not violating the legal prohibition against imposing curriculum on states and school districts. And so we funded the development of voluntary national standards in history, the arts, geography, civics, science, economics, foreign languages, and English. We did this energetically but without specific congressional authorization; the absence of authorization unfortunately lessened the projects' credibility and longevity.

The Department of Education was committed to both standards and choice (choice was even higher on the agenda of Republicans than standards, because Republicans generally opposed national standards, which suggested federal meddling). At meetings of top staff in the department, I sat in on many discussions of school choice in which the question was not whether to support choice, but how to do so. The issue of choice had never been important to me, but I found myself trying to incorporate the arguments for choice into my own worldview. I reasoned that standards would be even more necessary in a society that used public dollars to promote school choice. The more varied the schools, the more important it would be to have common standards to judge whether students were learning. I began to sympathize with the argument for letting federal dollars follow poor students to the school of their choice. If kids were not succeeding in their regular public school, why not let them take their federal funds to another public school or to a private—even religious— school? Since affluent families could choose their schools by moving to a better neighborhood or enrolling their children in private schools, why shouldn't poor families have similar choices?

In the decade following my stint in the federal government, I argued that certain managerial and structural changes—that is, choice, charters, merit pay, and accountability—would help to reform our schools. With such changes, teachers and schools would be judged by their performance; this was a basic principle in the business world. Schools that failed to perform would be closed, just as a corporation would close a branch office that continually produced poor returns. Having been immersed in a world of true believers, I was influenced by their ideas. I became persuaded that the business-minded thinkers were onto something important. Their proposed reforms were meant to align public education with the practices of modern, flexible, high-performance organizations and to enable American education to make the transition from the industrial age to the postindustrial age. In the 1990s, I found myself in step with people who quoted Peter Drucker and other management gurus. I dropped casual references to "total quality management" and the Baldridge Award, both of which I learned about by listening to David Kearns during my stint in the Department of Education.

During this time, I wrote many articles advocating structural innovations. In the past, I would have cast a cold eye on efforts to "reinvent the schools" or to "break the mold," but now I supported bold attempts to remake the schools, such as charter schools, privatization, and specialized schools of all kinds. I maintained that we should celebrate the creation of good schools, no matter what form they took or who developed them.

Both the Bush administration and the Clinton administration advocated market reforms for the public sector, including deregulation and privatization. Bill Clinton and the New Democrats championed a "third way" between the orthodox policies of the left and the right. People in both parties quoted *Reinventing Government* by David Osborne and Ted Gaebler as a guide to cutting down bureaucracy and injecting entrepreneurship into government.[10] Months after his inauguration, President Clinton tasked Vice President Al Gore to devise ways to "reinvent" the federal bureaucracy, and he did. With the help of David Osborne, Gore created the National Partnership for Reinventing Government, whose purpose was to adapt private sector management techniques to the public sector. Many of its recommendations involved privatizing, cutting jobs, and implementing performance agreements in which agencies would receive autonomy from regulations in exchange for meeting targets.[11]

Similar ideas began to percolate in the world of public education. The new thinking—now ensconced in both parties—saw the public school system as obsolete, because it is controlled by the government and burdened by bureaucracy. Government-run schools, said a new generation of reformers, are ineffective because they are a monopoly; as such, they have no incentive to do better, and they serve the interests of adults who work in the system, not children. Democrats saw an opportunity to reinvent government; Republicans, a chance to diminish the power of the teachers' unions, which, in their view, protect jobs and pensions while blocking effective management and innovation.

This convergence explained the bipartisan appeal of charter schools. Why shouldn't schools be managed by anyone who could supply good schools, using government funds? Free of direct government control, the schools would be innovative, hire only the best teachers, get rid of incompetent teachers, set their own pay scales, compete for students (customers), and be judged solely by their results (test scores and graduation rates). Good schools under private management would proliferate, while bad schools would be closed down by market forces (the exit of disgruntled parents) or by a watchful government. Some of the new generation of reformers—mainly Republicans, but not only Republicans—imagined that the schools of the future would function without unions, allowing management to hire and fire personnel at will. With the collapse of Communism and the triumph of market reforms in most parts of the world, it did not seem to be much of a stretch to envision the application of the market model to schooling.

Like many others in that era, I was attracted to the idea that the market would unleash innovation and bring greater efficiencies to education. I was certainly influenced by the conservative ideology of other top-level officials in the first Bush administration, who were strong supporters of school choice and competition. But of equal importance, I believe, I began to think like a policymaker, especially a federal policymaker. That meant, in the words of a book by James C. Scott that I later read and admired, I began "seeing like a state," looking at schools and teachers and students from an altitude of 20,000 feet and seeing them as objects to be moved around by big ideas and great plans.[12]

Anyone who is a policymaker, aspires to be a policymaker, or wants to influence policymakers must engage in "seeing like a state." It is inevitable. Policymaking requires one to make decisions that affect people's lives without their having a chance to cast a vote. If no one thought like a state, there would probably be no highways or public works of any kind. Those who make the most noise would veto almost everything. It is the job of representative government to make decisions without seeking a majority vote from their constituents on every single question. Anyone who recommends a change of federal or state policy engages in "seeing like a state." Improvement also depends on having a mix of views and new ideas to prevent the status quo from becoming ossified. Those who make policy are most successful when they must advance their ideas through a gauntlet of checks and balances, explaining their plans, submitting them to a process of public review, and attempting to persuade others to support them. If the policymaker cannot persuade others, then his plans will not be implemented. That's democracy.

How can I distinguish between thinking like a historian and seeing like a state? A historian tries to understand what happened, why it happened, what was the context, who did what, and what assumptions led them to act as they did. A historian customarily displays a certain diffidence about trying to influence events, knowing that unanticipated developments often lead to unintended consequences. A policymaker, on the other hand, is required to plan for the future and make bets about a course of action that is likely to bring about improvements. Policymakers have a theory of action, even if they can't articulate it, and they implement plans based on their theory of action, their guess about how the world works. Historians are trained to recognize assumptions and theories and to spot their flaws.

Market reforms have a certain appeal to some of those who are accustomed to "seeing like a state." There is something comforting about the belief that the invisible hand of the market, as Adam Smith called it, will bring improvements through some unknown force. In education, this belief in market forces lets us ordinary mortals off the hook, especially those who have not figured out how to improve low-performing schools or to break through the lassitude of unmotivated teens. Instead of dealing with rancorous problems like how to teach reading or how to improve testing, one can redesign the management and structure of the school system and concentrate on incentives and sanctions. One need not know anything about children or education. The lure of the market is the idea that freedom from government regulation is a solution all by itself. This is very appealing, especially when so many seemingly well-planned school reforms have failed to deliver on their promise.

The new corporate reformers betray their weak comprehension of education by drawing false analogies between education and business. They think they can fix education by applying the principles of business, organization, management, law, and marketing and by developing a good data-collection system that provides the information necessary to incentivize the workforce—principals, teachers, and students—with appropriate rewards and sanctions. Like these reformers, I wrote and spoke with conviction in the 1990s and early 2000s about what was needed to reform public education, and many of my ideas coincided with theirs.

I have long been allied with conservative scholars and organizations. My scholarly work at Teachers College and later at New York University was supported by conservative foundations, principally the John M. Olin Foundation, which never sought to influence anything I wrote. My close friend Checker Finn took over the helm of the Thomas B. Fordham Foundation in 1996, and I was a member of its board until 2009. We previously worked together as organizers of the Educational Excellence Network in 1981, which advocated for a solid curriculum and high standards.

In 1999, I became a founding member of the Koret Task Force at the Hoover Institution at Stanford University; the task force supports education reforms based on the principles of standards, accountability, and choice. Most of the members of the task force are forceful advocates of school choice and accountability. John Chubb and Terry Moe wrote a highly successful book promoting choice. Caroline Hoxby, Eric Hanushek, Paul Peterson, Paul Hill, Checker Finn, Bill Evers, and Herbert Walberg are well-known scholars and/ or advocates of choice, competition, and accountability. In a debate at Hoover, Don Hirsch and I argued against Hoxby and Peterson that curriculum and instruction were more important than markets and choice.[13] I enjoyed the camaraderie of the group, and I loved the intellectual stimulation I encountered at the Hoover Institution. But over time I realized that I was no longer fully supportive of the task force's aims. When I told my colleagues that I felt I had to leave, they urged me to stay and debate with them. I did for a time, but in April 2009 I resigned.

I grew increasingly disaffected from both the choice movement and the accountability movement. I was beginning to see the downside of both and to understand that they were not solutions to our educational dilemmas. As I watched both movements gain momentum across the nation, I concluded that curriculum and instruction were far more important than choice and accountability. I feared that choice would let thousands of flowers bloom but would not strengthen American education. It might even harm the public schools by removing the best students from schools in the poorest neighborhoods. I was also concerned that accountability, now a shibboleth that everyone applauds, had become mechanistic and even antithetical to good education. Testing, I realized with dismay, had become a central preoccupation in the schools and was not just a measure but an end in itself. I came to believe that accountability, as written into federal law, was not raising standards but dumbing down the schools as states and districts strived to meet unrealistic targets.

The more uneasy I grew with the agenda of choice and accountability, the more I realized that I am too "conservative" to embrace an agenda whose end result is entirely speculative and uncertain. The effort to upend American public education and replace it with something market-based began to feel too radical for me. I concluded that I could not countenance any reforms that might have the effect—intended or unintended—of undermining public education. Paradoxically, it was my basic conservatism about values, traditions, communities, and institutions that made me back away from what once was considered the conservative agenda but has now become the bipartisan agenda in education.

Before long, I found that I was reverting to my once familiar pattern as a friend and supporter of public education. Over time, my doubts about accountability and choice deepened as I saw the negative consequences of their implementation.

As I went back to work in my freshly painted office and reviewed the historical record of my intellectual wanderings, deviations, and transgressions, I decided to write about what I had learned. I needed to explain why I had returned to my roots as a partisan of American public education. I wanted to describe where we have gone astray in our pursuit of worthy goals. We as a society cannot extricate ourselves from fads and nostrums unless we carefully look at how we got entangled in them. We will continue to chase rainbows unless we recognize that they are rainbows and there is no pot of gold at the end of them. We certainly cannot address our problems unless we are willing to examine the evidence about proposed solutions, without fear, favor, or preconceptions.

It is time, I think, for those who want to improve our schools to focus on the essentials of education. We must make sure that our schools have a strong, coherent, explicit curriculum that is grounded in the liberal arts and sciences, with plenty of opportunity for children to engage in activities and projects that make learning lively. We must ensure that students gain the knowledge they need to understand political debates, scientific phenomena, and the world they live in. We must be sure they are prepared for the responsibilities of democratic citizenship in a complex society. We must take care that our teachers are well educated, not just well trained. We must be sure that schools have the authority to maintain both standards of learning and standards of behavior.

In this book, I will describe the evidence that changed my views about reforms that once seemed promising. I will explain why I have concluded that most of the reform strategies that school districts, state officials, the Congress, and federal officials are pursuing, that mega-rich foundations are supporting, and that editorial boards are applauding are mistaken. I will attempt to explain how these mistaken policies are corrupting educational values. I will describe the policies that I believe are necessary ingredients in a good system of public education. I will not claim that my ideas will solve all our problems all at once and forever. I will not offer a silver bullet or a magic feather. I do claim, however, that we must preserve American public education, because it is so intimately connected to our concepts of citizenship and democracy and to the promise of American life. In view of the money and power now arrayed on behalf of the ideas and programs that I will criticize, I hope it is not too late.

CHAPTER TWO

Hijacked! How the Standards Movement Turned Into the Testing Movement

IN THE FIRST DECADE of the twenty-first century, the leading reform ideas in American education were accountability and choice. These ideas were at the heart of President George W. Bush's No Child Left Behind program, which he signed into law in January 2002. No Child Left Behind—or NCLB—changed the nature of public schooling across the nation by making standardized test scores the primary measure of school quality. The rise or fall of test scores in reading and mathematics became the critical variable in judging students, teachers, principals, and schools. Missing from NCLB was any reference to what students should learn; this was left to each state to determine.

I was initially supportive of NCLB. Who could object to ensuring that children mastered the basic skills of reading and mathematics? Who could object to an annual test of those skills? Certainly not I. Didn't all schools test their students at least once annually?

As NCLB was implemented, I became increasingly disillusioned. I came to realize that the law bypassed curriculum and standards. Although its supporters often claimed it was a natural outgrowth of the standards movement, it was not. It demanded that schools generate higher test scores in basic skills, but it required no curriculum at all, nor did it raise standards. It ignored such important studies as history, civics, literature, science, the arts, and geography. Though the law required states to test students eventually in science, the science scores didn't count on the federal scorecard. I saw my hopes for better education turn into a measurement strategy that had no underlying educational vision at all. Eventually I realized that the new reforms had everything to do with structural changes and accountability, and nothing at all to do with the substance of learning. Accountability makes no sense when it undermines the larger goals of education.

How did testing and accountability become the main levers of school reform? How did our elected officials become convinced that measurement and data would fix the schools? Somehow our nation got off track in its efforts to improve education. What once was the standards movement was replaced by the accountability movement. What once was an effort to improve the quality of education turned into an accounting strategy: Measure, then punish or reward. No education experience was needed to administer such a program. Anyone who loved data could do it. The strategy produced fear and obedience among educators; it often generated higher test scores. But it had nothing to do with education.

Tests should follow the curriculum. They should be based on the curriculum. They should not replace it or precede it. Students need a coherent foundation of knowledge and skills that grows stronger each year. Knowledge and skills are both important, as is learning to think, debate, and question. A well-educated person has a well-furnished mind, shaped by reading and thinking about history, science, literature, the arts, and politics. The well-educated person has learned how to explain ideas and listen respectfully to others.

In the 1980s and early 1990s, efforts to revive liberal education in the schools seemed to be gaining ground; many states were reviewing their academic expectations with an eye to strengthening them in all grades. In 1991 and 1992, the agency that I headed in the U.S. Department of Education awarded grants to consortia of professional groups of teachers and scholars to develop voluntary national standards in history, English language arts, science, civics, economics, the arts, foreign languages, geography, and physical education.[1] I acted at the direction of Secretary Lamar Alexander, who believed as I did that all children should have access to a broad education in the arts and sciences.

The efforts to establish voluntary national standards fell apart in the fall of 1994, when Lynne V. Cheney attacked the not-yet-released history standards for their political bias. As chairperson of the National Endowment for the Humanities, Cheney had funded their development along with the Department of Education. Cheney's scathing critique in the *Wall Street Journal* opened up a bitter national argument about what history, or rather, *whose* history, should be taught.[2]

Cheney lambasted the standards as the epitome of left-wing political correctness, because they emphasized the nation's failings and paid scant attention to its great men. The standards document, she said, mentioned Joseph McCarthy and McCarthyism nineteen times, the Ku Klux Klan seventeen times, and Harriet Tubman six times, while mentioning Ulysses S. Grant just once and Robert E. Lee not at all. Nor was there any reference to Paul Revere, Alexander Graham Bell, Thomas Edison, Jonas Salk, or the Wright brothers. Cheney told an interviewer that the document was a "warped and distorted version of the American past in which it becomes a story of oppression and failure."[3]

Editorialists and radio talk shows across the country weighed in on the dispute, some siding with Cheney, others defending the standards. Every major newspaper and newsmagazine covered the story of the angry ideological conflict. The controversy quickly became a debate about the role of minority groups and women in American history, which was placed in opposition to the role of great white men. Radio host Rush Limbaugh said the standards should be "flushed down the toilet," but they were endorsed by many editorial boards and historians.[4]

Unfortunately, the historians at the University of California at Los Angeles who supervised the writing of the history standards did not anticipate that their political views and their commitment to teaching social history through the lens of race, class, and gender would encounter resistance outside the confines of academe. They insisted that their critics were narrow-minded conservatives who opposed the standards' efforts to open American history to a diversity of cultures.

Meanwhile, in D.C., the administration changed from George H. W. Bush to Bill Clinton, and in the turnover, there was no provision for oversight of the standards, no process by which they might be reviewed and revised, again and again, to remove any hint of political bias. After Cheney raised a ruckus about the history standards, elected officials in Washington wanted nothing to do with them. The Clinton administration disowned them, pointing out that it had not commissioned them. In January 1995, the U.S. Senate passed a resolution condemning them by a vote of 99–1 (the lone dissenter, a senator from Louisiana, thought the resolution was not strong enough).[5] After the vitriolic front-page battle over the history standards, the subject of standards, curriculum, and content became radioactive to political leaders.

I was disappointed by the national history standards, but unlike Cheney I thought they could be fixed by editing. When the controversy first exploded into public view, I told *Education Week* that the document was a very good start, but "they should keep working on it, make it more parsimonious, and get out whatever seems to be biased in terms of politics. It shouldn't have a whiff of political partisanship from the left or the right." I wrote a letter to the *New York Times*, which had editorially supported the standards, warning that the history standards had to be "depoliticized," because they were jeopardizing the bipartisan movement to set voluntary national standards.[6] In the *Chronicle of Higher Education*, I argued that the history standards should be revised, not abandoned. I worried that the controversy would "lead to the demise of the entire effort to set national standards, even in less contentious fields, such as mathematics and science." I insisted that national standards would succeed only as long as they were voluntary and nonpartisan and avoided "any effort to impose 'correct' answers on disputed questions." I concluded that the project to develop national standards was at a crossroads; either we as a nation would recognize that much more time was needed to do it right, or the entire effort would be abandoned. I predicted, "The questions that will soon be answered are: Will we learn from our mistakes and keep trying? Or will we give up?"[7]

In hindsight, it is clear that we gave up, in reaction to the media firestorm. The politicians whose leadership and endorsement were needed to establish national standards lost interest. Senators, congressmen, and governors watched the spectacle and determined that it was political suicide to get involved in the contretemps. To Republicans, national standards were anathema, a policy that would turn our education system over to leftist academics, a point that Lynne Cheney drove home again and again in her newspaper articles and public appearances. To Democrats, national standards sounded like a good idea—after all, Bill Clinton had run for office with a promise to establish national standards and assessments[8]—but after the debacle associated with the history standards, the Clinton administration backed away from national standards.

Even as the history standards came into disrepute, the Clinton administration was writing its own legislation to promote standards and accountability. Having seen the political disaster that erupted around the national history standards, administration strategists concluded that it would be politically impossible to forge federally directed academic standards, even voluntary ones. So they punted: The law they wrote said that every state should write its own standards, pick its own tests, and be accountable for achievement. The task of identifying what students should learn—the heart of curriculum standards—was left to each state.

The Clinton administration's Goals 2000 program gave the states federal money to write their own academic standards, but most of the state standards were vague when it came to any curriculum content. It seemed that the states had learned from the battle over the history standards that it was better to say nothing than to provoke controversy by setting out any real curriculum standards. Most state standards were windy rhetoric, devoid of concrete descriptions of what students should be expected to know and be able to do. One exception was Massachusetts, which produced stellar state standards in every subject area. But most states wrote social studies standards in which history was mentioned tangentially, with few or no references to names, events, or ideas. The states seemed to understand that avoiding specifics was the best policy; that standards were best if they were completely noncontroversial; and that standards would survive scrutiny only if they said nothing and changed nothing.

A few examples should suffice. A typical middle-school history standard says that "students will demonstrate an understanding of how ideas, events, and conditions bring about change." A typical high school history standard says that "students will demonstrate an understanding of the chronology and concepts of history and identify and explain historical relationships." Or, "explain, analyze, and show connections among patterns of change and continuity by applying key historical concepts, such as time, chronology, causality, change, conflict, complexity, and movement."[9] Since these statements do not refer to any actual historical event, they do not require students to know any history. They contain no historical content that students might analyze, debate, or reflect on. Unfortunately, they are typical of most state standards in history. The much-maligned voluntary national history standards of 1994, by contrast, are intellectually challenging, because they expected students to discuss the causes and consequences of the American Revolution, the Great Depression, world wars, and other major events in American history. Without specificity and clarity, standards are nothing more than vacuous verbiage.

State standards for the English language arts are similarly vapid. Few states refer to a single significant work of literature that students are expected to read. In most states, the English standards avoid any mention of specific works of fiction or nonfiction or specific major authors. Instead, they babble about how students "interact with text," apply "word analysis and vocabulary skills to comprehend selections," "relate reading to prior knowledge and experience and make connections to related information," "make text-to-text, text-to-self, and text-to-world connections," use "language processes" as "meaning-making processes," engage in "meaningful literacy activities," and "use effective reading strategies to achieve their purposes in reading." Students should certainly think about what they read, but they should read something worth thinking about.[10]

The standards movement died in 1995, when the controversy over the national history standards came to a high boil. And the state standards created as a substitute for national standards steered clear of curriculum content. So, with a few honorable exceptions, the states wrote and published vague documents and called them standards. Teachers continued to rely on their textbooks to determine what to teach and test. The tests and textbooks, written for students across the nation, provided a low-level sort of national standard. Business leaders continued to grouse that they had to spend large amounts of money to train new workers; the media continued to highlight the mediocre performance of American students on international tests; and colleges continued to report that about a third of their freshmen needed remediation in the basic skills of reading, writing, and mathematics.

When Governor George W. Bush of Texas was elected president in 2000, he decided that education reform would be his first priority. He brought with him the Texas plan: testing and accountability. Bush's No Child Left Behind program melded smoothly with a central feature of the Clinton administration's Goals 2000 program:

namely, leaving it to the states to set their own standards and pick their own tests. Under the terms of NCLB, schools that did not demonstrate adequate progress toward the goal of making every student proficient in math and English by 2014 would be subject to increasingly onerous sanctions. But it was left to each state to decide what "proficiency" meant. So the states, most of which had vague and meaningless standards, were left free to determine what children should learn and how well they should learn it.[11] In effect, they were asked to grade themselves by creating tests that almost all children could eventually pass. NCLB was all sticks and no carrots. Test-based accountability—not standards—became our national education policy. There was no underlying vision of what education should be or how one might improve schools.

NCLB introduced a new definition of school reform that was applauded by Democrats and Republicans alike. In this new era, school reform was characterized as accountability, high-stakes testing, data-driven decision making, choice, charter schools, privatization, deregulation, merit pay, and competition among schools. Whatever could not be measured did not count. It was ironic that a conservative Republican president was responsible for the largest expansion of federal control in the history of American education. It was likewise ironic that Democrats embraced market reforms and other initiatives that traditionally had been favored by Republicans.

Nothing better portrayed the new climate than a charged battle during and after the 2008 presidential campaign over the definition of the term "reformer." During the campaign, the *New Republic* chided Democratic candidate Barack Obama for waffling on education reform. A real reformer, said this usually liberal magazine, was someone who supports competition between schools, charter schools, test-based accountability, performance pay for teachers, and No Child Left Behind, while being ready to battle the teachers' unions. This agenda, the article asserted, was shared by influential center-left think tanks in Washington, D.C., such as the Center for American Progress.[12]

After Obama's election, the media vigorously debated the new president's likely choice for secretary of education. For a brief time, it appeared that the new president might pick his main campaign adviser on education, scholar Linda Darling-Hammond of Stanford University. This prospect alarmed the champions of corporate-style reform, because Darling-Hammond was known as an advocate of teacher professionalism and a critic of Teach for America; the new breed of reformers thought she was too friendly with the teachers' unions. Consequently, writers in the *New York Times*, the *Washington Post*, the *Chicago Tribune*, and other publications warned President-elect Obama not to choose Darling-Hammond, but to select a "real" reformer who supported testing, accountability, and choice. True reformers, said the pundits and editorialists, fought the teachers' unions and demanded merit pay based on student test scores. True reformers closed low-performing schools and fired administrators and teachers. True reformers opposed teacher tenure. Never mind that these had long been the central tenets of the Republican approach to education reform.[13]

This rhetoric represented a remarkable turn of events. It showed how the politics of education had been transformed. The same views might as well have appeared in conservative journals, such as *National Review* or the *Weekly Standard*. Slogans long advocated by policy wonks on the right had migrated to and been embraced by policy wonks on the left. When Democratic think tanks say their party should support accountability and school choice, while rebuffing the teachers' unions, you can bet that something has fundamentally changed in the political scene. In 2008, these issues, which had been the exclusive property of the conservative wing of the Republican Party since Ronald Reagan's presidency, had somehow managed to captivate education thinkers in the Democratic Party as well.

WHERE DID EDUCATION REFORM GO WRONG? Ask the question, and you'll get different answers, depending on whom you ask. But all roads eventually lead back to a major report released in 1983 called *A Nation at Risk*.

It is important to understand *A Nation at Risk* (ANAR), its role in the rise and fall of the standards movement, and its contrast with No Child Left Behind. *ANAR* encouraged states and the nation to craft genuine curriculum standards in many subjects; this movement foundered when the history standards came under attack. Consequently, education leaders retreated into the relative safety of standardized testing of basic skills, which was a poor substitute for a full-fledged program of curriculum and assessments. In the trade-off, our education system ended up with no curricular goals, low standards, and dumbed-down tests.

A *Nation at Risk* was a response to the radical school reforms of the late 1960s and early 1970s. Whoever remembers that era fondly is sure to dislike *ANAR*; conversely, whoever was skeptical toward the freewheeling reforms of those years is likely to admire *ANAR*. No one who lived in that time will forget the proliferation of experiments and movements in the nation's schools. Reformers differed mainly in terms of how radical their proposals were. The reforms of the era were proffered with the best of intentions; some stemmed from a desire to advance racial equity in the classroom and to broaden the curriculum to respect the cultural diversity of the population. Others were intended to liberate students from burdensome requirements. Still others proceeded in the spirit of A. S. Neill's *Summerhill*, where any sort of adult authority was strictly forbidden. Tear down the walls between the classrooms, said some reformers. Free the children, free the schools, abolish all rules and requirements. Let the English teacher teach math, and the math teacher teach English. Let students design their own courses and learn whatever they feel like learning whenever (or if ever) they feel like learning. Get rid of graduation requirements, college entrance requirements, grades, tests, and textbooks. Down with the canon. On it went, with reformers, radicals, and revolutionaries competing to outdo one another.[14]

And then one day in 1975, the *New York Times* reported on its front page that scores on the SAT—the nation's premier college entrance examination—had fallen steadily for over a decade.[15] The College Board, which sponsors the SAT, appointed an august commission to consider the likely causes of the score decline. The SAT commission in 1977 found plenty of reasons, including the increased numbers of minority students taking the test, whose test scores on average were lower than those of traditional test takers. But, said the commission, the test score decline was not entirely explained by the changing ethnic composition of the test takers. Some erosion in academic learning had probably been caused by large social forces, such as increased television viewing and the rising divorce rate, as well as political upheavals, such as the Vietnam War and Watergate. Significantly, the commission also concluded that changes in the schools' practices had contributed to the steady slippage of SAT scores, especially in the verbal portion. Students were taking fewer basic academic courses and more fluffy electives; there was less assignment of homework, more absenteeism, and "less thoughtful and critical reading"; and, the commission noted, "careful writing has apparently about gone out of style."[16] The SAT report was soon followed by doleful federal reports about the state of the nation's schools, documenting falling enrollments in math and science and in foreign language study.[17]

Then in 1983 came *A Nation at Risk*, the all-time blockbuster of education reports. It was prepared by the National Commission on Excellence in Education, a group appointed by President Reagan's secretary of education, Terrel Bell. Bell was a subversive in the Reagan cabinet, a former school superintendent and a bona fide member of the education establishment. Whenever the president launched into a lecture about his desire to restore school prayer or to promote vouchers, Secretary Bell was notably silent.[18]

The report was an immediate sensation. Its conclusions were alarming, and its language was blunt to the point of being incendiary. It opened with the claim that "the educational foundations of our society are presently being eroded by a rising tide of mediocrity that threatens our very future as a Nation and a people. What was unimaginable a generation ago has begun to occur—others are matching and surpassing our educational attainments." The nation, it warned, has "been committing an act of unthinking, unilateral educational disarmament." Beset by conflicting demands, our educational institutions "seem to have lost sight of the basic purposes of schooling, and of the high expectations and disciplined effort needed to attain them."[19]

In the years since *A Nation at Risk* was published, academics, educators, and pundits have debated whether the report was an accurate appraisal of academic standards or merely alarmist rhetoric by the Reagan administration, intended to undermine public education. The language was flamboyant, but that's how a report about education gets public attention. If it had been written in the usual somber, leaden tones of most national commissions, we would not be discussing it a generation later. *A Nation at Risk* was written in plain English, with just enough flair to capture the attention of the press. Its argument and recommendations made sense to nonspecialists. People who were not educators could understand its message, which thoughtfully addressed the fundamental issues in education. The national news media featured stories about the "crisis in education." The report got what it wanted: the public's attention.

A Nation at Risk was notable for what it did not say. It did not echo Reagan's oft-expressed wish to abolish the U.S. Department of Education. It did not support or even discuss his other favorite education causes: vouchers and school prayer. It did not refer to market-based competition and choice among schools; it did not suggest restructuring schools or school systems. It said nothing about closing schools, privatization, state takeover of districts, or other heavy-handed forms of accountability. It referred only briefly, almost in passing, to testing. Instead, it addressed problems that were intrinsic to schooling, such as curriculum, graduation requirements, teacher preparation, and the quality of textbooks; it said nothing about the governance or organization of school districts, because these were not seen as causes of low performance.

Far from being a revolutionary document, the report was an impassioned plea to make our schools function better in their core mission as academic institutions and to make our education system live up to our nation's ideals. It warned that the nation would be harmed economically and socially unless education was dramatically improved for *all* children. While it did not specifically address issues of race and class, the report repeatedly stressed that the quality of education must improve across the board. What was truly at risk, it said, was the promise that "all, regardless of race or class or economic status, are entitled to a fair chance and to the tools for developing their individual powers of mind and spirit to the utmost."[20] To that end, the report recommended stronger high school graduation requirements; higher standards for academic performance and student conduct; more time devoted to instruction and homework; and higher standards for entry into the teaching profession and better salaries for teachers.

The statistics it cited showed declining SAT scores from 1963 to 1980, as well as a decline in the number and proportion of high-scoring students on that test; lowered scores on standardized achievement tests; poor performance on international assessments; large numbers of functionally illiterate adults and seventeen-year-olds; the expansion of remedial courses on college campuses; and the cost of remedial training to the military and businesses.[21]

The primary cause of this inadequate academic performance, the commission said, was the steady erosion of the *content* of the curriculum: "Secondary school curricula have been homogenized, diluted, and diffused to the point that they no longer have a central purpose. In effect, we have a cafeteria-style curriculum in which the appetizers and desserts can easily be mistaken for the main courses. Students have migrated from vocational and college preparatory programs to 'general track' courses in large numbers." The proportion in this general track—neither academic nor vocational—had grown from 12 percent in 1964 to 42 percent in 1979. This percentage exceeded that of enrollment in either the academic or the vocational track. This "curricular smorgasbord," combined with extensive student choice, led to a situation in which only small proportions of high school students completed standard, intermediate, and advanced courses. Second, the commission cited data to demonstrate that academic expectations had fallen over time—that students were not doing much homework, that high school graduation requirements were minimal, that college entry requirements had fallen, and that students were not taking as many courses in math and science as their peers in other nations.[22]

Although the report offered many recommendations, the most consequential, listed first in the report, was that high school graduation requirements should be strengthened. All high school students, the commission urged, should study what it called "The Five New Basics." This was to consist of four years of English, three years of mathematics, three years of science, three years of social studies, and one-half year of computer science. In addition, college-bound students should study at least two years of a foreign language. The commission proposed that foreign language study begin in elementary school and that schools include courses in the arts and vocational education in addition to the new basics.[23]

The commission did not just list the subjects to be studied; it succinctly defined the essential goals of each subject, without using jargon. For example, the commission said that the teaching of English "should equip graduates to: (a) comprehend, interpret, evaluate, and use what they read; (b) write well-organized, effective papers; (c) listen effectively and discuss ideas intelligently; and (d) know our literary heritage and how it enhances imagination and ethical understanding, and how it relates to the customs, ideas, and values of today's life and culture." The teaching of mathematics "should equip graduates to: (a) understand geometric and algebraic concepts; (b) understand elementary probability and statistics; (c) apply mathematics in everyday situations; and (d) estimate, approximate, measure, and test the accuracy of their calculations." In addition to the traditional course of study for college-bound students, the commission recommended that "new, equally demanding mathematics curricula" be developed "for those who do not plan to continue their formal education immediately."[24] Again, none of this was revolutionary; the commission called on schools to educate all students well and to prepare them for whatever path they chose after high school.

A Nation at Risk proposed that four-year colleges and universities raise their admissions requirements. It urged scholars and professional societies to help upgrade the quality of textbooks and other teaching materials. It called on states to evaluate textbooks for their quality and to request that publishers present evidence of the effectiveness of their teaching materials, based on field trials and evaluations.

A Nation at Risk urged "significantly more time" for learning. High school students, it said, should receive more homework. *ANAR* called on school districts and states to lengthen the school day (to seven hours) and the school year (from the current 180 days to as many as 200 or 220 days). It called for firm, fair codes of conduct and for special classes or schools for children who were continually disruptive.

Those preparing to teach, said the commission, should be expected to meet high educational standards, by demonstrating not only their aptitude for teaching but also their competence in an academic discipline. Teachers' salaries should be increased and should be "professionally competitive, market-sensitive, and performance-based." Decisions about salary, tenure, promotion, and retention should be tied to peer review "so that superior teachers can be rewarded, average ones encouraged, and poor ones either improved or terminated."[25] The report recommended differential pay for teachers in relation to their quality, but proposed that judgments about teacher quality include peer review.

The commission correctly observed that "learning is the indispensable investment required for success in the 'information age' we are entering."[26] And it was right to say that those who are uneducated or poorly educated would be effectively excluded from material rewards and the chance to participate fully in our shared political and civic life. It was right to point to the curriculum as the heart of the matter, the definition of what students are expected to learn.

When the curriculum is incoherent and insubstantial, students are cheated.

A *Nation at Risk* was certainly not part of a right-wing plot to destroy public education or a precursor to the privatization movement of the 1990s and early twenty-first century.[27] Nor did it offer simple solutions to complex problems or demand the impossible. Every one of its recommendations was within the scope of the schools as they existed then and as they exist now, and none had any potential to harm public education. The report treated public education as a professional, purposeful enterprise that ought to have clear, attainable goals.

Some critics complained that the commission should have paid more attention to social and economic factors that affect educational outcomes, such as poverty, housing, welfare, and health.[28] That's a fair criticism. But the commission was asked to report on the quality of education in the nation's schools, so it focused on the academic aspects of education. When critics said *ANAR* unfairly blamed the nation's economic woes in the early 1980s on the schools, they took their argument too far, as if schools have nothing at all to do with a nation's economic health. When the economy subsequently improved, the critics asked, "Why aren't the schools getting credit for the upturn?" The critics confused the relationship between schools and the economy. Of course schools create human and social capital. Of course they are not the immediate cause of good times or bad times. Schools did not cause the Great Depression, nor can they claim credit for boom times. But economists have long recognized that good schools are important for a nation's future economic, civic, social, and cultural development.

The one consequential error of *A Nation at Risk* was its implication that the fundamental problems of American education resided solely in the nation's high schools and could be corrected by changes to that institution. The report assumed that elementary schools and junior high schools or middle schools were in fine shape and needed no special attention. But a closer look might have persuaded the commission that many students arrived in high school without the foundation of basic skills and knowledge essential to a good high school education. If the high school curriculum was a smorgasbord, the curriculum in the early grades was equally haphazard, lacking in coherence or content. This meant that students began their freshman year of high school with widely varying levels of preparation, many without even the most rudimentary knowledge of history, science, literature, or other subjects. The commission blamed the high schools for the undereducated students who arrived at their doors. Whatever its deficiencies, the high school was not the cause of the poor preparation of its first-year students.

Today, when we contrast the rhetoric of A Nation at Risk with the reality of the No Child Left Behind legislation of 2002, A Nation at Risk looks positively idealistic, liberal, and prescient. A Nation at Risk was a report, not a legal mandate; if leaders in states and school districts wanted to implement its recommendations, they could; but they were also free to ignore the report and its recommendations. No Child Left Behind, however, was a federal law; any state or district that refused to comply with its mandates risked losing millions of dollars targeted to its neediest students. A Nation at Risk envisioned a public school system that offered a rich, well-balanced, and coherent curriculum, similar to what was available to students in the academic track in successful school districts. No Child Left Behind, by contrast, was bereft of any educational ideas. It was a technocratic approach to school reform that measured "success" only in relation to standardized test scores in two skill-based subjects, with the expectation that this limited training would strengthen our nation's economic competitiveness with other nations. This was misguided, since the nations with the most successful school systems do not impose such a narrow focus on their schools.

Whereas the authors of A Nation at Risk concerned themselves with the quality and breadth of the curriculum that every youngster should study, No Child Left Behind concerned itself only with basic skills. A Nation at Risk was animated by a vision of good education as the foundation of a better life for individuals and for our democratic society, but No Child Left Behind had no vision other than improving test scores in reading and math. It produced mountains of data, not educated citizens. Its advocates then treated that data as evidence of its "success." It ignored the importance of knowledge. It promoted a cramped, mechanistic, profoundly anti-intellectual definition of education. In the age of NCLB, knowledge was irrelevant.

By putting its emphasis on the importance of a coherent curriculum, A Nation at Risk was a precursor to the standards movement. It recognized that what students learn is of great importance in education and cannot be left to chance. When the standards movement collapsed as a result of the debacle of the national history standards, the reform movement launched by *ANAR* was left without a strategy. To fill the lack, along came the test-based accountability movement, embodied by the No Child Left Behind law.

So, the great hijacking occurred in the mid-1990s when the standards movement fell apart. The passage of No Child Left Behind made testing and accountability our national education strategy. The controversies over national standards showed that a national consensus would be difficult to achieve and might set off a political brawl. State education departments are averse to controversy. Most states settled for "standards" that were bland and soporific to avoid battles over what students should learn. Education reformers in the states and in the federal government endorsed tests of basic skills as the only possible common ground in education. The goal of testing was higher scores, without regard to whether students acquired any knowledge of history, science, literature, geography, the arts, and other subjects that were not important for accountability purposes.

Whereas *A Nation at Risk* encouraged demands for voluntary national standards, No Child Left Behind sidestepped the need for any standards. In spirit and in specifics, they are not closely related. *ANAR* called for sensible, mainstream reforms to renew and repair our school system. The reforms it recommended were appropriate to the nature of schools: strengthening the curriculum for all students; setting clear and reasonable high school graduation requirements that demonstrate students' readiness for postsecondary education or the modern workplace; establishing clear and appropriate college entrance requirements; improving the quality of textbooks and tests; expecting students to spend more time on schoolwork; establishing higher requirements for new recruits into the teaching profession; and increasing teacher compensation.

These recommendations were sound in 1983. They are sound today.

CHAPTER THREE

The Transformation
of District 2

IN THE HALF-DOZEN YEARS after the release of *A Nation at Risk* in 1983, almost every state established a task force, study group, or commission to discuss school reform. When President George H. W. Bush took office in January 1989, he convened a national summit of governors to agree on a course of action. The participants set specific goals for the year 2000, which included a pledge that "all children in America will start school ready to learn"; American students would be first in the world in math and science; at least 90 percent of students would graduate from high school; all children would master "challenging subject matter"; all adults would be literate and prepared to compete in the global economy; and every school would be free of drugs, alcohol, and violence. Worthy goals all, but none was attained by the year 2000.

In retrospect, it seems curious that elected officials would set such ambitious targets for achieving ends over which they had so little control and for which the solutions were neither obvious nor at hand. Perhaps the leaders were mimicking corporate America, where it is customary to set numerical targets for sales, profits, and other easily quantifiable outcomes. Or perhaps they just underestimated the difficulty of attaining their admirable goals.

Still, the dire warnings about mediocre academic performance continued to grab headlines, and something had to be done. The George H. W. Bush administration urged the public to support the

31

national goals and promoted voluntary national academic standards. The Clinton administration came to office committed to national standards and tests. But enthusiasm for national standards waned in the wake of the noisy controversy over the history standards. In 1997, President Clinton proposed voluntary national testing. However, Republicans took control of Congress in the November 1994 elections and refused to authorize it, and national standards and tests were a dead issue.

For a time in the 1990s, the most promising idea for school improvement was "systemic school reform."[1] Leading scholars said student performance would improve only when all the parts of the education system were working in tandem to support higher student achievement. That meant that public officials and educators should establish a curriculum, set standards for proficiency in those subjects, base tests on the curriculum, expect teachers to teach it, choose matching textbooks, and realign the entire education system around the curricular goals. The scholars recognized that school reform begins with determining what children should know and be able to do (the curriculum) and then proceeds to adjust other parts of the education system to support the goals of learning. This approach makes sense; it is what top-performing nations do.[2]

Some states made a stab at systemic reform, but it was difficult to realign so many moving parts, especially when the results seemed remote to school officials who wanted them now, not years from now. Perhaps the greatest obstacle to systemic reform was that it required numerous stakeholders—textbook publishers, test publishers, schools of education, and so on—to change, which turned out to be an insurmountable political obstacle. Few states or districts had anything resembling a curriculum or syllabus—that is, a coherent, clear description of what students were expected to learn in each subject in each grade. The curriculum was supposed to be the linchpin of systemic reform, the starting point for instruction, teacher education, assessment, and professional development. Absent a curriculum, systemic reform and alignment made no sense.

So the search went on for the idea, the program, the innovation that would lift achievement, not just one student at a time, nor even one school at a time, but in an entire district, particularly one with many poor and low-performing students. The challenge, which no school district had mastered, was "scaling up" isolated success to include almost all students.

One urban district was said to have solved the puzzle of raising achievement across the board with a diverse enrollment, including a substantial number of poor students. That district—Community School District 2 in New York City—became a national symbol of success in the late 1990s.

District 2 was one of New York City's thirty-two community school districts.[3] It stretched from the southern tip of Manhattan to the midsection of the island, including the affluent Upper East Side. Although the district contained public housing projects and pockets of poverty, especially in parts of Chinatown on the Lower East Side, it also encompassed some of the city's wealthiest neighborhoods. In some neighborhoods, the public schools were so desirable that families moved to their zone, and real estate advertisements used them as lures for tenants and buyers.

District 2 was only a small part of the much larger school district of New York City, but it included nearly fifty schools and about 20,000 students. In the late 1990s, the district's remarkable achievements were documented by a consortium of prominent scholars, who told the story of District 2's success at national conferences, in major education journals, and ultimately on national television. The centerpiece of the District 2 strategy was a reading program called Balanced Literacy, which was copied by other cities and had a major influence on textbook publishers.

District 2 is important because it caught the attention of the corporate reformers who came to prominence at the turn of the twenty-first century. They became convinced that District 2 was the model for success in an urban district, that Balanced Literacy was the key to District 2's success, and that other districts would experience similar improvement if every teacher were compelled to adopt District 2's methods unquestioningly. They believed that District 2 had closed the achievement gaps among different groups of students. To business-minded reformers, District 2 provided a template that could be standardized and imposed by tough managers to achieve fast results, meaning higher test scores.

The story of District 2 began in 1987, when Anthony Alvarado was appointed as its district superintendent. Tony Alvarado was well known in the New York City school system as a dynamic, articulate, and charismatic leader. He had previously served for ten years as superintendent of District 4 in Harlem, where he had introduced small schools and a choice program, both of which attracted middle-class students from private schools and from other districts. Test scores rose during his tenure in this impoverished district, lifting it from last in the city to near the middle of the pack. In 1983, the New York City Board of Education named Alvarado chancellor for the entire public school system. However, the following year he resigned when it was revealed that he had borrowed large sums of money from subordinates.[4]

The charming, irrepressible Alvarado reemerged in 1987 as superintendent of District 2. There he embarked on a reform program even more ambitious than the one he had led in District 4. Determined to turn the district into an exemplar of school reform, he opened small schools and choice programs to draw in middle-class students. He engaged literacy consultants from Australia and New Zealand to lead intensive district-wide professional development in Balanced Literacy, which soon became the district's lingua franca.

The debut of Balanced Literacy in District 2 followed a decade of sniping between partisans of phonics and what was known as "whole language." During the late 1970s and the 1980s, whole language emerged as a popular national movement among many teachers, reading supervisors, and teacher educators. It emphasized student-centered activities, figuring out words in context, and reading experiences; it opposed explicit instruction in phonics, spelling, grammar, punctuation, or any other sort of linguistic analysis. Whole-language advocates caricatured critics as elitists and racists for their insistence on "arbitrary, 'proper' language."[5]

Critics of whole language were appalled by its methods, especially its disregard for teaching phonics and the conventions of standard English. In 1967, Harvard scholar Jeanne S. Chall supposedly had settled the ceaseless argument about teaching children to read. In her comprehensive study, *Learning to Read: The Great Debate*, she concluded that beginning readers needed to learn how to decode the symbols and sounds of language.[6] In 1985, the National Academy of Education, which included the nation's leading scholars, stated that "on the average, children who are taught phonics get off to a better start in learning to read than children who are not taught phonics," but the polemical battle between the factions went on unabated.[7] Not until the late 1990s, with the publication of reports from the National Academy of Sciences and the National Institute of Child Health and Human Development, was there an apparent consensus that beginning readers should learn the sounds and symbols of language.[8]

Balanced Literacy was supposed to bridge the differences between the warring camps, but it is a hybrid that differs from both its predecessors. While Balanced Literacy may integrate elements of phonics and whole language, it focuses mainly on reading strategies and teaching children to identify and practice them. It places a premium on children's mastery of certain prescribed techniques (e.g., predicting what they will read, visualizing what they will read, inferring the meaning of what they have read, reading alone, reading in a group, etc.).

Large blocks of time are set aside each day for literacy instruction, in which children engage in structured activities such as shared reading, guided reading, independent reading, word study, writing, and reading aloud. During this time, the teacher functions as a facilitator, moving from group to group and conferring with students. Direct whole-class instruction is generally limited to a mini-lesson at the start of the literacy block. Each classroom has its own library, with books for different reading levels, and students choose the books they want to read or are assigned books to read in small groups. Children participate in cooperative learning activities in classrooms decorated with student work. Each classroom typically has a rug, where the children sit together, interacting with each other and with the teacher.

Balanced Literacy has a well-defined structure and methodology. The teacher is not supposed to stand at the front of the classroom and instruct the entire class beyond the mini-lesson, nor is the teacher's desk placed at the front of the classroom. Children are expected to teach one another. The hoped-for result is a joyful buzz as children engage in varied learning activities. Teachers are supposed to teach the prescribed strategies and procedures, and the students (alone or in groups) are expected to practice their reading strategies and refer to them by name. A student might say, for example, "I am visualizing," "I am summarizing," "I am making a text-to-self connection," "I am making a prediction," or "I am making an inference." In theory, students who become conscious of reading strategies become better readers.[9] In some districts, Balanced Literacy is implemented flexibly, with room for teacher discretion; in others, all elements are strictly prescribed and closely monitored by supervisors.[10]

Such approaches had been criticized in the early days of Balanced Literacy. In 1987, educators P. David Pearson and Janice A. Dole warned, "We have to consider the possibility that all the attention we are asking students to pay to their use of skills and strategies and to their monitoring of these strategies may turn relatively simple and intuitively obvious tasks into introspective nightmares." They suggested that "what really determines the ability to comprehend anything is how much one already knows about the topic under discussion in a text."[11] Knowing reading strategies is not enough; to comprehend what one reads, one must have background knowledge.

Once District 2 officials adopted Balanced Literacy as the district's pedagogy, the entire staff was required to learn a new vocabulary, new ways of teaching, and new ways of interacting with one another. Alvarado became an evangelist for the idea that the job of all teachers and principals, indeed all staff members, was to focus relentlessly on instruction, by which he meant faithfully implementing Balanced Literacy and, later, the district's mandated mathematics program. Every principal was expected to be an instructional leader, not just the manager of the building. Professional development was not an isolated activity, but a daily routine in every school. Every month, principals attended a day-long conference on instructional improvement. Principals accompanied district officials on "walk-throughs," visiting every classroom to ensure that teachers were using the district-approved methods and that the expected improvements were taking place.

Alvarado made sure his principals and teachers were trained in Balanced Literacy and used only the new methods. Those who did not were quietly encouraged to transfer to other districts. Over the course of his eleven-year tenure in District 2, Alvarado replaced two-thirds of the district's principals and about half the teacher workforce.[12]

By the mid-1990s, the district rose from a middling performance to second place among the city's thirty-two community school districts on state tests of reading and mathematics. This impressive growth got the attention of eminent researchers Lauren Resnick of the Learning Research and Development Center at the University of Pittsburgh and Richard F. Elmore of the Harvard Graduate School of Education. Resnick is a cognitive scientist with a deep interest in standards and assessments; Elmore, a scholar of organizational behavior. Resnick and Elmore are among the most respected scholars in education.

Impressed by the district's gains, Resnick and Elmore joined with Alvarado to document how the district became successful and why it ought to be considered a national model. In 1995, Resnick, Elmore, and Alvarado requested funding from the U.S. Department of Education for their unique venture, which they called a study of "High Performance Learning Communities." They received a grant of $6,177,462 to document "The District 2 Story: A Human Resources Theory of School Improvement."[13]

Over the next few years, Resnick, Elmore, and their colleagues—a team that included five members of the District 2 staff, half a dozen researchers, and a large number of graduate students—turned out some two dozen research studies and reports, as well as conference papers and videos. Several of the studies were published in major education journals. The dramatic improvements in student achievement, they said, were due to the district's heavy investment in professional development and its determination to make every teacher and principal responsible for improving instruction.

The district put most of its discretionary funding into teacher training and principal training, on which it spent between 3 percent and 12 percent of its budget, far more than any other district in the city and more than most districts in the nation.[14] Alvarado made a conscious choice to invest in professional development rather than reduce class size. He even eliminated most classroom aides to free up additional funds for professional development.

In 1987, when Alvarado took charge of the district, it had nearly 18,000 students, almost all in elementary and middle schools. (At that time, high schools were controlled by central headquarters, not by community school districts, but Alvarado received permission to open some small high schools in his district.) The student enrollment was 26 percent white, 15.4 percent African American, 24.5 percent Hispanic, and 34 percent Asian. English was a second language for about 20 percent of the students.[15] About half the students came from families whose income was below the official poverty line. The district included a large number of middle-class students, even before Alvarado opened small alternative schools and programs for gifted students.

The scholars attributed District 2's improvements over the course of Alvarado's tenure to his decision to focus "professional development and accountability almost entirely on reading and literacy improvements." The gains, they said, "place District 2 second among all the community districts in New York City, although it has a substantially poorer and more diverse student population than many districts with lower scores."[16]

The studies produced by this unusual partnership between scholars and practitioners were almost uniformly celebratory. One paper admiringly described the district's philosophy of "continuous improvement," which allowed it to maintain its "central focus on high quality instruction."[17] Others praised the district's practice of teaching principals to be instructional leaders. A paper on "closing the gap" between advantaged and disadvantaged students concluded that District 2's strategic focus on instruction was "having powerful effects on student achievement—especially literacy. Furthermore, professional development, District 2's espoused route to improving teacher quality, appears to be having the desired effect on teaching and therefore on achievement, beyond the strong impact of SES [socioeconomic status]."[18]

One study, however, reached different conclusions. The authors of this paper ("Professional Development and the Achievement Gap in Community School District #2") found that in literacy, where the district recorded its biggest gains, classrooms with high proportions of relatively affluent students were likely to have higher test scores. After surveying teachers about the time they spent in professional development and comparing this to the achievement gains of their students, the authors concluded that "engagement in professional development . . . does not appear to have significant influence on student achievement in either literacy or mathematics." This finding contradicted the conclusions of other studies in the project.[19]

Nonetheless, the multiple studies of District 2 gave it national stature. Here was a district that did the right things and got the right results: It engaged in sustained, large-scale instructional improvement, promoted collaboration among teachers, trained its leaders, kept the focus on learning for students and professionals, and made remarkable gains.

According to Elmore and his colleague Deanna Burney, what made District 2 successful was its relentless focus on instruction and professional development; its cultivation of teacher and principal support; its experimentation with new approaches; and the conscious encouragement of "collegiality, caring, and respect" among all staff members. Improvement relied on professionals who were willing "to take the initiative, to take risks, and to take responsibility for themselves, for students, and for each other."[20]

Elmore and Burney anticipated that skeptics might attribute District 2's success to demography, rather than pedagogical strategy. They contended that the district's strategy of investing in teacher training had "clearly paid off in terms of overall improvement." After all, the district had risen to second place in the city, an impressive accomplishment, even though it was "among neither the most affluent or homogeneous districts in the city nor among the poorest." (In fact, District 2 was one of the most affluent districts in the city and became even more so during Alvarado's tenure.) They detailed the demographics and achievement data for every school in the district in 1995. Of its forty-three schools, including elementary schools, intermediate schools, and a few small high schools, thirteen were majority white; six, majority Asian; six, a combined majority of whites and Asians; and eighteen, majority African American and Hispanic. That is, more than half the schools in District 2 had an enrollment that was majority white and/or Asian. This was quite unusual in New York City, where nearly three-quarters of the city's students were African American and Hispanic. The highest-performing schools in District 2 were those with a majority of white and/or Asian students. The lowest-performing schools were highly segregated; even though a majority of the district's students were white and Asian, nine schools were more than 75 percent African American and Hispanic.[21]

Elmore and Burney described these disparities as "school-level variability" and explained District 2's method for dealing with it. The five or six top-performing schools were considered "Free-Agents" and left alone; the next group of schools—some twenty of them—were considered "With-the-Drill," meaning that they were making progress but needed some support to master the Balanced Literacy strategies; then came the "Watch-List," some thirteen schools that needed lots of extra attention to push them toward the correct path. Last were five schools that were so problematic that they were categorized as "Off-the-Screen." These five schools were not identified, but they probably included some of the schools that were more than 75 percent African American and Hispanic, particularly those where fewer than 10 percent of students reached the top quartile of achievement on reading tests during this period.[22]

The final report of the Resnick-Elmore-Alvarado collaboration was presented to the U.S. Department of Education in 2001. With only minor caveats, the final report lauded District 2's "content-driven reform," "standards-based education," professional development, continuous improvement, commitment to adult learning, and significant academic gains in literacy and mathematics. The report acknowledged that District 2 "enjoys a lower proportion of impoverished students than many urban districts, which may account for some portion of their success" and that it was "in the wealthiest quartile" of urban districts in the nation. But, the authors insisted, the district's favorable demographic composition "is clearly not the only factor. Achievement levels have risen over the last 13 years, despite the fact that the socio-economic composition of the district has remained relatively static."[23] It was true that achievement levels had risen, but the socioeconomic composition of the district and its schools had also undergone significant change.

Critics soon emerged to challenge the scholars' narrative. In February 2001, *Education Week*, the most widely read weekly newspaper in the education field, published two side-by-side critical commentaries about District 2 on the same day. Louisa C. Spencer, a retired environmental lawyer who had spent the previous four years as a volunteer tutor in a District 2 elementary school, complained that large numbers of the students in her school—which was 80 percent African American and Hispanic—were not learning to read. She attributed their failure to the Balanced Literacy program. Spencer charged that the district's methods produced "the most fearful waste of precious time in the school day," while failing to teach phonics and to offer a "substantive, sequenced" curriculum. The victims of this failure, she wrote, were the poorest children.[24]

The other article was by Lois Weiner, a professor who prepared urban teachers at New Jersey City University. Weiner was a parent activist at P.S. 3 in District 2, which she described as a highly progressive alternative school with an unusual degree of parent involvement. She claimed that district administrators were stifling teachers and parents at P.S. 3 by mandating "constructivist" materials and specific instructional strategies. (Constructivism is a theory that students construct their own knowledge; in its extreme forms, constructivism eschews direct instruction, focusing instead on activities, processes, and social interaction among students.) Weiner said that "P.S. 3 parents by and large favor ideas associated with 'constructivist' learning," but "they are suspicious of packages that presume any single method or approach could be best for every child and teacher in our school." When Alvarado "fired our new principal (the third in four years) in the sixth week of school, despite the expressed collective wishes of parents and teachers, we realized that we no longer have a choice about whether to accept the package District 2 delivers. We watch, powerless, as staff developers trained and paid by the district office report back to supervisors if teachers don't follow mandates about instruction." She continued, "The degree of micromanagement is astounding." Those who challenged the district office's mandates, she said, risked getting an unsatisfactory rating or being fired. Weiner contended that "opposition from parents is building against the new math curriculum," which was supposed to be field-tested with control groups, but instead was mandated for every classroom. Teachers were expressly prohibited from using other math textbooks or materials, and some were clandestinely "photocopying pages of now-banned workbooks."[25]

The response to the articles was swift in coming. Two of the district's former superintendents (Alvarado and Elaine Fink) and the acting superintendent (Shelley Harwayne) wrote letters to the editor of *Education Week*. By 2001, when the articles were published, Alvarado was chancellor of instruction in San Diego (he left District 2 in 1998), and Fink too was there, training principals for the San Diego schools. The three vigorously defended District 2's record and described the critical authors as biased representatives of "the left and the right" who had ignored "facts and the hard reality of educational outcomes."[26]

The district's mathematics curriculum provoked controversy in 2001. A group of angry District 2 parents and professors from New York University's Courant Institute of Mathematical Sciences met to protest the district's constructivist method of teaching mathematics. What did a constructivist math lesson look like? The National Council of Teachers of Mathematics (NCTM) offers lesson plans in which students are supposed to think deeply, work collaboratively, and discover their own ways of solving problems. For example, a constructivist mathematics teacher might use the card game Krypto to "develop number sense, computational skill, and an understanding of the order of operations." In this game, students must perform operations on five numbers (say, 3, 2, 6, 1, 9) in order to arrive at a target number, such as 10. The lesson plan says, "Ask students to work on this individually for 45 seconds, which is usually enough time for most students to find at least one solution. Then, ask them to work with a partner for another 90 seconds. They should compare solutions, noting any differences. If neither of them found a solution, they should work together to find one. If they both found solutions, they should work together to find a third solution."[27] Constructivist programs such as TERC (used in District 2) and Everyday Mathematics (used in many cities) emphasize multiple solutions to problems. However, students who do not have a firm grasp of basic arithmetic are seldom able to find their own solutions.[28]

At a forum convened to air their grievances, District 2 parents complained that they had to hire tutors because their children were not learning basic skills. The mathematicians warned that students who lacked computational skills were not prepared to succeed in mathematics courses in high school or college. One parent said that "the district leaders have a mentality of a sect." After the first meeting, parents and mathematicians formed a new organization, NYC HOLD, which lobbied vigorously against the math curriculum by writing articles, convening meetings, and managing a Web site to disseminate critical studies.[29]

Weiner was not assuaged by the district's frosty dismissal of her article in *Education Week*. At the 2002 annual meeting of the American Educational Research Association, she accused researchers and district leaders of fabricating the District 2 mystique through a public relations campaign. The following year, she published a long article titled "Research or 'Cheerleading'? Scholarship on Community School District 2, New York City." She charged that the research team had ignored District 2's racial and social segregation and taken a cheerleading role, "promoting reforms they have aided in implementing and assessing." District 2, she pointed out, was atypical of New York City; in the year 2000, its combined white-Asian enrollment was 65 percent, while in the city as a whole it was only 27 percent. District 2's alleged success, she maintained, was a function of demography, not pedagogy.[30]

Resnick defended her team's conclusions, saying that its relationship with district officials was never a secret, and they never pretended to conduct "an arm's length investigation," but rather fostered collaboration between scholars and practitioners in a "new form of research and development."[31]

In 2005, the Public Broadcasting Service, in a program called *Making Schools Work*, narrated by Hedrick Smith, singled out District 2 as "a pioneering effort at district-wide reform and a watershed in the two-decade effort to improve America's schools." The program omitted the meetings of angry parents, the controversy over the constructivist mathematics program, the debate about demographics, and questions about the imposition of Balanced Literacy. The teachers who complained about micromanagement got short shrift. Viewers learned only that some teachers complained "about the extra work forced on them, lack of respect for their professional opinion and the pressure to comply with Alvarado or risk being pushed out."[32]

In 1998, Alvarado was hired as chancellor of instruction in San Diego. There he oversaw the implementation of the programs that had brought him national acclaim in District 2: Balanced Literacy and constructivist mathematics. When Chancellor Joel Klein of New York City selected reading and math programs in late 2002, he copied those in use in San Diego, believing that they would produce rapid test score gains. So the programs inaugurated in District 2 came home to New York City, to be mandated across the city's public schools, only four years after Alvarado left for the West Coast.

Certainly reading scores improved in District 2 under Alvarado's leadership. However, the cause of these gains is not easily ascertained. Resnick and Elmore thought it was because of the pedagogical approach that was mandated across the district. A study by another group of scholars concluded that school choice in District 2 was responsible for higher scores in reading.[33] Still others attributed the improved results to Alvarado's charisma and the strong staff he assembled. But relatively little attention has been paid to the remarkable economic boom and demographic changes in the district during the 1990s. These shifts surely influenced the district's educational gains.

Alvarado's tenure in District 2 stretched from 1987 to 1998. This was a period of population growth and rapid gentrification in District 2, when many neighborhoods were changing and slum buildings were replaced by high-rise luxury apartment buildings.

Once-impoverished sections in Chelsea, Soho, Tribeca, the far West Side, and the Lower East Side became fashionable, expensive neighborhoods. Even the Bowery, long known for its flophouses for indigents, was transformed into a stretch of luxury apartment buildings.

District 2 was not a typical urban district nor was it a typical New York City district. In a city where more than half the population was African American or Hispanic, the population of District 2 was overwhelmingly white (in 1990, 5 percent was African American, 10 percent Hispanic, 13 percent Asian, and 72 percent white; in 2000, 4 percent was African American, 9 percent Hispanic, 15 percent Asian, and 70 percent white).[34]

District 2 was also very wealthy: The average family income in District 2 rose from $150,767 in 1990 to $169,533 in 2000 (in inflation-adjusted dollars). Over the same decade, the average family income in New York City increased slightly from $62,818 to $63,424. While 23 percent of families in New York City had an income over $75,000 in both 1990 and 2000, the proportion of District 2 families in the same category rose from 39 percent in 1990 to 43 percent in 2000.[35]

The researchers who studied the district believed that District 2's socioeconomic composition was "relatively static" during the period of its test score gains, but this was incorrect. From the late 1980s to the late 1990s, as the district gentrified, District 2 enrollment grew from 18,000 to 22,000 students. Nearly 90 percent of the new enrollment in District 2 consisted of white and Asian students; the largest growth was among white students. The district saw increases in groups that tend to score higher, and declines in the proportion of groups that tend to have lower scores, that is, African Americans and Hispanics. District 2 was becoming even more affluent and whiter than other urban districts in the city and the nation.

From 1988 to 1998, the ethnic composition of District 2's schools significantly diverged from that of the city as a whole. The proportion of white students increased, while the proportion of African American and Hispanic students declined (Asian students remained the same, at about one-third). By the late 1990s, District 2 had approximately twice the proportion of white students, three times the proportion of Asian students, half the proportion of African American students, and a smaller share of Hispanic students, as compared to the city's schools as a whole. The students in

District 2 were approximately 65 percent white and Asian, and 35 percent African American and Hispanic. At the same time, enrollment in the New York City public schools was almost the reverse, at 63 percent African American and Hispanic, and 27 percent white and Asian.[36]

The schools of District 2 had a large achievement gap among students of different racial and ethnic backgrounds. In 1999, when the state introduced new tests, the following proportions of fourth-grade students met state standards (levels 3 and 4) in reading: 82 percent of whites, 61 percent of Asians, 45.7 percent of African Americans, and 37.8 percent of Hispanics. On the state mathematics test, 79.6 percent of whites, 87 percent of Asians, 50.3 percent of African Americans, and 51.9 percent of Hispanics met the standards.[37]

In eighth grade, the gaps were just as large or larger. Eighty percent of white students met state standards in reading, as compared to 61 percent of Asian students, 53 percent of African American students, and 40 percent of Hispanic students. In mathematics, 68.8 percent of white students, 70.6 percent of Asian students, 25.2 percent of African American students, and 24.4 percent of Hispanic students met the standards. Although its minority students scored higher than those in most other districts, District 2 did not close the achievement gaps. The gaps among racial and ethnic groups ranged from 30 percentage points to more than 40.[38]

The researchers who turned District 2 into a national symbol of how to "scale up" reform could not know what we know now; the 2000 census figures were not available to them then. They attributed the gains solely to pedagogical reforms. They were unable to see that demographic and economic transformation buoyed the district's improvements. Armed with new data, researchers should continue to analyze the effects of this transformation on District 2's schools.

There was much to admire about District 2. It was a fine school district that saw consistent gains on city and state tests. It had inspired leadership; many excellent schools; a smaller number of low-performing and highly segregated schools; a choice program that attracted white and middle-class students to the public schools; and a mandated pedagogy in reading.

When the new corporate-style reform leaders learned about District 2, they thought they had found the secret to raising achievement across the board. They believed that District 2 had successfully closed the achievement gap among students of different racial and ethnic groups, and that this could translate into a formula. This formula, they believed, could be transplanted elsewhere to get results quickly. The time for debate about what to do and how to proceed was over.

CHAPTER FOUR

Lessons from San Diego

WHAT HAPPENED IN SAN DIEGO from 1998 to 2005 was unprecedented in the history of school reform. The school board hired a non-educator as superintendent and gave him carte blanche to overhaul the district's schools from top to bottom. Major foundations awarded millions to the district to support its reforms. Education researchers flocked to San Diego to study the dramatic changes. The district's new leaders set out to demonstrate that bold measures could radically transform an entire urban district and close the achievement gap between students of different racial and ethnic groups.

The San Diego reforms were based on New York City's District 2 model. A few years later, they became the model for New York City's schools during the Bloomberg era.

In 1998, in response to San Diego's business community, the city's school board selected Alan Bersin, a former federal prosecutor, as city superintendent. Bersin immersed himself in education issues, consulted with education experts at Harvard University, and quickly learned about District 2 in New York City and its visionary leader, Anthony Alvarado. Bersin invited Alvarado to join him as chancellor for instruction in San Diego. Together, this team launched a radical venture in school reform. Intent on closing the achievement gap, the two introduced changes into every classroom, disciplined resistant teachers, and fired reluctant principals. And they did so to national acclaim, while alienating significant numbers of teachers and principals and creating a national exemplar of the "get-tough" superintendent.

With about 140,000 students, San Diego was the eighth-largest district in the nation, second in California only to Los Angeles. Its enrollment in 1998 was 36.2 percent Hispanic/Latino, 16.7 percent African American, 28.2 percent white, and 18.3 percent Asian-Filipino–Pacific Islander.[1] The district enrolled many recent arrivals from Mexico and Asia, as well as many students from affluent sections of the city, such as La Jolla.

San Diego was a surprising place to launch a major reform effort, because the district was widely perceived in the 1990s as one of the nation's most successful urban school systems. In 1996, two years before Bersin was hired, *Education Week* noted that San Diego had a "national reputation as an innovative urban district with a commitment to reform."[2] Michael Casserly, the executive director of the Council of the Great City Schools (a national organization that represents urban districts in Washington, D.C.), expressed amazement that San Diego was the setting for an ambitious reform agenda: "You don't have a school district that is broken, you have a school district that many cities would envy. If other cities had the performance levels of San Diego they would call it a victory."[3] The city's stellar reputation had been due in large part to Tom Payzant, a talented educator who led the district from 1982 to 1993. When Payzant left to join the Clinton administration, he was succeeded by Bertha Pendleton, a thirty-five-year veteran of the San Diego schools, who was the system's first female and first African American superintendent.

Known as a conservative city, San Diego hosted the Republican National Convention in 1996. That spring, the city's business leaders were aghast when the teachers' union launched a strike seeking higher wages and a larger role in decision making at each school. The strike was settled after a week, with the union winning a 14 percent salary increase and a commitment to school-based decision making. To the union, the agreement was by no means extravagant, since the highest teachers' salary would rise to only $55,000 by 1998; even with the increase, few teachers could afford to buy homes in the district.[4] The business community fumed, however, believing that Superintendent Pendleton had capitulated to the union. The business leaders decided it was time the schools had a tough leader. Elections to the city's five-member school board were held every two years. The San Diego Chamber of Commerce raised money to back three candidates whose platform supported strong accountability for students, teachers, and principals, which meant an end to social promotion and a push to remove principals and senior administrators for poor performance. The business community's slate prevailed in November 1996, and this board hired Bersin in 1998.

Bersin was no ordinary change agent. A native of Brooklyn, he was educated at Harvard, Oxford University (where he was a Rhodes Scholar), and Yale Law School. He served as the U.S. attorney for the southern district of California from 1993 to 1998 and as the Clinton administration's "border czar," overseeing enforcement of immigration and drug laws. A friend of President Bill Clinton and Vice President Al Gore, Bersin was well connected to business and political elites in the city, state, and nation. The business community concluded that Bersin—known as fearless and decisive—was just the man to shake up the school system. The school board voted 4–0 to hire Bersin (one member abstained). The San Diego Education Association (SDEA)—the teachers' union—was unhappy about having been excluded from the selection process. The business community, however, didn't care how the union felt, because it considered the union to be a self-serving adult interest group that cared more about money and power than about children.

Bersin and Alvarado formed a partnership, in which Bersin was responsible for politics and relations with the public, while Alvarado was in charge of the instructional agenda. Admiring scholars called them "the dynamic duo from Gotham City." The pair moved quickly and assertively to reorganize the school system and change its culture.[5]

Bersin and Alvarado mandated a uniform way of teaching reading: the Balanced Literacy method that had been used by District 2 in New York City. All principals and teachers were required to participate in professional development training to learn the techniques of Balanced Literacy. Every elementary teacher was required to teach reading for three hours every morning, using only Balanced Literacy methods. Principals were expected to be instructional leaders and required to spend at least two hours each day visiting classrooms, observing teachers, and making sure they used the Balanced Literacy method—and nothing else.

The two leaders eliminated the system's five area superintendents, each in charge of a geographical area, and replaced them with seven "instructional leaders," each in charge of a "learning community" of twenty-five principals from schools that were not geographically contiguous. Alvarado trained the instructional leaders, who reported directly to him. They, in turn, trained the principals.

Bersin promptly downsized the central office bureaucracy by 104 people and used the savings to put Balanced Literacy coaches in every school.[6] The teachers' union objected, fearing that the coaches would act as spies for the administration. Eventually every school had one or more centrally trained coaches, staff developers, resource teachers, or content administrators, whose job was to diffuse the district's philosophy of reform into every classroom.

From the outset, the union objected to the heavy-handed, fast-paced Bersin-Alvarado style of management, which centralized decision making and made no pretense of collaborating with teachers. Bersin and Alvarado were not interested in incrementalism. They wanted wholesale change, directed centrally and implemented quickly. In May 1999, some 2,000 teachers demonstrated at a school board meeting to protest the administration's top-down mandates.[7]

In June 1999, Bersin ordered the immediate demotion of fifteen administrators—thirteen principals and two assistant principals—whom he described as "ineffective" leaders. The school board unanimously supported his decision. The administrators were informed of their humiliation at a school board meeting, escorted to their schools by armed police officers, told to remove their personal items, and then directed to leave the premises. Most of those demoted were not in charge of low-performing schools. The episode had a chilling effect on other staff members. A raw display of force, it seemed calculated to send a warning to those who did not promptly comply with the leadership's mandates. (Some of the demoted administrators later sued the district for denying them due process and eventually won a judgment against the school district in a federal appeals court.)[8]

To ensure a steady supply of principals who were trained in the strategies of Balanced Literacy, Alvarado turned to Elaine Fink, his former District 2 deputy. In 2000, he appointed Fink to run the new Educational Leadership Development Academy at the University of San Diego, which would train principals for the San Diego public schools. Alvarado also imported consultants from Australia, New Zealand, and District 2 to lead professional development sessions for principals and teachers on Balanced Literacy.

In the spring of 2000, Bersin presented his formal plan to the school board. Titled "Blueprint for Student Success in a Standards-

Based System," the document stressed the themes of "prevention, intervention, and retention" and summarized the activities that Bersin and Alvarado were pursuing and planned to pursue. Now, nearly two years into the reform era, mathematics was added to literacy as a core subject. The emphasis in the plan was on intensive professional development. Properly trained teachers sharing the same practices, the same ideas, and the same language, it was believed, would lift student achievement. The Blueprint added summer school, longer school days, and other support for students who needed extra time.

The Blueprint borrowed heavily from District 2's program of Balanced Literacy and constructivist mathematics. The Blueprint decreed that every school would adopt the district's new literary framework; three middle schools would have a double-period mathematics block. Low-performing students in middle and high schools would be required to attend a two- or three-period literacy block termed "genre studies." The central bet of the Blueprint strategy was that, over the long run, "as the base of instruction across the whole system rises, so will the academic achievement of all students."[9]

The cost of implementing the Blueprint was substantial. The annual cost of professional development rose from $1 million to about $70 million. The district paid for the reforms partly by shifting control over federal Title I funds from individual schools to the central office. (Title I is a federal program whose purpose is to improve the achievement of disadvantaged students.) In 1999, the schools controlled some $18 million in Title I monies; by 2001, that funding dropped to $3 million. During the same period, the Title I funds directly controlled by central headquarters rose from less than $3 million to more than $20 million. Bersin and Alvarado fired over six hundred classroom aides funded through Title I and used the savings to support the Blueprint reforms. In District 2, Alvarado had similarly redirected Title I funds, calling it "multipocket budgeting."[10] Bersin raised more than $50 million from foundations, including the Gates Foundation, the Hewlett Foundation, the Carnegie Corporation of New York, and the Broad Foundation. Several foundation grants had a specific contingency: The money would be available only as long as Bersin and Alvarado remained in charge of the district.[11]

On March 14, 2000, the San Diego school board voted on the Blueprint. Thousands of teachers and parents showed up for the meeting, most to demonstrate vociferously against the Blueprint.

Bersin insisted that the district's academic performance was dismal. The San Diego Chamber of Commerce praised the Blueprint; John Johnson, president of the local Urban League, said that "collaboration, input, and buy-in" were fine and well, but sometimes "leaders must exercise leadership and move ahead."[12] Critics complained about the superintendent's plan to fire six hundred classroom aides, as well as the narrowing of the curriculum to just literacy and mathematics. Behind all the complaints was a simmering resentment that the leadership had not consulted teachers or parents when forging their plans.

The board approved the Blueprint by a vote of 3–2. The vote revealed a bitter split on the school board. Bersin and the Blueprint had the solid support of the three members of the board—Ron Ottinger, Edward Lopez, and Sue Braun—who had run for office with the endorsement of the business community. The other two members—Frances O'Neill Zimmerman and John de Beck—had the support of the teachers' union, and they consistently opposed Bersin's initiatives. Divisions within the board became open and personal, as the pro- and anti-Bersin forces argued over every decision and shift in policy. Every significant vote came out 3–2, with the pro-Bersin majority always prevailing.

Many teachers in the district were upset by the heavy-handedness with which the reforms were implemented. Even those who were fully supportive of Balanced Literacy and constructivist mathematics felt disrespected by the leadership's lack of collaboration and consultation. Terry Pesta, the president of the SDEA and a thirty-year veteran of the school system, complained about Bersin and Alvarado's approach: "It's been that style of leadership since day one," he told an interviewer. "Everything's been dictatorial. It's 'Our way is the only way.'" Pesta claimed that "morale among our members is at an all-time low" and that teachers felt they were being evaluated not on how well they teach, but "on how well they're being a team player."[13] Teachers were often told that if they were not good team players, they were not good teachers.

A study of the San Diego reforms reported that principals and teachers often questioned the rationale for the leadership's choices: "Why *this* instructional content, why *this* model of leadership?" "Why is the method of instruction associated with Balanced Literacy better than what we have been doing?" "Why are district leaders *telling* us what to do instead of *asking* us?" The answer from Bersin and Alvarado, reiterated again and again, was that Balanced Literacy would close the achievement gap.[14] The implication was that anyone who resisted Bersin and Alvarado's agenda was opposed to social justice. San Diegans did not know that their model, District 2, had not closed the achievement gap.

Bersin disdained school-based decision making, site-based management, and other means of involving teachers in matters of curriculum or instruction. He disparaged the research on school reform that spoke of cultivating teacher "buy-in," that is, persuading teachers to embrace changes wholeheartedly. He was insistent, passionate, and impatient, sincerely believing, as did Alvarado, that their program was in the best interests of children. One of Bersin's favorite expressions was: "You don't cross a chasm in two leaps." A study commissioned by the Bersin administration in 2004 defined the Bersin-Alvarado strategy with these three axioms: "1) Do it fast, 2) Do it deep, 3) Take no prisoners."[15]

This strategy assumes that the central planners know exactly what to do and how to do it. It relies on command-and-control methods rather than consensus. It brooks no dissent. It requires absolute loyalty. It rejects the conventional belief that incremental reforms are more successful in the long run, especially when they are shaped by consultation with those who are expected to implement them. For Alvarado, this was an abrupt change from his earlier roles in District 4, where he was known for giving schools autonomy, or in District 2, where he was known for working closely with teachers to implement his instructional agenda.

Bersin made no apologies for his aggressive imposition of the reform agenda. He said, "There was no other way to start systemic reform. You don't announce it. You've got to jolt a system. I understood that. You've got to jolt a system, and if people don't understand you're serious about change in the first six months, the bureaucracy will own you. The bureaucracy will defeat you at every turn if you give it a chance." Bersin treated the teachers and their union as part of "the bureaucracy."[16]

Many principals and teachers did not like the changes. During the Bersin years, 90 percent of the district's principals were replaced. Teacher attrition was high. Before the reform era, about 250 of the district's 9,000 teachers resigned each year. In the first two years of the new regime, teacher resignations and retirements doubled to nearly 500. In 2002–2003, about 1,000 teachers accepted the district's offer of early retirement. Altogether, more than a third of the district's teachers left between 1998 and 2005. Some scholars thought this offered "real advantages for reform" because those who enter the district knowing about its program are less likely to offer resistance and "are likely to be 'believers.'"[17]

This pattern bore only a slight resemblance to Alvarado's path in District 2. There, he did not fire teachers and principals outright, but quietly pushed out those who did not support his reforms. About half the district's teachers and two-thirds of its principals left during his eleven-year tenure; most retired or relocated to schools in other districts in New York City. In District 2, he made staff changes without fanfare and without humiliating anyone. Alvarado cultivated a close working relationship with the United Federation of Teachers in New York City; this relationship facilitated his ability to transfer out the teachers he did not want. In San Diego, by contrast, the Bersin-Alvarado team was continually at war with the SDEA.

In District 2, Alvarado described his reforms as a "multi-stage process," in which principals and teachers reflected on teaching practice, tried out ideas, and refined their teaching strategies over time; he recognized that teachers would be at different levels of experience, and some would need more direction than others. During his tenure in District 2, Alvarado told Richard Elmore of Harvard, "Eighty percent of what is going on now in the district I could never have conceived of when we started this effort. Our initial idea was to focus on getting good leadership into schools, so we recruited people as principals who we knew had a strong record of involvement in instruction. . . . Then we wanted to get an instructional sense to permeate the whole organization. . . . So we settled on literacy. Since then, we've built out from that model largely by capitalizing on the initiative and energy of the people we've brought in. They produce a constant supply of new ideas that we try to support."[18]

As leader of District 2, Alvarado stressed the importance of "collegiality, caring, and respect" among staff members: "We care about and value each other, even when we disagree. Without collegiality on this level you can't generate the level of enthusiasm, energy, and commitment we have." He worried about outsiders reducing the lessons of District 2 to a set of management principles. Imposing these principles without recognizing the importance of its culture of "commitment, mutual care, and concern" wouldn't work, he suggested then, because changes in management cannot affect people's underlying values. District administrators, he insisted, could not impose change. Rather, the changes must originate with teachers, students, administrators, and parents as they work together to solve problems.[19]

But when Alvarado moved to San Diego, this philosophy did not move with him. Bersin hired Alvarado to bring about change fast and to get results, not to embark on a multistage process that might take eight to ten years. Bersin assumed that Alvarado had perfected his formula for success, one ready for full implementation throughout the San Diego schools, not someday, but at once. The mandated professional development sessions were not opportunities for reflection and collegiality, but a time for teachers to be told what to do and how to do it. Unquestioning compliance was expected.

In the fall of 2000, three of the five school board members stood for reelection. One, Frances O'Neill Zimmerman, was an outspoken opponent of Superintendent Bersin. A Democrat from affluent La Jolla, Zimmerman was a parent of two children in the San Diego public schools and had worked as a substitute teacher in the system. Zimmerman objected to Bersin and Alvarado's coercive, top-down approach. The typical school board race at that time cost about $40,000, but leading business figures in the city contributed over $700,000 in an effort to defeat Zimmerman. Walmart heir John Walton of Arkansas, a supporter of charter schools and vouchers, and Los Angeles billionaire Eli Broad each contributed more than $100,000 to the anti-Zimmerman campaign. Television commercials attacked Zimmerman for "leading the fight against San Diego's back-to-basics reform plan."[20] This appeal was misleading, because neither Balanced Literacy nor constructivist mathematics was a "back-to-basics" method.

The business-funded onslaught against Zimmerman failed. She was reelected (with a bare majority), but the board nonetheless continued to have a 3–2 majority in Bersin's favor.

In 2002, the school board election was again a battleground between pro- and anti-Bersin forces. The SDEA and the statewide California Teachers Association spent $614,000 in an effort to oust Bersin's supporters.[21] But the election produced the same 3–2 majority favoring Bersin and the Blueprint. The climate for reform, however, had cooled, as the state's budget crisis was causing major cutbacks in funding. Elements of the Blueprint were put on hold, and the district offered early retirement to teachers to reduce payroll expenses.

Although Bersin's supporters won at the polls in 2002, Bersin decided that he needed to tone down the simmering hostility of the teachers and their union. A few weeks after the school board election, Bersin announced that Alvarado's role in the district would be curtailed, a move widely viewed by critics as sacrificing Alvarado in an effort to appease angry teachers. This change, said Bersin, was "a mutual decision based on a joint and shared assessment of where we are" in reforming the schools. But there was no placating the critics. John de Beck, the newly reelected member of the anti-Bersin bloc on the school board, responded to the news: "Good riddance. . . . But [his] leaving is not going to make a difference. We've had four years of Alan Bersin's top-down management and now he wants to pass off all his problems on Tony and use him as a scapegoat. Alvarado is not the problem, the superintendent is the problem." De Beck had retired after thirty-six years in the San Diego school system; he saw himself as a voice for teachers and class-size reduction, but Bersin considered him a union spokesman. In February 2003, Alvarado announced his departure, although he still had nearly two years left on his contract.[22]

As Alvarado's influence waned and then ended, the district loosened its demands for instructional uniformity and moved on to a program of structural and organizational change, including small high schools and charter schools. As state budget cuts loomed, Bersin empowered principals to decide where to make cuts. In another show of flexibility, Bersin no longer required high schools to place low-performing students in the three-hour literacy block ("genre studies") that was detested by students and teachers alike, enrolled mostly minority students, and had shown no results.

In the 2004 school board election, Bersin finally lost his slim margin of control to a new board, which had three anti-Bersin votes. Apparently, the voters wanted a change. One of the new members, Mitz Lee, ran on a platform demanding Bersin's ouster. Bersin announced his resignation in January 2005. The Blueprint era was over. The new board dismissed the peer coaches, suspended most of the professional development activities, and replaced Bersin with Carl Cohn, a respected educator who had previously led the Long Beach, California, schools and emerged from retirement to take over the San Diego schools.

The San Diego story didn't end with Bersin's departure. Researchers had begun analyzing the results of the Blueprint long before Bersin resigned. Some studies were commissioned by Bersin, others by the school board. Scholars came to San Diego to witness for themselves this much-heralded experiment in urban school reform. Those who favored the Blueprint's methods were impressed by the district's rising test scores in reading and baffled by the teachers' complaints.

Early on, the San Diego school board had commissioned the American Institutes for Research (AIR) to evaluate the Blueprint. In 2002, AIR praised the Blueprint but reported that teachers were unhappy about the fast pace of implementation. AIR said that most teachers did not feel respected by district staff and were enjoying teaching less since the reforms started. Many complained of "a climate of fear and suspicion" and of being "exhausted, stressed out, and in some cases, fearful of losing their jobs if they do not perform under this new program." A second AIR report, in 2003, concluded that the Blueprint's academic results were mixed and that further gains might be jeopardized by continuing teacher opposition and impending budget cuts. The biggest academic gains were posted in reading in elementary school, where three-hour literacy sessions were required in every school. Yet in mathematics, the same students showed no gains. The largest improvement was among English-language learners and nonwhite students, who were the primary focus of the Blueprint reforms. However, the reading and mathematics scores of high school students in San Diego had actually declined relative to the rest of the state.[23]

AIR concluded that teacher resistance to the Blueprint was a large obstacle. "Teacher buy-in is critical for the success of school reform efforts," it said, citing other research showing that "teachers who perceived decision making as being top-down tended to resist schoolwide reform efforts." The study found that teachers had "rather negative reactions to both the district and to the Blueprint itself." Elementary school teachers and high school teachers differed: Nearly half the elementary teachers believed that their students were learning more, but only 16 percent of high school teachers did. The most experienced teachers were the most negative toward both the district leadership and the Blueprint. The study's authors had expected that the teachers' negative attitudes would "soften over time," but this did not occur.[24]

By contrast, many education researchers treated San Diego as the mecca of education reform, waxing enthusiastic about Bersin and

Alvarado's relentless imposition of change. They liked the changes that were made and the swiftness with which they were imposed.

Researcher Amy Hightower wrote one of the earliest studies. She concluded that the leaders' "top-down, non-incremental approach to change" was necessary. Waiting for teachers and principals to agree to their plans would have been a waste of time and a risk, allowing the status quo to mobilize against them. She approved of the "big boom" and the "jolt" to the system because the leaders were building a "culture of learning," acting on "principled knowledge." Hightower was predisposed to agree with the reforms, so she concluded that it was commendable to impose them without consulting the teachers who were expected to implement them.[25]

Larry Cuban of Stanford University and Michael Usdan of the Institute for Educational Leadership were cautious in their praise. They expressed hope over "the beginnings of a genuine district culture of professional norms," yet noted Bersin and Alvarado's "unrelenting top-down managerial direction at an accelerator-to-the-floor pace" and teachers' unhappiness. The head of the SDEA told them that the reform was "being done *to* us, not *with* us," but Bersin countered that the union was just part of the old, discredited status quo. Cuban and Usdan were uncertain "whether the consequences of the 'boom' theory of changing the system in the initial year have left raw, unhealed wounds that will continue to fester and undermine both the direction and institutionalizing of these reforms or whether the agenda of change has taken hold among principals and teachers sufficiently for the initial trauma to heal, leaving a few unpleasant but distant memories that will fade as new cadres of teachers and principals enter the system." They said that "it is too early to answer this key question."[26]

Bersin invited Frederick M. Hess of the American Enterprise Institute to gather researchers to study the district's reforms. The project was called the San Diego Review. The team presented its findings at a public conference in San Diego in the fall of 2004 and published them the next year in a book titled *Urban School Reform: Lessons from San Diego*. By the time the essays appeared, Bersin's time in office was finished, so the book ended up as a sort of valedictory to the Blueprint. Most of the essays hailed the Blueprint and Bersin's take-no-prisoners style of implementation. Teacher resistance was discussed but was largely attributed to the intransigence of the teachers' union.

The biggest surprise in the San Diego Review was an analysis of the academic results by economist Margaret E. Raymond of Stanford University and researcher Daphna Bassok. They found that "San Diego students were helped moderately" by the Blueprint, "but other districts were able to generate larger gains over equivalent periods of time." San Diego consistently scored higher than the state average from 1999 to 2003, but its rate of change "lagged slightly behind the rate of change statewide." Only the middle schools made the same progress as other urban districts in California, but the gains were small. Raymond and Bassok noted that in light of the many interventions in middle schools, "such as genre studies, literacy blocks, and extended days, it is surprising to see such limited growth."[27]

The study observed that San Diego's reading scores in elementary school had improved since 1998, especially for low-income students and students in the lowest-performing schools. For those students, scores rose in kindergarten, first grade, and second grade, but not in third grade. In high schools, improvement in reading was "minimal at best," as there were no gains between 1998 and 2002 on state tests. In mathematics, the gains occurred mainly in the years *prior* to the adoption of the Blueprint and were smaller than the gains in other urban districts in California. Although there were bright spots, it was a dispiriting summary of the academic changes in San Diego, as compared to the rest of the state, during the reform era.[28]

Analyzing test scores from 1999 to 2002, Julian Betts of the University of California at San Diego came to different conclusions. He declared that the reforms were so successful in helping low-performing students in elementary schools that they could serve as a model for the state and the nation. Betts and his colleagues found that the gains were largest in elementary schools, moderate in middle schools, but nonexistent in high schools. In fact, the double- and triple-length classes in high school seemed to diminish achievement. The most effective reform strategies were summer school and the "extended day reading program," in which low-performing students received additional instruction for three ninety-minute periods each week, before or after school. Targeting low-performing schools with extra resources and a longer school year was also effective.[29]

As Bersin's term of office came to an end, the *San Diego Union-Tribune*, which had consistently supported him, summarized the seven tumultuous years of his superintendency. It was a mixed scorecard. Charter schools were flourishing. New buildings were going up. The number of high-scoring schools increased, and the number of low-scoring schools declined. Elementary schoolchildren made significant progress, but not as much as those in comparable urban districts across the state, such as Santa Ana, Fresno, Garden Grove, Long Beach, and Los Angeles. The reforms "largely fizzled in middle and high schools." The district's dropout rate increased almost every year starting in 1999 and grew by 23 percent during Bersin's tenure.[30]

UP TO THIS POINT in the narrative, everything I learned about the Bersin years had appeared in books, essays, research studies, and news articles. I wasn't sure what I thought about the reforms, because the picture was unclear. Some of the nation's most respected educators praised the Blueprint as a transformative strategy and potential national model for urban education reform. But the achievement gains were mixed, and there was something troubling about the frequent reports of teachers' resistance. So I began my own inquiries.

In reading the Hess collection (*Urban School Reform*), I noticed that no one wrote about the curriculum in the schools. Many of the studies referred to the district's strong curriculum but none actually described it. So I contacted Hess to ask about the curriculum for the arts, literature, history, civics, science, foreign languages, and other subjects. He referred me to Sheila Byrd, a well-known curriculum expert, who was originally engaged to write on the subject for the San Diego Review. She sent me her unpublished paper. In it, she wrote that San Diego never implemented the state's academic curriculum frameworks and had chosen instead to focus on "intensive professional development" for teachers and principals. San Diego emphasized "*how* teachers should be teaching at the expense of conveying *what* students should be learning." Consequently, she noted in the paper, "many teachers expressed frustration with what they viewed as the enforcement of loosely defined teaching strategies that sidestepped content and had been developed without their input."[31]

In an e-mail to me, Byrd said she learned after agreeing to write the paper that five years after the reforms started, San Diego "didn't have a curriculum. They had just started to create one," but what was emerging was only about literacy and it "was not promising." District officials had not been able to explain what the curriculum was, nor was there documentation of a systematic plan to develop one. Some schools had developed a few draft "curriculum maps," but only in literacy. She said that at the San Diego Review conference in 2004, there was a panel discussion on high schools "and not one word about standards or curriculum escaped the panelists' lips. It was all about administrative reorganization, etc." Finally, Byrd wrote, a parent got up and asked, "Why aren't you discussing what students are or aren't being taught?" The parent described how weak her child's courses had been. Said Byrd, "Panelists basically brushed her off."[32]

In January 2007, I visited San Diego to interview teachers, principals, union leaders, school board members, and central office administrators. Some of the principals had been removed by Bersin and Alvarado, and some had been hired and promoted by them. I spent time with the new superintendent, Carl Cohn, had dinner with Bersin, and later, when I returned to New York City, spoke at length with Alvarado. He was mortified by the public humiliation of the fifteen administrators and wanted to make clear that he had nothing to do with it.

The teachers and principals said they had not objected to Balanced Literacy or to the intensive professional development. San Diego had been a "whole-language" district before the Blueprint, so this approach was not unfamiliar to them. Yet they uniformly were bitter about the high-handed way in which the reforms were imposed on them. Teachers, especially veterans, spoke about being harassed. They complained about mandates and directives that narrowed what they were permitted to teach. The Bersin era, several said, was a "reign of terror." Those who didn't go along were bullied. Teachers were punished by grade switching: A first-grade teacher might be reassigned on short notice to teach sixth grade, while a sixth-grade teacher would be reassigned to teach kindergarten or first grade. Principals spoke in hushed voices about the abrupt public removal in June 1999 of the fifteen administrators. The theory behind these tactics, several said, was "culture shock," keeping everyone on edge, afraid, insecure.

One principal who was promoted to the central office by Bersin spoke with regret about the district's 90 percent turnover in principals. When the fifteen administrators were fired, he said, it sent a message: "Comply or be destroyed." The influx of large numbers of new principals brought new problems. They had no "deep reservoir of experience" and felt "intense pressure to push change," so they "bludgeoned people" when they walked through classrooms, thinking that by taking harsh actions, they could forcibly change people's beliefs. "People complied because of fear," he said. "All up and down the system, there was *fear*." The introduction of five hours daily of literacy and math in high school, he said, was a disaster. "That meant eliminating all electives, other courses. The kids hated it."

This administrator was blunt about his time as a principal under the Blueprint. Putting coaches in every school, he said, was "a great idea, badly implemented." The coaches sowed animosity, especially among experienced teachers. The coaches made teachers feel less competent, not respected. Teachers saw them as policemen and did not trust them. They came into classrooms to inspect the "word walls," the "leveled libraries," and the mandatory student-made posters, all elements of Balanced Literacy. The general sense among teachers was that the coaches were there to catch teachers making mistakes and to report them, not to help them.

He described the reforms as a regime of thought control. "We learned to walk the tightrope regarding teacher talk." He and his teachers learned to say over and over: "I am a reflective practitioner, I am a reflective practitioner." He said, "Survival became paramount. Everyone was afraid of speaking out. We were muzzled." He survived, he said, because his teachers united to protect him, and he protected them.

A principal who was promoted during the Blueprint era complained about the "minute-to-minute schedule. If kids are reading something they really enjoy, it is hard to stop and move on to the next assignment. But we were closely monitored and had no choice." Another who was hired during the Blueprint days said, "It was great pedagogy, but they got the people stuff all wrong. Their sense of urgency sometimes spilled over and provoked a sense of anxiety [in teachers], then hostility." She said, "They came to 'kick ass.' They never listened. It was bad the way they got rid of principals, the way it was done. It undermined trust." She added that people in the schools generated an active rumor mill about what was allowed and what was prohibited, some of which was untrue.

A retired principal wistfully described the elementary school she had founded. It was an English-Spanish dual-language school with a newspaper, a bank, a currency, and a court, mostly run by the children. When the new era began, all these innovative programs had to go, because the school had to concentrate only on literacy and math. The instructional leader assigned to her school came from New York City. "She made me feel incompetent," she said. "She saw nothing good. The hardest part was to go back to the teachers and cushion the news. Everyone was demoralized." She said, "If you gave her any information, it was bad, she wrote you up for an infraction. Or if you asked a question, it was bad. She was always demanding that I write up the teachers: 'Document them, fire them!'" When the principal retired, the entire staff left the school. Her dream died.

A National Board–certified teacher who was a former Teacher of the Year for the district spoke contemptuously of the regimented language, the scripted talk, such as "I am a reflective practitioner." Teachers were not allowed to question the leadership's strategy. "We bonded, we spoke in code words. They spied on us, videotaped our staff development meetings, with the camera pointed at the audience, not the presenters. Sometimes we agreed that no one would talk. We would sit quietly, in a form of passive noncompliance. It was a totalitarian atmosphere. We were subversive. We knew what they wanted to hear. We would be punished if we didn't parrot the words they wanted to hear," she said.

A high school teacher spoke with derision about the three-hour block of time for "genre studies." Everyone knew the classes were for "dummies," he said, and the kids felt stigmatized. He spoke of the introduction of a physics course in ninth grade ("ActivePhysics"), based on comic books. It was dumbed-down physics and was eventually dropped. Then there was "Algebra Exploration," which was "fuzzy math for kids who failed algebra." He said that the system turned principals into "Stepford wives," doing the bidding of the central office.

Two kindergarten teachers described the reading test—Developmental Reading Assessment—as "the monster to which we fed our kids." One asked, "Why would we have a three-hour literacy block for kindergarten children when they don't know how to hold a book? Why teach reading to a four-year-old?" They complained about the inconsistency of the professional development, which often seemed to be devoted to "the latest rage, the idea of the moment." One consultant said, "Move the desks to the corner and they will learn to read." Another said, "If you use purple paper, they will learn to read." Even the children were supposed to master the pedagogical jargon. The consultants wanted children to say things like, "I can make a text-to-text connection! I can make a text-to-self connection!"

From the moment Bersin was hired, he and the SDEA were at loggerheads. The union accused him of harassing teachers, and he accused them of blocking reform. They were both right. In June 2001, the union surveyed its members about the reforms; most responded. When asked "Do you believe the Blueprint and other reform efforts instituted by Superintendent Bersin will improve the overall quality of education in San Diego?" 78 percent said "no." When asked to describe teacher morale, 0.3 percent answered "excellent"; 6 percent said "good"; 29 percent said "only fair"; and 63 percent said "poor." When asked "Do you have confidence in the current Superintendent and his administration?" 93 percent said "no." When asked to offer one word that best described "the Superintendent and his administration's attitude toward teachers and parents in this district," the most frequently cited words were "dictator," "arrogant," "disrespectful," "dictatorial," "dictatorship," "condescending," and so on.[33]

When I visited the district's headquarters, I met with Bersin's replacement, Carl Cohn, and top members of the central administration, most of whom had been appointed by Bersin and Alvarado. My conversation with Cohn was informal and candid. The staff members enthused about the historic successes of the Blueprint. When I met with the former director of curriculum and instruction, she wanted me to know how valuable she found Balanced Literacy. She said, "You won't believe this, but we had fourth graders who didn't know the difference between point of view and perspective. So we had to stop and teach it to them." I wrote that down and said nothing. I did not want to admit that I didn't know the difference between point of view and perspective either. I began to understand what the teachers had been telling me about the district's demand that everyone mouth the same jargon.

As I interviewed San Diego educators, I heard recurrent rumors about stress-related illnesses among teachers, which they called "Bersinitis." Seeking evidence, I called the San Diego office of Kaiser Permanente, the major health-care organization in California, and spoke to a psychiatric social worker. She told me that from 1999 to 2005, San Diego teachers came to the clinic "in droves" with "work-related depression and anxiety due to a hostile work environment." She said they were "under pressure by their principals to raise scores." She said the phenomenon ended when Cohn took over. From 2005 to 2007 (when I spoke to her), not a single teacher appeared with a similar problem.[34]

Alan Bersin told me over dinner in San Diego that there was no responsible alternative to swift, top-down reform and that the Blueprint had become deeply institutionalized in the San Diego schools. Brilliant, charming, and self-assured, Bersin said that school-based decision making is a terrible idea, and that elected school boards are obstacles to reform. He explained that reform could happen in public schools only by pushing hard, without waiting for consensus. If you wait for consensus, he said, reform won't happen.

But is this a replicable strategy? How many districts are likely to turn complete control over to a leader who is prepared to forge ahead without gaining the support of the teachers who must implement the program? How many districts are likely to disregard the views of teachers, parents, and others who might disagree with the leadership's ideas about "reform"?

The political genius of the San Diego approach was what I call a left-right strategy. Bersin's instructional reforms employed and empowered the pedagogical left; he directed millions of dollars in professional development contracts to those who were deeply versed in Balanced Literacy and constructivist math. At the same time, Bersin's accountability reforms and organizational policies—firing principals, demanding higher test scores, fighting the teachers' union, attacking the bureaucracy, and opening charter schools—delighted the business community and those on the right who believe that public agencies, especially schools, are overflowing with waste, inefficiency, and incompetence and are greatly in need of accountability, competition, and choice.

In the end, were the gains in the elementary years worth the rancor created by Bersin's "take no prisoners" style? Surely I would have found enthusiastic supporters of the Blueprint if I had interviewed more teachers and principals. But I also have no doubt that the bitterness I encountered was genuine; whether it represented 70 percent of the staff, 60 percent, or only 50 percent was immaterial. Almost every study—including the AIR studies—documented that a majority of teachers were angry and disaffected. You can't lead your troops if your troops do not trust you.

Carl Cohn published an essay just three months after we met in San Diego, echoing what he told me in our informal conversation. Ostensibly criticizing the No Child Left Behind legislation, Cohn could not resist comparing the federal law to the Blueprint: "I inherited a district in which the driving philosophy over the previous six years had, similarly, been to attack the credibility of any educator who spoke out against a top-down education reform model. These attacks allowed those in charge to portray themselves as the defenders of children, to justify any means to promote their model of improving student achievement, and to view their critics through the same apocalyptic lens of good and evil that has characterized many of our national debates." Such an approach, he cautioned, was counterproductive. "In San Diego, it produced a climate of conflict that is only now beginning to improve." Any genuine school reform, he argued, "is dependent upon empowering those at the bottom, not punishing them from the top."[35]

School reform will continue to fail, Cohn warned, until we recognize that "there are no quick fixes or perfect educational theories. School reform is a slow, steady labor-intensive process" that depends on "harnessing the talent of individuals instead of punishing them for noncompliance with bureaucratic mandates and destroying their initiative." He predicted that "ground-level solutions, such as high-quality leadership, staff collaboration, committed teachers, and clean and safe environments, have the best chance of success. These solutions are not easily quantified. They cannot be experimented on by researchers or mandated by the federal government."

Cohn observed that the leaders of the Blueprint forged ahead without listening to the very people whose cooperation was necessary for ultimate success. They ignored the fundamental importance of trust among those who make schooling effective: students, teachers, principals, and administrators. In my conversation with him, Cohn cited the work of sociologists Anthony Bryk and Barbara Schneider, who maintain in their study *Trust in Schools* that successful school reform depends on an atmosphere of trust. Trust "foments a moral imperative to take on the hard work of school improvement." Trust, not coercion, is a necessary precondition for school reform.[36]

Did the get-tough policy produce results? Did it lead to higher student test scores? These may not be the right questions. It makes more sense to ask whether a policy of coercion can create good schools. Can teachers successfully educate children to think for themselves if teachers are not treated as professionals who think for themselves? Can principals be inspiring leaders if they must follow orders about the most minute details of daily life in classrooms? If a get-tough policy saps educators of their initiative, their craft, and their enthusiasm, then it is hard to believe that the results are worth having.

CHAPTER FIVE

The Business Model in New York City

In the first decade of the new century, New York City became the national testing ground for market-based reforms. Mayor Michael Bloomberg and his chancellor, Joel Klein, applied business principles to overhaul the nation's largest school system, which enrolled 1.1 million children. Their reforms won national and even international acclaim. They reorganized the management of the schools, battled the teachers' union, granted large pay increases to teachers and principals, pressed for merit pay, opened scores of charter schools, broke up large high schools into small ones, emphasized frequent practice for state tests, gave every school a letter grade, closed dozens of low-performing schools, and institutionalized the ideas of choice and competition (albeit without vouchers). In 2007, only five years after mayoral control of the schools was authorized by the state legislature, New York City won the Broad Prize as the most improved urban school district in the nation.

In the fall of 2001, media mogul Michael Bloomberg was elected mayor of New York City. One of the wealthiest men in the world, Bloomberg had achieved renown as a businessman and philanthropist. As a candidate, he vowed to gain control of the public schools and to make them successful. His campaign literature maintained that the system was "in a state of emergency" and noted, "remarkably, $12 billion—30% of our city's total expenditures, a sum greater than the school spending in Chicago and Los Angeles combined—is not enough to teach 1.1 million public school students or to provide safe, clean and appropriately equipped school facilities." He vowed to remake the system with management reforms, incentives, merit pay, testing, and accountability.[1]

When Bloomberg ran for mayor, the schools were overseen by a seven-member Board of Education, which was appointed by six different elected officials. Each of the city's five borough presidents (from Manhattan, Brooklyn, the Bronx, Queens, and Staten Island) selected one member of the central board. The remaining two members of the board were appointed by the mayor. Since this arrangement became law in 1969, every mayor had sought to regain the power to select the Board of Education. For nearly a century prior to 1969, the city's mayors had appointed every single member of the Board of Education; usually the members of the board were distinguished citizens and community leaders.[2] Once appointed, however, the board was an independent agency, and its members had fixed terms and the power to hire the school superintendent and oversee his policies and budget.

Mayor Bloomberg did not want an independent board. He wanted full, direct control of the schools, with no meddlesome board to second-guess him.

In June 2002, the state legislature turned control of the public school system over to Bloomberg, who promptly established the New York City Department of Education (DOE) to manage the schools. The legislation continued a central board of education, while giving the mayor a majority of appointees, who would serve at his pleasure; Bloomberg renamed it the Panel for Educational Policy and made clear that he considered it of no importance. When he introduced the members at a press conference, he said, "They don't have to speak, and they don't have to serve. That's what 'serving at the pleasure' means."[3] He sold the Board of Education's headquarters in Brooklyn to a real estate developer and moved the new department's headquarters to the Tweed Courthouse, adjacent to his offices at City Hall. Henceforth, the shorthand term for the New York City Department of Education was simply "Tweed."

Thus, the DOE was housed in a magnificent building that symbolized the infamous Tweed Ring. Moreover, there was this irony:

William Marcy Tweed, aka the boss of Tammany Hall, had led the effort to abolish the New York Board of Education in 1871 and turn the school system into a municipal department, making it easier to control and to loot. Boss Tweed's Department of Public Instruction banned the purchase of books from the Harper Brothers publishing company as punishment for Thomas Nast's cartoons lampooning the Tweed Ring in *Harper's Weekly*. In 1873, after the Tweed Ring was exposed, the state legislature reestablished an independent Board of Education, appointed by the mayor. And from 1873 until 1969, the mayor appointed every member of the central board.[4]

A few weeks after he gained control, Mayor Bloomberg offered the top education job in the nation's largest city to Joel Klein, a lawyer who had served as assistant attorney general in the Justice Department during the Clinton administration. During his time as head of the antitrust division, Klein won national attention for his efforts to break up the software giant Microsoft. A brilliant and accomplished lawyer and prosecutor, he had little experience in education.

Soon after being appointed, Klein visited Alan Bersin, the school superintendent in San Diego, who had come to the job with the same background as lawyer, prosecutor, and former official in the Clinton administration.[5] Like Bersin, Klein adopted a "left-right" strategy: He selected instructional programs that pleased the pedagogical left, awarded large contracts to vendors of these programs, and created large numbers of jobs for consultants and coaches who were knowledgeable about progressive approaches. And he satisfied the business community by vigorously promoting choice and accountability.

Klein spent the winter of 2002 fashioning his reform agenda. He first brought in the management consulting firm McKinsey & Company, then turned to investment banker Ron Beller, a former partner at Goldman Sachs. *BusinessWeek* admiringly described how Mayor Bloomberg had "terrorized New York's educational establishment" by recruiting leaders from corporate America, such as controversial business legend Jack Welch, former chairman of General Electric, to spearhead the effort to apply business principles to public education.[6]

In January 2003, on Martin Luther King Jr. Day, the mayor announced his reform program, which he called Children First. It consisted of several parts:

First, the administration declared that in fall 2003, it would install a uniform reading and mathematics program in almost every school (235 of the city's 1,200 schools were exempt because they were relatively high-performing schools). His new Department of Education mandated Balanced Literacy, the same method that was pioneered in District 2 and later implemented in San Diego. The math program consisted of two McGraw-Hill products, *Everyday Mathematics* and *Impact Mathematics*, which are nontraditional, constructivist programs. Each school was assigned literacy coaches and mathematics coaches to monitor and enforce strict implementation of the new mandates. In addition, the DOE mandated citywide use of the Teachers College "workshop model" and imposed it in a highly prescriptive manner, with group work required in all lessons and each day's activities defined in precise order and detail.[7]

Second, the mayor and chancellor declared their intention to eliminate the city's thirty-two community school districts (although these districts were continued in the law) and to replace them with ten large regions, each headed by a regional superintendent. Local instructional superintendents (known as "LISes") would each oversee ten to twelve schools and report to the regional superintendent. In addition, there would be regional instructional specialists and community school district superintendents (even though the districts now existed only on paper), all of whom would report to the regional superintendents. Financial matters were to be separated entirely from instruction and handed over to six regional operating centers (or "ROCs"). The city's educators and parents had to learn a new vocabulary of acronyms and a new system of governance.

Third, the Bloomberg administration announced the creation of a privately funded Leadership Academy to mentor new principals and train people from various fields who wanted to become principals. The mayor raised $75 million in private philanthropic funds for a three-year program to train ninety people each year. To head this academy, Klein hired a business executive with no previous experience in education and put together a board whose star member was Jack Welch.[8] In its initial three years, the academy produced about 150 principals. After the first three years, the DOE assumed responsibility for the academy.

Fourth, the mayor promised there would be greater parental involvement in the schools, but the new structure actually reduced parental involvement. With the elimination of local school boards and the central board, where each of the city's five boroughs had a representative, parents found it difficult to contact anyone in authority about issues that affected their children. Local community education councils made up of parents replaced the community school boards in each district, but they were seldom, if ever, consulted about decisions that affected schools in their communities. Many parents became frustrated by their inability to influence decisions that affected their children or their school. Klein directed principals to hire a parent coordinator, but the coordinators worked for the principal, not for parents.

The reorganization was a corporate model of tightly centralized, hierarchical, top-down control, with all decisions made at Tweed and strict supervision of every classroom to make sure the orders flowing from headquarters were precisely implemented. The general perception was that the mayor planned to run the school system like a business, with standard operating procedures across the system. Klein surrounded himself with noneducators, most of whom were lawyers, management consultants, and business school graduates. Many of the young aides to the chancellor were only a few years out of college or graduate school and had no experience in education but received six-figure salaries.[9]

The Children First reforms were introduced into the public schools in the fall of 2003. The mandated pedagogy was soon immersed in controversy. Many teachers complained of micromanagement, since they had to follow the new directives about how to teach even if they had been successful with different methods. They resented their supervisors' close scrutiny of bulletin boards in classrooms and hallways, as well as the requirement that elementary classrooms be equipped with a rug and a rocking chair, which were aspects of the Balanced Literacy approach.[10]

Despite frequent references by the mayor and the chancellor to a citywide uniform curriculum, there was no uniform curriculum, except in mathematics. Minimal attention was paid to science, history, literature, geography, civics, the arts, or other subjects. Instead, Tweed mandated a citywide pedagogy, which imposed a rigid orthodoxy about *how* to teach. Eventually, in response to complaints from parents and civic groups about the lack of attention to non-tested subjects, the DOE developed a curriculum in science and in the arts, but the schools were held accountable only for test scores in reading and math.

The first major controversy for the Bloomberg administration occurred because of its choice of reading program. When the DOE

mandated Balanced Literacy as its single method of teaching reading, seven prominent reading researchers from local universities
wrote a private letter to Klein, warning that he had made a mistake.
They counseled that this method was unproven and unlikely to succeed, especially with the neediest children. He replied a week later
by releasing a letter in support of his choice, signed by one hundred education professors; the lead signatory to the letter was Lucy
Calkins, a professor at Teachers College who would later receive
large contracts from the DOE to train thousands of teachers in her
reading methods and the Teachers College "workshop model."[11]

At the mayor's insistence, a school was opened on the ground
floor of the Tweed Courthouse, the headquarters of the Department
of Education. The mayor believed that having children in their midst
would remind the administrators why they were there. The DOE
spent $7.5 million to create classrooms in its building. Called City
Hall Academy, the school was not large enough to be a real school.
Instead, groups of about one hundred students rotated in for a two-
week period to study the city and then return to their regular school.

In the spring of 2006, the chancellor decided to reshuffle the
school system yet again. The initial reorganization—with its ten
tightly managed regions—included a pilot program for twenty-six
schools (mostly small high schools)—called the "autonomy zone,"
where the schools agreed to meet performance goals in exchange
for a modicum of freedom from the system's mandates. Now Klein
invited additional principals to escape the micromanagement of the
ten regions he had established and join this autonomy zone, which
he renamed the "empowerment zone." About a quarter, or 350, of
the city's schools applied, and 331 were admitted. This was a prelude to even bigger changes.

A year later, in 2007, Klein launched another reorganization of
the school system, the third in four years. He declared his earlier
program of tight centralization a success, abolished the regions,
and eliminated all direct supervision of the schools. Superintendents retained their titles but were not expected to visit schools
unless directed to do so by the chancellor or in response to falling
test scores. There was no public discussion or review of the sweeping changes in school governance. It was announced and done. To
accomplish this reorganization, Klein relied on outside consultants,
including Sir Michael Barber of England and the corporate restructuring firm of Alvarez & Marsal. Barber, who had been a key adviser

to the government of Tony Blair in Britain, urged a strategy of top-down accountability, plus market reforms that included choice, competition, school autonomy, and incentives. Alvarez & Marsal had previously managed the troubled St. Louis public school system, collected a $5 million fee, and decamped not long before the system was declared a failure and taken over by the state of Missouri.

In the new order, all principals would be "empowered" to take responsibility for their schools, which were part of a community district in name only. Every school would be "autonomous." The principals were directed either to affiliate with an internal or external "support organization," which would provide services to schools but not supervise them, or to join the empowerment zone, where no one would supervise them. Most principals chose to join support organizations led by experienced educators, while others joined with private agencies like New Visions for Public Schools or the City University of New York. Of course, the schools were not really autonomous, because Tweed still determined the examination schedule, still administered interim assessments, still controlled personnel policy, still issued detailed rules and regulations, still controlled admissions procedures, and still imposed mandates that affected daily life in every school. Moreover, after three intensive years of professional development devoted to the compulsory reading and mathematics programs of the first reorganization, few schools were willing or able to exercise autonomy on matters of curriculum and instruction.

The major decisions of the school system that affected children's lives were made at headquarters. For example, the DOE gave a $15.8 million no-bid contract for eighteen months to Alvarez & Marsal to devise cost-cutting measures. A&M executives rearranged the school system's bus routes in January 2007, with disastrous consequences. Thousands of children were stranded without transportation to school during the coldest days of the year. Children as young as five were suddenly ineligible for school bus service and told to take a public bus; siblings were sent to different bus stops. The resulting confusion was not only a major embarrassment for the DOE, but one of the rare occasions when Tweed was criticized by the city's tabloid press.[12]

After the 2007 reorganization of the school system, no school-level supervision was needed, because the Department of Education intended to judge every school solely by its results—that is, whether it raised test scores. In 2003, Tweed thought it could get higher scores by micromanaging the schools. By 2007, administration officials decided they could get better results by replacing supervision with a tightly aligned accountability program of incentives and sanctions. At headquarters, new job titles proliferated, mimicking titles in the corporate sector. Instead of superintendents and deputy superintendents, there was a "chief accountability officer," a "chief knowledge officer," a "chief talent officer," a "chief portfolio officer," "senior achievement facilitators," and other corporate-sounding titles; most high-level officials at the DOE were noneducators.[13]

Large contracts were awarded to companies that specialized in test-preparation activities, such as Princeton Review and Kaplan Learning. Beginning in September each year, the elementary and middle schools dedicated large blocks of time to practice for the state tests that were administered in January and March. Once the tests were finished, there was time for other subjects, but it was difficult to maintain the same level of student motivation, because teachers and students knew the tests were the primary measures of their success or failure.

Test scores in reading and mathematics became the be-all and end-all of public education in grades three through eight. Reading and mathematics were the only subjects that mattered, because they were the only subjects that counted for city, state, and federal accountability. In 2005, the National Assessment of Educational Progress (NAEP) survey of science found that two-thirds of New York City's eighth-grade students were "below basic," the lowest possible ranking. Arts education suffered too. When the system was reorganized in 2007, Tweed eliminated a program that earmarked $67.5 million specifically for arts education, and the funds were released to the schools as discretionary. An official DOE survey of the arts in the schools in 2008 revealed that only 4 percent of the city's elementary schools met the state's requirements for arts education. By 2009, nearly a third of the schools had no arts teachers.[14] Because accountability was restricted only to reading and mathematics, there was little reason for elementary and middle schools to pay much attention to subjects that did not count, such as the arts, physical education, science, history, and civics.

The Bloomberg-Klein reforms were part of the national zeitgeist. They embodied the same ideas as the federal No Child Left Behind legislation. The principles behind them—test-based accountability and choice—were exactly the same. Children First was the New

York City version of No Child Left Behind, in spirit and in practice. The basic idea shared by Mayor Bloomberg in New York City and the George W. Bush administration and Congress was that a relentless focus on testing and accountability would improve the schools. Schools that failed to produce higher scores would suffer increasingly severe sanctions, their principals might be fired, and the schools might be closed. After the passage of No Child Left Behind, President Bush saw the modest score gains on national tests as a major element in his legacy. Similarly, Mayor Bloomberg wanted to prove that his stewardship of the schools had produced dramatic results.

Although I initially supported the mayor's takeover of the schools, I was increasingly disturbed by the lack of any public forum to question executive decisions and by the elimination of all checks and balances on executive power. In the spring of 2004, I joined with Randi Weingarten, president of the New York City United Federation of Teachers, to write an opinion piece in the *New York Times* decrying the autocratic nature of the school system. We said that under this new system, the public had been left out of public education.[15]

It is true that decisions can be made more quickly when only one person is in charge of the schools. The mayor and chancellor staunchly maintained that any attempt by the state legislature to erode the mayor's total authority over the schools or to reestablish an independent board—especially one where members had fixed terms—would destroy mayoral control. Chancellor Klein told a legislative hearing, "If you have divided authority, what you have is no one in charge. An independent board would return this city to the politics of paralysis."[16] However, school reform without public oversight or review is contrary to basic democratic principles. In a democracy, every public agency is subject to scrutiny. Removing all checks and balances may promote speed, but it undermines the credibility and legitimacy of decisions, and it eliminates the kind of review that catches major mistakes before it is too late. While Mayor Bloomberg and Chancellor Klein are men of integrity, unchecked power in the wrong hands can facilitate corruption and malfeasance. Even officials of the highest integrity must be subject to checks and balances to ensure that they listen to those they serve.

The need for checks and balances surely occurred to the state legislature when it changed the legislation in 2002, because it preserved a board of education in the law, giving the mayor the power to appoint eight of its thirteen members, while the borough presidents appointed the other five. Mayor Bloomberg treated the board as an advisory group whose advice he never sought. The old Board of Education had been a powerful body, with the power to hire the chancellor, to veto his decisions, and to fire him. But the new Panel for Educational Policy was a rubber stamp for the mayor and chancellor.

Only on one occasion, in March 2004, did the panel presume to disagree with the mayor, over the issue of social promotion, the practice of promoting children to the next grade even if they have not mastered the skills and knowledge that they need to succeed in the next grade. When the mayor wanted to end social promotion in third grade, some members of the panel expressed their concern about the hasty adoption of this policy and the lack of planning to help children who were retained; on the day of the vote, the mayor fired two of his appointees and engineered the dismissal of a third, guaranteeing passage of his proposal. The media called that evening the "Monday Night Massacre." After the meeting, Bloomberg defended his actions. He said, "Mayoral control means mayoral control, thank you very much. They are my representatives, and they are going to vote for things that I believe in." The members of the panel appointed by the mayor never again objected to any mayoral priority.[17]

Over the next few years, the DOE ended social promotion not only in grade three, but also in grades five, seven, and eight, and eventually in all grades. However, the number of children actually left back under the new retention policy didn't change from what was customary in the past. Surprisingly, even fewer students were retained than in the past. A 2009 study of the city's small high schools by Clara Hemphill and Kim Nauer reported that "a huge proportion of students arrive in ninth grade with the skills that are two, three or even four years below grade level," an observation that raises questions about whether social promotion ever really ended.[18]

As it happened, the city's policy of ending social promotion converged with the state's unannounced decision to make it easier for students to reach level 2 on state tests between 2006 and 2009. The city used the results of the state tests to determine which students should be held back; any student scoring at level 1, the very bottom, was supposed to be retained. The state began annual testing of grades three through eight in 2006 (previously it had tested only grades four and eight).

In 2006, significant numbers of New York City students scored at level 1 and were subject to retention. By 2009, very few students were at level 1. The number of students at level 1 dropped so low that level 1 could hardly be considered a performance level. In 2006, 70,090 students in grades three through eight were at level 1 in mathematics; by 2009, that number had fallen to 14,305. In reading, the number of level 1 students fell from 46,085 to 11,755. In seventh-grade math, 18.8 percent were at level 1 in 2006, but by 2009, only 2.1 percent were. In sixth-grade reading, 10.1 percent were at level 1 in 2006, but by 2009, only 0.2 percent were.[19]

Why did the number of students at level 1 plummet? Because the state lowered the bar and made it easier for students to reach level 2. On the sixth-grade reading test in 2006, students needed to earn 41 percent of the points to attain level 2; by 2009, students in that grade needed only 17.9 percent. In seventh-grade math, students needed to earn 36.2 percent of the points on the test to advance to level 2 in 2006, but by 2009, they needed to earn only 22 percent. The standards to advance from level 1 to level 2 dropped so low that many students could get enough correct answers to pass to level 2 by randomly guessing.[20]

So, while public declarations about ending social promotion sounded good in theory, in practice there was no change from before. Thanks to the state's lowering of standards on its tests, it became easier for students to earn the score necessary to escape level 1. In the meantime, parents grew angry because their concerns were ignored. The "Monday Night Massacre"—when social promotion was allegedly ended—spurred a parent rebellion against the mayor and the chancellor. Parents realized that there was no public forum in which their views would be heard or heeded.

Parent activists regularly expressed their frustration on the New York City Public School Parents' blog.[21] There, parents complained about overcrowding, large classes, the expansion of charter schools into public school facilities, the excessive time devoted to testing, profligate spending by Tweed, no-bid contracts, and changes in the policies governing the admission of children to kindergarten, gifted programs, middle schools, and high schools. Parent groups such as Class Size Matters, the Chancellor's Parent Advisory Council, the Coalition for Educational Justice, the Campaign for Better Schools, and community education councils (which were composed of parent leaders) wanted a greater voice in how the schools were run. But no one was listening.

When mayoral control of the schools was set to expire in 2009, it was parent groups that were most vociferous in seeking limits on the mayor's power to control the schools. But the mayor lined up overwhelming political support for continuing his control of the public schools, financed in part by millions of dollars from the Gates Foundation and the Broad Foundation.[22] The only group that might have stymied his goal was the United Federation of Teachers. More than 80 percent of its membership expressed strong disapproval of the mayor's and chancellor's approach in a poll taken in June 2008. But the union leadership was grateful to the mayor, because he had awarded the teachers a 43 percent salary increase and a generous boost to their pensions. Randi Weingarten, the union's president, endorsed continuation of mayoral control. Despite the protests of parent groups and objections by state senators largely from minority communities, the state legislature renewed the mayor's grant of power in 2009.[23]

THE ORIGINAL ANNOUNCEMENT of the Children First agenda made only a passing reference to charter schools, but they emerged as one of the administration's signature initiatives. Charter schools are privately managed but receive public funding. Previous leaders of the school system had opposed charter schools, believing that they would drain away students and money from the regular public schools. The city had only a few of them when Klein took office. He energetically authorized new charter schools, and within a few years, the DOE reached the state-legislated cap of fifty charter schools. In 2007, Mayor Bloomberg persuaded the legislature and newly elected Governor Eliot Spitzer to permit New York City to open an additional fifty charter schools. During his reelection campaign in 2009, he promised to open another one hundred new charter schools, so that by 2013, 100,000 students would be in charters.

Once Tweed embraced charter schools, they received priority treatment. The chancellor placed many charter schools into regular public school buildings, taking classrooms and facilities away from the host schools and igniting bitter fights with the regular schools' parent associations. In 2006, when Courtney Sale Ross, widow of Steve

Ross, chairman of Time Warner, proposed to open a charter school, the DOE offered her space in a successful public school for gifted children on the Lower East Side of Manhattan, called NEST+M (New Explorations in Science, Technology, and Mathematics). However, the school's parent association led a noisy public fight against inserting the Ross Global Academy Charter School into its building. Eventually Chancellor Klein abandoned his efforts to put the charter school into the NEST+M building. Instead, he ousted the celebrated City Hall Academy from the basement of Tweed, relocated it to Harlem, and gave the coveted space to Courtney Sale Ross's charter school. City Hall Academy was quietly closed in 2007, and the Ross Global Academy eventually moved to larger quarters.[24]

Klein frequently celebrated the successes of charter schools, appeared at their celebrations to praise them, and hailed them as superior to the regular public schools over which he presided. In announcing the authorization of additional charter schools in 2009, Klein said, "Charter school students' achievements are proof that all students can succeed given the right opportunity. I am thrilled that these additional charter schools will enable even more families to choose the rigorous education that these schools provide."[25] He did not consider his comments to be a negative reflection on his stewardship of the regular public schools, whose test scores did not match those of the charters. Compared to regular public schools, the charter schools typically had smaller classes and more resources, especially if they had philanthropic sponsors.

Most charter schools were located in low-income neighborhoods, and their students were chosen by lottery. Critics complained that they were "enrolling only the best students and ignoring disadvantaged populations," since only the most motivated students were likely to apply for admission to a charter school. A state-funded group that advocates for the rights of homeless students complained that homeless families were shut out of charter schools, because they had difficulty meeting the deadlines and following through with the application process. Of 51,316 public school students in the city who were homeless, only 111 were enrolled in charter schools. In one impoverished neighborhood, where there were nine homeless shelters, the Achievement First East New York Charter School did not enroll a single homeless student.[26]

Another strategy the DOE enthusiastically embraced was small high schools. When the DOE was established, the system had about one hundred large high schools, some with enrollments as large as 3,000 to 5,000 students. It also had about seventy-five small high schools that had been created during the 1990s as part of the progressive small-school movement led by innovative educator Deborah Meier. Many of the large high schools boasted historic traditions as portals for immigrant children. They enrolled significant numbers of students who spoke little or no English and came from impoverished circumstances. Many of these high schools were extremely low-functioning, and in the era of high expectations, they were notable mainly for overcrowding, large class sizes, poor attendance rates, and low graduation rates, as well as their deteriorated physical condition. It was not clear whether their low performance was due to their size, the learning problems of their students, the extreme poverty of the families they served, their instructional programs, their leadership, or neglect by central authorities.

Within the space of a few years, Chancellor Klein had closed nearly two dozen of the city's large high schools and opened two hundred new small high schools, funded by hundreds of millions of dollars from the Bill & Melinda Gates Foundation, the Carnegie Corporation, and the Open Society Institute. By 2009, these schools enrolled about 25 percent of the city's high school pupils. The DOE reported that graduation rates and attendance rates were higher in these schools than in the large high schools they replaced. However, the new small high schools were permitted in their first two years to admit smaller proportions of special education students and English-language learners, as compared to large high schools; this contributed to their improved outcomes.[27]

The Department of Education clearly favored the small high schools it had created, and looked on the large high schools as relics. As small schools multiplied, the large high schools became more overcrowded and enrolled disproportionate shares of students with high needs. The more the large high schools struggled, the more they became candidates for closure. In 2009, the study by Hemphill and Nauer found that the small high schools eventually enrolled "roughly the same proportion of students" who were at risk of dropping out as other high schools; after a few years of operation, as their student population came to resemble those in other schools, their initially stellar attendance rates and graduation rates declined. The small schools, the authors said, experienced high teacher turnover and principal turnover—in some schools, nearly half the teachers quit in a one-year period, as did nearly half the 124 principals hired for the first group of small high schools. As compared to students in the large high schools, students in the small high schools were far more likely to receive a local diploma (which represents the bare minimum of state requirements) than a Regents diploma (which requires the student to pass five state examinations).

The small high schools, said Hemphill and Nauer, have strengths but also "significant limitations," including their inability to provide special education services, support for English-language learners, an array of courses in music and the arts, extracurricular and sports programs, advanced courses, and vocational programs. Nor did choice serve all children well. The authors noted that many thirteen-year-olds might lack the "good judgment or activist parents" to make wise decisions, and school officials routinely rejected requests to transfer once a choice was made. Hemphill and Nauer pointed out that "the gains for students at the small schools came at the expense of other students, some of whom were even needier than those who attended the new small schools." The authors concluded that "the small high schools are no panacea," and "school choice, by itself, won't improve schools."[28]

A typical student entering ninth grade could choose from about one hundred high schools in his or her borough. Citywide, he could choose from more than four hundred high schools. Most of the new small schools were theme schools, centered on a specific profession or specialty. This produced some offbeat results, such as a high school for future firefighters; a school for the hospitality industry; a school for urban planners; a school for architecture; a school for the business of sports; a school for the violin; several schools for social justice, peace, and diversity; and other schools for the health professions, writers, leaders, the arts, law, technology, communications, journalism, and media. Adults like the idea of themes, but few children starting ninth grade are prepared to select a profession or career specialty.

As it elevated the concept of school choice, the Department of Education destroyed the concept of neighborhood high schools. Getting into the high school of one's choice became as stressful as getting into the college of one's choice. Should students apply to the school for peace and justice or the school for law or the school for stagecraft? Students were expected to list their top twelve preferences. Most got into one of the twelve, but thousands got into none at all. Neighborhoods were once knitted together by a familiar local high school that served all the children of the community, a school with distinctive traditions and teams and history. After the neighborhood high school closed, children scattered across the city in response to the lure of new, unknown small schools with catchy names or were assigned to schools far from home. Hemphill and Nauer found that some students traveled up to ninety minutes to get to school each day. At Harry S. Truman High School, which is part of the nation's largest residential development—Co-op City in the Bronx—with 55,000 residents, only 5 percent of its students live in Co-op City; 45 percent of its freshmen commute more than forty-five minutes to get there.[29]

Meanwhile, a sad story was acted out in one high school after another. As a high school for 3,000 students was closed down, it would be replaced by four or five small schools for 500 students. What happened to the missing students? Invariably, they were the lowest-performing, least motivated students, who were somehow passed over by the new schools, who did not want kids like them to depress the school's all-important scores. These troublesome students were relegated to another large high school, where their enrollment instigated a spiral of failure, dissolution, and closing. The DOE set into motion a process that acted like a computer virus in the large high schools. As each one closed, its least desirable students were shunted off into yet another large high school, starting a death watch for the receiving school.[30]

After the DOE turned to autonomy and choice as its main initiatives, it lost interest in the instructional reforms of 2003. The unifying idea of the new reform agenda was accountability. The DOE introduced a program of rating and evaluating every school. It surveyed parents, teachers, and students about their satisfaction with their school and their principal. The surveys usually revealed high levels of satisfaction because everyone knew the ratings would affect their school's grade, its status, its potential bonuses, even its survival. The DOE hired a group of British educators to perform quality reviews of every school, but these reviews did not count in the school's grade. Soon, everyone was rating and grading and evaluating everyone else, but little attention was given to helping schools do a better job. The bottom line of accountability was rewards (for higher scores) and sanctions (for not getting higher scores). The DOE offered incentives to improve test scores: There were bonuses for principals and teachers if their school's scores went up, and there was even a pilot program to pay students to raise their test scores.

In 2007, the mayor negotiated an agreement with the United Federation of Teachers to award schoolwide bonuses to teachers in about two hundred schools if their school's scores went up; he called it "merit pay," but the union insisted it was not. Merit pay, said the union, set teacher against teacher in a competition for dollars. In a merit pay school, Ms. Smith might earn more than Mr. Jones in the classroom next door. But in the schoolwide bonus plan, a committee at each school decided how to divide the bonus among all union members on the staff, including non-teaching personnel, and all might receive exactly the same stipend, if the school committee so chose. Or the committee might award bonuses to all the teachers or only to those teachers whose test scores were higher. The schoolwide bonus plan was not quite merit pay, but it was a significant step in that direction. It ensured that teachers would concentrate their attention on those all-important scores in reading and mathematics. In exchange for agreeing to the bonus plan, the union won a generous enhancement of teacher pensions, allowing teachers to retire five years earlier than before, at the age of fifty-five with twenty-five years of service. Prior to this agreement, teachers hired after 1973 had to work thirty years or wait until they were sixty-two to retire with full pension.[31]

The accountability movement entered a new phase in the fall of 2007, when the DOE revealed what it called progress reports for each school. Each school received a single letter grade, from A to F. This approach mirrored the grading system introduced in Florida by then-governor Jeb Bush a few years earlier. Most of each school's grade was based on year-to-year changes in standardized test scores (its "progress"), as compared to a group of schools that were demographically similar; if a school's scores went up, it was likely to win an A or B. If they remained flat or slipped, the school was almost certain to get a C, D, or F.

Some excellent schools, known for their sense of community and consistently high scores, received an F because their scores dipped a few points. Some very low-performing schools, even some schools the State Education Department ranked as persistently dangerous, received an A because they showed some improvement.

To add to the confusion, the city's grades were inconsistent with the ratings issued by the State Education Department in accordance with No Child Left Behind. If schools failed to meet their adequate yearly progress goals under the federal NCLB law, they were called SINI schools, or "schools in need of improvement." If schools consistently performed poorly, the state called them SURR schools, or "schools under registration review." In the first year that school grades were issued, the city awarded an A or B to about half of the 350 schools the state said were SINI or SURR. More than half of the fifty schools that received an F from the city were in good standing with the state and the federal law. The next year, 89 percent of the F schools were in good standing according to NCLB standards, as were 48 percent of D schools.[32]

In 2009, the city's accountability system produced bizarre results. An amazing 84 percent of 1,058 elementary and middle schools received an A (compared with 23 percent in 2007), and an additional 13 percent got a B. Only twenty-seven schools received a grade of C, D, or F. Even four schools the state said were "persistently dangerous" received an A. The Department of Education hailed these results as evidence of academic progress, but the usually supportive local press was incredulous. The *New York Post* called the results "ridiculous" and said, "As it stands now, the grades convey nearly no useful information whatsoever." The *New York Daily News* described the reports as a "stupid card trick" and "a big flub" that rendered the annual school reports "nearly meaningless to thousands of parents who look to the summaries for guidance as to which schools serve kids best."[33]

The debacle of the grading system had two sources: First, it relied on year-to-year changes in scores, which are subject to random error and are thus unreliable. Second, the scores were hugely inflated by the state's secret decision to lower the points needed to advance on state tests. Consequently, the city's flawed grading system produced results that few found credible, while the Department of Education was obliged to pay teachers nearly $30 million in bonuses—based on dumbed-down state tests—as part of its "merit pay" plan.[34]

How could parents make sense of the conflicting reports from the city, state, and federal accountability systems? Should they send their children to a school that got an A from the city, even though the state said the same school was low-performing and persistently dangerous? Should they pull their child out of a highly regarded neighborhood school where 90 percent of the kids passed the state exams but the city gave it an F? The city had no plan to improve low-performing schools, other than to warn them that they were in danger of being closed down. Shame and humiliation were considered adequate remedies to spur improvement. Pedro Noguera of New York University observed that the Department of Education failed to provide the large schools with the support and guidance they needed to improve. "They don't have a school-change strategy," Noguera said. "They have a school-shutdown strategy." Chancellor Klein acknowledged that opening and closing schools was an essential element in the market-based system of school choice that he preferred. He said, "It's basically a supply-and-demand pattern. . . . This is about improving the system, not necessarily about improving every single school." But there was no reason to believe that closing a school and opening a new one would necessarily produce superior results; in fact, half of the city's ten worst-performing schools on the state math tests in 2009 were new schools that had been opened to replace failing schools.[35]

Having promised to make dramatic improvements in the school system, both Mayor Bloomberg and Chancellor Klein pointed with pride to the gains recorded on state tests, calling them evidence of historic change. When the mayor's reforms were launched in September 2003, 52.5 percent of fourth-grade students were at levels 3 and 4 on the state tests in reading. By 2007, that proportion had risen to 56.0 percent, a gain of 3.5 percentage points (this was a much smaller increase than in the four years from 1999 to 2003, when the scores rose by 19.7 percentage points). In eighth-grade reading, where there had been no progress in the previous years, the proportion of students meeting state standards grew from 32.6 percent to 41.8 percent, an impressive improvement. In mathematics, the Bloomberg administration celebrated an increase in the fourth-grade proficiency rate from 66.7 percent in 2003 to 74.1 percent in 2007, a gain of 7.4 percentage points (again, this was a smaller gain than in the four years before mayoral control, when the number climbed from 49.6 percent to 66.7 percent, or 17.1 percentage points). Eighth-grade scores in mathematics shot upward from 34.4 percent meeting standards in 2003 to 45.6 percent in 2007.[36] Laudatory articles celebrating the Bloomberg miracle appeared in *Forbes*, *The Economist*, *Time*, *Newsweek*, *U.S. News & World Report*, and *USA Today*. The stories reported the remarkable transformation of the New York City public schools. And the city's schools won the Broad Prize in 2007, because of the improved test scores.

It was a shock, therefore, when the federal NAEP released reading and math scores for eleven cities, including New York City, in November 2007. The NAEP scores for 2003–2007 encompassed the first four years of the new regime and provided an independent check on the city's claims of historic gains.

On the NAEP, students in New York City made no significant gains in reading or mathematics between 2003 and 2007, except in fourth-grade mathematics. In fourth-grade reading, in eighth-grade reading, and in eighth-grade mathematics, the NAEP scores showed no significant change. Nor was there any narrowing of the achievement gap among students from different racial groups. Except in fourth-grade mathematics, there were no gains for black students, white students, Asian students, Hispanic students, or lower-income students. The *New York Times* published a front-page story about the NAEP report, titled "Little Progress for City Schools on National Test."[37]

The New York City Department of Education responded to the stagnant results on the federal tests with a press release claiming that "New York City students made impressive gains" on NAEP. The flat scores on the national tests, the chancellor explained to reporters, reflected that students prepared for the state tests, which were aligned with the state standards. But both the state and the federal tests assessed generic skills in reading and mathematics, not specific content (such as works of literature); the skills should have been transferable. If they were not transferable and were useful only for taking state tests, then students were not prepared to read college textbooks, job-training manuals, or anything else that was not specific to the state tests.[38]

Using private funding, the city launched a publicity blitz to proclaim its increased test scores and graduation rates. The graduation rates were even more malleable than the test scores, as there were so many ways to adjust them up or down. It all depended on which students were counted or not counted. Does one count only students who graduate in four years or students who take more than four years? Does one count GED diplomas that students obtain outside of regular school? What about August graduates?

According to the state, the New York City graduation rate increased from 44 percent to 56 percent between 2003 and 2008. On its face, this was an impressive improvement, but the rate was inflated in various ways, such as excluding students who left city high schools without a diploma and were counted as "discharges" rather than dropouts. (Many discharges would be considered dropouts by federal standards.) The graduation rate was also artificially increased by a dubious practice called "credit recovery," a covert form of social promotion for high school students. Under credit recovery, students who failed a course or never even showed up for it could get credit by turning in an independent project, whose preparation was unmonitored, or by attending a few extra sessions. A principal told the *New York Times* that credit recovery was the "dirty little secret of high schools. There's very little oversight and there are very few standards."[39]

Among those who did graduate, many were poorly educated. Three-quarters of the city's high school graduates who enrolled in the two-year community colleges of the City University of New York were required to take a remedial course in reading, writing, or mathematics; this was an improvement over the statistics for 2002, before mayoral control, when 82 percent required remediation. But in the earlier period, no one claimed that social promotion had ended.[40]

Testing was always important in the New York City schools, but it assumed even more importance in the age of data-driven accountability. The DOE centralized admissions to gifted and talented programs, presumably in the interest of equity, requiring all applicants to take the same standardized intelligence tests; only those who reached the 90th percentile gained admission to a gifted program. But the new approach halved the number of children in such programs and halved the proportion of African American and Hispanic children accepted from 46 percent to only 22 percent.[41] Any education researcher could have predicted this result, because children from advantaged homes are far likelier to know the vocabulary on a standardized test than children who lack the same advantages.

Because of its concentration on raising test scores in reading and mathematics, the Department of Education consistently paid less attention to other subjects. The media, too, closely followed reading and math test scores but ignored such subjects as science and social studies, even though the state tested these subjects. When science and social studies were tested in 2008, twenty-eight of New York City's thirty-two districts placed in the bottom 10th percentile of the state's districts in science, and twenty-six districts were in the bottom 10th percentile in social studies. In fact, eighteen districts scored in the bottom 5th percentile statewide in both science and social studies. Not a single district scored at or above the 50th percentile in science, and only one (District 26 in Queens) exceeded the 50th percentile in social studies.[42] This was a sobering reflection on the narrowness of what was taught in New York City's public schools. But no one noticed or cared, because those subjects were not part of the city, state, or federal accountability programs. Thus, as the city concentrated intently on raising test scores in reading and mathematics, the other essential ingredients of a good education were missing.

Test score gains do not always last. In 2005, when test scores rose sharply across the city on state tests (as they did in other urban districts in the state), Mayor Bloomberg "trumpeted the results as an election-year affirmation of his stewardship of the public schools," as the *New York Times* described it. The mayor and Chancellor Klein made "a triumphant visit" to P.S. 33 in the Bronx to praise the school's astonishing gains. The proportion of fourth graders meeting state standards on the reading test more than doubled, rising by a staggering 46.7 points in a single year to 83.4 percent. The mayor lauded the good work of the principal. Soon after the principal's star turn, she retired with a $15,000 bonus, which added thousands a year for life to her pension. The following year, P.S. 33's astonishing gains evaporated. The meteoric rise and fall of test scores at the school was mysterious.[43]

Psychometricians are generally suspicious of dramatic changes in test scores. New York University's Robert Tobias, who was testing director of the New York City schools for thirteen years, was skeptical about sharp gains in test scores and their relation to test-preparation activities. At a City Hall hearing in 2005, Tobias criticized "unhealthy over-reliance on testing as a facile tool for educational reform and political advantage" and said, "Much of this test preparation is not designed to increase student learning but rather to try to beat or game the test."[44]

In the future, it is certainly possible that test scores and graduation rates will continue to rise. Or maybe they won't. Of course, it is better to see scores go up than to see them fall. But when the scores are produced by threats of punishment and promises of money, and when students cannot perform equally well on comparable tests for which they have not been trained, then the scores lose their meaning. Scores matter, but they are an indicator, not the definition of a good education.

Mayoral control in New York City had a mixed record. State test scores went up, and spending went up even faster. From 2002 to 2009, the overall budget for public education grew from $12.7 billion annually to $21.8 billion.[45] With such a huge jump, New York City's successes may have been a testament to the value of increased school spending. Did mayoral control bring greater accountability? No, because there was no way to hold the mayor or the chancellor accountable. Standing for reelection once every four years is not a sufficient form of accountability for the mayor, especially when there are so many other issues for voters to consider. The chancellor answered only to the mayor, so he could not be held accountable either. When there were major foul-ups, such as the misrouting of school buses by Alvarez & Marsal in the dead of winter, no one was held accountable.

Mayoral control is not a guaranteed path to school improvement. On the 2007 NAEP, the cities with the highest scores were Charlotte, North Carolina, and Austin, Texas, neither of which had mayoral control. And two of the three lowest-performing cities— Chicago and Cleveland—had had mayoral control for more than a decade. Clearly many factors affect educational performance other than the governance structure.

No governance reform alone will solve all the problems of the schools. A poorly constructed governance system, as New York City had during the era of decentralization from 1969 to 2002, can interfere with the provision of education. But absolute control by the mayor is not the answer, either. It solves no problems to exclude parents and the public from important decisions about education policy or to disregard the educators who work with students daily. Public education is a vital institution in our democratic society, and its governance must be democratic, open to public discussion and public participation.

CHAPTER SIX

NCLB: Measure and Punish

THREE DAYS AFTER HIS INAUGURATION in 2001, President George W. Bush convened some five hundred educators in the East Room of the White House to reveal his plan to reform American education. The plan, which he called No Child Left Behind, promised a new era of high standards, testing, and accountability in which not a single child would be overlooked. It was ironic that the Bush plan borrowed its name from Marian Wright Edelman of the Children's Defense Fund, who intended it to refer to children's health and welfare, not to testing and accountability. Edelman's fund trademarked the slogan "Leave No Child Behind" in 1990 as a rallying cry for its campaign to reduce the number of children living in poverty.[1]

The White House meeting was a thrilling event, as are all events at this grand and glorious mansion. Visiting the White House always gives me goose bumps. I went to the White House for the first time in 1965, when Lyndon B. Johnson was president, for a formal state dinner honoring the president of a small Caribbean nation (I was there because my then-husband was active in Democratic politics). Dressed in a long evening gown, I was escorted inside by a stiff-backed Marine in full dress uniform. Nearly a decade later, I was invited to discuss education issues at a small luncheon with President Gerald Ford, along with sociologists Nathan Glazer and James Coleman. In 1984, I was one of about forty educators invited to meet with President Ronald Reagan in the Cabinet Room. A couple of times, when I was an assistant secretary of education, I met

President George H. W. Bush (at our first meeting, in an irreverent mood, I pulled up a chair next to him behind his desk in the Oval Office so I could get a great picture, and he cheerfully obliged me). During the Clinton years, I was invited to the White House on several occasions to discuss Bill Clinton's education initiatives. I once was invited to watch him address hundreds of high school students in Maryland, and he had them cheering as he urged them to do their homework, study harder, and take tougher courses. It was an amazing demonstration of personal charisma.

So, on January 23, 2001, when the new President Bush presented his plans for school reform, I was excited and optimistic. The president pledged that his focus "would be on making sure every child is educated" and that "no child will be left behind—not one single child." No doubt everyone in the room agreed with that sentiment, though no one was quite certain how it would happen. The president described his principles: first, that every child should be tested every year in grades three through eight, using state tests, not a national test; second, that decisions about how to reform schools would be made by the states, not by Washington; third, that low-performing schools would get help to improve; and fourth, that students stuck in persistently dangerous or failing schools would be able to transfer to other schools.

These four principles, described in a concise 28-page document, eventually became the No Child Left Behind legislation, a document of nearly 1,100 pages. NCLB, as it came to be known, was the latest iteration of the basic federal aid legislation, known originally as the Elementary and Secondary Education Act of 1965.

Soon after President Bush took office in 2001, large bipartisan majorities in Congress approved NCLB. Under ordinary circumstances, Republicans would have opposed the bill's broad expansion of federal power over local schools, and Democrats would have opposed its heavy emphasis on testing. But reports of a "Texas miracle" and bipartisan support for the principle of accountability enabled the legislation to sail through.

The legislative leaders of both parties stood proudly with the president as he signed NCLB into law on January 8, 2002. Democrats liked the expansion of the federal role in education, and Republicans liked the law's support for accountability and choice (although the law did not permit students to take their federal funding with them to private schools, as many Republicans wanted). Republican John Boehner of Ohio called the law his "proudest achievement." Democratic senator Edward Kennedy of Massachusetts called the legislation "a defining issue about the future of our nation and about the future of democracy, the future of liberty, and the future of the United States in leading the free world."[2]

In retrospect, NCLB seems foreordained, because there were so many precedents for it in the states and in Congress in the previous decade. In the 1990s, elected officials of both parties came to accept as secular gospel the idea that testing and accountability would necessarily lead to better schools. Of course, testing was necessary to measure student academic performance and to determine whether it was moving forward, sliding backward, or standing still. At the time, few realized that the quality of the tests was crucial. Elected officials assumed the tests were good enough to do what they were supposed to do—measure student performance— and that a test is a test; they did not give much thought to such technical issues as validity or reliability. Everyone, it seemed, wanted "accountability." By accountability, elected officials meant that they wanted the schools to measure whether students were learning, and they wanted rewards or punishments for those responsible.

School reform was a politically popular issue. In 1988, President George H. W. Bush said he wanted to be the "Education President," and many governors in the 1980s and 1990s claimed the mantle of "Education Governor." Among them were James Hunt in North Carolina, Bill Clinton in Arkansas, Lamar Alexander in Tennessee, Richard Riley in South Carolina, George W. Bush in Texas, Booth Gardner in Washington State, and Roy Romer in Colorado. Some governors made their mark as education reformers by expanding funding for pre-kindergarten or raising teachers' salaries (or both), but most of the time their reforms consisted of new requirements for testing and accountability.

In Washington, the calls for testing and accountability grew louder during the 1990s. The first President Bush released his America 2000 program in 1991, recommending voluntary national standards and voluntary national testing, but it was never authorized by the Democratic majority in Congress. President Clinton came to office promising to create a system of national standards

and national tests, but he was stymied by a Republican majority in Congress. Clinton's Goals 2000 program, enacted before
Republicans took control of Congress in the fall of 1994, encouraged states to develop their own standards and tests. It became a
ritual for Republicans and Democrats alike to bemoan the lack of
accountability in American public education and to grouse that no
teacher, principal, or student was held accountable for poor test
scores.

In that light, the large test score gains in Texas over the previous half-dozen years must have impressed Congress. Not only were
increasing numbers of students passing the state tests, according
to the Texas state education department, but the achievement gap
between white students and minority students was steadily shrink-
ing, as was the number of students dropping out before high school
graduation. So when President George W. Bush arrived in Washington with a plan based on what appeared to be a successful model of
accountability in Texas, members of both parties were willing and
ready to sign on, so long as they could add one or two or three of
their own priorities to the bill. Almost everyone wanted an accountability plan, and almost everyone embraced the main elements of
the one President Bush set forth.

A few scholars had warned in 2000 that the gains in Texas
were a mirage; they said the testing system actually caused rising numbers of dropouts, especially among African American and
Hispanic students, many of whom were held back repeatedly and
quit school in discouragement. These scholars insisted that the
state's rising test scores and graduation rates were a direct result
of the soaring dropout rate: As low-performing students gave up on
education, the statistics got better and better. In separate studies,
Walt Haney of Boston College and Stephen Klein of RAND maintained that the dramatic gains in Texas on its state tests were not
reflected on other measures of academic performance, such as the
SAT and NAEP, or even the state's own test for college readiness.
Haney argued that the Texas high-stakes testing system had other
negative effects. As teachers spent more time preparing students
to take standardized tests, the curriculum was narrowed: Such
subjects as science, social studies, and the arts were pushed aside
to make time for test preparation. Consequently, students in Texas
were actually getting a worse education tied solely to taking the
state tests.[3]

In its eagerness to endorse education reform, Congress paid no attention to these red flags and passed a program that was closely aligned with the Texas model.

NCLB was complex and contained many programs. Its accountability plan included these features:

1. All states were expected to choose their own tests, adopt three performance levels (such as basic, proficient, and advanced), and decide for themselves how to define "proficiency."

2. All public schools receiving federal funding were required to test all students in grades three through eight annually and once in high school in reading and mathematics and to disaggregate (i.e., separate) their scores by race, ethnicity, low-income status, disability status, and limited English proficiency. Disaggregation of scores would ensure that every group's progress was monitored, not hidden in an overall average.

3. All states were required to establish timelines showing how 100 percent of their students would reach proficiency in reading and mathematics by 2013–2014.

4. All schools and school districts were expected to make "adequate yearly progress" (AYP) for every subgroup toward the goal of 100 percent proficiency by 2013–2014.

5. Any school that did not make adequate progress for every subgroup toward the goal of 100 percent proficiency would be labeled a school in need of improvement (SINI). It would face a series of increasingly onerous sanctions. In the first year of failing to make AYP, the school would be put on notice. In the second year, it would be required to offer all its students the right to transfer to a successful school, with transportation paid from the district's allotment of federal funds. In the third year, the school would be required to offer free tutoring to low-income students, paid from the district's federal funds. In the fourth year, the school would be required to undertake "corrective action," which might mean curriculum changes, staff changes, or a longer school day or year. If a school missed its targets for any

   subgroup for five consecutive years, it would be required
   to "restructure."
6. Schools that were required to restructure had five
   options: convert to a charter school; replace the principal and staff; relinquish control to private management; turn over control of the school to the state; or "any
   other major restructuring of the school's governance."
   (Most states and districts ended up choosing the last,
   most ambiguous alternative, hoping to avoid the other
   prospects.)
7. NCLB required all states to participate in the federal
   National Assessment of Educational Progress (NAEP),
   which would henceforth test reading and mathematics
   in grades four and eight in every state every other year
   (before NCLB, state participation in NAEP was voluntary, and some states did not participate; also, the NAEP
   reading and math tests were not administered every other
   year). The NAEP scores, which had no consequences
   for any student or school or district, served as an external
   audit to monitor the progress of the states in meeting
   their goals.[4]

Although the law contained a host of other programs and priorities (most notably, a requirement that all children be taught by a
"highly qualified teacher"), the central focus of NCLB was accountability. It was the issue that brought together Republicans and Democrats. Had there not been bipartisan agreement on accountability,
NCLB would never have become law. Both parties believed that
accountability was the lever that would raise achievement.

Over the next few years, most complaints about NCLB focused
on funding. Some states complained that the federal government did not give them enough extra money to do what the law
required. Federal funding for elementary and secondary programs
was increased by nearly 60 percent in the early years of NCLB, but
Democrats complained that it was way below what was needed and
what Congress had authorized. I remember thinking at the time that
the law only required the schools to teach reading and math effectively, so why should that be a huge additional cost? Isn't that what
they should have been doing anyway? Could there be a more fundamental responsibility of schools than to teach everyone basic skills?

Then there were periodic outbursts by parents and activists against excessive testing and even some organized protests against mandatory state tests. I was not sympathetic to the anti-testing movement. I didn't see why anyone would object to an annual test of reading and mathematics.

My support for NCLB remained strong until November 30, 2006. I can pinpoint the date exactly because that was the day I realized that NCLB was a failure. I went to a conference at the American Enterprise Institute in Washington, D.C.—a well-respected conservative think tank—to hear a dozen or so scholars present their analyses of NCLB's remedies. Organized by Frederick M. Hess and Chester E. Finn Jr., the conference examined whether the major remedies prescribed by NCLB—especially choice and after-school tutoring—were effective. Was the "NCLB toolkit" working? Were the various sanctions prescribed by the law improving achievement? The various presentations that day demonstrated that state education departments were drowning in new bureaucratic requirements, procedures, and routines, and that none of the prescribed remedies was making a difference.

Choice was not working, they all agreed. The scholars presented persuasive evidence that only a tiny percentage of eligible students asked to transfer to better schools. In California, less than 1 percent of eligible students in "failing" schools sought to transfer to another school; in Colorado, less than 2 percent did; in Michigan, the number of transfers under NCLB was negligible; in Miami, where public school choice was already commonplace, less than ½ of 1 percent asked to move because of NCLB; in New Jersey, almost no eligible students transferred, because most districts had only one school at each grade level, and the state's urban districts did not have enough seats available in successful schools to accommodate students from "failing" schools. Julian Betts of the University of California at San Diego questioned whether choice was even a successful strategy, because his own studies found that choice had little or no effect on student achievement.[5]

The scholars suggested many reasons why students were not transferring out of allegedly failing schools. In the first year or two, the letters informing parents of their right to switch their children to a better school were unclear or arrived too late, after the school year had already started. Even when the letters were clear and arrived on time, some parents did not want to send their children on a bus to a faraway school. In some districts, there were already so many public school choice programs that NCLB added nothing new. In others, there were far more eligible students than seats.

But what was especially striking was that many parents and students did not want to leave their neighborhood school, even if the federal government offered them free transportation and the promise of a better school. The parents of English-language learners tended to prefer their neighborhood school, which was familiar to them, even if the federal government said it was failing. A school superintendent told Betts that choice was not popular in his county, because "most people want their local school to be successful, and because they don't find it convenient to get their children across town."[6] Some excellent schools failed to meet AYP because only one subgroup—usually children with disabilities—did not make adequate progress. In such schools, the children in every other subgroup did make progress, were very happy with the school, did not consider it a failing school, and saw no reason to leave.

Thus, while advocates of choice were certain that most families wanted only the chance to escape their neighborhood school, the first four years of NCLB demonstrated the opposite. When offered a chance to leave their failing school and to attend a supposedly better school in another part of town, less than 5 percent—and in some cases, less than 1 percent—of students actually sought to transfer.

Free after-school tutoring (called Supplementary Educational Services, or SES) fared only a bit better than choice, according to the papers presented that day. In California, 7 percent of eligible students received tutoring; in New Jersey, 20 percent did; in Colorado, 10 percent; and in Kentucky, 9 percent. The law implicitly created a "voucher" program for tutoring companies, a marketplace where tutoring companies and school districts could compete for students. Any organization could step forward to register with state departments of education to provide tutoring, whether they were a public school, a school district, a community group, a mom-and-pop operation, a faith-based agency, a for-profit corporation, a college, or a social services organization. Across the nation, nearly 2,000 providers registered to offer tutoring to needy students. But no more than 20 percent of eligible students in any state actually received it, even though it was free and readily available.

Why so little interest in free tutoring? The tutoring agencies blamed the districts for not giving them space in the public schools, and the public schools blamed the tutoring agencies for demand-ing space that was needed for extracurricular activities. The tutors complained about the cost of liability insurance, and the districts complained that some of the tutoring companies were ineffective or were offering students gifts or money if they signed up for their classes. It also seemed likely that large numbers of low-performing students did not want a longer school day, even though they needed the extra help.

As I listened to the day's discussion, it became clear to me that NCLB's remedies were not working. Students were offered the choice to go to another school, and they weren't accepting the offer. They were offered free tutoring, and 80 percent or more turned it down. Enough students signed up to create handsome profits for tutoring companies, but the quality of their services was seldom monitored. I recalled a scandal in New York City when investiga-tors discovered that a tutoring company, created specifically to take advantage of NCLB largesse, was recruiting students by giving money to their principals and gifts to the children; several of the firm's employees had criminal records.[7]

Adult interests were well served by NCLB. The law generated huge revenues for tutoring and testing services, which became a siz-able industry. Companies that offered tutoring, tests, and test-prep materials were raking in billions of dollars annually from federal, state, and local governments, but the advantages to the nation's stu-dents were not obvious.[8]

At the conference, I was on a panel charged with summing up the lessons of the day. I proposed that the states and the federal government were trying to assume tasks for which they were ill suited. I suggested that they should flip their roles, so that the fed-eral government was gathering and disseminating reliable informa-tion on progress, and the states were designing and implementing improvements. Under NCLB, the federal government was dictating ineffectual remedies, which had no track record of success. Nei-ther Congress nor the U.S. Department of Education knows how to fix low-performing schools. Meanwhile, the law required the states to set their own standards and grade their own progress; this led to vastly inflated claims of progress and confusion about standards, with fifty standards for fifty states. Every state was able to define proficiency as it saw fit, which allowed states to claim gains even when there were none. The proper role of the federal government is to supply valid information and leave the remedies and sanctions to those who are closest to the unique problems of individual schools.

What I learned that day fundamentally changed my view of No Child Left Behind. When I realized that the remedies were not working, I started to doubt the entire approach to school reform that NCLB represented. I realized that incentives and sanctions were not the right levers to improve education; incentives and sanctions may be right for business organizations, where the bottom line—profit— is the highest priority, but they are not right for schools. I started to see the danger of the culture of testing that was spreading through every school in every community, town, city, and state. I began to question ideas that I once embraced, such as choice and account- ability, that were central to NCLB. As time went by, my doubts mul- tiplied. I came to realize that the sanctions embedded in NCLB were, in fact, not only ineffective but certain to contribute to the privatization of large chunks of public education. I wonder whether the members of Congress intended this outcome. I doubt that they did. In a bill whose length exceeds 1,000 pages, it is unlikely that many members of Congress read it thoroughly and fully understood all the eventual consequences.

The most toxic flaw in NCLB was its legislative command that all students in every school must be proficient in reading and math- ematics by 2014. By that magical date, every single student must achieve proficiency, including students with special needs, students whose native language is not English, students who are homeless and lacking in any societal advantage, and students who have every societal advantage but are not interested in their schoolwork. All will be proficient by 2014, or so the law mandates. And if they are not, then their schools and teachers will suffer the consequences.

The term "proficiency"—which is the goal of the law—is not the same as "minimal literacy." The term "proficiency" has been used since the early 1990s by the federal testing program, the National Assessment of Educational Progress, where it connotes a very high level of academic achievement. The federal assessment refers to four levels of achievement. The lowest is "below basic," which means a student who is unable to meet the standards for his or her grade. The next level is "basic," which means that a student has partially mastered the expectations for the grade. Then comes "proficient," indicating that a student has fully mastered the standards for the grade. And at the very top of the performance levels is "advanced," which represents truly superior achievement. On the 2007 NAEP for fourth-grade reading, 33 percent of the nation's students were below basic; 34 percent were basic; 25 percent scored proficient; and 8 percent were advanced. In that same year, 28 percent of students in eighth grade were reading at the proficient level, and an additional 3 percent were advanced.[9] Now, in a nation where only one-third of students meet the federal standard for proficiency, we are expected to believe that fully 100 percent will meet that standard by 2014. It will not happen. Unless, that is, the term "proficiency" is redefined to mean functional literacy, minimal literacy, or something akin to a low passing mark (say, a 60 on a test with a 100-point scale, a score that once would have merited a D, at best).

The goal set by Congress of 100 percent proficiency by 2014 is an aspiration; it is akin to a declaration of belief. Yes, we do believe that all children can learn and should learn. But as a goal, it is utterly out of reach. No one truly expects that all students will be proficient by the year 2014, although NCLB's most fervent supporters often claimed that it was feasible.[10] Such a goal has never been reached by any state or nation. In their book about NCLB, Finn and Hess acknowledge that no educator believes this goal is attainable; they write, "Only politicians promise such things." The law, they say, is comparable to Congress declaring "that every last molecule of water or air pollution would vanish by 2014, or that all American cities would be crime-free by that date."[11] I would add that there is an important difference. If pollution does not utterly vanish, or if all cities are not crime-free, no public official will be punished. No state or municipal environmental protection agencies will be shuttered, no police officers will be reprimanded or fired, no police department will be handed over to private managers. But if all students are not on track to be proficient by 2014, then schools will be closed, teachers will be fired, principals will lose their jobs, and some—perhaps many—public schools will be privatized. All because they were not able to achieve the impossible.

The consequence of mandating an unattainable goal, Finn and Hess say, is to undermine states that have been doing a reasonably good job of improving their schools and to produce "a compliance-driven regimen that recreates the very pathologies it was intended to solve."[12] It makes little sense to impose remedies that have never been effective and to assume that they will produce better than reasonably good results.

But the most dangerous potential effect of the 2014 goal is that it is a timetable for the demolition of public education in the United States. The goal of 100 percent proficiency placed thousands of public schools at risk of being privatized, turned into charters, or closed. And indeed, scores of schools in New York City, Chicago, Washington, D.C., and other districts were closed because they were unable to meet the unreasonable demands of NCLB. Superintendents in those districts boasted of how many schools they had closed, as if it were a badge of honor rather than an admission of defeat.

As 2014 draws nearer, growing numbers of schools across the nation are approaching an abyss. Because NCLB requires states to promise that they will reach an impossible goal, the states have adopted timetables agreeing to do what they can't do, no matter how hard teachers and principals try. Most have stretched out the timetable—putting off the biggest gains for the future—to stave off their inevitable failure. The school officials who wrote the timetables in the early years of implementation must have hoped or expected that they would be retired and gone long before 2014 arrived. With every passing year that brought the target date closer, more and more public schools failed to make AYP and were labeled as "failing." Even though some states lowered the cut scores (or passing marks) on their tests to make it easier for schools to meet their target, many still failed to make AYP toward 100 percent proficiency for every subgroup. And in states that maintained high standards and did not lower the cut scores, even more schools fell behind.

In the school year 2006–2007, 25,000 schools did not make AYP. In 2007–2008, the number grew to nearly 30,000, or 35.6 percent of all public schools. That number included more than half the public schools in Massachusetts, whose students scored highest in the nation on the rigorous tests of the National Assessment of Educational Progress.[13] As the clock ticks toward 2014, ever larger numbers of public schools will be forced to close or become charter schools, relinquish control to state authorities, become privately managed, or undergo some other major restructuring.

To date, there is no substantial body of evidence that demonstrates that low-performing schools can be turned around by any of the remedies prescribed in the law. Converting a "failing" school to a charter school or handing it over to private management offers no certainty that the school will be transformed into a successful school. Numerous districts have hired "turnaround specialists," but most of their efforts have been unavailing. In 2008, the federal government's education research division issued a report with four recommendations for "turning around chronically low-performing schools," but the report acknowledged that every one of its recommendations had "low" evidence to support it.[14] It seems that the only guaranteed strategy is to change the student population, replacing low-performing students with higher-performing students. Sometimes this happens with bells and whistles, as the old "failing" school is closed and then reopened with a new name, a new theme, and new students. But such a strategy is meaningless because it evades the original school's responsibility to its students. Rather than "leaving no child behind," this strategy plays a shell game with low-performing students, moving them out and dispersing them, pretending they don't exist.

Studies conducted by the Center on Education Policy (CEP) in Washington, D.C., concluded that "restructuring," the final sanction of the law, was ineffective. In the spring of 2008, according to one CEP study, California contained more than 1,000 schools that were restructuring. The study found that "federal restructuring strategies have very rarely helped schools improve student achievement enough to make AYP or exit restructuring." No matter which strategy the state or school district applied, the "failing" schools were seldom able to improve their status.[15]

In 2007–2008, according to another CEP study, more than 3,500 public schools across the nation were in the planning or implementation stage of restructuring, an increase of more than 50 percent over the previous year. In the five states covered by the study, very few schools chose to convert to a charter school or private management. Somewhere between 86 percent and 96 percent chose the ambiguous "any-other" (i.e., "do something") clause in the law, so as not to abandon their status as a regular public school. Even though few schools chose the most drastic penalties, "none of the five federal restructuring options were associated with a greater likelihood of a school making AYP overall or in reading or math alone. *In other words, there is no statistical reason to suspect that any one of the federal restructuring options is more effective than another in helping schools make AYP*" (italics added). None of the few successful schools was able to identify a single strategy that was essential to improving its achievement. And even the schools that had improved enough to exit restructuring worried about failing yet again to make adequate yearly progress, as the date grew nearer in which they would be expected to meet the impossible goal of 100 percent proficiency.[16]

California gambled that the provisions of the law would be eased over time, so state officials agreed that its schools would increase the proportion of students expected to meet standards by 2.2 percent each year from 2002 to 2007. After 2007, they projected an impossible increase of 11 percentage points per year to reach full proficiency by 2014. Twenty-two other states followed a similar pattern, choosing a low rate of anticipated academic score gains in the early years of implementation, then predicting a sharp annual growth rate between 2008 and 2014.[17] With the sudden and steep raising of the bar, more and more schools began to fail. In 2008, a team of researchers funded by the National Science Foundation predicted that by 2014, nearly 100 percent of California's elementary schools would fail to make adequate yearly progress. Richard Cardullo, a biologist from the University of California at Riverside, observed, "To use an analogy from the housing world, the balloon payment is about to hit." Because of disaggregation of the scores by subgroups, Cardullo said, "the lowest-performing subgroup will ultimately determine the proficiency of a school, district, or state."[18]

Most states devised ways to pretend to meet the impossible goal. Since the law granted each state the power to establish its own standards, choose its own tests, and define proficiency as it wished, most states reported heartening progress almost every year. Mississippi claimed that 89 percent of its fourth graders were at or above proficiency in reading, but according to NAEP, only 18 percent were. Only a handful of states maintained high standards that were comparable to the federal tests: Maine, Massachusetts, Missouri, South Carolina, and Wyoming. G. Gage Kingsbury of the Northwest Evaluation Association told the *New York Times* that states that set their proficiency standards prior to passage of NCLB tended to set high standards, thinking "that we needed to be competitive with nations like Hong Kong and Singapore. But our research shows that since NCLB took effect, states have set lower standards."[19]

Some policymakers complained that it wasn't fair to compare state test scores to NAEP, since the former "counts," and the latter does not. Presumably students try harder on the tests that count than on those that don't. Only states and a few urban districts get NAEP scores; no school or student ever learns how they did on

NAEP, which is considered a "low-stakes" or "no-stakes" exam. To shed light on this problem, the Thomas B. Fordham Institute commissioned the Northwest Evaluation Association to compare state test scores based on a computerized assessment used by twenty-six states. The resulting study, *The Proficiency Illusion*, found that the definition of proficiency "varies wildly from state to state, with 'passing scores' ranging from the 6th percentile to the 77th."[20] A student in Colorado might pass the state tests with ease, but if the family moved to New Mexico or Massachusetts, the same student might be in academic difficulty.

Among the states with the lowest expectations for proficiency, according to this study, were Colorado, Wisconsin, Michigan, New Jersey, Delaware, North Dakota, Illinois, and Ohio. In the foreword to the study, Chester E. Finn Jr. and Michael J. Petrilli concluded that "the testing enterprise is unbelievably slipshod. It's not just that results vary, but that they vary almost randomly, erratically, from place to place and grade to grade and year to year in ways that have little or nothing to do with true differences in pupil achievement. . . . The testing infrastructure on which so many school reform efforts rest, and in which so much confidence has been vested, is unreliable—at best."[21]

And yet, despite the "slipshod" nature of the tests, despite the random variability among them, despite the fact that they diverge dramatically in quality, the lives of students, teachers, and principals —and the fate of schools—are to be based on them.

One of the unintended consequences of NCLB was the shrinkage of time available to teach anything other than reading and math. Other subjects, including history, science, the arts, geography, even recess, were curtailed in many schools. Reading and mathematics were the only subjects that counted in calculating a school's adequate yearly progress, and even in these subjects, instruction gave way to intensive test preparation. Test scores became an obsession. Many school districts invested heavily in test-preparation materials and activities. Test-taking skills and strategies took precedence over knowledge. Teachers used the tests from previous years to prepare their students, and many of the questions appeared in precisely the same format every year; sometimes the exact same questions reappeared on the state tests. In urban schools, where there are many low-performing students, drill and practice became a significant part of the daily routine.

In New York City, teachers told a journalist that they eliminated social studies, art, and science for a month before the state reading and mathematics tests to concentrate on test-prep activities. One teacher said her students don't know who the president was during the Civil War, "but they can tell you how to eliminate answers on a multiple-choice test. And as long as our test scores are up, everyone will be happy." Her principal directed her to "forget about everything except test prep." Another teacher said that the principals are partially evaluated on test scores, so "naturally they want the scores up, [and] that's our priority. Actual education is second."[22]

In Texas, which was the model for No Child Left Behind, students became better and better at answering multiple-choice questions on the Texas Assessment of Knowledge and Skills, known as TAKS; the passing rates on the ninth-, tenth-, and eleventh-grade tests steadily increased. But when eleventh-grade students were asked to write a short answer about a text they were given to read, half of them were stumped. Whether in low-performing districts or high-achieving ones, students were unable to write a thoughtful response to a question that asked them to present evidence from what they read. They had mastered the art of filling in the bubbles on multiple-choice tests, but they could not express themselves, particularly when a question required them to think about and explain what they had just read.[23]

The Center on Education Policy conducted studies of "curriculum narrowing." In 2007, CEP surveyed a nationally representative group of school districts and found that 62 percent had increased the time devoted to reading and mathematics in elementary schools, while 44 percent reported that they had reduced the amount of time spent on science, social studies, and the arts.[24] There are just so many hours and minutes in the school day, and if more time is devoted to testing and test preparation, then less time will be available to teach subjects that will not be on the state tests. Yet lack of attention to history, science, and the arts detracts from the quality of education, the quality of children's lives, the quality of daily life in school, and even performance on the tests. Ironically, test prep is not always the best preparation for taking tests. Children expand their vocabulary and improve their reading skills when they learn history, science, and literature, just as they may sharpen their mathematics skills while learning science and geography. And the arts may motivate students to love learning.

Linda Perlstein's *Tested: One American School Struggles to Make the Grade* describes the year she spent in an elementary school in Annapolis, Maryland, where the children were lower-income, African American, and Hispanic. The school and its staff were obsessed with the state test scores. The children were carefully taught how to answer questions that were likely to appear on the state test. But they knew little or nothing about their nation, state, or city. They knew nothing about history, geography, or current affairs. They guessed at math questions. Their general knowledge about science was appallingly low. Their teachers worked conscientiously to get the children ready for the state tests; consequently, they did well on the state tests, which consumed everyone's energy all year, but they lacked the vocabulary and general knowledge to succeed in high school. In Perlstein's narrative, earnest, hardworking teachers and a dedicated principal did their best to meet the requirements of state and federal law. They succeeded, but the children were being trained, not educated.[25]

Did NCLB work? It could never "work," in that its goal of 100 percent proficiency by 2014 was out of reach, unless states deliberately dumbed down the meaning of proficiency. This goal has negative consequences for thousands of schools, whose teachers are struggling valiantly each day to do what no nation has ever done before. Furthermore, its simpleminded and singular focus on test scores distorts and degrades the meaning and practice of education.

As it happened, NCLB did not even bring about rapidly improving test scores. To the contrary, test score gains on the National Assessment of Educational Progress—the only national yardstick for this period—were modest or nonexistent in the four years after the adoption of the law. In fourth-grade reading, NAEP scores went up by 3 points from 2003 to 2007, less than the 5-point gain from 2000 to 2003, before NCLB took effect. In eighth-grade reading, there were no gains at all from 1998 to 2007. In mathematics, the 5-point gain by fourth-grade students from 2003 to 2007 did not match their 9-point gain from 2000 to 2003. In eighth-grade mathematics, the story was the same: The gain from 2000 to 2003 (5 points) was larger than the gain from 2003 to 2007 (3 points).[26] Scores were higher after the implementation of NCLB, but the rate of improvement slowed. Even if one insists on starting the clock on the day the law was signed in January 2002, well before the nation's schools understood what the law required, the gains have been modest at best.

Similarly, the achievement gaps between black and white students narrowed more before the implementation of NCLB than in the years afterward. Black fourth-grade students had a 13-point gain in mathematics from 2000 to 2003, but only a 6-point gain from 2003 to 2007; white fourth-grade students had a 10-point gain from 2000 to 2003, but only a 5-point gain from 2003 to 2007. In fourth-grade reading, black student scores were up by 8 points from 2000 to 2003 but increased only 6 points from 2003 to 2007. White scores in the same grade were up by 4 points from 2000 to 2003 and by 3 points from 2003 to 2007. In eighth-grade reading, white and black scores were virtually unchanged over the past decade.[27]

For the lowest-performing students, those who scored in the bottom 10th percentile, the gains registered after NCLB took effect were smaller than in preceding years. In fourth-grade reading, the bottom 10th percentile saw a gain of 6 points from 1998 to 2003; these students gained 5 points from 2003 to 2007. Low-performing students in eighth grade saw no improvement in their reading scores: From 1998 to 2003, their scores went up by 1 point, and from 2003 to 2007, they were unchanged. In mathematics, the scores of low-performing students in fourth grade soared by 13 points from 2000 to 2003; they went up by 5 points from 2003 to 2007. In eighth-grade mathematics, the story was similar: Scores rose by 7 points from 2000 to 2003, and by 5 points from 2003 to 2007.[28]

Although NCLB was surrounded with a great deal of high-flown rhetoric when it was passed, promising a new era of high standards and high accomplishment, an era when "no child would be left behind," the reality was far different. Its remedies did not work. Its sanctions were ineffective. It did not bring about high standards or high accomplishment. The gains in test scores at the state level were typically the result of teaching students test-taking skills and strategies, rather than broadening and deepening their knowledge of the world and their ability to understand what they have learned.

NCLB was a punitive law based on erroneous assumptions about how to improve schools. It assumed that reporting test scores to the public would be an effective lever for school reform. It assumed that changes in governance would lead to school improvement. It assumed that shaming schools that were unable to lift test scores every year—and the people who work in them—would lead to higher scores. It assumed that low scores are caused by lazy teachers and lazy principals, who need to be threatened with the loss of their jobs. Perhaps most naively, it assumed that higher test scores on standardized tests of basic skills are synonymous with good education. Its assumptions were wrong. Testing is not a substitute for curriculum and instruction. Good education cannot be achieved by a strategy of testing children, shaming educators, and closing schools.

CHAPTER SEVEN

Choice: The Story of an Idea

When I was a child in Houston in the 1940s and 1950s, everyone I knew went to the neighborhood public school. Every child on my block and in my neighborhood went to the same elementary school, the same junior high school, and the same high school. We carpooled together; we cheered for the same teams; we went to the same after-school events; we traded stories about our teachers. I went to Montrose Elementary School until fifth grade, when my family moved to a new neighborhood and I enrolled in Sutton Elementary School. Then, along with everyone else who lived nearby, I went to Albert Sidney Johnston Junior High School and San Jacinto High School.

At that time, there were few private schools in Houston. When I was five years old, my parents tried to enroll me in the Kinkaid School, which was directly across the street from our home. I was interviewed by Mrs. Kinkaid, the school's founder. She rejected me. My parents said she turned me down because she didn't like Jews (Kinkaid today has a nondiscriminatory admissions policy). I don't know if they were right, but I heard the story many times, and my parents became passionate advocates of public education. Ever after, in our home, private education was considered an appropriate alternative only for those kids who failed to behave or succeed in public school. Two of my five brothers were sent away to military school; the experience was supposed to "straighten them out." If they learned to behave and apply themselves, they were told, they could come back to public school.

At the end of my sophomore year in high school in May 1954, the U.S. Supreme Court issued its historic decision against school segregation, *Brown v. Board of Education*. The Houston schools were segregated, and the local school board had no intention of complying with the decision. Anyone who spoke up on behalf of racial integration was likely to be called a communist or a pinko. Over the next decade, political leaders in some Southern states declared that they would never desegregate their schools, that they would hold out forever against the Court's decision. Some school districts in the South responded to the Court's pressure to desegregate by adopting "freedom of choice" policies. Under "freedom of choice," students could enroll in any public school they wanted. Big surprise: White students remained enrolled in all-white schools, and black students remained in all-black schools.

When the federal government and the federal courts began compelling segregated districts to reassign black and white pupils to integrated schools, public officials in some Southern states embraced a new form of choice. They encouraged the creation of private schools to accommodate white students who did not want to attend an integrated school. These "schools of choice" were also known as "segregation academies." In Virginia, which had a policy of "massive resistance" to desegregation, the state gave tuition grants to students to enroll in a private school of their choice.

During the 1950s and 1960s, the term "school choice" was stigmatized as a dodge invented to permit white students to escape to all-white public schools or to all-white segregation academies. For someone like me, raised in the South and opposed to racism and segregation, the word "choice" and the term "freedom of choice" became tainted by their use as a conscious strategy to maintain state-sponsored segregation.

Given that I was only a junior in high school at the time, I knew nothing about Milton Friedman's 1955 piece "The Role of Government in Education." It was only many years later, long after I left college, that I encountered his classic essay. Almost everyone who supports vouchers and school choice is familiar with Friedman's argument that government should fund schooling but not run the schools. Friedman proposed that government supply vouchers to every family so every student could attend a school of choice.

A brilliant economist at the University of Chicago, Friedman won the Nobel Prize in 1976 for his scholarly economic studies. He gained renown as a libertarian who opposed government regulation and championed the private marketplace.

In his essay, Friedman maintained that the ultimate objective of society should be to maximize the freedom of the individual or the family. Toward that end, government should provide a voucher to parents to subsidize the cost of their children's schooling, which they could spend in any school—whether run by a religious order, a for-profit business, a nonprofit agency, or public authorities—so long as the school met "specified minimum standards." He predicted that "a wide variety of schools will spring up to meet the demand" and that competitive private enterprise was "likely to be far more efficient in meeting consumer demands" than any government agency. The introduction of competition, he believed, would "meet the just complaints of parents" who were sending their children to religious schools and paying twice for education, once in taxes and again in tuition fees. Friedman expected that vouchers would "stimulate the development and improvement" of nonpublic schools, as well as "promote a healthy variety of schools." Not only would public school systems become more flexible in response to competition, but the competition would "make the salaries of school teachers responsive to market forces."[1]

When Milton Friedman was writing his essay about vouchers in the early 1950s, the hot-button issue in education was whether Catholic schools should be allowed to receive federal aid. Congress was stymied in its efforts to legislate any federal aid to education, because of deep divisions about whether to include Catholic schools. Catholics and their allies in Congress insisted that Catholic schools should participate in any program that was enacted. Public school organizations, such as the National Education Association, and advocates of the separation of church and state adamantly opposed any federal aid to religious schools. Catholics complained that to exclude their children would be religious discrimination, denying them benefits for which they were already taxed.

State and federal courts issued several highly contested (and inconsistent) decisions in the late 1940s about whether states could reimburse Catholic schools for textbooks, school transportation, tuition, and other expenses. The dispute reached a fever pitch when former first lady Eleanor Roosevelt and New York City's Cardinal Francis Spellman engaged in a vitriolic public exchange about the issue. Protestant and Jewish groups waded in to oppose any aid to religious schools. One noted polemicist, Paul Blanshard, warned that the rise of Catholic power threatened American freedom.[2] To resolve this contentious issue, Friedman recommended vouchers, which parents could use for tuition at any approved school, including religious ones.

In a footnote, Friedman acknowledged that he discovered only after he had finished writing his essay that Southern states were adopting his proposal ("public financing but private operation of education") to evade complying with the *Brown* decision against segregation. He recognized that this was a problem for his proposition, but this did not deter him. While he deplored segregation and racial prejudice, he simply did not like government compulsion, even in a good cause. In a true choice system, he insisted, where all schools were privately operated, all students would be enrolled in schools their parents had chosen. There would be all-white schools, all-black schools, and mixed schools. Those who opposed segregation, he suggested, should try to persuade others to adopt their views, and in time the segregated schools would disappear.

When Congress passed the landmark Elementary and Secondary Education Act in 1965, it decided to permit needy students in religious schools to receive federal aid for remedial services.[3] Extending federal funding to poor children in parochial schools was not an act of benevolence, but a necessary political compromise to garner votes from urban Democrats who represented large numbers of Catholic constituents. Nor was it a concession to Friedman's voucher proposal. In fact, the federal government used the funding from the 1965 act to force Southern districts to dismantle segregated public schools, threatening to withhold federal dollars if they did not desegregate. This approach was the very opposite of Friedman's goal of maximizing individual freedom through school choice.

As the federal government kept up the pressure for desegregation and as resistance to mandatory busing increased, some school districts attempted to encourage voluntary desegregation through choice. They opened magnet schools—schools with specialized offerings in the arts or sciences or other fields—to encourage white students to attend urban schools that would otherwise be heavily nonwhite. But until the election of Ronald Reagan in 1980, the issue of school choice remained far outside the mainstream, mainly because it was viewed by the media and elected officials as a means to permit white students to escape court-ordered racial desegregation.

After Reagan was elected, he advocated school choice, specifically vouchers. Reagan was directly influenced by Friedman's ideas.
When Friedman retired from the University of Chicago in 1977,
he moved to California and affiliated with the Hoover Institution
at Stanford University. He and his wife, Rose, wrote a best-selling
book, *Free to Choose*, which was the basis for a ten-part documentary on public television. Reagan agreed with Friedman's advocacy
of freedom, deregulation, market-based solutions, and privatization,
and Friedman became one of Reagan's advisers.

President Reagan's legislative proposals for vouchers were
not intended for all children—as Friedman had urged—but for
low-performing students, to make the voucher idea politically palat-
able. In his second term, Reagan backed away from vouchers and
promoted public school choice, making the choice idea even less
threatening. Reagan's first secretary of education, Terrel H. Bell, who
had been a public school administrator in Utah, did not join in Reagan's advocacy of vouchers and school prayer. Nor was Bell thrilled
with Reagan's desire to disestablish the U.S. Department of Education, which had been elevated to cabinet-level status in the last year
of Jimmy Carter's administration.[4] After Bell resigned in 1985, he
was succeeded by William J. Bennett as secretary of education. Bennett enthusiastically embraced school choice and included it as one
of his "three C's" of education: content, character, and choice.

Throughout Reagan's two terms in office, the Democratic Party
controlled the House of Representatives, and the party was closely
allied with the two national teachers' unions, the National Education Association (NEA) and the American Federation of Teachers
(AFT). The unions opposed school choice, which they saw as a
threat to public education and a step toward privatization. Congress
rebuffed Reagan's proposals for school choice, as well as his plan
to eliminate the Department of Education. However, the concept
of school choice found a home among free-market-oriented foundations and think tanks, such as the Heritage Foundation, the Cato
Institute, the John M. Olin Foundation, and the Lynde and Harry
Bradley Foundation. The foundations and think tanks incubated a
generation of scholars and journalists who advocated school choice
long after the end of the Reagan administration. State and local
think tanks devoted to free-market principles sprouted up across the
nation, inspired in large measure by Friedman's writings, to continue
the battle for school choice.[5]

Although Friedman's idea of a market-driven approach to schooling made no headway in Congress, its partisans campaigned for referenda in several states. But whenever vouchers were put to a statewide vote, they were rejected by large margins. Voucher advocates blamed the political clout of the teachers' unions for these losses, but it was clear nonetheless that most voters turned down the chance to implement vouchers. Public school choice programs, however, began to gain ground at the same time that vouchers were soundly rejected. In the 1980s, a few local school districts adopted public school choice plans, including Cambridge, Massachusetts, Montclair, New Jersey, and District 4 in East Harlem, New York City. In the late 1980s, Minnesota became the first to adopt a statewide program of "open enrollment," permitting students to transfer to public schools in districts other than their own, and high school juniors and seniors to enroll in a public or private institution of higher education.

As the 1990s opened, the choice movement gained new momentum. First, John E. Chubb and Terry M. Moe's *Politics, Markets, and America's Schools* restarted the campaign for school choice with powerful and contemporary arguments; second, the nation's first voucher program was established in Milwaukee by Wisconsin's state legislature in 1990; and third, the charter school movement was born.

In their widely noted book, Chubb and Moe contended that public education was incapable of ever reforming itself, because the institution was "owned" by vested interests, including "teachers' unions and myriad associations of principals, school boards, superintendents, administrators, and professionals—not to mention education schools, book publishers, testing services, and many other beneficiaries of the institutional status quo." So long as the public schools were subject to democratic control, they argued, the interest groups would protect the status quo, and the schools could never be fundamentally changed. Poor academic performance was "one of the prices Americans pay for choosing to exercise direct democratic control over their schools."[6]

The only way to bring about fundamental change in schooling, they asserted, was through a system of school choice. School choice would make it possible to break the iron grip of the adult interest groups, unleash the positive power of competition, and achieve academic excellence. They boldly claimed that "reformers would do well to entertain the notion that choice *is* a panacea." Choice "has the capacity *all by itself* to bring about the kind of transformation that, for years, reformers have been seeking to engineer in myriad other ways."[7]

Chubb and Moe wanted to sweep away "the old institutions" and replace them with a new system in which almost all "higher-level authority" outside the school was eliminated. In their new system, the state would set certain minimum requirements (related, for example, to graduation, health and safety, and teacher certification); any group or organization or nonpublic school could apply to the state and receive a charter to run a school. Local districts could continue to run their own schools but would have no authority over schools with state charters. Each state would decide on a formula for scholarships for every child, depending on need, and every student would be free to enroll in any school in the state. Every school would be free to set its own admissions policy, subject to nondiscrimination law, and to expel students who did not follow its rules. The state would hold schools accountable for meeting certain procedural requirements (such as providing full and accurate information to the public) but *not* for academic achievement. Chubb and Moe wrote: "When it comes to performance, schools are held accountable from below, by parents and students who directly experience their services and are free to choose."[8] Chubb and Moe's proposal set off a firestorm in educational journals, where it was denounced as advocacy for vouchers. Of course, it was advocacy for vouchers, but in retrospect, it is clear that Chubb and Moe forecast the rise of the charter movement.

Chubb and Moe's controversial book kept the voucher movement in the forefront of discussion, if not implementation. Although Congress consistently rejected vouchers, and voters consistently turned them down in state referenda, two urban districts—Milwaukee and Cleveland—saw vouchers as a way to raise student achievement. Voucher proponents confidently predicted that vouchers would empower low-income parents, expand the educational opportunities available to African American families, and improve the regular public schools, which would be compelled to compete for students. It seemed like a win-win situation: gains for the kids who left public schools and gains for the public schools, which would get better when they competed for students.

In Milwaukee, African American activists—led by former Milwaukee school superintendent Howard Fuller and state legislator Polly Williams—allied themselves with the Milwaukee-based

Bradley Foundation to seek vouchers for low-income children. With the support of Republican Wisconsin governor Tommy Thompson, Democratic Milwaukee mayor John Norquist, and the city's business leadership, the Wisconsin legislature approved a voucher program for Milwaukee in 1990. At first, the Milwaukee voucher program enabled low-income students to attend only nonreligious private schools. Even this limited option encountered stiff opposition. Opponents of vouchers included the elected state superintendent of education, unions representing teachers and administrators, the local branch of the NAACP, People for the American Way, and the American Civil Liberties Union.

The anti-voucher forces mounted a lengthy legal challenge in state courts, but the pro-voucher forces ultimately prevailed. In June 1998, the Wisconsin Supreme Court upheld the legality of the voucher program and permitted religious schools to accept voucher students. The U.S. Supreme Court refused to review the state court's decision, thereby removing the legal cloud that hung over the program. After the courts ruled the program constitutional and allowed voucher students to attend religious schools, it rapidly expanded. Before 1998, there were 2,000 students in the voucher program; a decade later, 20,000 students in Milwaukee were using vouchers to attend nonpublic schools, nearly 80 percent of which were religious schools.[9]

In Cleveland, the situation was similar to that of Milwaukee. African American parent activists were angry about the persistently poor performance of their children and discouraged by the lack of progress after years of pursuing desegregation. Encouraged by Akron industrialist David Brennan and Republican governor George Voinovich, the Ohio legislature enacted a voucher program for Cleveland in 1995. Some 2,000 scholarships were awarded by lottery, with preference given to low-income families. Students could attend any state-approved school, including religious schools. As in Milwaukee, opponents challenged the program in state and federal courts. The legal battle ended in 2002 when the U.S. Supreme Court ruled in *Zelman v. Simmons-Harris* that the Cleveland program did not violate the Establishment Clause of the Constitution, because the benefits of the program went to individuals to exercise free choice between secular and religious schools. Although the Court split 5–4, its approval gave a green light to state-subsidized voucher programs that included religious schools.

Opponents braced for the creation of new voucher programs in urban districts, but only one such program was started in the wake of the *Zelman* decision. In 2003, the Republican-led Congress established a voucher program for nearly 2,000 students in the District of Columbia. About two-thirds enrolled in Catholic schools.

At the very moment that the voucher movement achieved a victory in the highest court in the land, the movement seemed to lose steam. It was not that proponents of school choice had lost heart, but that they had found a new vehicle that was less troublesome than vouchers: charter schools. Unlike vouchers, which might involve religious schools, charters raised no constitutional issues. Beginning in the early 1990s, friends of school choice campaigned to persuade state legislatures to pass laws authorizing charter schools.

The idea was simple, and it was closely related to the Chubb and Moe plan: Any group or organization could apply for a charter for three to five years from the state or a state-authorized chartering agency, agree to meet certain minimum requirements and academic targets, and receive public funding for its students. What was the difference between voucher schools and charter schools? Students could use vouchers to enroll in any private school, whether it was religious or nonsectarian; the schools remained private schools. Charter schools, however, were considered public schools under private management; they were required to be nonsectarian.

In the 1990s, three versions of school choice emerged: voucher schools, privately managed schools, and charter schools. All of these schools receive public funds to educate students but are not regular public schools and are not run by a government agency.

Voucher schools are private schools that might or might not be religious in nature. Children with public vouchers enroll in them by choice. The vouchers usually cover only a portion of the tuition. Voucher schools exist only where they have been authorized by the state legislature (Milwaukee and Cleveland) or Congress (the District of Columbia).

Privately managed schools are public schools that an outside entity operates under contract with a school district. They may be run by for-profit firms or by nonprofit organizations. Usually the districts turn over low-performing schools to private managers, hoping they might succeed where the district has not. The private firms, in essence, work for the district but are given a certain amount of leeway to make changes in staffing and programs. If the district is dissatisfied with the results, it may terminate the contract and regain control of the school or assign it to a different management organization.

Charter schools are created when an organization obtains a charter from a state-authorized agency. The charter gives the organization a set period of years—usually five—to meet its performance goals in exchange for autonomy. In some states, such as California, regular public schools may convert to charter status, thus seceding from their school district to become an independent district of one school. Charter schools may be managed by nonprofit groups or for-profit businesses. They may be managed by a national organization or by a local community group.

In 1988, Ray Budde, a professor of educational administration in Massachusetts, first proposed the idea of charter schools. Budde published a paper called "Education by Charter: Restructuring School Districts." Budde wanted teams of teachers to apply for charters to run schools within the district. Each charter would have a specific set of goals and a specific term (say, three to five years) and would be rigorously evaluated to see what it had accomplished before the charter was renewed. In his plan, those who received a charter would have a bold vision and would take risks to explore the unknown. They would be expected to work on the cutting edge of research and knowledge, not to replicate what others were doing. Budde believed that the charter concept would lead to a restructuring of school districts, flattening their organizational chart while enabling teachers to take charge of decisions about curriculum, management, and instruction.[10]

In the same year, Albert Shanker, president of the American Federation of Teachers, put forward a similar idea of his own. In a speech at the National Press Club, Shanker suggested that groups of teachers should be able to run their own schools within regular schools and to pursue innovative ways of educating disaffected students. The reform movement inspired by the *Nation at Risk* report, he said, was raising standards and was working well for about a quarter of students; the successful students were the ones "who are able to learn in a traditional system, who are able to sit still, who are able to keep quiet, who are able to remember after they listen to someone else talk for five hours, who are able to pick up a book and learn from it—who've got all these things going for them." But the old ways, he insisted, were not working for the majority of kids.[11]

Shanker suggested that any group of six or more teachers should be able to submit a proposal to start a new school. "Do not think of a school as a building, and you can see how it works," he said. Such a group of teachers could set up a school within their own school that would try out different ways "of reaching the kids that are now not being reached by what the school is doing." Proposals for new schools would be reviewed by a panel jointly run by the union and the school district. These new schools would be research programs with a five- to ten-year guarantee that they could try out their ideas. The schools would be schools of choice for both the teachers and the students. But before they were approved, the other teachers in the building would have to agree to them, so that the new schools would not be in a hostile environment. This approach, Shanker said, was "a way of building by example. It's a way not of shoving things down people's throats, but enlisting them in a movement and in a cause." He pledged to take this idea to all of his locals around the country.[12]

At the union's national convention, Shanker described his proposal for teacher-led autonomous schools within schools. He made clear that these new schools would be experimental, tasked with solving important problems of pedagogy and curriculum, and expected to produce findings that would help other schools. He did not want anyone "to go off and do his own thing." While he originally called these schools "opt-for schools," someone sent him Budde's essay, which used the term "charter schools." Shanker liked the name and used it in his speech. The new charter schools should be evaluated, he said, although he hoped it would not be done with "the crazy standardized tests that are driving us all to narrow the curriculum."[13]

Over the next twenty years, as the charter movement spread, its supporters liked to point to Shanker as a founding father. The association with Shanker was intended to reassure people that charters were public schools, that they were not a threat to public education, and that they were not vouchers. But those who invoked his name routinely overlooked the fact that Shanker withdrew his endorsement of charter schools in 1993 and became a vociferous critic. As he watched the charter movement evolve, as he saw new businesses jump into the "education industry," he realized that the idea he had so enthusiastically embraced was being taken over by corporations, entrepreneurs, and practitioners of "do your own thing." He abandoned his dream that charters would be led by teams of teachers who were akin to medical researchers, seeking solutions to difficult pedagogical and social problems. He came to see charter schools as dangerous to public education, as the cutting edge of an effort to privatize the public schools.

When Baltimore handed over nine public schools to a for-profit business called Education Alternatives Inc. in 1992, Shanker was appalled. When Republican governor John Engler of Michigan endorsed charter legislation, Shanker denounced him for ignoring his state's poor curriculum and standards. In his paid weekly column in the *New York Times*, he repeatedly condemned charter schools, vouchers, and for-profit management as "quick fixes that won't fix anything."[14]

After he turned against charter schools, Shanker steadfastly insisted that the biggest problem in American education was the absence of a clear national consensus about the mission of the schools. He repeatedly decried the lack of a national curriculum, national testing, and "stakes" attached to schooling; these, he said, were huge problems that would not be solved by letting a thousand flowers bloom or by turning over the schools to entrepreneurs.

Ironically, as charter schools evolved, the charter movement became increasingly hostile to unions. Charter operators wanted to be able to hire and fire teachers at will, to set their own salary schedule, to reward teachers according to their performance, to control working conditions, and to require long working hours; with few exceptions, they did not want to be subject to a union contract that interfered with their prerogatives as management. The Green Dot charter organization was one of the few that was willing to accept teachers' unions in its schools. The United Federation of Teachers in New York City opened its own charter schools, to prove that its contract was not an obstacle to charter management. But the overwhelming majority of other charter operators did not want a unionized teaching staff.

Charter schools had an undeniable appeal across the political spectrum. Liberals embraced them as a firewall to stop vouchers. Conservatives saw them as a means to deregulate public education and create competition for the public education system. Some educators, sharing Shanker's original vision, hoped that they would help unmotivated students and reduce dropouts. Some entrepreneurs looked at them as a gateway to the vast riches of the education industry. Ethnic groups embraced them as a refuge in which to teach their cultural heritage without deference to a common civic culture. According to their boosters, not only would charter schools unleash innovation and produce dramatic improvements in academic achievement, but competition would cause the regular public schools to get better.

In 1991, Minnesota became the first state to pass a law authorizing the creation of charter schools. The following year, the nation's first charter school opened in St. Paul. City Academy High School was a paradigm of what Shanker had hoped a charter school would be: It aimed to help youngsters who had not succeeded in a regular public school. Its students, ages fifteen through twenty-one, had dropped out of school. They were from home situations marked by poverty or substance abuse. The school began with 30 students and eventually grew to about 120 students. In addition to academic classes, it offered job skills training, counseling, and other individualized social services. While City Academy is not a research laboratory for public education, it is certainly serving students who would otherwise be on the streets with no prospects.

From there, the charter movement took off. In 1993, Jeanne Allen, the conservative Heritage Foundation's chief education analyst, established a new organization—the Center for Education Reform—to lead the battle for charter schools across the nation. The centrist Democratic Leadership Council endorsed the idea of charters, too, because it was an ingenious way to promote public school choice, to "reinvent" government, and to break the grip (as its chairman, Senator Joseph Lieberman of Connecticut, wrote) of "ossified bureaucracies governing too many public schools."[15] In 1994, as part of President Clinton's education legislation, Congress established a program to award federal dollars to spur the development of new charter schools. By fall 2001, some 2,300 charter schools had opened their doors, enrolling nearly half a million students. By 2009, the Center for Education Reform reported that there were about 4,600 charter schools with 1.4 million students. As of that date, forty states and the District of Columbia had charter schools; 60 percent of all charter school students were located in six states: California, Arizona, Texas, Florida, Michigan, and Ohio.

Charter schools proliferated in urban districts, where academic performance was lowest and the demand for alternatives was greatest. In the fall of 2008, twelve communities had at least 20 percent of their public school students in charter schools. Nearly a third of all students in Washington, D.C., Dayton, Ohio, and Southfield, Michigan, were enrolled in charter schools. The district with the largest proportion in charter schools was New Orleans, where 55 percent of students were in charters. New Orleans was a unique case, because its public school system had been decimated by Hurricane Katrina in 2005, and officials decided to place their bets on charters and privately managed schools when rebuilding the education system.[16]

As charter schools grew in popularity, the demand for vouchers ebbed. Charter schools met virtually the same needs as vouchers. They competed with the regular public schools. They offered choices to families. They freed the schools from the regulatory control of a school district. They included schools that were focused on specific cultures, whether Afrocentric or Greek or Native American or Hebrew or Arabic.

Charter schools came closer to the ideal set forth by Chubb and Moe than to the one proposed by Shanker. He had wanted charter schools started by teachers to concentrate on solving the problems of low-achieving, unmotivated students. But it soon became clear that charter schools could be started by anyone who could persuade the state or a state-approved agency to grant them a charter. Charters were opened by social service agencies, universities, teachers, parents, philanthropists, hedge-fund managers, for-profit firms, charter-management organizations, community groups, and other groups and individuals. Depending on the state, they might include public schools that converted to charter status, religious schools that removed the religious symbols, or tuition-charging private schools that decided to become tax-supported public charters. Some charters had efficient management teams that ran first-rate schools, but others were operated by minimally competent providers who collected public money while offering bare-bones education to gullible students. And a few were opened by get-rich-quick schemers who saw easy pickings.

The advocates of choice—whether vouchers or charters—predicted that choice would transform American education. They were certain that choice would produce higher achievement. They based their case for choice on the failings of the public schools, pointing to low test scores, low graduation rates, and the achievement gap between children of different racial groups. They invoked the clarion call of *A Nation at Risk* as proof that America's schools were caught in a downward spiral; only choice, they argued, could reverse the "rising tide of mediocrity," though the report itself never made that claim. They were confident that when schools compete, all students gain. Parents would surely vote with their feet for the good schools. Good schools would thrive, while bad schools would close. Some advocates believed that choice was indeed a panacea. Having chosen their schools, students would get a superior education, and the regular public schools would improve because of the competition. The basic strategy was the market model, which relied on two related assumptions: belief in the power of competition and belief in the value of deregulation. The market model worked in business, said the advocates, where competition led to better products, lower prices, and leaner bureaucracies, so it would undoubtedly work in education as well.

I GOT CAUGHT UP in the wave of enthusiasm for choice in education. I began to wonder why families should not be able to choose their children's schools the way they choose their place of residence, their line of work, their shoes, or their car. In part, I was swept along by my immersion in the upper reaches of the first Bush presidency, where choice and competition were taken for granted as successful ways to improve student achievement. But I also wanted to help Catholic schools, as a result of my contact with the great sociologist James Coleman in the early 1980s. His work convinced me that these schools were unusually successful in educating minority children. When I became assistant secretary of education in charge of research, I was invited to speak to the National Catholic Education Association. I asked my staff to gather information comparing the performance of Hispanic and African American students in Catholic and public schools. I learned that minority kids who attended Catholic schools were more likely to take advanced courses than their peers in public schools, more likely to go to college, and more likely to continue on to graduate school. The Catholic schools could not afford to offer multiple tracks, so they expected all students to do the same coursework. I became interested in seeing whether there was any way public policy could sustain these schools. Long after I was out of office, I coauthored an opinion piece with William Galston, who had served as President Clinton's domestic policy adviser, proposing a national school choice demonstration project in at least ten cities.[17]

At the same National Catholic Education Association conference in 1991, the sociologist Father Andrew Greeley predicted that the first voucher would arrive on the day that the last Catholic school closed. He knew that Catholic schools, despite their great success in educating working-class and poor children, were struggling to survive. He knew that help was not on the way. What he did not know—and what I did not realize—was that the new charter school movement would undercut Catholic schooling. Charter schools offered an alternative not only to regular public schools, but to Catholic schools, which were burdened by rising costs. As more and more states opened charter schools, more and more Catholic schools closed their doors. Between 1990 and 2008, some 1,300 Catholic schools that had once enrolled 300,000 children were shuttered.[18] Many of them would have shut down anyway because of changing demographics and the diminished number of low-paid religious teachers to staff them, but competition with free charter schools was very likely a contributing factor.

There was an undeniable appeal to the values associated with choice: freedom, personal empowerment, deregulation, the ability to chart one's own course. All of those values appealed to me and many others. The anti-choice side was saddled with defending regulation, bureaucracy, and poor academic results. How much easier it was to promise (and hope for) the accomplishments, successes, and rewards that had not yet been achieved and could not yet be demonstrated, but were surely out there on the other side of the mountain.

Not long after the Milwaukee voucher program started in 1990, researchers began to debate whether vouchers were improving student achievement. The Wisconsin State Education Department hired John Witte of the University of Wisconsin to evaluate the Milwaukee program. Witte found that the voucher students were not making large gains. Voucher supporters denounced his findings because he was appointed by the Wisconsin state superintendent, who was a well-known critic of vouchers.[19] One study followed another, with a predictable pattern: The critics of vouchers almost always found small or no gains, while supporters of vouchers almost always found significant gains. Each side criticized the other's research methodology. Each said the other was ideologically biased and not to be trusted.

The same exchanges occurred in Cleveland, where a voucher program started in 1995. The critics saw little or no progress. The supporters said the critics were wrong. One side found promising gains; the other side saw no gains.

By 2009, studies by different authors came to similar conclusions about vouchers, suggesting an emerging consensus. Cecelia E. Rouse of Princeton University and Lisa Barrow of the Federal Reserve Bank of Chicago published a review of all the existing studies of vouchers in Milwaukee, Cleveland, and the District of Columbia. They found that there were "relatively small achievement gains for students offered educational vouchers, most of which are not statistically different from zero." They could not predict whether vouchers might eventually produce changes in high school graduation rates, college enrollment, or future wages. But they did not find impressive gains in achievement. Nor was there persuasive evidence that the public school systems that lost voucher students to private schools had improved. Since no one claimed that the voucher programs had produced dramatic changes, Rouse and Barrow cautioned against anticipating that voucher programs were going to produce large academic gains in the future.[20]

A team of researchers that included both supporters and critics of vouchers launched a five-year longitudinal study of the Milwaukee program. In the first year of the study, they found that students in the regular public schools and those in the voucher schools had similar scores. Students in the fourth grade in voucher schools had lower scores on state tests of reading, math, and science than students in regular schools, while voucher students in eighth grade had higher scores. Neither group demonstrated high performance. At all grades, both public school students and voucher students were well below the 50th percentile nationally, mainly around the 33rd percentile, which was typical of low-income students.[21]

In 2009, the same research team released another study that found no major differences between students in voucher schools and those in regular public schools. The research group included the strongly pro-voucher Jay P. Greene of the University of Arkansas and John Witte, who was considered a critic of vouchers. The researchers found "no overall statistically significant differences between MPCP [voucher] and MPS [Milwaukee Public Schools] student achievement growth in either math or reading one year after they were carefully matched to each other." Perhaps there would be different outcomes in the future, but this was not the panacea that voucher supporters had promised and hoped for.[22]

The District of Columbia voucher program—the D.C. Opportunity Scholarship Program—was created by the Republican-controlled Congress in 2003. The scholarship, worth $7,500, could be used for tuition and fees at a private or religious school. The vouchers were awarded by lottery; priority was given to students attending "schools in need of improvement"—so-called SINI schools. Congress mandated annual evaluations of the program. The first evaluation in 2008 reported that in the first two years of the program (2004 and 2005), there was no statistically significant difference in test scores of reading and math between students who won the lottery and those who entered the lottery but did not win. However, the third-year evaluation of the voucher program (released in 2009) found that there was "a statistically significant positive impact on reading test scores, but not math test scores." The reading scores represented a gain of more than three months of learning.[23]

Supporters of vouchers were ecstatic about the third-year evaluation because at last they had hard evidence that vouchers would benefit students. They glossed over the finding that these gains were limited to certain groups of students. The students who experienced gains in reading were those who entered the program from schools that were *not* in need of improvement, those who entered the program in the upper two-thirds of the test score distribution, and those who entered in grades K–8. Females also seemed to benefit, though that finding was not as robust as the others. The groups that did not experience improvement in reading (or math) were boys, secondary students, students from SINI schools, and students in the lowest third of the test score distribution. The students who did not see any gains were those in the highest-priority groups, the ones for whom the program was designed: those with the lowest test scores and those who had previously attended SINI schools.[24]

Test results were not the only source of concern about voucher schools. When a team of reporters from the *Milwaukee Journal Sentinel* examined the voucher schools in Milwaukee in 2005, they uncovered unanticipated problems. Applicants to run a voucher school did not need any particular credentials, nor did their teachers. The journalists visited 106 of 115 voucher schools (nine voucher schools would not let them in); they found good schools and awful schools, Catholic schools, Muslim schools, and evangelical Christian schools.

The reporters judged that about 10 percent of the voucher schools were excellent, and the same proportion showed "alarming deficiencies." Among the last group was Alex's Academics of Excellence, which had been opened by a convicted rapist and remained open despite allegations that staff members used drugs on school grounds. At another school, the Mandella School of Science and Math, the founder went to jail for padding the school's enrollment and stealing some $330,000 in public funds; he used part of his ill-gotten gains to buy two Mercedes, while his teachers went unpaid. Those schools and two others were eventually closed by the authorities, not because of parents voting with their feet to take their children out of bad schools, and not because the academic program was abysmal, but because of financial improprieties. One of the voucher schools that reporters visited was opened by a man with an expired license as a substitute teacher who had previously worked as a school security guard and a woman who had previously been a teacher's aide. They collected $414,000 annually in public funds for the eighty pupils enrolled in their sparsely furnished rented space. When reporters visited the school, only fifty students were present, and instruction was minimal.[25]

But on the whole, the reporters concluded that "the voucher schools feel, and look, surprisingly like schools in the Milwaukee Public Schools district." Student performance in the Milwaukee public schools increased in the first two years after vouchers were introduced—possibly because the new competition spurred teachers to prepare students for the state tests. After that, achievement in the regular schools stalled. As the competition got stiffer, there were no more improvements in the public schools. This was not the momentous result that voucher advocates had predicted.

The one notable consequence of the voucher program was that (in the words of the *Journal Sentinel* reporters) "it opened the door for the spread of other forms of school choice, including charter schools, which have taken innovative paths and have been growing rapidly in enrollment." As students enrolled in the voucher schools, charter schools, and interdistrict choice programs, enrollment in the Milwaukee public schools plummeted. In 1998, the district had about 100,000 students. A decade later, enrollment in the regular public schools dropped just below 80,000. Vouchers, charters, and choice were rapidly eroding the public education system.[26]

A similar phenomenon occurred in Washington, D.C. As charter schools grew, enrollment in the District of Columbia's public schools dropped sharply. When the first charter school opened in the district in 1997, the public schools enrolled nearly 80,000 students. By 2009, the number of students enrolled in public schools dropped to only 45,000, while fifty-six charter schools enrolled 28,000 children, over a third of the students in the district (with an additional 1,700 students in voucher schools).[27] The media regularly pummeled the district's public schools as the worst in the nation, while the highest officials in the federal and local government lauded charter schools as the leading edge of school reform. Little wonder that parents voted with their feet to abandon the public schools.

The 2007 report of the federal National Assessment of Educational Progress had disturbing implications for Milwaukee's public schools. That assessment found that the test scores of African American students in Wisconsin's public schools were among the lowest in the nation, comparable to those of African American students in Mississippi and Alabama in both reading and mathematics in fourth and eighth grades. The gap between white and African American students in Wisconsin was one of the largest in the nation. This reflected poorly on Milwaukee, where two-thirds of the African American students in Wisconsin attended school. According to choice theory, vouchers were supposed to improve the public schools, but the NAEP results showed that the performance of African American students in Milwaukee continued to lag.[28]

In sum, twenty years after the initiation of vouchers in Milwaukee and a decade after the program's expansion to include religious schools, there was no evidence of dramatic improvement for the neediest students or the public schools they left behind.

CHARTER SCHOOLS WERE THE JEWELS of the school choice movement. They were far more popular than vouchers and multiplied rapidly. By 2010, about 30,000 students in the nation were using publicly funded vouchers, while some 1.4 million students were enrolled in about 4,600 charter schools. Every president lauded charter schools, from George H. W. Bush to Bill Clinton to George

W. Bush to Barack Obama. Charter schools appealed to a broad spectrum of people from the left, the right, and the center, all of whom saw charters (as others had previously seen vouchers) as the antidote to bureaucracy and stasis and as the decisive change that would revolutionize American education and dramatically improve educational achievement. Charter schools represented, more than anything else, a concerted effort to deregulate public education, with few restrictions on pedagogy, curriculum, class size, discipline, or other details of their operation.

The charter school sector had its problems, which was not surprising in light of its explosive growth. In 2004, the California Charter Academy, the largest charter school chain in California, collapsed in bankruptcy, stranding 6,000 students in sixty storefront schools at the beginning of the fall term. The founder of the organization, a former insurance company executive, allegedly collected $100 million from the state to finance his statewide chain of charter schools.[29]

Pennsylvania passed a charter law in 1997. Ten years later, there were 127 charter schools, nearly half in Philadelphia. The city adopted what is known as the "diverse provider model," in which district schools compete with charter schools and privately managed schools (operating under contract to the district and not entirely free of districtwide mandates). Researchers from the RAND Corporation noted that achievement had improved in Philadelphia, but "with so many different interventions under way simultaneously in Philadelphia, there is no way to determine exactly which components of the reform plan are responsible for the improvement." The RAND team concluded in 2008 that students in charter schools made gains that were statistically indistinguishable from the gains they experienced while attending traditional public schools. They found no evidence that the local public schools were performing any differently because of competition with the charter schools. In 2007, the same researchers had analyzed Philadelphia's experiment in privatizing schools. They found that the privately managed schools—including for-profit and nonprofit managers—did not, on average, exceed the performance of regular public schools. In 2009, Philadelphia officials announced that the privatization experiment had not worked; of twenty-eight privately managed schools, they said, six elementary and middle schools outperformed the regular public schools, but ten were worse than district-run schools.[30]

The *Philadelphia Inquirer* reported that at least four charters were under federal criminal investigation for nepotism, conflicts of interest, and financial mismanagement. The managers of other charters in Pennsylvania created private companies to sell products or services to their schools or placed relatives on the payroll. One charter, the *Inquirer* found, paid millions of dollars in rent, salaries, and management fees annually to a for-profit company owned by the charter's chief executive officer. Cyber-charters, which offered online instruction to students at home, were receiving full payment for each student and amassing multimillion-dollar reserves; in virtual charter schools, relatively small numbers of teachers can "instruct" hundreds or even thousands of students online, generating huge profits for the charter company. Special education funding was also an issue in Pennsylvania, because charters collected payments for special education students but were not required to spend all the money they received on special education services.[31]

When charters get outstanding results, researchers inevitably ask whether they enroll a fair share of the neediest students. Some charters specifically serve English-language learners or special education students, and some do have their fair share. But in many instances, charters avoid students with high needs, either because they lack the staff to educate them appropriately or because they fear that such students will depress their test scores. A 2008 study by Jack Buckley and Mark Schneider of the charter schools in Washington, D.C., showed that they enroll substantially smaller numbers of children with high needs than do the regular public schools. On the one hand, the D.C. charters have a disproportionately high number of poor children, but on the other, "the vast majority of charters have proportionally fewer special education and English language learning students." A small number of charters target these groups, they said, but most do not. English-language learners were underrepresented in twenty-eight of thirty-seven charters, and special education students were underrepresented in twenty-four of thirty-seven charters, as compared to their proportions in the District of Columbia public schools.[32]

Nonetheless, some charter schools unquestionably have achieved outstanding results. In Texas, the School of Science and Technology in San Antonio was the only middle school in that city to earn a rating of "exemplary" from the state. About 20 percent of charter schools were considered excellent by state evaluators, and another 20 percent were struggling to survive, while the remaining 60 percent were somewhere in between.[33]

The charter schools with the most impressive record of success are the KIPP (Knowledge Is Power Program) schools, which have been called culture-changing schools, because they aim to teach students not just academics but also self-discipline and good behavior. KIPP was launched in 1994 by two teachers, David Levin and Michael Feinberg, after they completed their two-year assignment in the Teach for America program in Houston. Feinberg opened a KIPP school in Houston, and Levin opened one in the South Bronx in New York City. Both schools achieved exceptional results. Generously funded by foundations, Levin and Feinberg opened dozens more KIPP schools across the nation, specifically to prepare poor minority students for college. Fifteen years after the organization was founded, there were eighty-two KIPP schools with approximately 20,000 students.[34]

Almost every KIPP school is a charter school, and most are middle schools (grades five through eight). In contrast to regular public schools, KIPP schools have longer days (nine and a half hours), some Saturday classes, and three weeks of summer school; typically, a KIPP school provides 60 percent more time in school than a regular public school. Students, parents, and teachers sign a contract agreeing to fulfill specific responsibilities. The central organization does not define KIPP's pedagogy and curriculum; it leaves these decisions to individual school leaders.

In the demands they make on students, teachers, and parents, the KIPP schools are reminiscent of the American public schools of the 1940s, or even the 1920s, before the onset of class-action lawsuits and union contracts. In those days, it was not unusual to encounter schools with strict disciplinary codes and long working hours (though not nine-and-a-half-hour days).

Despite its successes, KIPP has its detractors. Critics question the applicability of the KIPP model to public education in general. One persistent question is whether KIPP enrolls all kinds of students, as regular public schools must. Like other successful charter schools, KIPP admits students by lottery; by definition, only the most motivated families apply for a slot. Charters with lotteries tend to attract the best students in poor neighborhoods, leaving the public schools in the same neighborhood worse off because they have lost some of their top-performing students. They also tend to enroll fewer of the students with high needs—English-language learners and those needing special education.[35]

The students who remain in KIPP schools for four or more years tend to achieve large test score gains. Most KIPP schools consistently outperform traditional public schools in the same neighborhood. But KIPP schools often have a high attrition rate. Apparently many students and their parents are unable or unwilling to comply with KIPP's stringent demands. A 2008 study of KIPP schools in San Francisco's Bay Area found that 60 percent of the students who started in fifth grade were gone by the end of eighth grade. The students who quit tended to be lower-performing students. The exit of such a large proportion of low-performing students—for whatever reasons—makes it difficult to analyze the performance of KIPP students in higher grades. In addition, teacher turnover is high at KIPP schools, as well as other charter schools, no doubt because of the unusually long hours. Thus, while the KIPP schools obtain impressive results for the students who remain enrolled for four years, the high levels of student attrition and teacher turnover raise questions about the applicability of the KIPP model to the regular public schools.[36]

KIPP has demonstrated that youngsters from some of the toughest neighborhoods in the nation can succeed in a safe and structured environment, if they have supportive parents and are willing to work hard, spend long days in school, and comply with the school's expectations. Thus far, public schools have not copied their methods. Regular public schools must accept everyone who applies, including the students who leave KIPP schools. They can't throw out the kids who do not work hard or the kids who have many absences or the kids who are disrespectful or the kids whose parents are absent or inattentive. They have to find ways to educate even those students who don't want to be there. That's the dilemma of public education.

The theory of the charter movement is that competition with the regular public schools will lead to improvements in both sectors, and that choice is a rising tide that lifts all boats. But in reality, the regular public schools are at a huge disadvantage in competition with charter schools. It is not only because charter schools may attract the most motivated students, may discharge laggards, and may enforce a tough disciplinary code, but also because the charters often get additional financial resources from their corporate sponsors, enabling them to offer smaller classes, after-school and enrichment activities, and laptop computers for every student. Many charter schools enforce discipline codes that would likely be challenged in court if they were adopted in regular public schools; and because charter schools are schools of choice, they find it easier to avoid, eliminate, or counsel out low-performing and disruptive students.

Yet, even with their advantages, charter schools—like all new schools—face daunting challenges. Reformers declare their intention to open new schools as though this would solve the problems of low-performing schools. But new schools cannot be mass-produced or turned out with a cookie-cutter design. Opening a new school is difficult. It involves starting with or recruiting a strong leader and a capable faculty, obtaining facilities, developing a program, assembling a student body, creating an effective administrative structure, and building a culture. Getting a new school up and running may take as many as five years. Some will succeed, some will be no different from the schools they replaced, and others will fail.

Reformers imagine that it is easy to create a successful school, but it is not. They imagine that the lessons of a successful school are obvious and can be easily transferred to other schools, just as one might take an industrial process or a new piece of machinery and install it in a new plant without error. But a school is successful for many reasons, including the personalities of its leader and teachers; the social interactions among them; the culture of the school; the students and their families; the way the school implements policies and programs dictated by the district, the state, and the federal government; the quality of the school's curriculum and instruction; the resources of the school and the community; and many other factors. When a school is successful, it is hard to know which factor was most important or if it was a combination of factors. Even the principal and teachers may not know for sure. A reporter from the local newspaper will arrive and decide that it must be the principal or a particular program, but the reporter will very likely be wrong. Success, whether defined as high test scores or graduation rates or student satisfaction, cannot be bottled and dispensed at will. This may explain why there are so few examples of low-performing schools that have been "turned around" into high-performing schools. And it may explain why schools are not very good at replicating the success of model schools, whether the models are charters or regular public schools. Certainly schools can improve and learn from one another, but school improvements—if they are real—occur incrementally, as a result of sustained effort over years.

HAVE CHARTER SCHOOLS LIVED up to the promises of their promoters? Given the wide diversity of charter schools, it's hard to reach a singular judgment about them. In terms of quality, charter schools run the gamut. Some are excellent, some are dreadful, and most are somewhere in between. It is in the nature of markets that some succeed, some are middling, and others fail.

In 2004, a furious controversy erupted between advocates and opponents of charter schools when it turned out that the federal government had tested a national sample of charter schools in 2003 but had not released its findings. The federal government did not release the data on charter school performance when it announced the results for states and the nation in November 2003. The charter scores went unnoticed until the results were discovered on the federal testing agency's Web site by staff members of the American Federation of Teachers. They learned that NAEP showed no measurable differences on tests of reading and mathematics between fourth-grade students from similar racial/ethnic backgrounds in charter schools and in regular public schools. Among poor students, fourth graders in regular public schools outperformed those in charter schools in both subjects. Overall, charter and public students performed similarly in reading, but public school students performed better in mathematics. The AFT published its own analysis in August 2004, which raised the question of why the testing data about charters had not been released in a timely manner. The effectiveness of charter schools was especially important, the AFT team argued, because the No Child Left Behind legislation proposed to improve low-performing public schools by turning them into charter schools. If charter schools were no more successful than regular public schools, then the "remedy" made no sense. The AFT leaked its discovery to Diana Jean Schemo, an education reporter at the *New York Times*, whose front-page story stated that "the findings, buried in mountains of data the Education Department released without public announcement, dealt a blow to supporters of the charter school movement, including the Bush administration."[37]

The data wars were on! Charter school supporters were outraged and took out a full-page ad in the *New York Times* to complain about the unfairness of judging charter schools that were serving far more disadvantaged students than their peers in regular public schools and to stress that the federal data said nothing about whether charter students were making gains. In December 2004, Harvard University economist Caroline M. Hoxby published a comprehensive study comparing charter schools and their nearby public schools. Hoxby analyzed the performance of virtually every charter elementary school student in the nation and found that they were more likely to be proficient in both reading and math than public school students, and that the charter school advantage increased with the age of the charter schools; students in charter schools that had been operating for more than nine years showed the largest gains.[38]

But that was not the end of the data wars. Critics of charter schools associated with the left-leaning think tank Economic Policy Institute (EPI) published *The Charter School Dust-Up*, reviewing the evidence as well as the controversy over the NAEP charter report, and concluded that charter schools were a risky venture in education. The critics quoted one of the leading charter boosters, Chester E. Finn Jr., who wrote:

> Some of the best schools I've ever been in are charter schools, some of which are blowing the lid off test scores in such vexed communities as Boston, New York, and Chicago. And some of the worst—and flakiest—schools I've ever been in are charter schools. Yet people are choosing them.[39]

The EPI authors said that the question to be answered was not whether charter schools, on average, outperform regular public schools, "but rather whether the underperformance of some charter schools is a price worth paying for the overperformance of others." They were particularly concerned that the response of charter supporters to the flap over the NAEP scores "reflects an unfortunate shift of some charter school advocacy from a pragmatic quest to identify school improvement strategies to an ideological prejudice against regular public schools." They recalled that one of the original goals of the charter movement was to engage in experimentation to see what works best, but the repeated claim that charter schools were superior to regular schools suggests that "experimentation is not necessary because charter school operators already know what works."[40]

In the years that followed, study after study compared educational performance in private schools and public schools, or charter schools and regular public schools. The only surprise was how small and usually insignificant were the gains recorded by any sector.

On a Friday in July 2006, the U.S. Department of Education quietly released a study comparing students in public and private schools. The timing suggested that the department did not want to call attention to the study, which found that public school students performed as well as or better than comparable children in private schools. Private school students scored higher on average, but their advantage disappeared when they were compared to public school students with similar characteristics. In mathematics, fourth-grade students in public schools were nearly half a year ahead of their peers in private schools. Only in eighth-grade reading did private school students surpass their public school counterparts.[41]

In the same year, another study appeared comparing the performance of students in public schools, private schools, and charter schools on the 2003 NAEP mathematics assessment. The authors, Christopher Lubienski and Sarah Theule Lubienski, maintained that mathematics scores offered a clearer indication of the school's effectiveness than reading scores, because mathematics is influenced less by the child's home experiences than reading. After controlling for demographic and other variables, the study found that the advantages of private schools and charter schools disappeared and, in some instances, demonstrated the superiority of regular public schools. The researchers concluded that the regular public schools performed "relatively well when compared to demographically similar private and charter schools, without the remedy of major, private-style structural reforms in their governance and management."[42]

When the 2007 NAEP test results were released, they showed that students in charter schools had lower scores than students in public schools in fourth-grade reading, fourth-grade mathematics, and eighth-grade mathematics. Only in eighth-grade reading did charter school students score the same as public school students. When students were compared by race and ethnicity, there was little difference in the test scores of students in charter schools and regular public schools (except that eighth-grade Hispanic students in charter schools did better in math). As *Education Week* reported, "The picture that emerges from the growing data set appears mixed for charter schools. While many analysts urge caution in using NAEP to judge the 4,300-school charter sector, the latest data do not bolster the early hopes of charter advocates that the sector as a whole would significantly outperform regular public schools."[43]

Meanwhile, studies of charter schools compared to regular public schools continued to appear, and they reached dissimilar conclusions.

A 2009 study by Thomas Kane and colleagues compared Boston's charter schools, pilot schools (which have a high degree of autonomy in budget, staffing, and curriculum but are still part of the district), and traditional public schools and reached a verdict favorable to charters. Charters in Massachusetts have an impressive record of success; in 2008, four of the top ten public schools on the state's test of eighth-grade mathematics were charter schools, as were three of the top ten on the state's test of tenth-grade mathematics. The study concluded that charters "appear to have a consistently positive impact on student achievement" in both middle schools and high schools. The gains were especially large in middle school mathematics, where students moved from the 50th to the 69th percentile in performance in one year—about half the size of the black-white achievement gap. Part of the study compared students who won the lottery to those who applied but did not win the lottery. Sociologist Jennifer Jennings admired the study but pointed out that the lottery portion of the study included only the most successful of the city's charter schools—zero of five charter elementary schools, four of thirteen charter middle schools, and three of eleven charter high schools. The remainder were "not oversubscribed enough to require a lottery." The Kane report acknowledged that "substantial" gains were found in "high-demand Charter Schools with complete records" and warned that "these results should not be interpreted as showing that Boston Charters always produce test score gains."[44] It showed that successful charter schools are very successful; it did not show that all charters are successful.

Given their outstanding results, charters in Boston enjoy a good reputation. Some are exemplary schools. But an analysis by the *Boston Globe* in 2009 determined that compared to regular public schools, Boston's charter schools enrolled a smaller percentage of students who were in special education or who were English-language learners. English-language learners were nearly one-fifth of the public school enrollment, yet the city's charters (with only one exception) contained fewer than 4 percent of such students. Six of Boston's sixteen charters had not a single English-language learner. The *Globe* wondered whether charters achieved "dazzling" test scores "because of innovative teaching or because they enroll fewer disadvantaged students."[45] This analysis by no means diminishes the accomplishments of Boston's top charter schools—such as Academy of the Pacific Rim, Boston Collegiate, Boston Prep, and Roxbury Prep—but it leaves open the question of how to educate the neediest students and which schools will do so.

A national study in 2009 concluded that students in most charter schools performed no better than those in traditional public schools. Researchers at Stanford University, led by economist Margaret E. Raymond, analyzed data from 2,403 charter schools in fifteen states and the District of Columbia (about half of all charters and 70 percent of all charter students in the nation at the time) and found that 37 percent had learning gains that were significantly below those of local public schools; 46 percent had gains that were no different; and only 17 percent showed growth that was significantly better. More than 80 percent of the charter schools in the study performed either the same as or worse than the local public schools. Raymond concluded, "This study reveals in unmistakable terms that, in the aggregate, charter students are not faring as well as their TPS [traditional public school] counterparts. Further, tremendous variation in academic quality among charters is the norm, not the exception. The problem of quality is the most pressing issue that charter schools and their supporters face." She commented to *Education Week*, "If this study shows anything, it shows that we've got a two-to-one margin of bad charters to good charters." The Stanford study created demographic matches between students in charter schools and local public schools. The results were sobering, especially since the study was funded by such pro-charter groups as the Walton Family Foundation and the Michael and Susan Dell Foundation.[46]

In the same year, however, Caroline Hoxby and her colleagues at Stanford reached a starkly different conclusion. In a study of New York City charter schools, Hoxby determined that disadvantaged students who attended charter schools for nine consecutive years, from kindergarten to eighth grade, closed most of the "Scarsdale-Harlem" achievement gap. She compared students who won the lottery with students who entered but did not win, matching equally motivated students, to demonstrate that the charters did not attain great results by "creaming" the best students. This finding suggested to editorialists at the *Wall Street Journal*, the *Washington Post*, and other national media that charter schools were the silver bullet that could finally solve the most deep-seated problems of urban education.[47]

A summary of research on charter schools by Tom Loveless and Katharyn Field of the Brookings Institution in 2009 found, as one might expect, a large divide between advocates and critics of these schools. Some researchers found positive effects, some found negative effects, but on the whole "none of the studies detects huge effects—either positive or negative." Their review also indicated that charters probably promoted racial segregation, since parents chose schools "with a racial profile matching their own." The authors predicted that the real debate about charter schools was ideological and would not easily be resolved. They concluded,

> As so often happens with competing ideologies, the empirical evidence on charter schools has not yet settled the theoretical arguments about their existence. We need better research on charter schools, it is true, a non-controversial recommendation endorsed by blue ribbon commissions. But we should not be overly optimistic that better data will settle the charter school debate. Future research will be of varying quality, the data will be mixed and difficult to interpret, and the findings subject to different interpretations. Just as it is unreasonable to expect charter schools to solve all of the problems of American education, it is unreasonable to expect research to settle all of the theoretical disputes about market-based education and school choice.[48]

Buoyed by hope and the endorsement of important political figures, enthusiasm for charter schools far outstripped research evidence for their efficacy, as scholars Buckley and Schneider noted. They predicted that the demand for "evidence-based reform" was on a collision course with the demand for more charter schools. While they saw cause for optimism in some charters, they concluded that the push for charters was "characterized by too many promises that are only, at best, weakly supported by evidence . . . even the most basic descriptions of charter schools are often infused with hype. In turn, the creation of charter schools has become more than a reform; it has become a *movement*."[49]

Regardless of competing research studies, the charter school sector continued to expand rapidly, as states and districts turned to private agencies and entrepreneurs to solve the problems of education. As more charter schools opened, advocacy for charters in Washington and state capitals grew stronger, supported by major foundations, including the Gates Foundation and the Broad Foundation, and wealthy entrepreneurs. Everyone knew the charter sector was big, bold, diverse, and getting bigger, bolder, and more diverse. Their quality ranged from excellent to awful. That's what happens when an industry is deregulated and the sluice gates are opened to release a huge flow of innovation, entrepreneurship, and enterprise. So, ironically, at the very time that the financial markets were collapsing, and as deregulation of financial markets got a bad name, many of the leading voices in American education assured the public that the way to educational rejuvenation was through deregulation.

WHAT IS THE SECRET of successful charter schools, those that consistently record high standardized test scores? The higher scores may be the product of longer hours and weeks, dedicated teachers, motivated students, excellent curricula, and outstanding leaders. The scores may be affected by an encompassing culture that demands persistent effort and parental engagement. And they may be a result of peer effects. In other words, motivated students perform best when surrounded by other motivated students. Students may take their schoolwork more seriously when they are in a school where almost all their classmates are trying their best to do well and disruptive behavior is not tolerated.

So this is the emerging scenario, particularly in urban districts. Charter schools enroll the most motivated students in poor communities, those whose parents push them to do better. Regular public schools in the same communities get the students who did not win the lottery, plus all the less motivated students. When the students who lost the lottery return to their public schools in poor neighborhoods, they will attend classes with a mix of peers, including some who just want to get by and some who are not interested in schoolwork. This seems likely to depress the academic performance of the motivated students.

What lessons can public schools learn from the charter schools? Should they create more selective schools to hold on to motivated students? Should they separate their students by ability to prevent the unmotivated from negatively affecting the performance of the motivated? If they have longer hours and weeks, will that cause unmotivated students to become more motivated? How should regular public schools educate those who are not highly motivated and those who are not at all interested in their schoolwork, as well as those who are working hard and want a good education? These are the problems that Albert Shanker once imagined would be studied and perhaps even solved by innovative charter schools.

As currently configured, charter schools are havens for the motivated. As more charter schools open, the dilemma of educating *all* students will grow sharper. The resolution of this dilemma will determine the fate of public education.

The question for the future is whether the continued growth of charter schools in urban districts will leave regular public schools with the most difficult students to educate, thus creating a two-tier system of widening inequality. If so, we can safely predict that future studies will "prove" the success of charter schools and the failure of regular schools, because the public schools will have disproportionate numbers of less motivated parents and needier students. As charter schools increase in number and able students enroll in them, the regular public schools in the nation's cities will be locked into a downward trajectory. This would be an ominous development for public education and for our nation.

WITH THE ELECTION of Barack Obama as president, it seemed certain that federal support for vouchers was a dead issue, at least for the foreseeable future. For supporters of school choice, it mattered little, as they shifted their allegiance to charter schools as the vehicle that would inject market forces and competition into American education. And soon after he entered office, President Obama heartened charter school advocates by urging state legislatures to remove the caps on charter schools. The Obama administration's Department of Education advised states that they would not be eligible for nearly $5 billion in discretionary funds unless they eliminated any legal limits on the expansion of charter schools.[50]

This was puzzling. Here was a president who had been elected on a promise of change, yet he was picking up the same banner of choice, competition, and markets that had been the hallmark of his predecessors. There was little evidence that charter schools were generically better than public schools. Nothing in the record suggested that the entire sector was successful, that *any* charter school was better than *any* public school. Lost, it seemed, was the original vision of charter schools, in which they were supposed to help solve some of the hardest problems of public education. As originally imagined, charters were intended not to compete with public schools, but to support them. Charters were supposed to be research and development laboratories for discovering better ways of educating hard-to-educate children. They were not intended to siphon away the most motivated students and families in the poorest communities, but to address some of the public schools' most urgent problems.

In their current manifestation, charters are supposed to disseminate the free-market model of competition and choice. Now charters compete for the most successful students in the poorest communities, or they accept all applicants and push the low performers back into the public school system. Either approach further disables regular public schools in those communities by leaving the lowest-performing and least motivated students to the regular public schools. It matters not that the original proponents of charter schools had different goals. It does matter, though, that charter schools have become in many communities a force intended to disrupt the traditional notion of public schooling. The rhetoric of many charter school advocates has come to sound uncannily similar to the rhetoric of voucher proponents and of the most rabid haters of public schooling. They often sound as though they want public schools to fail; they want to convert entire districts to charter schools, each with its own curriculum and methods, each with its own private management, all competing for students and public dollars.

If there is one consistent lesson that one gleans by studying school reform over the past century, it is the danger of taking a good idea and expanding it rapidly, spreading it thin. What is stunningly successful in a small setting, nurtured by its founders and brought to life by a cadre of passionate teachers, seldom survives the transition when it is turned into a large-scale reform. Whether charter schools are a sustainable reform, whether they can proliferate and at the same time produce good results, is a question yet to be resolved. Whether there is the will to close low-performing charters remains to be seen. Whether there is an adequate supply of teachers who are willing to work fifty-hour weeks is unknown. The biggest unknown is how the multiplication of charter schools will affect public education.

In barely twenty years, the idea of school choice rapidly advanced in the public arena and captivated elite opinion. Given the accumulating evidence of its uneven results, this was surprising. Even more surprising was how few voices were raised on behalf of the democratic vision of public education.

CHAPTER EIGHT

The Trouble with Accountability

In the 1990s, accountability became the watchword of public officials and business leaders. Governors, corporate executives, the first Bush administration, and the Clinton administration agreed: They wanted measurable results; they wanted to know that the tax dollars invested in public education were getting a good return. Governors wanted better schools to attract new industries to their state, and business leaders complained that the nation was losing its competitive edge in the global economy. In 1989, President George H. W. Bush invited the nation's governors to a national summit on education to set a course of action. The federal and state leaders agreed on six ambitious national goals for the year 2000 and established the National Education Goals Panel to monitor progress toward the goals.

President Clinton enthusiastically supported the national goals (he had drafted the language for them at the Bush summit) and added two more for good measure. In 1997, Clinton asked Congress to authorize voluntary national testing in reading and mathematics for students in fourth and eighth grades, but Congress—controlled by Republicans—refused. Clinton's proposed national tests disappeared and so did the national goals. None of the goals that had been proclaimed to much fanfare in 1990 was reached by the year 2000, and the Goals Panel quietly vanished.

Undaunted, the second President Bush persuaded a willing Congress to pass his No Child Left Behind legislation in 2001. Democrats and Republicans alike agreed on the importance of accountability for teachers, principals, and schools, especially if their students were not achieving. The administration and Congress agreed that testing would spur school improvement. Unlike the first President Bush's six national goals or Clinton's eight national goals, NCLB contained one goal: All children would be "proficient" in reading and mathematics by 2014. This time, however, the goal was not merely a devoutly desired wish, but a federal mandate, with real consequences for schools whose students did not meet it.

NCLB opened a new era of testing and accountability in American public schools. Educators and parents who objected to the new emphasis on testing were outraged. They railed against the tests, they filed lawsuits, they protested, all to no avail. Politicians dismissed them as anti-testing fanatics, and the courts rejected their lawsuits.

The anti-testing forces lashed out against the wrong target. Testing was not the problem. Tests can be designed and used well or badly. The problem was the misuse of testing for high-stakes purposes, the belief that tests could identify with certainty which students should be held back, which teachers and principals should be fired or rewarded, and which schools should be closed—and the idea that these changes would inevitably produce better education. Policy decisions that were momentous for students and educators came down from elected officials who did not understand the limitations of testing.

The information derived from tests can be extremely valuable, if the tests are valid and reliable. The results can show students what they have learned, what they have not learned, and where they need to improve. They can tell parents how their children are doing as compared to others of their age and grade. They can inform teachers whether their students understood what they were taught. They can enable teachers and school administrators to determine which students need additional help or different methods of instruction. They can identify students who need help in learning English or special education services. They can inform educational leaders and policymakers about the progress of the education system as a whole. They can show which programs are making a difference and which are not, which should be expanded and which should be terminated.

They can help to direct additional support, training, and resources to teachers and schools that need them.

The federal tests—the National Assessment of Educational Progress, or NAEP—measure the progress over time of students in the nation, states, and a number of urban districts. International assessments offer insight into how students compare to their peers in other countries. Most selective colleges rely on admissions tests to find out whether prospective students are prepared to meet their academic expectations, though they always look at test scores in tandem with grades, essays, and other indicators of students' ability. Many universities routinely test incoming students to determine whether they need remedial courses. Used judiciously, this is valuable information.

Tests have been a fixture in American education since the early decades of the twentieth century, when they were used to make decisions about matters such as promotion to the next grade, graduation, and college admissions. Schools regularly tested their students to see if they had mastered what they were taught. Students who didn't pass tests in history, geography, literature, and arithmetic were often "left back." Schoolteachers were sometimes required to pass a test of their knowledge when they entered the profession. But once they were hired, there were no more tests of their suitability or capacity.

Educational tests began to change in the 1920s, in response to new developments in the technology of testing. During World War I, the nation's leading psychologists designed intelligence tests to help the army sort recruits into their roles as officers or enlisted men. These new tests, the psychologists believed, were scientific and objective, in contrast to the tests written by school districts and teachers. The psychologists criticized tests with written answers, because their grading was necessarily subjective. Educators became persuaded that the new standardized, multiple-choice tests were the leading edge of scientific efficiency. The schools began to use them to classify students according to their ability. And the new tests had another advantage: They could be scored quickly and cheaply, often by machines, an important consideration at a time when enrollments were growing rapidly.

Today, NCLB requires every state to test students annually in grades three through eight in reading and mathematics. Due to technological advances, many states and districts have the capacity to attribute the test scores of specific students to specific teachers, and (with the active encouragement of the Obama administration) many will use this information to hold teachers accountable for the rise or fall of their students' scores. If testing inspires a degree of loathing, it is because it has become the crucial hinge on which turns the fate of students and the reputations and futures of their teachers, principals, and schools.

The problem with using tests to make important decisions about people's lives is that standardized tests are not precise instruments. Unfortunately, most elected officials do not realize this, nor does the general public. The public thinks the tests have scientific validity, like that of a thermometer or a barometer, and that they are objective, not tainted by fallible human judgment. But test scores are not comparable to standard weights and measures; they do not have the precision of a doctor's scale or a yardstick. Tests vary in their quality, and even the best tests may sometimes be error-prone, because of human mistakes or technical foul-ups. Hardly a testing season passes without a news story about a goof made by a major testing company. Sometimes questions are poorly worded. Sometimes the answers are wrongly scored. Sometimes the supposedly "right" answer to a question is wrong or ambiguous. Sometimes two of four answers on a multiple-choice question are equally correct.[1]

All tests have a margin of error, like opinion polls, and the same student could produce different scores when taking the same test on different days. The scores might not be wildly different, but they might be different enough to nudge the student's rating across the line from "not proficient" to "proficient," or drop her down a notch. So, a student who failed a test on Monday might pass if she took the same test on Wednesday. Maybe the student got a good night's sleep one day, but not the next; maybe she was distracted by a personal crisis—a spat with her best friend—one day, but not the next. Tests themselves differ from one another, even when they are designed to be as similar as possible. So a student could pass one test and fail another that was designed to be of equal difficulty. Testing experts frequently remind school officials that standardized test scores should be used not in isolation to make consequential decisions about students, but only in conjunction with other measures of student performance, such as grades, class participation, homework, and teachers' recommendations. Testing experts also warn that test scores should be used only for the purpose for which the test was designed: For example, a fifth-grade reading test measures fifth-grade reading skills and cannot reliably serve as a measure of the teacher's skill.

Testing experts know that tests have their limitations, and the testing companies themselves have publicly stated that the results of their exams should never be used as the sole metric by which important decisions are made. When students take the SAT for college admissions, their score on any given day is an estimate of their developed ability. If a student gets a 580 on his verbal SAT, that score is an approximation of his skills and knowledge; if he took the SAT a week later, he might get a 560 or a 600, or a score that is even higher or lower. The College Board reminds students, teachers, guidance counselors, and college admissions officers that the SAT score is not exact and that it might differ on another day or in response to coaching.[2]

The Committee on Appropriate Test Use of the National Research Council stated in an authoritative report in 1999 that "tests are not perfect" and "a test score is not an exact measure of a student's knowledge or skills." Because test scores are not an infallible measure, the committee warned, "an educational decision that will have a major impact on a test taker should not be made solely or automatically on the basis of a single test score."[3] This expert panel could not have dreamed that only two years later, a law would be passed that established harsh consequences not for test takers, but for educators and schools. Or that only ten years later, the president of the United States would urge states and school districts to evaluate teachers on the basis of their students' test scores.

Psychometricians are less enthusiastic than elected officials about using tests to make consequential judgments, because they know that test scores may vary in unpredictable ways. Year-to-year changes in test scores for individuals or entire classes may be due to random variation. Student performance may be affected by the weather, the student's state of mind, distractions outside the classroom, or conditions inside the classroom. Tests may also become invalid if too much time is spent preparing students to take them.

Robert Linn of the University of Colorado, a leading psychometrician, maintains that there are many reasons why one school might get better test scores than another. NCLB, he says, assumes that if school A gets better results than school B, it must be due to differences in school quality. But school A may have students who were higher achieving in earlier years than those in the other school. Or school A might have fewer students who are English-language learners or fewer students with disabilities than school B. School A, which is presumably more successful, may have a homogeneous student body, while the less successful school B may have a diverse student body with several subgroups, each of which must meet a proficiency target. Linn concludes, "The fact that the school that has fewer challenges makes AYP [adequate yearly progress] while the school with greater challenges fails to make AYP does not justify the conclusion that the first school is more effective than the second school. The first school might very well fail to make AYP if it had a student body that was comparable to the one in the second school."[4]

State testing systems usually test only once each year, which increases the possibility of random variation. It would help, Linn says, to administer tests at the start of the school year and then again at the end of the school year, to identify the effectiveness of the school. Even then, there would be confounding variables: "For example, students at the school with the higher scores on the state assessment might have received more educational support at home than students at school B. The student bodies attending different schools can differ in many ways that are related to performance on tests, including language background, socioeconomic status, and prior achievement."[5] The professional organizations that set the standards for testing—such as the American Psychological Association and the American Educational Research Association—agree that test results reflect not only what happens in school, but also the characteristics of those tested, including such elusive factors as student motivation and parental engagement. Because there are so many variables that cannot be measured, even attempts to match schools by the demographic profile of their student body do not suffice to eliminate random variation.

Given the importance of test scores, it is not surprising that teachers and school officials have devised various ways of gaming the testing system: that is, tricks and shortcuts to achieve the desired results, without improving education. When the purpose of testing is informational and diagnostic, there is no reason for teachers and administrators to alter the results except through improved instruction. But when the purpose of testing is accountability, then teachers and administrators understand that there are real consequences if the scores in their classroom or their school change. If scores go up, they may get a handsome bonus; if they go down, their school will be stigmatized, and they may lose their jobs. The intense pressure generated by demands for accountability leads many educators and school officials to boost the scores in ways that have nothing to do with learning.

The most reprehensible form of gaming the system is plain old-fashioned cheating. There have been many news stories about a teacher or principal who was fired for correcting students' answers before handing in the tests or leaking the questions in advance to students. In some instances, the cheating is systematic, not idiosyncratic. The *Dallas Morning News* analyzed statewide scores in Texas on the state's high-stakes TAKS test—which determines schools' reputations and teachers' rewards—and found evidence that tens of thousands of students cheated every year without being detected or punished. The cheating was especially pervasive on eleventh-grade tests, which students must pass to graduate. Most of the cheating uncovered by reporters was in Houston and Dallas and was more common in low-achieving schools, "where the pressure to boost scores is the highest." Cheating was found in charter schools at almost four times the rate of traditional public schools. In response to the story, Dallas school officials beefed up their school system's testing security, but Houston school officials slammed the newspaper's study as an effort "to dismiss the real academic progress in Texas schools."[6]

Many ways of gaming the system are not outright illegal, yet they are usually not openly acknowledged. Most principals know that the key to getting higher test scores is to restrict the admission of low-performing students, because they depress the school's test scores. As choice becomes more common in urban districts, principals of small schools and charter schools—both of which have limited enrollments—may exclude the students who are most difficult to educate. They may do it by requiring an interview with parents of applicants, knowing that the parents of the lowest-performing students are not as likely to show up as the parents of more successful students. They may do it by requiring that students write an essay explaining why they want to attend the school. They may ask for letters of recommendation from the students' teachers. They may exclude students with poor attendance records, since poor attendance correlates with poor academic performance. They may limit the number of students they admit who are English-language learners or in need of special education. All such requirements tend to eliminate the lowest performers.

Whenever there is competition for admission, canny principals have learned how to spot the kids who will diminish their scores and how to exclude them without appearing to do so.[7]

A lottery for admission tends to eliminate unmotivated students from the pool of applicants because they are less likely to apply. Principals know there is a wide range of ability within every racial and ethnic group, as well as among low-income students. A school can carefully weed out the lowest-performing students and still be able to boast that most or all of its students are African American, Hispanic, and low-income. Education researchers call this skimming or cream-skimming.[8] It is a very effective way for a school to generate high test scores regardless of the quality of its program. Schools of choice may improve their test scores by counseling disruptive students to transfer to another school or flunking low-performing students, who may then decide to leave. Not only do choice schools look better if they exclude laggards, but the traditional public schools look worse, because they must by law accept those who were not admitted to or were booted out of the choice schools.[9]

Another way a school can improve its test scores is to reduce the participation of low-performing students on the state tests. Such students may be encouraged to stay home on the day of the big test or may be suspended right before testing day. Sometimes these students are inappropriately assigned to special education to remove them from a subgroup (white or African American or Hispanic or Asian) where their low score might prevent that group from making AYP. Or the principal may assign low-performing students to a special education program that is unavailable in the school, thus ensuring that the student will transfer to a different school. In California, dozens of schools reclassified students by their race or English fluency or disability status, moving them from one category to another to improve their school's standing under NCLB (if schools have too few students in a specific group, that group's scores are not reported).[10] Presumably, schools that blatantly shift students from one category to another will be caught in the act at some point and sanctioned.

States can cleverly game the system to meet their testing targets by making the test content less challenging or by lowering the cut score (the passing mark) on state tests. State education officials tend to ignore critics who say the test is easier than previous tests, and outsiders seldom have enough information to verify their suspicions.

Actually, the test may be equally difficult as in previous years, but if the state education department lowers the cut score, then more students will pass. Typically, the state releases the test scores, the press reports the results, public officials step up to take credit for any gains, and editorials congratulate the schools on their stunning progress. When the technical data are released a few weeks later, few in the media have the technical expertise to ascertain whether the cut scores were lowered; even if testing experts discover that the scores were manipulated, no one pays attention. Also, states may test only a narrow range of the state's standards, so the test becomes predictable from year to year. All such tactics may produce a steady, even dramatic, increase in scores without improving any student's education.[11]

Yet another way to raise the proportion of students who reach "proficiency" is to expand the pool of test takers who are eligible for accommodations, that is, extra time or a dictionary or other special assistance. School officials may increase the number of students who are classified as disabled so they will get extra accommodations. Or state officials may decide that students who were formerly classified as English-language learners should continue to receive extra accommodations even *after* they passed an English examination and achieved proficiency in English.[12]

Districts, too, have incentives to game the system. In 2007, Cleveland celebrated improved test scores, but an investigation by the *Cleveland Plain Dealer* determined that the district, as well as others in Ohio, had "scrubbed" or tossed out the test scores of students who were not continuously enrolled during the school year. Not surprisingly, most of the scores that were scrubbed were from low performers. The newspaper's analysis found that "from 14 percent to 32 percent of the scores in grades 4 to 10 were eliminated in 2007."[13]

In the NCLB era, many states and districts reported outsized test score gains, but the gains were usually not real. The state education department in New York quietly changed the scoring of the state tests in mathematics and English language arts, which produced dramatic gains in the proportion who met state standards each year. Between 2006, when the state introduced a new test, and 2009, the proportion of students in grades three through eight who reached proficiency on the state math test leapt from 28.6 percent to an incredible 63.3 percent in Buffalo, from 30.1 percent to 58.2

percent in Syracuse, and from 57 percent to 81.8 percent in New York City. In the state as a whole, the proportion of students who were proficient jumped in these three years from 65.8 percent to 86.5 percent. To an unknowing public, these breathtaking increases were solid evidence that the schools were getting better and that more students were meeting high standards. But in reality, state officials made it easier to pass the tests. In 2006, a student in seventh grade was required to get 59.6 percent of the points on the test to meet state standards in mathematics; by 2009, a student in that grade needed only 44 percent to be considered proficient.[14] Most people would consider a score of 44 percent to be a failing grade, not evidence of proficiency.

A similar phenomenon affected New York's Regents examinations, on which students must score 65 to receive a high school diploma. Many students would have failed to reach this high bar, but state officials took care of their difficulty by adjusting the cut scores. The public probably assumed that a student who received a 65 had correctly answered 65 percent of the questions. But in algebra, a student would receive a passing score of 65 if he earned only 34.5 percent of the possible points. To win a 65 on the biology Regents, the student needed to earn only 46 percent of the possible points. With this intricate conversion formula, the Regents diploma was turned into a goal that almost every student could reach.[15] By making it easier to pass the Regents exams, state officials helped increase the graduation rate.

In 2009, the Civic Committee of the Commercial Club of Chicago released a study demonstrating that the city's claims of dramatic test score gains were exaggerated. Chicago school officials had boasted that from 2004 to 2008, the proportion of eighth-grade students who met state standards in reading had increased from 55 percent to 76 percent, and in mathematics it had grown from 33 percent to 70 percent (President Obama recited these statistics when he announced the appointment of Arne Duncan, Chicago's superintendent of schools, as U.S. secretary of education). The study concluded, however, that "these huge increases reflect changes in the tests and testing procedures—not real student improvement." In 2006 the state hired a new testing company, which introduced a new test and lowered the cut scores (mainly in eighth-grade mathematics), thus producing the illusion of remarkable gains. At the same time that Chicago's scores soared on the state tests, its scores on

NAEP (from 2003 to 2007) were flat. Meanwhile, student performance levels in high school remained disastrously low from 2001 to 2008, suggesting that any modest improvements in the elementary grades disappeared by high school.[16]

Of all the ways of gaming the system, the most common is test preparation. Most districts, especially urban districts where performance is lowest, relentlessly engage in test-prep activities. Some preparation for test-taking is valuable; reading and studying, learning new vocabulary, and solving math problems are good ways to get ready for the tests. But school districts have invested hundreds of millions of dollars in programs and training materials that teach students the specific types of questions that will appear on the state tests. For weeks or even months before the state test, children are drilled daily in test-taking skills and on questions mirroring those that are likely to appear on the state test.[17]

The consequence of all this practice is that students may be able to pass the state test, yet unable to pass a test of precisely the same subject for which they did not practice. They master test-taking methods, but not the subject itself. In the new world of accountability, students' acquisition of the skills and knowledge they need for further education and for the workplace is secondary. What matters most is for the school, the district, and the state to be able to say that more students have reached "proficiency." This sort of fraud ignores the students' interests while promoting the interests of adults who take credit for nonexistent improvements.

The National Research Council's Committee on Appropriate Test Use held that "all students are entitled to sufficient test preparation" so they are familiar with the format of the test, the subject matter to be tested, and appropriate test-taking strategies. Surely students should know what a multiple-choice question is and should not be stumped by the nature of the testing process. (By now, there must be very few children in the United States who are unfamiliar with the nature of standardized testing and test-taking strategies.) The committee cautioned, however, that the test results might be invalidated "by teaching so narrowly to the objectives of a particular test that scores are raised without actually improving the broader set of academic skills that the test is intended to measure."[18]

Daniel Koretz, a psychometrician at Harvard University, contends that coaching students for state tests produces test score inflation and the illusion of progress. He criticizes the common practice of teaching students certain test-taking tricks, such as how to eliminate obviously wrong answers on a multiple-choice question and then making a guess among the remaining choices. It is equally questionable, he says, to teach students "to write in ways that are tailored to the specific scoring rubrics used with a particular test." When teachers focus too narrowly on the test students are about to take, he writes, whatever they learn is likely to be aligned with that test and is not likely to generalize well to other tests of the same subject or to performance in real life.[19]

Koretz retested students in a district that had shown impressive gains; he found that the gains disappeared when the students took a different test of similar material, a test that had been used by the district in the recent past. Clearly the reported gains were illusory. The skills the students had learned were specific to the test and were not generalizable to unexpected situations. The scores had gone up, but the students were not better educated.[20]

Of what value is it to the student to do well on a state reading test if he cannot replicate the same success on a different reading test or transfer these skills to an unfamiliar context?

Excessive test preparation distorts the very purpose of tests, which is to assess learning and knowledge, not just to produce higher test scores. Koretz demonstrates that the problem with high-stakes testing—that is, test-based accountability—is that it corrupts the tests as measures of student performance. Koretz cites a well-known aphorism in social science known as Campbell's Law: "The more any quantitative social indicator is used for social decision-making, the more subject it will be to corruption pressures and the more apt it will be to distort and corrupt the social processes it is intended to monitor."[21] Written by sociologist Donald T. Campbell in 1975, this saying has become legendary as a description of the way organizations in every field change their behavior to meet external measures. As Koretz shows, the changes induced by accountability pressures corrupt the very purpose of schooling by causing practitioners to focus on the measure rather than on the goals of education.

Koretz offers many examples of goal distortion drawn from medicine, job training, industry, and other fields. Most cardiologists in New York stopped performing surgery on critically ill cardiac patients, he writes, after the state began issuing scorecards that reported mortality rates. To avoid getting a bad score, many doctors refused to operate on risky patients; some patients were turned away who might have survived surgery. Similarly, when the airline industry was required to report on-time arrivals, they manipulated the statistics by changing the expected duration of flights; as a result, the on-time statistics became meaningless.[22] Richard Rothstein has described how test-based accountability has corrupted education, narrowed the curriculum, and distorted the goals of schooling. By holding teachers accountable only for test scores in reading and mathematics, he writes, schools pay less attention to students' health, physical education, civic knowledge, the arts, and enrichment activities.[23] When faced with demands to satisfy a single measure, people strive to satisfy that measure but neglect the other, perhaps more important goals of the organization.

The pressure to increase test scores is likely to produce higher scores, whether by coaching or cheating or manipulating the pool of test takers. As long as the state or district superintendent continues to report good news about student performance, the public seems satisfied, and the media usually sees no reason to investigate whether the gains are real. State and local leaders want to claim credit for improvement, rather than determine whether the improvement was meaningful.

The starkest display of score inflation is the contrast between the state-reported test scores, which have been steadily (and sometimes sharply) rising since the passage of NCLB, and the scores registered by states on NAEP, the federal assessment program. NCLB permitted the states to write their own standards, pick their own tests, and decide for themselves how to define proficiency. The decision to let the states decide how well they were doing was a bow to federalism and local control, but it created a bizarre situation in which every state was left to determine what would be its passing mark and what percent of its students had reached it. Given the necessity to report gains, many states reported steady—and sometimes amazing—progress toward the mandated goal of 100 percent proficiency. Texas, for example, reported in 2007 that 85.1 percent of its students in grades four and eight were proficient readers, but on NAEP tests, only 28.6 percent were. Tennessee claimed that 90 percent of its students were proficient readers, but NAEP reported that 26.2 percent were. Similarly, Nebraska told the public that 90.5 percent of students in these grades were proficient, but NAEP said the number was 34.8 percent.[24]

NAEP monitors trends; if the state says its scores are rising but its scores on NAEP are flat, then the state reports are very likely inflated. In a choice between the state's self-reported scores and an audit test, the public should trust the audit test.

Most states were content to report their impressive gains to the public, congratulating themselves for their wise planning and implementation of standards-based reform. Once in a great while, however, a dissident voice was heard. This happened in 2007 in North Carolina, when a state commission was created to review the state's policies on testing and accountability. That commission reported that "there is too much time spent on testing" and recommended a reduction in the number of tests students were required to take. Sam Houston, chairman of the commission, said, "We're testing more but we're not seeing the results. We're not seeing graduation rates increasing. We're not seeing remediation rates decreasing. Somewhere along the way testing isn't aligning with excellence."[25]

However, few states or districts challenged the dominant paradigm of test-based accountability. It was the federal law, and they had to comply. NCLB fueled a growing demand for accountability, as well as a booming testing industry. Journalists referred to proponents of tough accountability as "reformers." These reformers, the new breed of corporate-style superintendents, were hailed for their willingness to crack down on teachers and principals and to close schools if their students' scores did not go up. Some states and districts introduced merit pay plans, which tied teacher compensation to their students' test scores. Some districts, such as Chicago, New York City, and Washington, D.C., closed schools in response to students' test scores; these same districts even gave cash payments to students in pilot programs if they increased their grades or scores. Others gave bonuses to principals or fired them, depending on their school's test scores.

One problem with test-based accountability, as currently defined and used, is that it removes all responsibility from students and their families for the students' academic performance. NCLB neglected to acknowledge that students share in the responsibility for their academic performance and that they are not merely passive recipients of their teachers' influence. Nowhere in the federal accountability scheme are there measures or indicators of students' diligence, effort, and motivation. Do they attend school regularly? Do they do their homework? Do they pay attention in class? Are they motivated to succeed? These factors affect their school performance as much as or more than their teachers' skill.[26]

Similarly, the authors of the law forgot that parents are primarily responsible for their children's behavior and attitudes. It is families that do or do not ensure that their children attend school regularly, that they are in good health, that they do their homework, and that they are encouraged to read and learn. But in the eyes of the law, the responsibility of the family disappears. Something is wrong with that. Something is fundamentally wrong with an account-ability system that disregards the many factors that influence stu-dents' performance on an annual test—including the students' own efforts—except for what teachers do in the classroom for forty-five minutes or an hour a day.

Accountability as we know it now is not helping our schools. Its measures are too narrow and imprecise, and its consequences too severe. NCLB assumes that accountability based solely on test scores will reform American education. This is a mistake. A good accountability system must include professional judgment, not simply a test score, and other measures of students' achievement, such as grades, teachers' evaluations, student work, attendance, and graduation rates. It should also report what the school and the district are providing in terms of resources, class sizes, space, well-educated teachers, and a well-rounded curriculum. Furthermore, a good accountability system might include an external inspection of schools by trained observers to evaluate their quality on a regular schedule, though not necessarily every single year. In a state or a large district, low-performing schools might be reviewed frequently, while schools that consistently get good reports might get a visit every few years. The object of inspection should not be to assay the school as a prelude to closing it or to impose a particular way of teaching, but to help the school improve.

Consider the distinction between what we might think of as "positive accountability," where low scores trigger an effort to help the school, and "punitive accountability," where low scores pro-vide a reason to fire the staff and close the school. In a strategy of positive accountability, district officials take decisive and consistent steps to improve low-performing schools. One example was the Chancellor's District in New York City, established by Chancellor Rudy Crew in 1996. Crew placed fifty-eight of the city's lowest-performing schools into a noncontiguous district and targeted them for intensive assistance. He saturated them with additional services and resources. He reduced class size, with no more than twenty students in kindergarten through third grade, and no more than twenty-five students in grades four through eight. He lengthened the school day. Students who needed extra help could get tutoring every afternoon. After-school activities extended the school day to 6 p.m. Each school was required to follow a prescribed curriculum and instructional program, with a heavy dose of literacy and mathematics. Extra pay was awarded to draw certified teachers to the Chancellor's District. Students in these schools registered significant improvement in reading, but not in mathematics (as compared to students in other low-performing schools). Eleven of the fifty-eight schools did not improve and were closed. The Chancellor's District was singled out for commendation by the Council of the Great City Schools for raising student achievement in the lowest-performing schools. After the school system was transferred to mayoral control in 2002, the district was abolished.[27]

Another (albeit mixed) example of positive accountability can be found in Florida, where the state gives a single letter grade, ranging from A to F, to all public schools. This is a practice I abhor, as I think it is harmful to stigmatize a complex institution with a letter grade, just as it would be ridiculous to send a child home with a report card that contained only a single letter grade to summarize her performance in all her various courses and programs. That said, after the grades are handed out, the state quickly steps in to help the D and F schools with technical support, consultants, coaches, and materials. As a result of the state's supportive response, most of the low-rated schools have improved. For nearly seven years, the state sanctioned F-rated schools by giving vouchers to their students, who could use them to attend a private or better-performing public school. In 2006, a Florida court declared the voucher program unconstitutional.[28]

In the original printing of this book, I offered the Atlanta public schools as a third example of positive accountability. I saluted Superintendent Beverly Hall for her record of steady and significant improvement over a decade. I was taken in, as were many other people. I wrote: "Not only did Atlanta see strong improvement in its state test scores and graduation rates (which are not always meaningful indicators), but Atlanta showed impressive gains on the National Assessment of Educational Progress. It was the only one of

eleven cities tested from 2003 to 2007 that showed significant progress in both reading and mathematics in fourth and eighth grades.
The American Association of School Administrators selected Hall as
its National Superintendent of the Year in 2009."

However, in 2011, an independent investigation commissioned
by Governor Sonny Perdue revealed that Atlanta's gains on state
tests were the result of systematic and widespread cheating by educators. Many principals and teachers confessed to changing student
answers on tests and engaging in other inappropriate practices. The
inquiry reported that "clear and significant warnings" were sounded
in 2005 and ignored. The investigators described "a climate of
fear, intimidation, and retaliation," which created "a conspiracy
of silence." The district leadership punished whistle-blowers, the
report said, and suppressed information about the cheating.[29] They
concluded that "Cheating was caused by a number of factors but
primarily by the pressure to meet targets in the data-driven environment." The report said that the targets set by the district were
"often unrealistic" and that the administration put "unreasonable
pressure" on principals and teachers to reach them. Principals who
reached their targets received public praise; those who missed them
were humiliated. Principals were told that they would be replaced
if they did not meet their targets within three years.[30] State officials said that those found guilty of cheating would face criminal
prosecution.

So, Atlanta ends up not as an example of positive accountability
but as an example of how the pressure to get higher test scores every
year may drive educators to desperate, illegal measures. When faced
with a choice of losing their job or finding a way to raise scores, some
people will resort to unethical measures that cheat children and that
put their own careers and reputations in jeopardy. Certainly, cheat-
ers should be punished; there should be no excuse for cheating. But
we should also recognize the harm generated by a system that produces illegal behavior, that raises suspicion about the validity of all
test scores, and that makes the measure more important than what is
being measured. The scope of cheating in the Atlanta public schools
was unprecedented. If anything, it was an alarming object lesson in
why the public and the media should no longer accept standardized
test scores as a reliable measure of teacher or school quality. It also
demonstrates why independent audits are absolutely necessary to
validate test scores; school districts cannot investigate themselves.

In the NCLB era, when the ultimate penalty for a low-performing school was to close it, punitive accountability achieved a certain luster, at least among the media and politicians. Politicians and non-educator superintendents boasted of how many schools they had shuttered. Their boasts won them headlines for "getting tough" and cracking down on bad schools. But closing down a school is punitive accountability, which should happen only in the most extreme cases, when a school is beyond help. Closing schools should be considered a last step and a rare one. It disrupts lives and communities, especially those of children and their families. It destroys established institutions, in the hope that something better is likely to arise out of the ashes of the old, now-defunct school. It accelerates a sense of transiency and impermanence, while dismissing the values of continuity and tradition, which children, families, and communities need as anchors in their lives. It teaches students that institutions and adults they once trusted can be tossed aside like squeezed lemons, and that data of questionable validity can be deployed to ruin people's lives.

The goal of accountability should be to support and improve schools, not the heedless destruction of careers, reputations, lives, communities, and institutions. The decision to close a school is a death sentence for an institution; it should be recognized as a worst-case scenario. The abject failure of a school represents the failure of those in charge of the district, not just the people who work in the school.

The trouble with test-based accountability is that it imposes serious consequences on children, educators, and schools on the basis of scores that may reflect measurement error, statistical error, random variation, or a host of environmental factors or student attributes. None of us would want to be evaluated—with our reputation and livelihood on the line—solely on the basis of an instrument that is prone to error and ambiguity. The tests now in use are not adequate by themselves to the task of gauging the quality of schools or teachers. They were designed for specific purposes: to measure whether students can read and can do mathematics, and even in these tasks, they must be used with awareness of their limitations and variability. They were not designed to capture the most important dimensions of education, for which we do not have measures.

This issue was addressed in 1988, when a group of esteemed members of the National Academy of Education, led by psychologist

Robert Glaser, commented on the value of the National Assessment of Educational Progress. They worried that NAEP might measure only reading, mathematics, and writing. They wrote, "While these competencies are important prerequisites for living in our modern world and fundamental to general and continuing education, they represent only a portion of the goals of elementary and secondary schooling." They represent neither the humanities nor the "aesthetic and moral aims of education" that cannot be measured. The scholars warned that "when test results become the arbiter of future choices, a subtle shift occurs in which fallible and partial indicators of academic achievement are transformed into major goals of schooling. . . . Those personal qualities that we hold dear—resilience and courage in the face of stress, a sense of craft in our work, a commitment to justice and caring in our social relationships, a dedication to advancing the public good in our communal life—are exceedingly difficult to assess. And so, unfortunately, we are apt to measure what we can, and eventually come to value what is measured over what is left unmeasured."[31]

Tests are necessary and helpful. But tests must be supplemented by human judgment. When we define what matters in education only by what we can measure, we are in serious trouble. When that happens, we tend to forget that schools are responsible for shaping character, developing sound minds in healthy bodies (*mens sana in corpore sano*), and forming citizens for our democracy, not just for teaching basic skills. We even forget to reflect on what we mean when we speak of a good education. Surely we have more in mind than just bare literacy and numeracy. And when we use the results of tests, with all their limitations, as a routine means to fire educators, hand out bonuses, and close schools, then we distort the purpose of schooling altogether.

CHAPTER NINE

What Would Mrs. Ratliff Do?

My FAVORITE TEACHER was Mrs. Ruby Ratliff. She is the teacher I remember best, the one who influenced me most, who taught me to love literature and to write with careful attention to grammar and syntax. More than fifty years ago, she was my homeroom teacher at San Jacinto High School in Houston, and I was lucky enough to get into her English class as a senior.

Mrs. Ratliff was gruff and demanding. She did not tolerate foolishness or disruptions. She had a great reputation among students. When it came time each semester to sign up for classes, there was always a long line outside her door. What I remember most about her was what she taught us. We studied the greatest writers of the English language, not their long writings like novels (no time for that), but their poems and essays. We read Shakespeare, Keats, Shelley, Wordsworth, Milton, and other major English writers. Now, many years later, in times of stress or sadness, I still turn to poems that I first read in Mrs. Ratliff's class.

Mrs. Ratliff did nothing for our self-esteem. She challenged us to meet her exacting standards. I think she imagined herself bringing enlightenment to the barbarians (that was us). When you wrote something for her class, which happened with frequency, you paid close attention to proper English. Accuracy mattered. She had a red pen and she used it freely. Still, she was always sure to make a comment that encouraged us to do a better job. Clearly she had multiple goals for her students, beyond teaching literature and grammar. She was also teaching about character and personal responsibility.

These are not the sorts of things that appear on any standardized test.

She loved her subject, and she enjoyed the respect the students showed her, especially since this was a large high school where students did not easily give respect to their teachers. Despite the passage of years, I still recall a class discussion of Shelley's "Ozymandias," and the close attention that thirty usually rowdy adolescents paid to a poem about a time and a place we could barely imagine. I wonder if Mrs. Ratliff has her counterparts today, teachers who love literature and love to teach it, or whether schools favor teachers who have been trained to elicit mechanical responses from their students about "text-to-self connections," "inferencing," "visualizing," and the other formalistic behaviors so beloved by au courant pedagogues. If Mrs. Ratliff were planning to teach these days, I expect that her education professors and supervisors would warn her to get rid of that red pen, to abandon her insistence on accuracy, and to stop being so judgmental. And they would surely demand that she replace those dated poems and essays with young adult literature that teaches adolescents about the lives of other adolescents just like themselves.

At our graduation, she made a gift of a line or two of poetry to each of the students in her homeroom. I got these two: "To strive, to seek, to find, and not to yield," the last line of Tennyson's "Ulysses," which we had read in class, and "among them, but not of them," from Byron's "Childe Harold's Pilgrimage," which we had not read in class. As she did in class, Mrs. Ratliff used the moment to show us how literature connected to our own lives, without condescending into shallow "relevance." I think these were the best graduation presents I got, because they are the only ones I remember a half century later.

I think of Mrs. Ratliff when I hear the latest proposals to improve the teaching force. Almost every day, I come across a statement by a journalist, superintendent, or economist who says we could solve all our problems in American education if we could just recruit a sufficient number of "great" teachers. I believe Mrs. Ratliff was a great teacher, but I don't think she would have been considered "great" if she had been judged by the kind of hard data that is used now. The policy experts who insist that teachers should be judged by their students' scores on standardized tests would have been frustrated by Mrs. Ratliff. Her classes never produced hard data. They didn't even produce test scores. How would the experts have measured what we learned? We never took a multiple-choice test. We wrote essays and took written tests, in which we had to explain our answers, not check a box or fill in a bubble. If she had been evaluated by the grades she gave, she would have been in deep trouble, because she did not award many A grades. An observer might have concluded that she was a very ineffective teacher who had no measurable gains to show for her work.

Data-driven education leaders say that academic performance lags because we don't have enough "effective" teachers, the ones whose students consistently improve their standardized test scores. The major obstacle to getting enough effective teachers and getting rid of ineffective teachers, they say, is the teachers' unions. Union contracts provide job security that prevents administrators from hiring and firing teachers at will. If there were no unions, no union contracts, and no tenure, then superintendents could get rid of bad teachers and hire only effective teachers. Without the union, teachers' salaries would be based on the test scores of their students, rather than on their seniority and credentials. According to theory, the higher compensation would attract outstanding teachers—the kind whose students will get higher scores—to the nation's classrooms. So long as the unions insist on a uniform salary scale that gives equal rewards to effective teachers and mediocre teachers, then outstanding teachers will leave teaching and outstanding college graduates will never enter the profession. The answer to the problem of ineffective teachers, or so goes the argument, is to eliminate the teachers' unions or at least render them toothless, then fire the teachers whose students get low scores.

To some economists and business leaders, this analysis makes sense because it reflects the way the free market supposedly works. In the free market, incentives and sanctions matter. Good performance gets rewarded, poor performance gets penalized, and employers have the power to hire and fire their employees. According to this theory, people work harder if the incentives are large enough, and they work harder if they fear being fired. What works in the private sector should also work in the public sector. Or so the theorists say, not taking note of the many instances when executives of failed corporations collected huge bonuses after the stockholders lost everything.

The test case for the theory that the schools should operate like the private sector is Washington, D.C. There, Michelle Rhee, the brash young chancellor of schools, emerged as a national symbol of a get-tough management style soon after she was hired by newly elected Mayor Adrian Fenty in 2007. Although Rhee had no experience running a school system, Mayor Fenty selected her soon after he gained control of the district's public schools. Chancellor Joel Klein of New York City recommended her to Fenty as someone who shared his views about school reform. The district's City Council turned the schools over to the mayor, because they were impressed by New York City's reforms and were desperate to improve their school system.

As a member of Teach for America, Rhee taught for three years in a Baltimore elementary school managed by Education Alternatives Inc., a for-profit organization that received a contract as part of an experiment in privatization. According to Rhee, during her second and third years of teaching, the proportion of her students who read on grade level leapt from 13 percent to 90 percent (critics were doubtful since the Baltimore records could not be located).[1] From her experience, she concluded that effective teachers could overcome poverty and other disadvantages; as she told *Newsweek* about the students she taught, "Those kids, where they lived didn't change. Their parents didn't change. Their diets didn't change. The violence in the community didn't change. The only thing that changed for those 70 kids was the adults who were in front of them every single day teaching them."[2] She subsequently created the New Teacher Project, an organization that recruits teachers for inner-city public schools.

As chancellor, Rhee made clear from the outset that "teachers are everything."[3] She moved quickly to introduce sweeping reforms. She fired central office staff, closed under-enrolled schools, reorganized low-performing schools, and ousted principals. She focused on recruiting strong teachers and getting rid of incompetent teachers. She offered a buyout to encourage teachers to resign. Her biggest target was teacher tenure, which she called "the holy grail of teacher unions." Job protection for teachers, she believed, was symptomatic of a culture that put "the interests of adults" over "the interests of children." She said that tenure "has no educational value for kids; it only benefits adults. If we can put veteran teachers who have tenure in a position where they don't have it, that would help us to radically increase our teacher quality."[4] In 2008, she offered the Washington Teachers' Union a deal: If teachers gave up their seniority and tenure, they would be eligible to receive salaries up to $130,000 a year, which would make them the highest-paid urban teachers in America. Those who chose to retain their tenure would not be eligible for the higher compensation. Rhee obtained a five-year commitment from several major foundations, including the Gates Foundation and the Broad Foundation, to support the supersize salaries. Rhee wanted the freedom to fire teachers who did not share her belief that all children, regardless of the disadvantages in their life, can post high test scores, and that the only impediment to academic success is not their family or their poverty but the quality of their teacher.[5]

Her direct assault on the teachers' union and on tenure won her lavish and admiring attention from the national media. The *Wall Street Journal* praised her fortitude for assailing the union and quoted her saying that it is "complete crap" to claim that poverty prevents students from learning.[6] As a result of her confrontational stand against the union, she was featured on national television and on the cover of *Time* magazine, where she was shown holding a broom.[7] To her admirers, she was a courageous reformer, prepared to do a clean sweep of a deeply dysfunctional school district; to her detractors, she was a witch with a broomstick.

Of course, if Rhee's policies are implemented, it will be years before anyone can evaluate their effects. Should teachers work without job security, like most workers in the private sector? Should the teachers' unions lose their power to protect their members against arbitrary firings? Should the salary schedule be abolished and replaced by merit pay based on students' test scores? And if all these things happened, would schools improve? Would students be better prepared for citizenship, college, and careers? Many like-minded reformers agreed with Rhee that school improvement hinged on breaking the unions, removing job security from teachers, and linking teacher pay to student test scores.

Although no one can predict whether Washington, D.C., will someday be the best urban school district in the nation, as Rhee pledged, there is a body of research and experience that is worth reviewing on these issues.

Let's start with the hardest question: Should teachers' unions exist? Do the protections they offer their members depress student achievement? Are they an "adult interest group," as their critics charge, whose priorities conflict with the needs of their students? Would schools improve if there were no unions to represent the teachers?

To answer these questions, I can no longer refer to Mrs. Ratliff, because she was not allowed to join a union. Texas was a "right to work" state, and there were no teachers' unions. As it happened, the teachers in Houston could have used a union to protect their academic freedom, because they were frequently harassed by an ultraconservative group called the Minute Women. Members of this organization would drop in unannounced to observe classes and sit in the back row to find out whether teachers expressed any unacceptable political opinions. Teachers were frightened by these vigilantes, but they could do nothing to stop their unwanted visits, because members of the group were elected to the city's school board. My beloved world history teacher, Miss Nelda Davis, was ridiculed in the press as politically suspicious by this group because she wanted to attend the convention of the National Council for the Social Studies, which the Minute Women deemed a leftist organization. They also thought the United Nations, the NAACP, the Urban League, and all other groups that advocated for desegregation or human rights were Communist fronts. My teachers needed protection of their basic rights but they didn't have it.

That's one important reason teachers joined unions: to protect their right to think, speak, and teach without fear. In my own research into the history of education in New York City, I discovered that teachers joined a teachers' organization for many reasons. In the early decades of the twentieth century, most teachers were women, and most supervisors and board members were men. Consequently, the administrators and politicians who controlled the schools had an unfortunate habit of imposing paternalistic decisions on teachers. The Board of Education fired female teachers if they got married. When teachers won the right to marry without losing their jobs, the Board of Education fired them if they got pregnant.[8] When the Board of Education finally relented on marriage and motherhood, female teachers organized to demand equal pay with male teachers. During World War I, the Board of Education fired some pacifist teachers, but the teachers had no teacher-led organization to defend them.

Most teachers joined a union to seek higher salaries and better working conditions. Teachers have historically been underpaid in comparison to people in other professions with similar levels of education. And most urban districts, where unionism got its start, have usually been burdened with aging facilities, overcrowded classrooms, and a shortage of supplies and resources. Individual teachers could do nothing to change these conditions, but acting collectively they could negotiate with political leaders to improve the schools.

Critics of teacher unions seem to be more plentiful now than ever before. Supporters of choice and vouchers see the unions as the major obstacle to their reforms. The *Wall Street Journal* regularly publishes editorials in opposition to teacher unionism, and the business press can be counted on to blame the unions for whatever is wrong with the schools. One would think, by reading the critics, that the nation's schools are overrun by incompetent teachers who hold their jobs only because of union protections, that unions are directly responsible for poor student performance, and that academic achievement would soar if the unions were to disappear.[9]

This is unfair. No one, to my knowledge, has demonstrated a clear, indisputable correlation between teacher unionism and academic achievement, either negative or positive. The Southern states, where teachers' unions have historically been either weak or nonexistent, have always had the poorest student performance on national examinations. Massachusetts, the state with the highest academic performance, has long had strong teacher unions. The difference in performance is probably due to economics, not to unionization. Where there are affluent communities, student performance tends to be higher, whether or not their teachers belong to unions. Some of the top-performing nations in the world are highly unionized, others are not. Finland, whose students score highest on international assessments of reading, has a teacher workforce that is nearly 100 percent unionized. Most high-performing Asian nations do not have large proportions of unionized teachers (though some do). Unionization per se does not cause high student achievement, nor does it cause low achievement.

While I have never been a member of any union, I was a friend of Albert Shanker, president of the American Federation of Teachers, whom I met after my history of the New York City schools was published. His successor, Sandra Feldman, was also my friend, and I am friends with her successor, Randi Weingarten, who was elected AFT president in 2008. At the behest of the AFT, I traveled to Eastern Europe in 1989 and 1990, as the Cold War ended, to meet with teachers and talk about civic education and democracy in Poland, Hungary, Czechoslovakia, and Romania. I worked with the leaders of Teachers Solidarity in Poland, which opposed the Communist regime and its puppet unions. As a result of these experiences, I came to believe that teachers, like other working people, should have the right to organize and to bargain collectively for their compensation, working conditions, and right to due process. Moreover, as a historian, I recognize the importance of the labor movement as a political force that has improved the lives of working people in many sectors of American life, including education.

Critics say the union contract makes it impossible for administrators to get rid of bad teachers. The union says it protects teachers against arbitrary dismissals. To be sure, it is not easy to fire a tenured teacher, but it can be done so long as there is due process in hearing the teacher's side of the story. But the issue should not take years to resolve. The AFT, which represents most urban districts, has supported peer review programs, in which teachers evaluate other teachers, offer to help them become better teachers, and, if they do not improve, "counsel them out" of the profession. When it comes to decisions about terminating a teacher, unions want to be part of the decision-making process. It is not in the interest of their members to have incompetent teachers in their midst, passing along poorly educated students to the next teacher. Since unions are not going to disappear, district officials should collaborate with them to develop a fair and expeditious process for removing incompetent teachers, rather than using the union as a scapegoat for low performance or for conditions in the school and society that are beyond the teachers' control.

Tenure is not a guarantee of lifetime employment but a protection against being terminated without due process. It does not protect teachers from being laid off in a recession, nor does it protect them from being fired for incompetence or misconduct. Why does due process matter? Teachers have been fired for all sorts of dubious and non-meritorious reasons: for being of the wrong race or religion, for being gay or belonging to some other disfavored group, for not contributing to the right politician, for not paying a bribe to someone for their job, for speaking out on an issue outside the classroom, for disagreeing with the principal, or simply to make room for a school board member's sister, nephew, or brother-in-law.

Teachers do not receive tenure automatically. Every state has its own requirements. Typically, tenure is awarded after three or four years of probationary status, during which time teachers are supposed to be observed and evaluated by their principal. The principal has the authority to deny tenure to any teacher for any reason.

Principals are supposed to carefully observe the performance of probationary teachers many times before awarding them tenure. Working with principals and unions, school boards should develop a thoughtful, deliberative process for evaluating probationary teachers. They should also put in place a peer review program to help struggling teachers, whether they are probationary or tenured.[10]

To a considerable extent, the teaching profession is self-selective. Between 40 percent and 50 percent of new teachers do not survive the first five years. Maybe they couldn't manage the classes; maybe they were disappointed by working conditions; maybe teaching was not for them; maybe they felt that they were unsuccessful; or maybe they decided to enter another profession. For whatever reason, the job is so demanding that nearly half of those who enter teaching choose to leave at an early stage in their career.

Unions have many critics, including some within their own ranks who complain that their leaders fail to protect teachers against corporate reformers. Other critics want the unions to become more assertive in policing their own ranks and getting rid of incompetents and malingerers. But the critics most often quoted in the media see unions as the major obstacle to education reform. They fault the unions for their resistance to using test scores to evaluate teachers. They want administrators to have the freedom to fire teachers whose students' test scores do not improve and to replace them with new teachers who might raise those scores. They want to use test scores as the decisive tool of evaluation. Their goal is a school system in which scores go up every year and in which teachers who don't contribute to that result can be promptly removed. In response to NCLB, which required steady improvement in test scores each year, many, including President Barack Obama, endorsed the idea of using students' test scores to evaluate their teachers.

In the NCLB era, the media attached the term "reformer" to those educators and officials who turned to market-based, data-driven reforms to produce higher scores. These free-market reformers advocated testing, accountability, merit pay, and charter schools, and most were notably hostile to unions. The unions objected to the reformers' efforts to judge teachers solely by their students' test scores, and the reformers sought to break the power of the unions. The reformers said that having "great" teachers or "effective" teachers was the key to their goals, and they wanted the union to get out of their way.

In the decade before NCLB, reformers agreed that the teacher was the key to educational improvement, but they pursued a different path. In 1996, five years before the passage of No Child Left Behind, the National Commission on Teaching & America's Future issued a report called *What Matters Most: Teaching for America's Future*. The chairman of the commission was Governor James B. Hunt Jr. of North Carolina. It included the presidents of the two major teachers' unions, business leaders, university presidents, and other educators. Its executive director was Linda Darling-Hammond, then of Teachers College, Columbia University.

The commission set a goal that by 2006, all children would be taught by excellent teachers. To reach this goal, the commission proposed higher standards for teacher education programs, high-quality professional development, more effective recruitment practices, a greater commitment to professionalism, and schools that support good teaching. The commission recommended additional compensation for teachers who won national board certification, received licenses to teach in another subject, or demonstrated greater pedagogical skills and content knowledge. But it specifically rejected schemes to connect teacher pay to students' test scores. The scores, the report warned, are only "crude measures" that "do not take into account the different backgrounds and prior performances of students, the fact that students are not randomly distributed across schools and classrooms, the shortcomings in the kinds of learning measured by current standardized tests, and the difficulty in sorting out which influences among many—the home, the community, the student him- or herself, and multiple teachers—are at play." It noted further that "attempts to link student test scores to rewards for teachers and schools have led to counterproductive incentives for keeping out or pushing out low-achieving students, retaining them in a grade so their scores look higher, or assigning them to special education where their scores don't count, rather than teaching them more effectively."[11]

After the passage of NCLB, however, everything changed. Efforts to improve teacher professionalism were swept away by the law's singular focus on raising test scores. Schools that did not meet this demand faced public humiliation and possible closure. Superintendents and principals were commanded by the law to get test scores higher every year until every student was proficient. The idea of teacher professionalism became an antique notion; far more compelling was the search for teachers who would get the scores up, especially in urban districts, where superintendents pledged to close the achievement gap between African American/Hispanic students and white/Asian students.

NCLB required that the scores rise in reading and mathematics in every grade from third through eighth, which meant that this year's fourth grade had to get a higher score than last year's fourth grade. It didn't take long for school officials to realize that they needed what were called "growth models," so the progress of individual children could be tracked over time. This way of measuring academic improvement was known as "value-added assessment" (VAA), a technique that was developed mainly by William Sanders of the University of Tennessee. A statistician and (at that time) adjunct professor in the university's College of Business Administration, Sanders had worked as a statistical consultant to agricultural, manufacturing, and engineering industries. His value-added method aimed to calculate the extent to which teachers contributed to the gains made by their students, as compared to other factors. Drawing on his studies, which were purely statistical in nature (i.e., not involving classroom observations), Sanders concluded that "the most important factor affecting student learning is the teacher. In addition, the results show wide variation in effectiveness among teachers. The immediate and clear implication of this finding is that seemingly more can be done to improve education by improving the effectiveness of teachers than by any other single factor. *Effective teachers appear to be effective with students of all achievement levels, regardless of the level of heterogeneity in their classrooms.*"[12] Sanders contrasted his method—which involved calculating the rate of progress that students make on standardized tests over a period of years—with what he called "a laissez faire approach," that is, "appropriate more resources and free educators to utilize their own professionalism."[13] The "laissez faire approach" sounded very much like the remedies proposed by the National Commission on Teaching & America's Future, although the commission would not have characterized its proposals as "laissez faire." In Sanders' view, this approach had created huge variability among schools and had failed. What was needed, Sanders insisted, was a rigorous, data-based analysis such as his own.

The idea of value-added assessment made sense, at least on the surface. If you compare the test scores of specific students from year to year, or from September to June, then you can pinpoint which students got the biggest gains and which made no gains at all. The scores of the students can be matched to their teachers, and patterns begin to emerge, making it possible to identify which teachers regularly get large gains in their classes, and which get few or none. Using the value-added scores, districts would be able to rank their teachers by their ability to increase gains. Those at the top would be considered the superstars, and those at the bottom would improve or get fired.

Value-added assessment is the product of technology; it is also the product of a managerial mind-set that believes that every variable in a child's education can be identified, captured, measured, and evaluated with precision. Computers make it possible to assemble the annual test scores of thousands of students and quickly analyze which students gained the most, which gained nothing, and which lost ground on standardized tests. Sanders the statistician soon became Sanders the educational measurement guru. As the methodology gained adherents, education policy increasingly became the domain of statisticians and economists. With their sophisticated tools and their capacity to do multivariate longitudinal analysis, they did not need to enter the classroom, observe teachers, or review student work to know which teachers were the best and which were the worst, which were effective and which were ineffective. Discussions of what to teach and what constituted a quality education receded into the background; those issues were contentious and value-laden, not worthy of the attention of the data-minded policy analysts. Using value-added models, the technical experts could evaluate teachers and schools without regard to the curriculum or the actual lived experiences of their students. What mattered most in determining educational quality was not curriculum or instruction, but data.

NCLB did not incorporate value-added assessment, and its failure to do so was grounds for frequent criticism. Of what value was it to know whether this year's fourth grade did better on the state test than last year's fourth grade? Wasn't it more important to determine whether the students in this year's fourth grade learned more by the time they moved to fifth grade? And wasn't it better still to be able to measure how much the scores of specific children had gone up or down over time? Even better was to link the scores of specific students to specific teachers. Of course, the missing consideration in the debates among economists and policymakers was the quality of the assessments. If the assessments were low-level, multiple-choice tests, and if teachers were intensely prepping their students for the tests, then could it really be said that these were measures of learning? Or that they were indicators of better teaching? Or were they instead measures of how well children had been drilled to respond to low-level questions?

Eric Hanushek of Stanford University studied the problem of how to increase the supply of high-quality teachers. Hanushek is a friend of mine, and one of the nation's best economists of education. In 2004, I invited him and his colleague Steven Rivkin to present a paper at a conference at the Brookings Institution. Reviewing a large number of studies, they noted that teachers' salaries, certification, education, and additional degrees had little impact on student performance. The variables that mattered most in the studies they reviewed were teachers' experience and their scores on achievement tests, but most studies found even these variables to be statistically insignificant. They cited studies showing that teachers in their first year of teaching, and to some extent their second as well, "perform significantly worse in the classroom" than more experienced teachers. Hanushek and Rivkin concluded that the best way to improve teacher quality was to look at "differences in growth rates of student achievement across teachers. A good teacher would be one who consistently obtained high learning growth from students, while a poor teacher would be one who consistently produced low learning growth." Since the current requirements for entry into teaching are "imprecise" or not consistently correlated with teaching skill, they argued, it made no sense to tighten up the credentialing process. Instead, "If one is concerned about student performance, one should gear policy to student performance." Hanushek and Rivkin projected that "having five years of good teachers in a row" (that is, teachers at the 85th percentile) "could overcome the average seventh-grade mathematics achievement gap between lower-income kids (those on the free or reduced-price lunch program) and those from higher-income families. In other words, high-quality teachers can make up for the typical deficits seen in the preparation of kids from disadvantaged backgrounds." In light of these findings, Hanushek and Rivkin recommended that states "loosen up" the requirements for entering teaching and pay more attention to whether teachers are able to get results, that is, better student performance on tests.[14]

At the conference, Richard Rothstein responded that the policy implications of the Hanushek-Rivkin paper were "misleading and dangerous." He objected to the authors' view that school reform alone could overcome the powerful influence of family and social environment. He dismissed their claims about closing the achievement gap between low-income students and their middle-class peers in five years, an assertion similar to one previously advanced by Sanders. Sanders said that students with teachers in the top quintile of effectiveness for *three* consecutive years would gain 50 percentile points as compared to those who were assigned to the lowest quintile. Rothstein said their reasoning was circular: "good teachers can raise student achievement, and teachers are defined as good if they raise student achievement." Thus, one cannot know which teachers are effective until after they had produced consistent gains for three to five straight years. But, said Rothstein, if these top teachers were then assigned to low-income schools, then middle-income schools would necessarily have less effective teachers. Rothstein found it hard to imagine how such a policy might be implemented.[15]

Yet there was something undeniably appealing about the idea that a string of "effective" or "top-quintile" teachers could close the achievement gap between low-income students and their middle-income peers and between African American students and white students. And there was something appalling about the idea that a string of mediocre or bad teachers would doom low-performing students to a life of constant failure, dragging them down to depths from which they might never recover. The bottom line was that the teacher was the key to academic achievement. A string of top-quintile teachers could, on their own, erase the learning deficits of low-income and minority students, or so the theory went.

This line of reasoning appealed to conservatives and liberals alike; liberals liked the prospect of closing the achievement gap, and conservatives liked the possibility that it could be accomplished with little or no attention to poverty, housing, unemployment, health needs, or other social and economic problems. If students succeeded, it was the teacher who did it. If students got low scores, it was the teacher's fault. Teachers were both the cause of low performance and the cure for low performance. The solution was to get rid of bad teachers and recruit only good ones. Of course, it was difficult to know how to recruit good teachers when the determination of their effectiveness required several years of classroom data.

A 2006 paper by Robert Gordon, Thomas J. Kane, and Douglas O. Staiger, titled "Identifying Effective Teachers Using Performance on the Job," took the argument a step further. Like Hanushek and Rivkin, these authors maintained that "paper qualifications," such as degrees, licenses, and certification, do not predict who will be a good teacher. The differences, they said, between "stronger teachers" and "weaker teachers" become clear only after teachers have been teaching for "a couple of years." Their solution was to recruit new teachers without regard to paper credentials and to measure their success by multiple means, including value-added measures of student scores, principal and parent evaluations, and classroom observations. They recommended that school districts pay bonuses to effective teachers who teach in high-poverty schools. And they recommended that the federal government provide grants to states to build data systems to "link student performance with the effectiveness of individual teachers over time." These recommendations were of more than academic interest, because one of the authors, Robert Gordon of the Center for American Progress, a Washington-based think tank, was subsequently selected by the Obama administration to serve as deputy director for education in the Office of Management and Budget, where he was able to promote his policy ideas. And sure enough, President Obama's education program included large sums of money for states to build data systems that would link student test scores to individual teachers, as well as funds for merit pay plans that would reward teachers for increasing their students' test scores. In choosing his education agenda, President Obama sided with the economists and the corporate-style reformers, not with his chief campaign adviser, Linda Darling-Hammond.[16]

The Gordon, Kane, and Staiger study followed teachers in their first, second, and third years. It concluded that students assigned to a teacher in the bottom quartile of all teachers (ranked according to their students' gains) lost on average 5 percentile points compared to similar students. Meanwhile, a student who was assigned to a teacher in the top quartile gained 5 percentile points. Thus, the difference between being assigned to a low- or high-rated teacher was 10 percentile points. Noting that the black-white achievement gap is estimated to be 34 percentile points, they reached this startling conclusion: "Therefore, if the effects were to accumulate, having a top-quartile teacher rather than a bottom-quartile teacher four years in a row would be enough to close the black-white test score gap."[17]

So, depending on which economist or statistician one preferred, the achievement gap between races, ethnic groups, and income groups could be closed in three years (Sanders), four years (Gordon, Kane, and Staiger), or five years (Hanushek and Rivkin). Over a short period of time, this assertion became an urban myth among journalists and policy wonks in Washington, something that "everyone knew." This particular urban myth fed a fantasy that schools serving poor children might be able to construct a teaching corps made up exclusively of superstar teachers, the ones who produced large gains year after year. This is akin to saying that baseball teams should consist only of players who hit over .300 and pitchers who win at least twenty games every season; after all, such players exist, so why should not such teams exist? The fact that no such team exists should give pause to those who believe that almost every teacher in almost every school in almost every district might be a superstar if only school leaders could fire at will.

The teacher was everything; that was the new mantra of economists and bottom-line school reformers. And not only was the teacher the key to closing the achievement gap, but the most effective teachers did not need to have any paper credentials or teacher education. There was no way to predict who would be a good teacher.[18] So there was no reason to limit entry into teaching; anyone should be able to enter the profession and show whether she or he could raise test scores.

Some scholars questioned whether value-added assessment should be used for consequential personnel decisions. Economist Dale Ballou wrote in 2002 that value-added assessment was "useful when viewed in context by educators who understand local circumstances," but that it was potentially dangerous when used for accountability and high-stakes personnel decisions. The tests were not accurate enough to serve as the basis for high-stakes decisions. Test scores, he wrote, were affected not only by students' ability and by random influences (such as the weather or students' emotional state), but also by statistical properties such as measurement error and random error. These errors affect student scores, and they get "noisier" (less reliable) when used to calculate gain scores and then to attribute the gains to a specific teacher. Gain scores, he pointed out, are influenced by factors other than teachers and schools; social and demographic factors affect not only the starting point but the "rate of progress" that students make. Yet, he noted, most value-added methods do not control for those non-school factors. Also problematic was that gain scores are not necessarily comparable, because test questions are not of equal difficulty. If the gains are not comparable, then the results are meaningless, he said. Ballou, who subsequently wrote articles with Sanders, warned that "there are too many uncertainties and inequities to rely on such measures for high-stakes personnel decisions."[19]

Another limitation of value-added assessment is that it applies only to those teachers for whom yearly test scores are available, possibly a minority of a school's staff. New teachers, those with less than three to five years of experience, cannot be evaluated, because there is not enough long-term test score data. Teachers of history, social studies, the arts, science, technology, physical education, and foreign languages cannot be evaluated, because their subjects are not regularly tested. Only teachers of reading and mathematics in elementary school and middle schools can be evaluated, and they can be evaluated only if scores are available from the previous year and only if they have been teaching for at least three years.

The idea of using value-added test scores to fire teachers or to award tenure posed another problem. In 2008, economist Dan Goldhaber and his assistant Michael Hansen asked whether teacher effectiveness, measured in this way, is stable over the years. Gold-haber said that if performance were extremely stable over time, then it would be a good idea to use students' scores for high-stakes decisions. But he discovered that teacher effects were unstable over time. Comparing thousands of North Carolina teachers, pre-tenure and post-tenure, Goldhaber found that 11 percent of teachers who were in the lowest quintile in their early years of teaching reading were in the highest quintile after they received tenure. Only 44 percent of reading teachers and 42 percent of math teachers in the top quintile before tenure were still in the top quintile in the post-tenure period. This meant that if an administrator assigned low-performing students to a top-quintile teacher, there was a good possibility that the teacher would not be a top-quintile teacher the next year. Some elementary teachers were more effective at teaching reading than math; others were more effective at teaching math than reading. An administrator who denied tenure to all teachers who were in the bottom quintile in either reading or math would terminate almost a third of the teachers. Moreover, almost a third of them would have eventually landed in the top two quintiles in reading, and about a quarter in the top two quintiles in math, had they not been terminated. Goldhaber also found that consistency of job performance and productivity became greater as teachers became more experienced.[20] Other studies of the stability of teacher effects reached the same conclusion: Most teachers who ranked in the top quintile one year were not the "best" teachers the next year, and most teachers who ranked in the lowest quintile one year got better results the next year.[21]

In other words, being an effective teacher is not necessarily a permanent, unchanging quality. Some teachers are outstanding year after year, when judged by increases in their students' test scores. Others are effective one year, but not the next, by the same measure. Some become better teachers over time. Some do not. Apparently, the test scores of their students reflected something other than what the teachers did, such as the students' ability and motivation, or the characteristics of a class or conditions in the school. Maybe the teacher had a great interaction with the class one year but not the next. Or maybe the students assigned to the teacher were not similar from year to year.

Economists Brian A. Jacob, Lars Lefgren, and David Sims identified another major problem with the claim that three or four or five years of great teachers in a row would wipe out the achievement gap. They said that learning gains do not all persist over time. Students forget, gains fade. After a year, only about 20 percent and at best only one-third of any gain due to teacher quality persists. After two years, unless there is continual reinforcement of learning, only one-eighth of the gain persists. The authors concluded, "Our results indicate that contemporary teacher value-added measures may overstate the ability of teachers, even exceptional ones, to influence the ultimate level of student knowledge since they conflate variation in short-term and long-term knowledge. Given that a school's objective is to increase the latter, the importance of teacher value-added measures as currently estimated may be substantially less than the teacher value-added literature indicates."[22]

If these studies are right, then the gains students make each year do not remain intact and accumulate. You can't just add up the gains of one year and multiply by three, four, or five. Teachers are very important, but students don't remember and retain everything they learn.

Another economist, Jesse Rothstein, tested three methods of calculating value added by teachers and determined that none of them was reliable. He surveyed data for 99,000 North Carolina fifth graders and asked what effect their current teachers had on their scores in third and fourth grades. This was a falsification test, a deliberate attempt to ask a question whose answer should have been "none," since a fifth-grade teacher cannot influence students' test scores in third and fourth grades. Yet he found that all three ways of calculating value added produced large effects on fourth-grade test scores, meaning that they were flawed. The reason for these results, he speculated, was that many students are not assigned to classes randomly, but according to their prior achievement. He reported that students' gains tended to decay, and that only a third of the teachers who were in the top quintile based on two years of data were in the top quintile based on a single year of data.[23] In sum, value-added modeling is rife with technical problems.

While economists traded arguments, prominent journalists joined the fray. Malcolm Gladwell, the best-selling author and writer for the *New Yorker*, wisely noted that teachers are not "solely responsible for how much is learned in a classroom, and not everything of value that a teacher imparts to his or her students can be captured on a standardized test." Nonetheless, he was impressed by the likelihood that three or four years of testing data would show which teachers are very good and which are very bad. The biggest problem in school reform, he argued, is "finding people with the potential to be great teachers." He cited the economists who had written that it doesn't matter if a teacher has certification, a master's degree, or high test scores. In light of all this, Gladwell concluded that "teaching should be open to anyone with a pulse and a college degree—and teachers should be judged after they have started their jobs, not before."[24]

Nicholas D. Kristof, a columnist for the *New York Times*, described education as "Our Greatest National Shame." He said that the national school system was broken, but he saw a bright spot on the horizon. First, he wrote, "good teachers matter more than anything; they are astonishingly important. It turns out that having a great teacher is far more important than being in a small class, or going to a good school with a mediocre teacher. A Los Angeles study suggested that four consecutive years of having a teacher from the top 25 percent of the pool would erase the black-white testing gap." The Los Angeles study to which he referred was the analysis by Gordon, Kane, and Staiger. Impressed by their study, Kristof held that entry credentials and qualifications don't matter, that it doesn't matter if prospective teachers had certification or a graduate degree, went to a better college, or had higher SAT scores. Predictably, he proposed "scrapping certification, measuring better through testing which teachers are effective, and then paying them significantly more—with special bonuses to those who teach in 'bad' schools."[25]

The theory seemed reasonable, but still and all, it was only a theory. The fact was that the theory had never been demonstrated anywhere. No school or school district or state anywhere in the nation had ever proved the theory correct. Nowhere was there a real-life demonstration in which a district had identified the top quintile of teachers, assigned low-performing students to their classes, and improved the test scores of low-performing students so dramatically in three, four, or five years that the black-white test score gap closed. Nor had any scholar adduced evidence that top-performing nations had opened the teaching profession to any college graduate who wanted to teach, without regard to their credentials or experience or qualifications.

One beneficiary of the ongoing debate about the importance of great teachers was Teach for America (TFA). This program began to attract national attention at the same time that growing numbers of economists questioned the value of traditional teacher-training requirements for entry into teaching. In what became an oft-told tale, Princeton student Wendy Kopp wrote a senior thesis in which she proposed the idea of a teacher corps composed of top-flight graduates from the nation's elite colleges and universities to teach for two years in schools enrolling low-income students. After her graduation, Kopp deployed her superb organizational skills to raise millions of dollars from corporations and philanthropists to create Teach for America, with the mission of closing the achievement gap. Its first class of 500 teachers went into classrooms in six low-income communities in 1990. By 2002, the TFA corps consisted of 2,500 teachers working at eighteen sites. Each year the number of applicants increased, and by 2009, there were nearly 7,500 corps members working in thirty-four urban and rural settings.[26] Some of the TFA graduates later founded their own charter schools, such as KIPP. Some remained in teaching. The most prominent TFA alumna was Michelle Rhee, the chancellor of the Washington, D.C., school system. Most left teaching after two years, but certainly the time they spent as urban teachers was an important life experience for an influential group of well-educated young men and women.

TFA is akin to the Peace Corps in its appeal to youthful idealism. But does TFA improve the quality of education in the poor urban and rural districts where its members have taught? Linda Darling-Hammond criticized TFA for sending inexperienced young people to teach the nation's most vulnerable children; Darling-Hammond had been the executive director of the National Commission on Teaching & America's Future, whose call for better-trained, more professional teachers was in direct opposition to the economists' critique of entry requirements and paper credentials. TFA seemed to be proof of the economists' views. TFA corps members received only a brief training period in the summer before their jobs commenced, yet were supposedly more successful than teachers with paper credentials and experience.

However, the evidence was far from conclusive. Researchers who examined the effects of TFA came to contradictory conclusions. A study in Arizona in 2002 held that TFA teachers had a negative impact on their students as compared to certified teachers.[27] A national evaluation in 2004 concluded that students with TFA teachers did as well in reading as those taught by a control group, and significantly better in mathematics. The study had a small sample size of forty-one TFA teachers and a control group of fifty-seven teachers. The gains for TFA teachers were significant but small: Their students' math scores rose from the 14th percentile to only the 17th percentile.[28]

Darling-Hammond led a study of 4,400 teachers and 132,000 students in Houston and concluded that certified teachers consistently produced significantly higher achievement than uncertified teachers, and that uncertified TFA teachers had a negative or nonsignificant effect on student achievement. TFA teachers who stayed long enough to gain certification performed as well as other certified teachers.[29] By contrast, a study of high school teachers in North Carolina concluded that TFA teachers were more effective than traditional teachers. It held that "the TFA effect . . . exceeds the impact of additional years of experience," especially in mathematics and science. However, another study of high school students in North Carolina determined that traditionally prepared secondary teachers were more successful than beginning teachers, including TFA corps members, who lacked teacher training.[30]

Thomas J. Kane, Jonah E. Rockoff, and Douglas O. Staiger studied different cohorts of New York City teachers (certified, uncertified, TFA, and Teaching Fellows) and concluded that certification doesn't make a difference in student test scores, but experience does, especially for newer teachers. They wrote that New York City's teachers "are no different from other teachers around the country. Teachers make long strides in their first three years, with very little experience-related improvement after that."[31]

Most studies find that new teachers are less effective than experienced teachers and that the first two years of teaching are the least successful. Most TFA teachers in urban districts leave after their two-year commitment ends, and 80 percent or more are gone after their third or fourth year.[32] Thus, many TFA teachers leave the field just at the point when teachers become most effective.

So is TFA the answer to the nation's need for large numbers of effective teachers? Can TFA meet its goal and close the achievement gap?

TFA is a worthy philanthropic effort to recruit bright young people to teach in beleaguered districts. The organization brings highly educated young people into the teaching profession, if only for a few years. If some choose to remain in teaching, that is a net plus. Those who leave will have a deeper understanding of the needs of the schools as they enter other walks of life, and that too is a net plus for them and for the schools.

But it is simply an illusion to see TFA as the answer to the nation's need for more and better teachers: The number of TFA teachers is insufficient to make a large difference in the teaching profession, and most will be gone after two or three years. TFA sends fewer than 10,000 new teachers each year into a profession with nearly 4 million members.

Similarly, it is an illusion to imagine that TFA will close the achievement gap. While some studies report significant gains for their students, none of the reported gains is large enough to close the gap that now exists between students of different racial groups. And since TFA members leave teaching at a higher rate than other new teachers, whatever gains they achieve cannot be sustained. A constant churn of new teachers into urban schools does not help the schools achieve the stability or the experienced teaching staff they need.

We should applaud the idealism of young people from our finest universities who want to devote two or three years to teaching. Nevertheless, the overwhelming majority of new teachers will not be drawn from elite institutions but will continue to come from state universities, where the quality of *their* education will determine their ability to improve the education of the next generation. The nation needs a steady infusion of well-educated teachers who will make a commitment to teaching as a profession. Every state university and teacher-preparation program should ensure that their graduates have a strong foundation in the liberal arts and sciences and are deeply grounded in the subjects they plan to teach.

To make teaching attractive to well-educated young people who are just starting their careers, teaching should offer good salaries and good working conditions. When a man or woman becomes a teacher, he or she should immediately have the support of mentors and colleagues. Simply knowing a lot about history or mathematics or reading theory is no guarantee that one can teach it well. On the other hand, too many teachers are immersed in pedagogy but are poorly educated in *any* subject matter. Teachers need both. They need to be well educated in whatever they plan to teach, preferably in more than one subject since assignments change. New teachers need to know about classroom management, interacting with children, helping children with special needs, communicating with parents, and working with colleagues. New teachers would also benefit if the schools in which they taught had a coherent curriculum, so they knew what they were expected to teach. And teaching would be enhanced if schools of education stopped insisting on pedagogical conformity and recognized that there are many ways to be a successful teacher.

When it is time for a principal to decide whether a teacher should get tenure, it should be treated as a weighty responsibility, not a routine matter. Given the availability of data about test score gains that every state now collects, it is inevitable that this information will become part of the tenure decision. Principals should know which teachers were very effective in teaching their students to read or do math, which teachers were effective on average, and which were extremely ineffective. Undoubtedly this information will become part of the principal's decision and should be used in conjunction with observations and peer evaluations. Presumably the principal will not grant tenure to a teacher whose students consistently failed to learn anything over a three- or four-year period.

Because the principal must decide which teachers will receive tenure, it is crucial that principals have prior experience as teachers and understand what good teaching is and how to recognize it. They will be called upon to evaluate and help struggling teachers, which they cannot do unless they have experience in the classroom. In recent years, a number of programs have recruited and trained new faces to serve as principals, some of them young teachers with only a few years of classroom experience or noneducators who have never been teachers. People with so little personal knowledge of good instruction—what it looks like, how to do it, and how to help those who want to do it—are likely to rely exclusively on data because they have so little understanding of teaching. This is akin to putting a lawyer in charge of evaluating doctors, or a corporate executive in charge of evaluating airline pilots. The numbers count for something, but on-site evaluation by an experienced, knowledgeable professional should count even more.

Should test score data be used to award bonuses or to fire teachers? Thus far, there is a paucity of evidence that paying teachers to raise test scores leads to anything other than teaching to the test. Teaching to the test predictably narrows the curriculum and inflates test scores, so it is not a good idea. Similarly, it may be a bad idea to base teacher terminations solely on test score data; the data must be supplemented by evaluations conducted by experienced educators. There are too many other confounding variables. Some states give their tests in midyear—which teacher should receive credit or blame for the students' scores? The one who taught them for nearly five months last year, or the one who taught them for nearly five months before the test was administered?

Districts such as Denver are giving bonuses not only to teachers who bring up their students' scores, but also to those who agree to work in "hard-to-serve" urban schools or accept "hard-to-staff" assignments (e.g., teachers of special education, middle-school mathematics, and English as a second language), or who improve their knowledge and skills (for instance, by getting an advanced degree in the subject they teach). That sort of performance-related pay seems likely to proliferate, especially since the Denver plan was adopted with the support of the local teachers' union.[33] Other districts, such as New York City, pay a schoolwide bonus if test scores go up, and a committee of teachers decides how to distribute it to staff members, which might include non-teaching personnel, such as the school secretary. This plan too was adopted with the support of the local teachers' union. But, like the garden-variety merit pay plan, the schoolwide bonus plan puts a premium on raising test scores and encourages teaching to the test.

A study of international compensation for teachers and principals by Susan Sclafani and Marc Tucker reports that some districts and nations have come up with a variety of compensation schemes to attract or retain teachers. These include signing bonuses for new teachers, housing stipends, reimbursement for college loans in exchange for teaching a certain number of years, even subsidies for home mortgages. Bonuses may be designed to encourage teachers to teach in areas where there is a shortage, such as special education, science, or mathematics. They may be used to attract teachers to schools in poor urban neighborhoods or rural districts or simply to honor teachers. Sclafani and Tucker predict that there will be increasing use of incentives based on the school system's needs and teachers' performance. But they warn that such incentive systems must be properly structured. If a signing bonus is big enough, it will attract applicants, but they won't remain in teaching if the work is not satisfying. They add, "Performance bonuses based on student performance on low level literacy tests in math and English won't produce high level performance in any subject." And, perhaps most important from two authors who support incentives, "money is not everything." Teachers, like other professionals, "need to feel competent, effective, and admired."[34]

Knowing that they are changing the lives of their students, one by one, is a source of satisfaction, to be sure. If teachers are treated with condescension by administrators, expected to work in badly maintained buildings, assigned to large classes of poorly prepared students, confronted by unruly students, and compelled to meet unrealistic goals, they are not likely to gain a sense of personal and professional satisfaction.

So, I wonder, what would Mrs. Ratliff do? Would any school today recognize her ability to inspire her students to love literature? Would she get a bonus for expecting her students to use good grammar, accurate spelling, and good syntax? Would she win extra dollars for insisting that her students write long essays and for grading them promptly? I don't think so. She was a great teacher. But under any imaginable compensation scheme, her greatness as a teacher—her ability to inspire students and to change their lives—would go unrewarded because it is not in demand and cannot be measured. And let's face it: She would be stifled not only by the data mania of her supervisors, but by the jargon, the indifference to classical literature, and the hostility to her manner of teaching that now prevail in our schools.

As we expand the rewards and compensation for teachers who boost scores in basic skills, will we honor those teachers who awaken in their students a passionate interest in history, science, the arts, literature, and foreign language? If we fail to attract and retain teachers like Ruby Ratliff, will we produce a better-educated citizenry? Will our schools encourage the innovative thinkers who advance society? It's not likely.

CHAPTER TEN

The Billionaire Boys' Club

In 1967, OFFICIALS at the Ford Foundation asked the Carnegie Corporation to join them in supporting a controversial project in New York City, which was intended to demonstrate a new form of school governance called community control. The theory behind the project in three small demonstration districts was that schools in an impoverished urban neighborhood would improve if they were governed by parents and members of the local community. Ford was attempting not to redesign the New York City public school system, but to respond to racial grievances in certain school districts in the city. The districts—ranging from one to several schools—were located in black and Hispanic neighborhoods and led by activists who had concluded that racial desegregation was never going to happen; they wanted community control and—in two of the three districts—"Black Power."[1]

As Carnegie was mulling Ford's request, a college friend recommended me for a part-time position at Carnegie. The program officer decided to take a chance on me, even though I had no experience and no advanced degrees. I was paid $5 an hour to do research and writing. One of my first assignments was to visit the demonstration districts and report what I learned. When I introduced myself as a representative of the Carnegie Corporation, I had no trouble meeting and interviewing the leaders. My access to key local activists was further assured because I was a friend of Preston Wilcox, an African American social worker in Harlem who was one of the intellectual leaders of the community control movement.

My report described the context, the issues, and the personalities but made no recommendations. I was far too junior to presume to make recommendations. Carnegie, being deeply averse to controversy, decided not to become Ford's partner in the rapidly escalating conflict between militant community leaders and the city's Board of Education.

Ocean Hill–Brownsville, one of the demonstration districts, soon asserted its authority by ousting nineteen white teachers and supervisors without due process. Demonstrations, protests, and inflammatory rhetoric followed, as did racial and religious tensions. In response to the actions by the demonstration districts, the teachers' union went on strike three times, ultimately closing down the city's public schools for two months in the fall of 1968. For years afterward, the city was deeply polarized by enmity lingering from the struggle for control of the schools. The Ford Foundation's president, McGeorge Bundy, and Mayor John Lindsay sided with the rebel districts. At the time, other cities were convulsed by riots and uprisings as minority communities protested against poverty, inferior schools, police brutality, and dilapidated housing. Bundy and Lindsay wanted to mollify the leaders of the demonstration districts and avoid violent upheavals.

Eventually, to settle the prolonged conflict, the state legislature passed legislation in 1969 decentralizing the schools and creating elected local school boards while eliminating the three upstart districts that had started the confrontation. In a symbolic slap at the mayor, the legislature allowed him to appoint only two members to the new seven-person board. Thus began an era of decentralization for the city's schools, a period that lasted from 1969 until 2002, when the legislature restored control to the city's mayor, going from one extreme—in which political authority was dispersed among many officials—to the other—in which the mayor was granted complete dominion over the schools.[2]

The decentralization controversy marked the beginning of my career as a historian. I decided to write an article about the tumultuous events I had witnessed. When I was unable to find a magazine willing to publish the article, I instead wrote a history of the New York City schools, *The Great School Wars*, which was published in 1974. Thus began a lifetime commitment to studying and writing about education. So I have the Carnegie Corporation to thank for its modest but important investment in my life and the Ford Foundation to thank for turning the politics of education into a raging controversy in the late 1960s.

Foundations exist to enable extremely wealthy people to shelter a portion of their capital from taxation, and then to use the money for socially beneficial purposes. Foundations support hospitals, the arts, scientific research, public health, universities, and a host of other worthy philanthropic activities. Foundations themselves may not engage in political advocacy, but they may legally fund organizations that do. They may also support research projects likely to advance the foundation's goals. Education has often been high on their agendas. The steel magnate and philanthropist Andrew Carnegie established more than 2,500 free public libraries in the United States and other countries. Julius Rosenwald, who made his fortune as an executive of Sears Roebuck, devoted a large portion of it to building thousands of schools for African American children in the South.[3]

The Ford Foundation was badly burned by its assertive role in the school wars of the 1960s. It was castigated by all sides for having ignited a conflagration between the city's Jews and blacks (Albert Shanker, the president of the teachers' union, was Jewish, as were a substantial number of the teachers he represented, while most of the leaders of the community control movement were black). Almost everyone blamed Ford for its role in the ugly conflict that swirled around the public schools. The leadership of the demonstration districts felt betrayed by Ford, because their efforts at community control were thwarted, and critics of decentralization blamed Ford for encouraging the militants who demanded community control.

Ford's experience during the decentralization controversy was a stark lesson to other foundations and to Ford itself about the dangers of trying to engineer social change. In an article titled "The Very Expensive Education of McGeorge Bundy," David Halberstam attributed the disasters in both the war in Vietnam and the New York City schools to the arrogance and elitism of the patrician Bundy. Taking note of this unpleasant episode, other foundations (and Ford) continued to support school reform, but at arm's length.[4]

Not until a quarter century later, in 1993, did another philanthropist make a bold commitment to school reform. At a White House ceremony, publishing magnate Walter H. Annenberg stood with President Bill Clinton and announced a five-year plan to give $500 million to improve public education. The Annenberg Challenge grants, matched by equal (or greater) amounts from private and public donors at each site, awarded funds to local nonprofit groups in eighteen cities, including Boston, Detroit, Chicago, Houston, Los Angeles, New York City, and Philadelphia, as well as rural areas, and set aside millions of dollars specifically for arts education. The Annenberg Challenge, the largest grant ever made to American schools at that time, generated enormous excitement among school reformers. Each site had its own locally designed plan, with its own strengths and weaknesses, and each had to navigate the politics of negotiating with City Hall and the school system. In New York City, the Annenberg gift was the catalyst for expanding a network of progressive small schools; other cities promoted schools within schools, small learning communities, leadership development, professional development for teachers, parent engagement, social services for students, and a variety of other strategies.[5]

When the Annenberg funding ended in 2001, it was clear that it had not transformed public education. Some of the urban districts improved, but there were so many other reforms taking place at the same time that it was difficult to attribute the improvements to the Annenberg Challenge. In Philadelphia, district officials pointed with pride to the Kearny Elementary School as a success story that could be credited to Annenberg funding and the district's own visionary decentralization plan. Others thought that Kearny's achievements might be due to its tireless principal, Eileen Spagnola. In any case, despite Kearny's success, Philadelphia continued to register poor academic results and was in such financial distress that the state of Pennsylvania took control of the district in 2001. Ironically, President George W. Bush visited Kearny on January 8, 2009, to mark the anniversary of the signing of the No Child Left Behind act and to hail the school as proof of the law's effectiveness. But a teacher at the school told a reporter that the law had not changed the school, which was already recognized as a model school before NCLB was enacted.[6]

Michael Casserly, executive director of the Council of the Great City Schools, remarked that the Annenberg program was "a terrific bad example. The grants were poorly conceived, poorly managed, and . . . disconnected from any ability to drive any broader policy changes. The lesson is: Don't do that again."[7] With the passage of No Child Left Behind in 2001, the Annenberg Challenge soon faded into memory.

The Annenberg Challenge, unlike the Ford Foundation's involvement in the New York City public schools, did not ignite explosive social and political conflicts. Nor did it frighten other foundations away from school reform. In fact, the winding down of the Annenberg Challenge was promptly followed by the largest expansion in history of philanthropic effort focused on public education. New foundations, created by astonishingly successful entrepreneurs, took on the mission of reforming American education. But unlike the Ford Foundation, which responded to a specific crisis, or the Annenberg Foundation, which kept hands off its grantees, the new foundations had a plan. They wanted nothing less than to transform American education. They would not leave local communities to design their own reforms and would not risk having their money wasted. Their boldness was unprecedented. Never in American history had private foundations assigned themselves the task of reconstructing the nation's education system.

The turn of the millennium marked a changing of the guard in the foundation world. In 1998, the top four foundations contributing to elementary and secondary schooling were the Annenberg Foundation, the Lilly Endowment, the David and Lucile Packard Foundation, and the W. K. Kellogg Foundation. These four foundations provided 30 percent of all the funds given by the top fifty donors. A scant four years later, in 2002, the top two philanthropies were the Bill & Melinda Gates Foundation and the Walton Family Foundation; these two foundations alone were responsible for 25 percent of all funds contributed by the top fifty donors in that year.[8]

The new titans of the foundation world were billionaire entrepreneurs and corporate leaders. They were soon joined in education philanthropy by another billionaire, Eli Broad, who made his fortune in home building and the insurance industry; he launched the Eli and Edythe Broad Foundation in 1999. Unlike the older established foundations, such as Ford, Rockefeller, and Carnegie, which reviewed proposals submitted to them, the new foundations decided what they wanted to accomplish, how they wanted to accomplish it, and which organizations were appropriate recipients of their largesse.

Gates, Walton, and Broad came to be called venture philanthropies, organizations that made targeted investments in education reform. Venture philanthropy is also referred to as "philanthrocapitalism," because it borrows concepts from venture capital finance and business management. Unlike Annenberg, who had distributed his huge gift to many intermediate organizations to do as they thought best, the venture philanthropists treated their gifts as an investment that was expected to produce measurable results, or in the argot of business, a "return on investment." They funded new, entrepreneurial organizations that shared their goals, and they created new organizations to receive their funding when none existed that met their purposes.

Each of the venture philanthropies began with different emphases, but over time they converged in support of reform strategies that mirrored their own experience in acquiring huge fortunes, such as competition, choice, deregulation, incentives, and other market-based approaches. These were not familiar concepts in the world of education, where high value is placed on collaboration. The venture philanthropies used their funds assertively to promote their goals. Not many school districts could resist their offers. School districts seldom have much discretionary money; they are usually either cutting the budget or mediating disputes over how to spend any new money. The money expended by a foundation—even one that spends $100 million annually—may seem small in comparison to the hundreds of millions or billions spent by public school districts. But the offer of a multimillion-dollar grant by a foundation is enough to cause most superintendents and school boards to drop everything and reorder their priorities.

And so it happened that the Gates, Walton, and Broad foundations came to exercise vast influence over American education because of their strategic investments in school reform. As their policy goals converged in the first decade of the twenty-first century, these foundations set the policy agenda not only for school districts, but also for states and even the U.S. Department of Education.

Before considering the specific goals and activities of these foundations, it is worth reflecting on the wisdom of allowing education policy to be directed or, one might say, captured by private foundations. There is something fundamentally antidemocratic about relinquishing control of the public education policy agenda to private foundations run by society's wealthiest people; when the wealthiest of these foundations are joined in common purpose, they represent an unusually powerful force that is beyond the reach of democratic institutions. These foundations, no matter how worthy and high-minded, are after all, not public agencies. They are not subject to public oversight or review, as a public agency would be. They have taken it upon themselves to reform public education, perhaps in ways that would never survive the scrutiny of voters in any district or state. If voters don't like the foundations' reform agenda, they can't vote them out of office. The foundations demand that public schools and teachers be held accountable for performance, but they themselves are accountable to no one. If their plans fail, no sanctions are levied against them. They are bastions of unaccountable power.

Such questions are seldom discussed in the mass media. Frederick M. Hess of the American Enterprise Institute has written that the major foundations—especially Gates, Broad, and Walton—are the beneficiaries of remarkably "gentle treatment" by the press, which suspends its skeptical faculties in covering their grants to school reform. "One has to search hard to find even obliquely critical accounts" in the national media of the major foundations' activities related to education, Hess reports. Furthermore, he writes, education policy experts steer clear of criticizing the mega-rich foundations; to date, not a single book has been published that has questioned their education strategies. Academics carefully avoid expressing any views that might alienate the big foundations, to avoid jeopardizing future contributions to their projects, their university, or the district they hope to work with. Hess observes that "academics, activists, and the policy community live in a world where philanthropists are royalty." Everyone, it seems, is fearful of offending the big foundations, so there is an "amiable conspiracy of silence. The usual scolds choose to give philanthropic efforts only a pro forma glance while training their fire on other, less sympathetic targets." Because of this deferential treatment, Hess concludes, "we don't really know how much money foundations give, what it gets spent on, how they decide what to fund, how they think about strategy, or what lessons they have drawn from experience."[9]

This "conspiracy of silence" makes it all the more imperative that journalists, scholars, and public officials carefully scrutinize the long-term vision and activities of the major foundations, as well as their changes over time. Before relinquishing control of public policy to private interests, public officials should be sure that they understand the full implications of the foundations' strategies.

The big three of education philanthropy—Gates, Broad, and Walton—deserve close attention because they, more than any other foundations, tend to act in concert and therefore exert unusual power in the area of urban school reform.

The Walton Family Foundation has been the strongest, most consistent force in the nation advancing school choice through its gifts. It was established by Sam Walton, the founder of Walmart, in 1987. As the company became the world's largest retail operation, the foundation's assets grew rapidly; they are sure to multiply in the future as older family members bequeath their assets. By 2007, the latest year in which data were available, the family's foundation had assets of $1.6 billion and made grants that year of $241 million, distributed mainly to organizations involved in K–12 education, the environment, and the Arkansas-Mississippi region. It spent about $116 million to support vouchers, charter schools, and various local initiatives. Not only did Walton give large grants to individual charter schools and charter school chains, but it supported organizations that engage in political advocacy for charters, vouchers, and choice. Although most members of the Walton family went to public schools and did well in life, their family foundation has been a major source of funding for the school choice movement for many years.

In 2007, the Walton Family Foundation awarded $82 million to charter schools, $26 million to school choice programs, and an additional $8 million to school reform activities in Arkansas and Mississippi. Among its major grants was $8 million (most of which was a low-interest loan) to the Brighter Choice Foundation, which manages charter schools in Albany, New York; $21 million (half of which was a low-interest loan) to Charter Fund Inc., a Colorado-based charter promoter; $3.9 million to the KIPP Foundation for its schools; and direct grants to hundreds of charter schools across the nation. In addition, the Walton Family Foundation made sizable gifts to organizations that advocate for vouchers, including the Alliance for School Choice ($1.6 million), Children's Educational Opportunity Foundation ($4 million), the Hispanic Council for Reform and Educational Options ($700,000), and the Black Alliance for Educational Options ($850,000). The foundation also aided organizations favored by the Broad Foundation and the Gates Foundation, including Teach for America ($283,000), New Leaders for New Schools ($1.2 million), and the New Teacher Project ($1 million). The foundation made grants to a few public school districts in Arkansas, but most such grants were relatively small, less than $20,000.[10]

As one reviews the contributions made by the Walton Family Foundation, it is obvious that the family members seek to create, sustain, and promote alternatives to public education. Their agenda is choice, competition, and privatization. Beyond making symbolic contributions to local school districts near their Arkansas headquarters, they favor market competition among schools. Their theory seems to be that the private sector will always provide better consumer choices than government, and that government can't be relied upon to provide good education. They seem to have concluded that the best way to help low-income children is to ensure that they have access to a variety of privately managed schools.

Is there any commonality between the Walmart business philosophy and the Walton funding of school choice? When Walmart comes into a small town, the locally owned stores on Main Street often close down, because they can't match Walmart's low prices. In education, the Waltons underwrite charter schools and voucher programs that compete with the government-run public school system. Some left-wing critics think the Waltons are pushing privatization so they can make money in the education industry, but that does not seem credible. It simply doesn't make sense that a family worth billions is looking for new ways to make money. But why should it be surprising that a foundation owned by one of the richest families in the United States opposes government regulation and favors private sector solutions to social problems? Why should it be surprising that a global corporation that has thrived without a unionized workforce would oppose public sector unions? Nor should it be surprising that the Walton Family Foundation has an ideological commitment to the principle of consumer choice and to an unfettered market, which by its nature has no loyalties and disregards Main Street, traditional values, long-established communities, and neighborhood schools.

THE BILL & MELINDA GATES FOUNDATION was established in 2000 by the world's richest man, Bill Gates, the creator of Microsoft, the world's leading software company. (The Bill & Melinda Gates Foundation is the successor to the William H. Gates Foundation, created in 1994, and some smaller Gates-family foundations.) Its assets of some $30 billion make it the largest foundation in the nation, if not the universe, and the pledge of another $30 billion or so to the Gates

Foundation by one of its trustees, the famed investor Warren Buffett, in 2006 ensured its future dominance of the world of philanthropy (these values were depressed by market turbulence in 2008–2009, but the Gates Foundation remains the largest in the nation).

The Gates Foundation has laudably addressed some of the biggest global problems, such as public health and poverty. It has committed its vast resources to eradicating malaria in poor countries, noting that 2,000 children in Africa die every day from the disease. With the foundation's willingness to support the world's best researchers, combined with its ability to move swiftly, it stands a better chance of reaching this admirable goal than any national or international organization.

Yet even this worthy goal has alarmed critics who worry about the foundation's overwhelming influence and power. The chief of malaria research for the World Health Organization, Dr. Arata Kochi, complained in 2008 that the Gates Foundation was stifling a diversity of views among scientists, because so many of the world's leading scientists in the field were "locked up in a 'cartel' with their own research funding being linked to those of others within the group," making it difficult to get independent reviews of research. The foundation's decision-making process, he charged, was "a closed internal process, and as far as can be seen, accountable to none other than itself." In a statement that had implications for the foundation's education initiatives, the scientist said that the powerful influence of the foundation "could have implicitly dangerous consequences on the policy-making process in world health."[11] In other words, the Gates Foundation was setting the international agenda, because of its unrivaled wealth, and unintentionally shutting out competing views.

In 2000, the Gates Foundation selected a problem in American education that it wanted to solve: boosting high school graduation rates and college entry rates, especially in urban districts. The foundation leaders decided that the primary obstacle to reaching these goals was the traditional comprehensive high school. Although foundation officials regularly claimed that their decision to support small schools was based on research, most of the research available at that time was written by advocates of small schools, so the foundation had no warning signs of the difficulties it would encounter in pursuing its agenda.

The Gates initiative began when the small schools movement had become the leading edge of school reform in urban districts, largely because of the Annenberg Challenge. The movement's ardent adherents believed that small schools were the cure to the problems of urban education. They said that students got lost in large high schools, that they would respond positively to the personalized attention they received in a small high school, and that they would thus be motivated to study, stay in school, graduate, and go to college.

The foundation agreed with this diagnosis. It promised that its schools—most with fewer than four hundred students—would promote rigor, relevance, and relationships. "Rigor" meant that all students would take challenging courses; "relevance" meant that their studies would be connected to their own lives; and "relationships" referred to the close connections between teachers and students that a small school makes possible. Gates pumped about $2 billion between 2000 and 2008 into its campaign to restructure the American high school. Its funding reached 2,600 schools in forty-five states and the District of Columbia. Some of the Gates schools were new, while others were created by dividing up existing large schools.[12]

It was never obvious why the Gates Foundation decided that school size was the one critical reform most needed to improve American education. Both state and national tests showed that large numbers of students were starting high school without having mastered basic skills. Perhaps in a small school these students would get noticed quickly and get more help than they would in a large high school. But the root causes of poor achievement lie not in the high schools, but in the earlier grades, where students fail to learn the skills they need to keep up with their peers and to achieve academic competence.

Certainly there were too many high schools that enrolled too many students, some with 3,000, 4,000, or even 5,000 adolescents in the same building. In urban schools, this was a recipe for disaster because many students needed extra assistance and personal attention. For students who need close relationships with concerned adults, a small high school is surely superior to the anonymity of the comprehensive high school.

But the foundation seemed unaware of the disadvantages of small high schools, that is, schools with fewer than four hundred students. Because of their size, they seldom have enough students or teachers to offer advanced courses in mathematics and science, electives, advanced placement courses, career and technical education, choir, band, sports teams, and other programs that many teenagers want.

Nor can most offer adequate support for English-language learners or students with special needs. For many students, the small high school was not the wave of the future, but a revival of the rural schools of yesteryear, with strong relationships but limited curriculum.

When Bill Gates spoke to the nation's governors in 2005, half a decade into the foundation's commitment to small high schools, he told them bluntly that "America's high schools are obsolete. By obsolete, I don't just mean that our high schools are broken, flawed, and under-funded—though a case could be made for every one of those points. By obsolete, I mean that our high schools—even when they're working exactly as designed—cannot teach our kids what they need to know today." They were designed fifty years ago, he said, "to meet the needs of another age," and they are "ruining" the lives of millions of students every year. He said, "In district after district, wealthy white kids are taught Algebra II while low-income minority kids are taught to balance a check book!" He recited woeful statistics about high dropout rates and low performance on international assessments. He insisted that the high school of the future must prepare all students to go to college. He believed this was likeliest to happen in small high schools. What should governors do? Set high standards for all; publish data showing which students were progressing to college and which were not; and intervene aggressively to turn around failing schools and open new ones.[13]

I was at the World Economic Forum at Davos, Switzerland, in 2006, where I heard Gates enthusiastically describe the high schools his foundation had created. In a public discussion with *New York Times* columnist Thomas Friedman, Gates told the world's political and financial leaders about the dramatic improvements these schools had achieved. He assured them that the key to their success was "relevance," making all learning real and immediate to each student.

But Gates did not mention that things were not going so well at home. The foundation had contracted with two major research organizations, the American Institutes for Research and SRI International, to evaluate its small high schools. The first AIR-SRI report in the summer of 2005 indicated problems on the horizon. It compared students in the new and redesigned high schools with students in comprehensive high schools that were planning a redesign. The students in the new small schools were doing well in language arts, as compared to those in the comprehensive high schools under study, but not in mathematics. And according to the executive summary, "the quality of student work in all of the schools [both large and small] we studied was alarmingly low." In mathematics, the researchers found that half the teacher assignments in both kinds of schools lacked rigor, and that students in the comprehensive schools outperformed those in the new schools by a significant margin.[14] But it was still too early to draw any firm conclusions.

More troubling still was the tumult at Manual High School in Denver. Manual, initially considered a flagship of the foundation's plan to reconstruct the American high school, was closing.

Manual, one of Denver's oldest high schools, had an enrollment of 1,100 students in 2000. After a quarter century of mandatory busing ended in the late 1990s, the enrollment became predominantly nonwhite and low-income; the school's performance dropped sharply, and its graduation rate fell to about 60 percent. The principal eliminated many Advanced Placement classes, and academic expectations dropped. In 2001, the Gates Foundation awarded more than $1 million to restructure Manual High School into three small, autonomous high schools, each on its own floor of the building. Manual was supposed to demonstrate the foundation's belief that personal relationships and high expectations would enable every student to prepare for college.

It didn't work out that way. Soon after the three new schools opened, the new principals began to squabble over the use of the cafeteria, the library, and the gym, even over the division of textbooks. The small schools did not offer the programs, classes, and activities that had been available in the larger school, and enrollment plummeted by nearly half as students interested in college, athletics, and music transferred to other schools. As enrollment contracted, so did the number of faculty, and the school went into a steep decline. In 2002, three-quarters of the students at Manual were low-income; by 2005, the proportion was 91 percent. After four years of the new schools, evaluators reported better attendance and improved relationships between students and teachers, but the academic results of the transformation were awful. Only 20 percent of those who started ninth grade in the fall of 2001 graduated four years later, and no student at the school reached the advanced level on state tests of reading and mathematics in 2003, 2004, or 2005. In February 2006, just weeks after Gates praised his foundation's small schools initiative to world leaders, the Denver Board of Education voted to shut down Manual for a year, renovate it, and redesign it.[15]

The fallout from Manual's demise was not pretty. The foundation's spokesman blamed the school district, the principals, and the school. A local Colorado foundation that was involved in the venture, however, commented that the foundation was shifting blame and was "as much implicated in the Manual failure as any other stakeholder." It said that the reforms were implemented hastily, with inadequate planning and involvement of those who were expected to carry it out. The Gates Foundation's insistence that the three new schools be autonomous caused conflict and competition for resources among the schools, when collaboration was needed.[16]

Even more embarrassing to the Gates Foundation was the dissension in its own backyard at Mountlake Terrace High School, a suburban school of 1,800 students a few miles outside Seattle, not far from the foundation's headquarters. The school had a dropout rate of one-third and looked for ways to improve. In 2000, the Gates Foundation offered the school a gift of $833,000 to convert itself into small autonomous schools; 83 percent of the faculty voted to accept the grant. Unlike Manual High School in Denver, the school spent two years planning the breakup into small schools.

In the fall of 2003, Mountlake reopened as five new schools, each with its own theme, and its problems began. A math teacher complained, "All the math teachers used to share rooms, calculators, math tiles. Now that we're broken up, we're spread throughout the building and we have to buy five sets of things." Students immediately began to stereotype the schools; one was for "stoners," another for jocks, still another for geeks. A student said that one school was "the preppy, white school," while another was the "Asian, gangsta, druggie school." The teachers wanted students to be able to move from school to school, or to take electives in another school, but the foundation was opposed to anything that would dilute the autonomy of each school. The teachers didn't like competing for students and "marketing" their small school to eighth graders, believing that this competition was "very divisive for staff."[17]

At the end of the inaugural year, both the principal and the vice principal of Mountlake High School left for other districts. And nearly a quarter of the staff—twenty-three of one hundred teachers—decided not to return to the school (the typical turnover rate was 5 percent to 10 percent annually). The foundation said it was beginning to understand that the problem was not structure but "teaching and learning." Teachers heard this and thought they were being blamed for the initiative's failure. In the fall of 2008, Mount-lake Terrace High School abandoned its small schools and reverted to being a comprehensive high school.[18]

The foundation's bold idea worked in some places, but not in others. If foundation officials had considered the work of Valerie E. Lee, a professor at the University of Michigan, they would not have been surprised. Lee and a colleague concluded in 1997 that very large high schools were burdened by weak social relations, that very small schools might not be able to offer a full curriculum, and that the ideal size for a high school was six hundred to nine hundred students.[19] Schools within schools and theme-based schools, Lee told the *Seattle Times*, promote increased social stratification, with the motivated students enrolled in one or two small schools, and the unmotivated students in the "loser academy."[20] She also found that breaking schools into subunits did not necessarily lead to instructional improvement.[21] In Chicago, where the Gates Foundation had invested $21 million to create new small high schools, the results were depressingly familiar: Students had higher attendance rates and were less likely to drop out of school, but the academic results in the new high schools were no different from those of regular high schools.[22]

The Gates Foundation liked to point to its work in New York City as one place where it saw good results. It invested more than $100 million to launch two hundred new small high schools. Some of the new schools worked well as compared to the large high schools they replaced. The early returns looked good: Attendance was up, dropouts were down, and the graduation rate at the small high schools was 78 percent, about double the rate of the large comprehensive high schools that were closed.[23] But a study by Aaron Pallas of Teachers College and Jennifer Jennings of Columbia University found that the new small high schools did not enroll the same mix of students who had attended the large schools. The students admitted to the new schools, compared to those enrolled in the large comprehensive schools that closed, already had higher attendance rates and higher test scores; they included more females and smaller numbers of English-language learners and special education students. Pallas and Jennings concluded that "the buildings may be the same, but the students are not."[24] A study by the Center for New York City Affairs at the New School found that the impressive graduation rates and attendance rates at the new small high schools dropped over time, and the schools experienced very high rates of teacher and principal turnover; furthermore, their graduates were more likely than their peers in large schools to receive "local diplomas" (signifying that they were not college-ready) instead of Regents diplomas. To obtain a Regents diploma, a student had to pass five exit examinations; a student could get a local diploma without passing the exit examinations.[25]

So what did the Gates Foundation learn from these problems? It discontinued the evaluations of its small school grants and increased its funding for "advocacy work."[26] In the fall of 2006, Erik W. Robelen reported in *Education Week* that the foundation had increased its giving to advocacy groups from $276,000 in 2002 to nearly $57 million in 2005. Writing about the foundation's efforts to "broaden and deepen its reach," Robelen noted that almost everyone he interviewed was getting Gates money, including the publication he works for. The advocacy groups funded by Gates included Achieve ($8.84 million); the Alliance for Excellent Education ($3 million); the Center on Education Policy ($963,000); the Council of Chief State School Officers ($25.48 million); Education Sector ($290,000); Education Trust ($5.8 million); the National Alliance for Public Charter Schools ($800,000); the National Association of Secondary School Principals ($2.1 million); the National Association of State Boards of Education ($224,000); the National Conference of State Legislatures ($682,000); the National Governors Association ($21.23 million); the Progressive Policy Institute ($510,000); and the Thomas B. Fordham Institute ($848,000).[27]

Gates' biggest grantees were developers of new and redesigned high schools, as well as charter schools. Beginning in 2000, Gates supplied nearly $100 million to charter management organizations. The foundation's largest grants overall went to the NewSchools Venture Fund in San Francisco ($57 million), Communities Foundation of Texas in Dallas ($57 million), New Visions for Public Schools in New York City ($52 million), KnowledgeWorks Foundation in Cincinnati ($41 million), Jobs for the Future Inc. ($37.62 million), the College Board in New York City ($30 million), the Chicago Public Schools ($28 million), Alliance for Education in Seattle ($26 million), and the Bay Area Coalition for Equitable Schools in Oakland ($26 million).[28]

The only dissident voice that Robelen cited in his article was Brita Butler-Wall, president of the Seattle school board, which had previously received $26 million from the Gates Foundation. She said, "I don't understand if the Gates Foundation sees itself as trying to support districts or lead districts. No one was elected by the Gates Foundation to run schools." Others quoted in the article quickly rebutted Butler-Wall; an education expert praised the foundation for doing exactly the right things, and my friend Chester E. Finn Jr., who heads the Thomas B. Fordham Institute (where I was a trustee for many years), said "every large foundation" tries to change the minds of public officials.[29] But never in the history of the United States was there a foundation as rich and powerful as the Gates Foundation. Never was there one that sought to steer state and national policy in education. And never before was there a foundation that gave grants to almost every major think tank and advocacy group in the field of education, leaving almost no one willing to criticize its vast power and unchecked influence.

In late 2008, the Gates Foundation announced that it was changing course. Its $2 billion investment in new small high schools had not been especially successful (although it was careful not to come right out and say that it was unsuccessful). The foundation had received an evaluation from AIR-SRI in August 2006—two years earlier—that found that its new high schools had higher attendance rates but lower test scores than similar schools in the same districts. The evaluation in 2005 found lower scores only in mathematics; the 2006 evaluation revealed lower scores in both reading and mathematics. Bill and Melinda Gates invited the nation's leading educators to their home in Seattle and told them that they planned to invest millions in performance-based teacher pay programs; creating data systems; supporting advocacy work; promoting national standards and tests; and finding ways for school districts to measure teacher effectiveness and to fire ineffective teachers. Reflecting on its investments of the past eight years, the foundation acknowledged that its emphasis on school structure "is not sufficient to ensure that all students are ready for college, career, and life." It promised that it would now focus on "teaching and learning inside the classroom."[30]

Early in 2009, Bill Gates released a statement with the foundation's goals for the year. He candidly admitted that "many of the small schools that we invested in did not improve students' achievement in any significant way." Some had higher attendance rates and graduation rates, but their graduates were often not ready for college. The schools that got the best results, he said, were charter schools—such as KIPP and High Tech High in San Diego—that have significantly longer school days than regular public schools. He also stressed the difference that a "great teacher makes versus an ineffective one." He fondly recalled his teachers at Lakeside, the private school he attended in Seattle, who "fueled my interests and encouraged me to read and learn as much as I could." It was clear that the richest foundation in the world planned to put its considerable resources into the proliferation of charter schools and into the issue of teacher effectiveness: how to improve it and how to terminate ineffective teachers.[31]

Given the foundation's significant investment in advocacy, it was improbable that anyone would challenge Bill Gates and tell him his new goals were likely to be as ill advised as the $2 billion he had poured into restructuring the nation's high schools. Who would warn him of the dangers of creating a two-tiered system in urban districts, with charter schools for motivated students and public schools for all those left behind? Who would raise questions about the sustainability of charter schools that rely on a steady infusion of young college graduates who stay for only a few years? Who would caution him of the dangers of judging teacher effectiveness solely by the ups and downs of scores on standardized tests of basic skills? Who would tell him that the data systems now in use—and the ones he was about to fund—would never identify as great the kinds of teachers who had inspired him when he was a student at Lakeside?

ELI AND EDYTHE BROAD attended Detroit public schools. He received a degree in accounting from Michigan State University. With his wife's cousin, Broad entered the home-building business and later bought a life insurance company that eventually became a successful retirement savings business called SunAmerica. That business was sold to AIG in 1999 for $18 billion, and Eli Broad became one of the richest men in the nation. He promptly created the Eli and Edythe Broad Foundation, which invests in education, the arts, and medical research. The foundation's assets as of 2008 were more than $2 billion.

Having been trained as an accountant and having made his fortune as an entrepreneur, Broad believes in measurement, data, and results. He created training programs for urban superintendents, high-level managers, principals, and school board members, so as to change the culture and personnel in the nation's urban districts. He wanted district leaders to learn strategic planning, budgeting, accountability, data-driven decision making, technology, human resources, and other skills to improve the functioning of big-city bureaucracies.

In 2006, Broad invited me to meet with him at his gorgeous penthouse apartment in New York City. He explained his philosophy of education management. He believes that school systems should run as efficiently as private sector enterprises. He believes in competition, choice, deregulation, and tight management. He believes that people perform better if incentives and sanctions are tied to their performance. He believes that school leaders need not be educators, and that good managers can manage anything if they are surrounded by smart assistants. Broad told an audience in New York City in 2009, "We don't know anything about how to teach or reading curriculum or any of that. But what we do know about is management and governance." The Broad education agenda emphasizes the promotion of charter schools, the adoption of corporate methods for school leadership, and changes in the way teachers are compensated.[32]

His foundation makes investments, not grants. He invested in Alan Bersin's tough management approach in San Diego, until Bersin lost his slim majority on the Board of Education. After Bersin was forced out by an elected school board, the Broad Foundation decided that it was risky to invest in cities where there was dissension on the school board; it preferred situations where the leadership had longevity and was insulated from conflict and dissenting voices. He invested heavily in Joel Klein's reforms in New York City, because mayoral control of the school system ensured stable leadership and minimal interference by constituency groups. Broad liked Klein's commitment to testing, accountability, merit pay, and charter schools, and the fact that he surrounded himself with other noneducators who had degrees in business, law, and management.[33]

The Broad Foundation invested in Oakland, California, after the state took over its school system in 2003 because of a large budget deficit. The state put a Broad-trained superintendent, Randy Ward, in charge of the Oakland schools. In the view of the foundation, the removal of the locally elected school board created an ideal situation for change, because there was no board to slow or block the rapid imposition of reforms favored by the foundation. The Broad

Foundation was betting that the reforms would take root before the elected school board regained control of the district.

Supporters of charter schools were enthusiastic about Ward. Jeanne Allen, president of the Center for Education Reform, a pro-charter advocacy group, wrote that Ward was perceived as "the man who was leading the single most important and break-the-mold education effort in America." Allen asked Joe Williams to visit Oakland and find out if it really was a national model for education reform. Williams, formerly an investigative reporter, is executive director of Democrats for Education Reform, a pro-charter group in New York City.[34]

In his report, Williams described how Oakland's elected board had been stripped of its power by the state after the schools had run up a debt of $100 million. After the state takeover, he wrote, the city became a "politics free zone" where bold reforms were possible. The previous superintendent had staked his reputation on introducing small schools, an innovation that was popular with Oakland teachers, students, and parents. Ward embraced the small schools but went farther; his school reform plan aimed to turn the district into a marketplace of school choice while overhauling the bureaucracy. He closed low-performing schools and opened charter schools. He attracted $26 million in grants from the Broad Foundation, the Gates Foundation, the Dell Foundation, and corporations based in Oakland.[35]

But three years after he arrived, Ward left to become superintendent of the San Diego County Schools. Reflecting on his three years in Oakland, he said, "We really took accountability very seriously. . . . We created an environment of a free market." He was replaced by Kim Statham, also a graduate of the Broad Superintendents Academy, who continued to close struggling schools and open charter schools (Statham was subsequently replaced by Vincent Matthews, another Broad-trained superintendent). Williams looked for indicators of the success of the high-profile reforms imposed by Ward. Test scores were up, though they were still far below the state average. Williams noted that Oakland's score gains "have generally coincided with statewide increases as well—increases fueled by districts absent the kind of revolutionary reforms that are underway in Oakland." And while Oakland had received extensive press attention on the national stage as an exciting arena for reform, the citizens of Oakland were less than enthusiastic. A poll commissioned by the Center for Education Reform, which sponsored Williams' trip to Oakland, found that "more than half of respondents overall (54 percent) and parents (52 percent) said the school system had either gotten worse or stayed the same in the last decade."[36]

By 2008, when the state began the process of returning the public schools to the locally elected school board, Oakland had 32 charter schools and 111 regular public schools for its 46,000 students. Seventeen percent of the district's children were enrolled in charter schools. An analysis by the pro-charter group, the California Charter Schools Association, reported in 2009 that twenty-two of the thirty-two charter schools posted higher test scores than similar district schools. But the charters had a few important advantages. First, they enrolled half as many special education students as the district schools (4.6 percent of charter students were classified as special education, compared to 10.45 percent in the district's schools). And second, they could quietly counsel students out. These differences helped boost charters' scores in comparison to the regular public schools. Responding to an article reporting higher test scores for charters, a teacher wrote: "I work at a 'small school' in East Oakland, and we share our campus with a charter school. We routinely get students showing up at our school mid-year who have been kicked out of the charter school next door, and show up at our door the next morning. The question of whether charter schools truly educate all students is an important one that cannot be ignored. With that said, I am currently applying to charter schools for next year, because I am so sick of all the OUSD [Oakland Unified School District] bureaucratic bull. This district is truly frustrating to work for. Simple payroll and HR issues can take months to resolve, not to mention all the incompetent people at the school and district level when they really should [be] fired!"[37] The teacher was describing a district that supposedly had experienced a deep cultural transformation, a purge of incompetent personnel, and a thorough reorganization of its management structure in the previous six years.

In the spring of 2009, Dan Katzir, the managing director of the Broad Foundation, reflected on what the foundation had learned after a decade of investing many millions in urban school reform. Katzir said he and his colleagues had learned that thousands of private sector managers—primarily MBAs—are eager to work in urban education, installing new operating procedures. They learned that human resource departments in big city school systems can be streamlined to hire teachers in a more timely fashion. They learned that charter schools such as KIPP, Aspire, Green Dot, and Uncommon Schools get great results for low-income and minority students. They also learned that some of their investments did not "pay off." They were disappointed that many of the principal-training programs they supported did not produce higher student achievement. They saw progress halted in San Diego and Oakland when the leadership changed. Having learned these lessons, the foundation identified opportunities for future investment. Katzir said the foundation would support efforts to extend the school day and school year; merit pay for teachers based on student test scores; national standards and tests; and charter schools. It would take care to invest in communities where there was a mayor in charge, an appointed school board accountable to the city council, or a "near unanimous" elected school board, so as to ensure stability and minimize conflict over the reform agenda.[38]

The Broad Foundation invested millions of dollars in charter schools and charter management organizations including KIPP, Green Dot, Aspire, Pacific Charter School Development, the New-Schools Venture Fund, and Uncommon Schools.[39]

It invested millions in organizations that bypass traditional routes into teaching and school leadership, including Teach for America and New Leaders for New Schools.

It invested millions in programs to train school board members, administrators, and superintendents, principally by funding its own training programs.

It invested millions to improve the management in school districts such as Chicago, Prince George's County in Maryland, Charlotte-Mecklenburg in North Carolina, Denver, the District of Columbia, New York City, and Long Beach, California.

It invested millions in advocacy and think tanks such as the Center for American Progress (whose leader John Podesta was co-chairman of President-elect Obama's transition team); the California Charter School Association; the Center for Education Reform; the Council for the Great City Schools; the Council of Chief State School Officers; the National Governors Association; the Thomas B. Fordham Institute; the American Enterprise Institute; the Black Alliance for Education Options; Education Sector; and Education Trust. Many of these groups also received funding from the Gates Foundation.

It invested millions to subsidize pay-for-performance programs for teachers in several cities, including Houston, Chicago, and Minneapolis, and in programs to pay students to get higher test scores and grades in New York City, Washington, D.C., and Chicago.

It invested millions to pay for public relations for the New York City Department of Education, and it underwrote coverage of K–12 education reform issues by the public television network, the Educational Broadcasting Corporation.[40]

The Eli and Edythe Broad Foundation has been extraordinarily generous in supporting the arts and medical research, without trying to redefine how art should be created or how medical research should be conducted. In education, however, the foundation's investments have focused on Eli Broad's philosophy that schools should be redesigned to function like corporate enterprises. Eli Broad made his vast fortune in industries for which he had no special training, and his foundation embraces the belief that neither school superintendents nor principals need to be educators. His foundation includes educators in its training programs, but it seems to prefer people with a private sector background. Presumably the educators who are trained by the Broad Foundation learn the skills and mindset of corporate executives, which they can utilize when they return to their districts.

The Broad Foundation pursues strategies that would deprofessionalize education, uses bonuses to motivate (or "incentivize") teachers and students, and seeks to replace neighborhood schools with a competitive marketplace of choices.

This agenda is now shared by the Gates Foundation, along with several other major foundations, including the Robertson Foundation (assets in excess of $1 billion) and the Michael and Susan Dell Foundation (assets in excess of $1 billion). Together, these foundations wield immense economic and political power. During the 2008 campaign the Gates and Broad foundations jointly contributed $60 million to launch a project to make education reform a national campaign issue, while advocating for national standards, a longer school day, and merit pay.[41]

The Gates-Broad agenda was warmly endorsed by the Obama administration. Both foundations had invested heavily in the programs of Arne Duncan, Obama's secretary of education, when he was superintendent of the Chicago public schools. Soon after his election, President Obama called for the elimination of state caps on charter schools and endorsed merit pay. Duncan appointed a high-level official from the Gates Foundation to serve as his chief of staff at the U.S. Department of Education. He traveled the country urging mayors to take control of their public schools, an item high on the Broad Foundation's agenda.

Secretary Duncan appointed James H. Shelton III, a former program officer for the Gates Foundation, to oversee the $650 million Invest in What Works and Innovation Fund. Shelton worked previously for McKinsey & Company as a management consultant and later launched education-related businesses. He had also been a partner in the NewSchools Venture Fund, which describes itself as "a venture philanthropy firm working to transform public education by supporting education entrepreneurs and connecting their work to systems change." The NewSchools Venture Fund helped to launch many charter management organizations and other nonprofit and for-profit agencies. The fund was a beneficiary of the Gates Foundation, the Broad Foundation, and many other foundations.[42]

As he began his term in office, Secretary Duncan had charge of $100 billion that Congress had authorized to benefit education in the wake of the economic crisis of 2008. Of the total, Duncan set aside $4.3 billion to promote education reform in what he called the "Race to the Top" fund. To design and manage the Race to the Top, Duncan selected Joanne S. Weiss, a partner and chief operating officer of the NewSchools Venture Fund. Weiss is an education entrepreneur who had previously led several education businesses that sold products and services to schools and colleges. The regulations for the Race to the Top fund excluded any states that limited the number of charter schools or that prohibited a linkage between teacher and principal evaluations and student test scores.

When the regulations for the Race to the Top were released in 2009, Michael Petrilli of the Thomas B. Fordham Institute described the new federal program as "NCLB 2: The Carrot That Feels Like a Stick." Petrilli liked ideas such as evaluating teachers based in part on test scores, pushing the expansion of charter schools, and expanding alternate routes into teaching. But the heavily prescriptive nature of the program, he said, marked the death of federalism. Instead of asking states for their best ideas, the Obama administration "has published a list of 19 of *its* best ideas, few of which are truly 'evidence-based,' regardless of what President Obama says, and told states to adopt as many of them as possible if they want to get the money. It's as if a bunch of do-gooders sat together at the NewSchools Venture Fund summit and brainstormed a list of popular reform ideas, and are now going to force them upon the states. (Wait, I think that *is* how this list got developed.)"[43]

Now that the ideas promoted by the venture philanthropies were securely lodged at the highest levels of the Obama administration, policymakers and journalists listened carefully to Bill Gates. In a 2009 interview with Fred Hiatt, editorial page editor of the *Washington Post*, Gates signaled a new direction for his foundation. Hiatt wrote, "You might call it the Obama-Duncan-Gates-Rhee philosophy of education reform." It also was the Bloomberg-Klein-Broad philosophy of education reform. Gates said that his foundation intended to help successful charter organizations such as KIPP replicate as quickly as possible and to invest in improving teacher effectiveness. Gates asserted that there was no connection between teacher quality and such things as experience, certification, advanced degrees, or even deep knowledge of one's subject matter (at least below tenth grade). So, he suggested, the money now going to pay teachers for degrees or pensions should go toward preventing attrition in their fourth and fifth years. A few months later, Gates told the National Conference of State Legislatures that "if the entire U.S., for two years, had top quartile teachers, the entire difference between us and Japan would vanish."[44]

As we saw in Chapter 9, the debate about teacher effectiveness is far from simple. It is not easy to identify the "best teachers." Some economists believe, like Bill Gates, that the best teachers are those who produce the biggest test score gains, so little else matters. Other economists say that a teacher who is "great" one year may not be great the next. Some social scientists question whether student test scores are reliable when used for high-stakes personnel decisions, but Gates apparently was not familiar with these debates. And common sense suggests that any system of measurement that produces a top quartile will also produce three other quartiles.

Thus, Gates proposes to concentrate on charter schools and teacher effectiveness, as does the Broad Foundation. With characteristic confidence, Gates asserts that effective teaching can be taught, although he offers no examples to prove his point. Given the dubious research on which his foundation invested nearly $2 billion in small schools, one can only hope that he examines the extensive research that challenges his views on teacher effectiveness. He might also ask himself whether schools focused only on standardized tests of basic skills will produce the high achievement and creative thinking that he values and that are necessary to maintain the nation's innovative edge and its productivity in the future.

The foundations justify their assertive agenda by pointing to the persistently low performance of public schools in urban districts. Having seen so little progress over recent years, they now seem determined to privatize public education to the greatest extent possible. They are allocating millions of dollars to increase the number of charter schools. They assume that if children are attending privately managed schools, and if teachers and principals are recruited from nontraditional backgrounds, then student achievement will improve dramatically. They base this conclusion on the success of a handful of high-visibility charter schools (including KIPP, Achievement First, and Uncommon Schools) that in 2009 accounted for about 300 of the nation's approximately 4,600 charter schools.[45]

Given the money and power behind charter schools, it seems likely that they are here to stay. If we continue on the present course, with big foundations and the federal government investing heavily in opening more charter schools, the result is predictable. Charter schools in urban centers will enroll the motivated children of the poor, while the regular public schools will become schools of last resort for those who never applied or were rejected. The regular public schools will enroll a disproportionate share of students with learning disabilities and students who are classified as English-language learners; they will enroll the kids from the most troubled home circumstances, the ones with the worst attendance records and the lowest grades and test scores.

But why not insist that future charters fulfill their original mission, the one Albert Shanker envisioned in 1988? Why shouldn't they be the indispensable institutions that rescue the neediest kids? Why shouldn't they be demonstration centers that show what can be done to help those who can't succeed in a regular school? Why not redesign them to strengthen public education instead of expecting them to compete with and undercut regular public schools?

Do we need neighborhood public schools? I believe we do. The neighborhood school is the place where parents meet to share concerns about their children and the place where they learn the practice of democracy. They create a sense of community among strangers. As we lose neighborhood public schools, we lose the one local institution where people congregate and mobilize to solve local problems, where individuals learn to speak up and debate and engage in democratic give-and-take with their neighbors. For more than a century, they have been an essential element of our democratic institutions. We abandon them at our peril.

Business leaders like the idea of turning the schools into a marketplace where the consumer is king. But the problem with the marketplace is that it dissolves communities and replaces them with consumers. Going to school is not the same as going shopping. Parents should not be burdened with locating a suitable school for their child. They should be able to take their child to the neighborhood public school as a matter of course and expect that it has well-educated teachers and a sound educational program.

The market serves us well when we want to buy a pair of shoes or a new car or a can of paint; we can shop around for the best value or the style we like. The market is not the best way to deliver public services. Just as every neighborhood should have a reliable fire station, every neighborhood should have a good public school. Privatizing our public schools makes as much sense as privatizing the fire department or the police department. It is possible, but it is not wise. Our society needs a sensible balance between public and private.

I do not here make an argument against private or religious schools. For over a century, our cities have struck a good balance between public schools, private schools, and religious schools. In particular, the Catholic schools in urban districts have played an effective role as alternatives for families that sought a religious education. Oftentimes, Catholic schools have provided a better civic education than public schools because of their old-fashioned commitment to American ideals and their resistance to the relativism that weakened the fabric of many public schools. Sadly, many Catholic schools have closed because of declining numbers of low-paid religious teachers, which forced their costs to rise, and because of competition from charter schools, which are not only free to families but also subsidized by public and foundation funds. Catholic schools have a wonderful record of educating poor and minority children in the cities. It is a shame that the big foundations have not seen fit to keep Catholic schools alive. Instead, they prefer to create a marketplace of options, even as the marketplace helps to kill off highly successful Catholic schools.

The market undermines traditional values and traditional ties; it undermines morals, which rest on community consensus. If there is no community consensus, then one person's sense of morals is as good as the next, and neither takes precedence. This may be great for the entertainment industry, but it is not healthy for children, who need to grow up surrounded by the mores and values of their community. As consumers, we should be free to choose. As citizens, we should have connections to the place we live and be prepared to work together with our neighbors on common problems. When neighbors have no common meeting ground, it is difficult for them to organize on behalf of their self-interest and their community.

With so much money and power aligned against the neighborhood public school and against education as a profession, public education itself is placed at risk. The strategies now favored by the most powerful forces in the private and public sectors are unlikely to improve American education. Deregulation contributed to the near collapse of our national economy in 2008, and there is no reason to anticipate that it will make education better for most children. Removing public oversight will leave the education of our children to the whim of entrepreneurs and financiers. Nor is it wise to entrust our schools to inexperienced teachers, principals, and superintendents. Education is too important to relinquish to the vagaries of the market and the good intentions of amateurs.

American education has a long history of infatuation with fads and ill-considered ideas. The current obsession with making our schools work like a business may be the worst of them, for it threatens to destroy public education. Who will stand up to the tycoons and politicians and tell them so?

CHAPTER ELEVEN

Lessons Learned

WE HAVE KNOWN FOR MANY YEARS that we need to improve our schools. We keep stumbling, however, because there is widespread disagreement about what should be improved, what we mean by improvement, and who should do it. A strong case for improvement was made by *A Nation at Risk*, which warned in 1983 that our students and our schools were not keeping up with their international peers. Since then, many reports and surveys have demonstrated that large numbers of young people leave school knowing little or nothing about history, literature, foreign languages, the arts, geography, civics, or science. The consequences of inadequate education have been recently documented in books such as Mark Bauerlein's *The Dumbest Generation*, Rick Shenkman's *Just How Stupid Are We?* and Susan Jacoby's *The Age of American Unreason*. These authors describe in detail the alarming gaps in Americans' knowledge and understanding of political issues, scientific phenomena, historical events, literary allusions, and almost everything else one needs to know to make sense of the world. Without knowledge and understanding, one tends to become a passive spectator rather than an active participant in the great decisions of our time.

Education is the key to developing human capital. The nature of our education system—whether mediocre or excellent—will influence society far into the future. It will affect not only our economy, but also our civic and cultural life. A democratic society cannot long sustain itself if its citizens are uninformed and indifferent about its history, its government, and the workings of its economy. Nor can it

223

prosper if it neglects to educate its children in the principles of science, technology, geography, literature, and the arts. The great challenge to our generation is to create a renaissance in education, one that goes well beyond the basic skills that have recently been the singular focus of federal activity, a renaissance that seeks to teach the best that has been thought and known and done in every field of endeavor.

The policies we are following today are unlikely to improve our schools. Indeed, much of what policymakers now demand will very likely make the schools less effective and may further degrade the intellectual capacity of our citizenry. The schools will surely be failures if students graduate knowing how to choose the right option from four bubbles on a multiple-choice test, but unprepared to lead fulfilling lives, to be responsible citizens, and to make good choices for themselves, their families, and our society.

For the past century or more, education reformers have tried out their ideas in the schools. A wide variety of reformers and reform movements have offered their own diagnoses and cures. With the best of intentions, reformers have sought to correct deficiencies by introducing new pedagogical techniques, new ways of organizing classrooms, new technologies, new tests, new incentives, and new ways to govern schools. In every instance, reformers believed that their solution was the very one that would transform the schools, make learning fun, raise test scores, and usher in an age of educational joy or educational efficiency. As one innovation follows another, as one reform overtakes the last, teachers may be forgiven if from time to time they suffer an acute case of reform fatigue.

This constant reform churn is not the approach typically found in countries with successful schools. In November 2006, I attended a meeting of the International Association for the Evaluation of Educational Achievement, an organization of scholars that has been studying school performance in many nations since the 1960s. Two respected testing experts, Ina V. S. Mullis and Michael O. Martin of Boston College, described the lessons learned from decades of mathematics assessments in dozens of nations. As I listened to their presentation, I copied this list of the essential ingredients of a successful education system: "a strong curriculum; experienced teachers; effective instruction; willing students; adequate resources; and a community that values education." In their published essay, Mullis and Martin summarized their findings:

> Education is an arduous process. Different countries use dif-
> ferent approaches, but effective education always requires
> enormous effort. Success requires developing a rigorous and
> progressive curriculum and providing all students with an
> equal opportunity to learn it. Success also depends on eco-
> nomic resources and a strong-willed society to ensure that
> students are ready to learn and that teachers are well pre-
> pared to provide instruction, as well as having the necessary
> facilities and materials.[1]

The fundamentals of good education are to be found in the classroom, the home, the community, and the culture, but reformers in
our time continue to look for shortcuts and quick answers. Unteth-
ered to any genuine philosophy of education, our current reforms
will disappoint us, as others have in the past. We will, in time, see
them as distractions, wrong turns, and lost opportunities. It is time
to reconsider not only the specifics of current reforms, but also our
very definition of reform.

Our schools will not improve if we continually reorganize their
structure and management without regard for their essential purpose. Our educational problems are a function of our lack of educational vision, not a management problem that requires the enlistment
of an army of business consultants. Certainly we should mobilize
expert managerial talent to make sure that school facilities are well
maintained, that teachers have adequate supplies, that noninstruc-
tional services function smoothly, and that schools are using their
resources wisely. But organizational changes cannot by themselves
create a sound education program or raise education to the heights
of excellence that we want.

The most durable way to improve schools is to improve curriculum and instruction and to improve the conditions in which teachers
work and children learn, rather than endlessly squabbling over how
school systems should be organized, managed, and controlled. It is
not the organization of the schools that is at fault for the ignorance
we deplore, but the lack of sound educational values.

Our schools will not improve if elected officials intrude into pedagogical territory and make decisions that properly should be made
by professional educators. Congress and state legislatures should
not tell teachers how to teach, any more than they should tell sur-
geons how to perform operations. Nor should the curriculum of the

schools be the subject of a political negotiation among people who are neither knowledgeable about teaching nor well educated. Pedagogy—that is, how to teach—is rightly the professional domain of individual teachers. Curriculum—that is, what to teach—should be determined by professional educators and scholars, after due public deliberation, acting with the authority vested in them by schools, districts, or states.

Our schools will not improve if we continue to focus only on reading and mathematics while ignoring the other studies that are essential elements of a good education. Schools that expect nothing more of their students than mastery of basic skills will not produce graduates who are ready for college or the modern workplace. Nor will they send forth men and women prepared to design new technologies, achieve scientific breakthroughs, or accomplish feats of engineering skill. Nor will their graduates be prepared to appreciate and add to our society's cultural achievements or to understand and strengthen its democratic heritage. Without a comprehensive liberal arts education, our students will not be prepared for the responsibilities of citizenship in a democracy, nor will they be equipped to make decisions based on knowledge, thoughtful debate, and reason.

Our schools will not improve if we value only what tests measure. The tests we have now provide useful information about students' progress in reading and mathematics, but they cannot measure what matters most in education. Not everything that matters can be quantified. What is tested may ultimately be less important than what is untested, such as a student's ability to seek alternative explanations, to raise questions, to pursue knowledge on his own, and to think differently. If we do not treasure our individualists, we will lose the spirit of innovation, inquiry, imagination, and dissent that has contributed powerfully to the success of our society in many different fields of endeavor.

Our schools will not improve if we rely exclusively on tests as the means of deciding the fate of students, teachers, principals, and schools. When tests are the primary means of evaluation and accountability, everyone feels pressure to raise the scores, by hook or by crook. Some will cheat to get a reward or to avoid humiliation. Schools may manipulate who takes the test and who does not; district and state officials may fiddle with the scoring of the test. Districts and states may require intensive test preparation that mirrors the actual state tests and borders on institutionalized cheating. Any test score gains that result solely from incentives are meaningless because gains that are purchased with cash are short-lived and have nothing to do with real education.

Our schools will not improve if we continue to close neighborhood schools in the name of reform. Neighborhood schools are often the anchors of their communities, a steady presence that helps to cement the bonds of community among neighbors. Most are places with a history, laden with traditions and memories that help individuals resist fragmentation in their lives. Their graduates return and want to see their old classrooms; they want to see the trophy cases and the old photographs, to hear the echoes in the gymnasium and walk on the playing fields. To close these schools serves no purpose other than to destroy those memories, to sever the building from the culture of its neighborhood, and to erode a sense of community that was decades in the making. Closing a school should be only a last resort and an admission of failure, not by the school or its staff, but by the educational authorities who failed to provide timely assistance.

Our schools will not improve if we entrust them to the magical powers of the market. Markets have winners and losers. Choice may lead to better outcomes or to worse outcomes. Letting a thousand flowers bloom does not guarantee a garden full of flowers. If the garden is untended, unsupervised, and unregulated, it is likely to become overgrown with weeds. Our goal must be to establish school systems that foster academic excellence in every school and every neighborhood.

Our schools cannot improve if charter schools siphon away the most motivated students and their families in the poorest communities from the regular public schools. Continuing on this path will debilitate public education in urban districts and give the illusion of improvement. In exchange for the benefits of deregulation, charter schools should use their autonomy from the usual rules and regulations to show what they can do to educate students who have been unable to learn in a traditional school. In the future, charter schools should be valued partners of traditional public schools. Charter schools should be designed to collaborate with traditional public schools in a common mission: the education of all children. In this mission, they should be allies, not enemies or competitors.

Our schools will not improve if we expect them to act like private, profit-seeking enterprises. Schools are not businesses; they are a public good. The goal of education is not to produce higher scores, but to educate children to become responsible people with well-developed minds and good character. Schools should not be expected to turn a profit in the form of value-added scores. The unrelenting focus on data that has become commonplace in recent years is distorting the nature and quality of education. There are many examples of healthy competition in schools, such as science fairs, essay contests, debates, chess tournaments, and athletic events. But the competition among schools to get higher scores is of a different nature; in the current climate, it is sure to cause teachers to spend more time preparing students for state tests, not on thoughtful writing, critical reading, scientific experiments, or historical study. Nor should we expect schools to vie with one another for students, as businesses vie for customers, advertising their wares and marketing their services. For schools to learn from one another, they must readily share information about their successes and failures, as medical professionals do, rather than act as rivals in a struggle for survival.

Our schools will not improve if we continue to drive away experienced principals and replace them with neophytes who have taken a leadership training course but have little or no experience as teachers. The best principals have had a long apprenticeship as educators, first as teachers, then as assistant principals, and finally as principals. The principal should be the school's "head teacher," the person who evaluates teachers and helps those who are struggling to teach well. If principals have not spent much time as teachers, they are not qualified to judge others' teaching, nor can they assist new teachers.

Our schools cannot be improved by blind worship of data. Data are only as good as the measures used to create the numbers and as good as the underlying activities. If the measures are shoddy, then the data will be shoddy. If the data reflect mainly the amount of time invested in test-preparation activities, then the data are worthless. If the data are based on dumbed-down state tests, then the data are meaningless. A good accountability system, whether for schools, teachers, or students, must include a variety of measures, not only test scores. To use a phrase I first heard from educator Deborah Meier, our schools should be "data-informed," not "data-driven."[2]

Our schools cannot be improved by those who say that money doesn't matter. Resources matter, and it matters whether they are spent wisely. The best-informed and most affluent parents make sure to enroll their children in schools that have small classes, a broad curriculum in the liberal arts and sciences, well-educated teachers, and well-maintained facilities. Ample resources do not guarantee success, but it is certainly more difficult for schools to succeed without them. If we are serious about narrowing and closing the achievement gap, then we will make sure that the schools attended by our neediest students have well-educated teachers, small classes, beautiful facilities, and a curriculum rich in the arts and sciences.

Our schools cannot be improved if we ignore the disadvantages associated with poverty that affect children's ability to learn. Children who have grown up in poverty need extra resources, including preschool and medical care. They need small classes, where they will get extra teacher time, and they need extra learning time. Their families need additional supports, such as coordinated social services that help them to improve their education, to acquire necessary social skills and job skills, and to obtain jobs and housing. While the school itself cannot do these things, it should be part of a web of public and private agencies that buttress families.

Our schools cannot be improved if we use them as society's all-purpose punching bag, blaming them for the ills of the economy, the burdens imposed on children by poverty, the dysfunction of families, and the erosion of civility. Schools must work with other institutions and cannot replace them.

IF THERE IS ONE THING ALL EDUCATORS KNOW, and that many studies have confirmed for decades, it is that there is no single answer to educational improvement. There is no silver bullet, no magic feather, no panacea that will miraculously improve student achievement. There are no grounds for the claim made in the past decade that accountability all by itself is a silver bullet, nor for the oft-asserted argument that choice by itself is a panacea. Accountability and choice may or may not raise test scores, but neither is a surefire way to improve education.

Higher test scores may or may not be a reliable indicator of better education. The overemphasis on test scores to the exclusion of other important goals of education may actually undermine the love of learning and the desire to acquire knowledge, both necessary ingredients of intrinsic motivation. Investing inordinate amounts of time in test-preparation activities may well drive up the scores. It would be surprising if scores did not rise when so much effort is expended to push them up. Yet at the same time that scores go up, the youngsters may be ignorant of current events, the structure of our government and other governments, the principles of economics, the fundamentals of science, the key works of literature of our culture and others, the practice and appreciation of the arts, or the major events and ideas that have influenced our nation and the world. Even as their scores go up, they may be devoid of any desire to deepen their understanding and knowledge and may have no interest in reading anything for their own enlightenment and pleasure. And so we may find that we have obtained a paradoxical and terrible outcome: higher test scores and worse education.

WHAT, THEN, CAN WE DO to improve schools and education? Plenty.

If we want to improve education, we must first of all have a vision of what good education is. We should have goals that are worth striving for. Everyone involved in educating children should ask themselves why we educate. What is a well-educated person? What knowledge is of most worth? What do we hope for when we send our children to school? What do we want them to learn and accomplish by the time they graduate from school?

Certainly we want them to be able to read and write and be numerate. Those are the basic skills on which all other learning builds. But that is not enough. We want to prepare them for a useful life. We want them to be able to think for themselves when they are out in the world on their own. We want them to have good character and to make sound decisions about their life, their work, and their health. We want them to face life's joys and travails with courage and humor. We hope that they will be kind and compassionate in their dealings with others. We want them to have a sense of justice and fairness. We want them to understand our nation and our world and the challenges we face. We want them to be active, responsible citizens, prepared to think issues through carefully, to listen to differing views, and to reach decisions rationally. We want them to learn science and mathematics so they understand the problems of modern life and participate in finding solutions. We want them to enjoy the rich artistic and cultural heritage of our society and other societies.

One could make the list of hoped-for outcomes even longer, but the point should be clear. If these are our goals, the current narrow, utilitarian focus of our national testing regime is not sufficient to reach any of them. Indeed, to the extent that we make the testing regime our master, we may see our true goals recede farther and farther into the distance. By our current methods, we may be training (not educating) a generation of children who are repelled by learning, thinking that it means only drudgery, worksheets, test preparation, and test-taking.

So let us begin with a vision of the education we want for our children and our society.

To move toward that vision, we should attend to the quality of the curriculum—that is, what is taught. Every school should have a well-conceived coherent, sequential curriculum. A curriculum is not a script but a set of general guidelines. Students should regularly engage in the study and practice of the liberal arts and sciences: history, literature, geography, the sciences, civics, mathematics, the arts, and foreign languages, as well as health and physical education.

Having a curriculum is not a silver bullet. It does not solve all our educational problems. But not having a curriculum indicates our unwillingness or inability to define what we are trying to accomplish. To paraphrase the Cheshire cat in *Alice in Wonderland,* if you don't know where you are going, any road will get you there. The curriculum is a starting point for other reforms. It informs teachers, students, parents, teacher educators, assessment developers, textbook publishers, technology providers, and others about the goals of instruction. It provides direction, clarity, and focus around worthy ends, without interfering with teachers' decisions about how to teach.

Other nations that outrank us on international assessments of mathematics and science do not concentrate obsessively on those subjects in their classrooms. Nations such as Japan and Finland have developed excellent curricula that spell out what students are supposed to learn in a wide variety of subjects.[3] Their schools teach the major fields of study, including the arts and foreign languages, because they believe that this is the right education for their students, not because they will be tested. They do the right thing without rewards and sanctions. Their students excel in the tested subjects because they are well educated in many other subjects that teach them to use language well and to wrestle with important ideas.

If we are willing to learn from top-performing nations, we should establish a substantive national curriculum that declares our intention to educate all children in the full range of liberal arts and sciences, as well as physical education. This curriculum would designate the essential knowledge and skills that students need to learn. In the last two years of high school, there should be career and technical studies for students who plan to enter the workforce after high school graduation. But they too should study the arts and sciences, so that they too may gain a sense of life's possibilities. Because we are all citizens of this democracy, because we will all be voters, we must all be educated for our responsibilities.

Some will object that a country as diverse as ours can't possibly have a national curriculum and will point to the debacle of the voluntary national history standards as evidence for their skepticism. The counterargument is that our nation had a de facto curriculum for most of the nineteenth century, when the textbooks in each subject were interchangeable. For the first half of the twentieth century as well, we had an implicit national curriculum that was decisively shaped by the college entrance examinations of the College Board; their highly respected examinations were based on a specific and explicit syllabus, designed by teachers and professors of each subject.

But what about the culture wars that will surely erupt if there is any attempt to decide what will be taught and learned in any subject? We can now see, with the passage of years, that it is possible to forge a consensus in every contested subject-matter terrain if the various factions accept the necessity of working together and the futility of trying to impose their views on everyone else.

There is reason to hope that the curriculum wars of the 1990s have ended, not in a victory for either side, but in a truce. Where once there were warring partisans of whole language and phonics, now there is a general recognition that children need both. Beginning readers must learn the sounds and symbols of language, and they should learn to love reading by hearing and reading wonderful literature. Teachers should make sure that all children have a steady diet of good—no, excellent—literature in their classrooms. I would go further, hopefully not harming the possible consensus, to insist that all children should learn grammar, spelling, and syntax, which will enable them to write well and communicate their ideas clearly. Knowing the basic parts of speech will improve students' ability to understand and use the English language well.[4]

Furthermore, I suggest a short reading list—not more than ten titles—of indispensable literary classics for each grade. Carol Jago, a high school English teacher and a past president of the National Council of Teachers of English, wrote a delightful explanation of how and why to teach the classics today.[5] Back in the days of the culture wars, it was taken as a given that any list would be oppressive, exclusive, and elitist, privileging some while leaving others out. One hopes we have moved beyond those contentious times and can at last identify essential writings that have stood the test of time and continue to be worthy of our attention.

Without the effort to teach our common cultural heritage, we risk losing it and being left with nothing in common but an evanescent and often degraded popular culture. Let us instead read, reflect on, and debate the ideas of Abraham Lincoln, Martin Luther King Jr., Henry David Thoreau, Elizabeth Cady Stanton, Walt Whitman, Emily Dickinson, Ralph Waldo Emerson, W. E. B. Du Bois, Herman Melville, Nathaniel Hawthorne, William Shakespeare, John Milton, John Locke, John Stuart Mill, Lewis Carroll, and many others whose writings remain important because of their ideas, their beauty, or their eloquence. Let us be sure that our students read the Declaration of Independence, the Constitution, and other basic documents of our nation's founding and development. Classic literature coexists happily with contemporary writings, especially when students are encouraged to engage in discussions about timeless issues such as the conflict between freedom and authority, the conflict between the rights of society and the rights of the individual, and the persistent dilemmas of the human condition. I do not suggest that it will be easy to shape lists of essential readings for every grade, only that it is necessary not to shirk this obligation if we wish to have excellent education for all. An English language arts curriculum without literature—real, named books of lasting importance—is no English curriculum at all.

In mathematics, the wars of the 1990s between traditionalists and constructivists have also subsided, although they flare up from time to time when parents discover that their children can't add or subtract. The National Council of Teachers of Mathematics, which initially emphasized the role of discovery learning and social interaction in learning, now recognizes that students must learn the basic facts of computation, which are necessary for successful problem solving and critical thinking. Many districts that mandate constructivist programs realize that they must also teach basic mathematical computation. A consensus is possible. The results of international assessments, in which American students have faltered over the years, have helped us to understand the importance of avoiding extremes and unnecessary polarization.

In the sciences, the ingredients for a solid, sequential curriculum are at hand, based on work already completed by the American Association for the Advancement of Science's Project 2061 and the National Research Council. Students should study science in every grade, but this is hard to achieve when there are not enough science teachers. The study of science is also hobbled by the theological and political debate about evolution, which shadows every effort to devise science curricula on a statewide basis. The first problem can be solved with determination and resources; it is not beyond our reach. The second is not easily resolved because it involves a conflict with deeply held religious beliefs. Education authorities must separate teaching about science from teaching about religion. They must clarify to parents and the public that these are not the same. In other words, science classes should teach science, as validated by scholarship, and religion classes should teach religion. This principle cannot be compromised without doing injury to both fields of study.

Even history can be rescued from the culture wars, which now, one hopes, are a distant memory. In contrast to the voluntary national history standards, which unleashed a national furor, Massachusetts, California, and a few other states have demonstrated that it is possible to develop a history curriculum that is challenging and lively. Arguments over *whose* history should be taught amused academics and polemicists in the 1990s but helped to stifle the study of history in the schools.

At present, most students plod dutifully and unenthusiastically through obligatory textbooks of 1,000 or more pages stuffed with facts but lacking in narrative or intellectual excitement. The great stories of brave men and women, of heroes and villains, of tragic decisions and extraordinary deeds, are gone. The textbooks avoid controversy—which would hurt sales—and maintain a studied air of neutrality, thus ensuring the triumph of dullness. In *The Language Police*, I wrote that the systematic sanitizing of textbooks had turned school into "the Empire of Boredom." The same children whose textbooks avoid controversy have easy access to eroticized violence and sensationalism on videos, television, the movies, and the Internet.[6]

History should be as exciting to young people as anything on television, but their textbooks turn it into a listless parade of names, themes, wars, and nations. Among all the subjects tested by the federal government, U.S. history is the one in which American students register the worst performance, even though almost all students are required to study it.[7] To restore excitement and vitality to this subject, teachers and curriculum designers must raise questions, provoke debates, explore controversies, and encourage the use of primary documents, narratives written by master historians, biographies, documentaries, and other visual records of important events and personalities. Biographies are a terrific way to introduce elementary-age children to history.

In the arts, we should agree that all children deserve the opportunity to learn to play a musical instrument, to sing, engage in dramatic events, dance, paint, sculpt, and study the great works of artistic endeavor from other times and places. Through the arts, children learn discipline, focus, passion, and the sheer joy of creativity. We should make sure that these opportunities and the resources to support them are available to every student in every school.

Many educators and parents worry that a national curriculum might be captured by "the wrong people," that is, someone whose views they do not share. I too worry that a national curriculum might be no better than the vacuum that now exists, might fail to lift our sights, and might fail to release us from the shackles of test-based accountability. There is also a long-standing, deep-seated fear in this country about the federal government taking control of the curriculum. This fear stems from the individualistic, libertarian strain in American history, which harbors a certain suspicion about "those bureaucrats" in Washington, D.C., who might try to impose wrongheaded ideas on our neighborhood schools. In fact, it is currently a matter of federal law that the U.S. Department of Education is not permitted to impose any curriculum on the schools. Thus, any national curriculum must be both nonfederal and voluntary, winning the support of districts and states because of its excellence.

Of course, a voluntary national curriculum might be established by private organizations, as the College Board did in the first four decades of the twentieth century. State officials might work together to create a curriculum that is national but not federal. As I write, the National Governors Association and the Council of Chief State School Officers, working with state education departments and groups such as Achieve, are trying to develop common standards in reading and mathematics for the nation's school. It remains to be seen whether these organizations, with all their political muscle, will be able to circumvent the pitfalls that have plagued previous efforts and avoid the empty blather that has made most state standards meaningless. If they draft standards only for reading and mathematics, then their effort may reinforce the skills-only approach to schooling that now prevails.

If it is impossible to reach consensus about a national curriculum, then every state should make sure that every child receives an education that includes history, geography, literature, the arts, the sciences, civics, foreign languages, health, and physical education. These subjects should not be discretionary or left to chance. Every state should have a curriculum that is rich in knowledge, issues, and ideas, while leaving teachers free to use their own methods, with enough time to introduce topics and activities of their own choosing. That would avoid unnecessary duplication from grade to grade and would guarantee that children in different districts—rural, suburban, and urban—are getting access to the same opportunities to learn.

Even now, about 1,000 schools use the Core Knowledge curriculum, which describes explicitly what shall be taught in the full range of liberal arts and sciences in each grade. Teachers in these schools spend about half their day teaching the Core Knowledge curriculum, not through rote drill but through projects and activities. The rest of the day is available for their own choices or for fulfilling local and state requirements.[8] Students who have the benefit of this kind of sequential, knowledge-rich curriculum do very well on the standardized tests that they must take. They do well on tests because they have absorbed the background knowledge to comprehend what they read.

Why is the curriculum important? It is a road map. Without a road map, you are sure to drive in circles and get nowhere. To be sure, some people like driving in circles, and some educators like teaching in a school without a curriculum. In a nation that prizes liberty, those schools should continue to do as they please. But most schools will want to know what teachers should teach and what students are expected to learn. A sound curriculum ensures that young people will not remain ignorant of the most essential facts and ideas of the humanities and sciences. Background knowledge is critical to understanding and learning; whether one studies history or science or any other field, background knowledge is crucial in enabling the student to quickly grasp and integrate new information.

To have no curriculum, as is so often the case in American schools, leaves schools at the mercy of those who demand a regime of basic skills and no content at all. To have no curriculum is to leave decisions about what matters to the ubiquitous textbooks, which function as our de facto national curriculum. To have no curriculum on which assessment may be based is to tighten the grip of test-based accountability, testing only generic skills, not knowledge or comprehension.

Why not leave well enough alone, and let the textbook publishers decide what all children should learn? To anyone who might be satisfied with this response, I say: Sit down and read a textbook in any subject. Read the boring, abbreviated pap in the history textbooks that reduces stirring events, colorful personalities, and riveting controversies to a dull page or a few leaden paragraphs. Read the literature textbooks with their heavy overlay of pedagogical jargon and their meager representation of any significant literature. Note that nearly half the content of these bulky, expensive books consists of glitzy graphics or blank space. Challenge yourself to read what your children are forced to endure, and then ask why we expect that textbooks—written and negotiated line by line to placate politically active interest groups in Texas and California—are up to the task of supplying a first-rate curriculum.[9]

One of the few states with an excellent curriculum in every subject is Massachusetts. Perhaps not coincidentally, students in Massachusetts have the highest academic performance in the nation on the National Assessment of Educational Progress and rank near the top when compared to their peers in other nations. When Massachusetts participated in the TIMSS international assessment in 2007, its fourth graders placed second in the world in science, surpassed only by Singapore, and its eighth graders tied for first in the world in science with students in Singapore, Chinese Taipei, Japan, and Korea.[10] When students in Minnesota took the TIMSS tests, eighth graders tied with Singapore in earth science; in mathematics, their performance was mediocre, like the nation's. William Schmidt, the U.S. coordinator for TIMSS, said that Minnesota has a strong curriculum in earth science, but not in mathematics. The lesson, he concluded, is that American students "can be the best in the world when we give them a curriculum that is focused and coherent and that is delivered by teachers well trained in the content being offered at that level."[11]

If our nation or states or districts have a good curriculum, we must ensure that our assessment systems reflect and reinforce what is taught. There is a maxim among educators that "what gets tested is what gets taught." The assessments used in our schools should be as good as the curriculum. I do not seek to abolish standardized, multiple-choice tests; they give a quick snapshot of student performance at a specific point in time. But they are not sufficient to measure student learning. To lift the quality of education, we must encourage schools to use measures of educational accomplishment that are appropriate to the subjects studied, such as research papers in history, essays and stories in literature, research projects in science, demonstrations of mathematical competence, videotaped or recorded conversations in a foreign language, performances in the arts, and other exhibitions of learning.

Nor should test scores be the sole measure of the quality of a school. Every state should establish inspection teams to evaluate the physical and educational condition of its schools, to ensure that a full curriculum is taught (not only the tested subjects), and to review the quality of teaching and learning. Inspectors should judge teaching and learning by observing it, not by using checklists to note whether students have "learning goals," teachers have "data binders," schools have "data inquiry teams," or other nonsensical requirements based on the jargon of the day.

The goal of evaluation should not be to identify schools that must be closed, but to identify schools that need help. The job of educational authorities is to solve problems, not evade them by shuttering schools. When schools are struggling, the authorities should do whatever is necessary to improve them. This may mean professional development for teachers, smaller classes, targeted programs in reading or other subjects, after-school activities, additional tutoring for students, extra supervisors, a better disciplinary policy, parent education classes, and other interventions that will strengthen the school's capacity to educate its students.

With a strong and comprehensive curriculum and a fair assessment and evaluation system in place, the schools must have teachers who are well qualified to teach the curriculum. Teachers must be well educated and know their subjects. To impart a love of learning, they should love learning and love teaching what they know. They should have professional training to learn how to teach what they know, how to manage a classroom, and how to handle the kinds of issues and problems they are likely to encounter as classroom teachers. As in many other aspects of education, we do not have ways to quantify whether a teacher loves learning, but we have some important signposts, such as their education, their command of the subject, and their skill in the classroom. Prospective teachers should be tested on their knowledge of what they will teach, and they should be regularly evaluated by their supervisors and peers.

To attract and retain the teachers we need, schools must offer compensation that reflects the community's respect for them as professionals. Many districts are trying various forms of performance pay, and we should watch those experiments closely. Some districts will offer higher salaries to attract teachers in fields where there are chronic shortages, such as science and mathematics. Others may offer bonuses to those who perform extra assignments. Differential pay schemes are in flux and are likely to continue changing for several years, as we learn more from current efforts. But whatever the results may be, no manipulation of salary schedules will suffice to overcome the absence of a sound curriculum, willing students, supportive parents, collegial administrators, and good working conditions.

If our schools had an excellent curriculum, appropriate assessments, and well-educated teachers, we would be way ahead of where we are now in renewing our school system. But even that would not be enough to make our schools all that they should be. Schools do not exist in isolation. They are part of the larger society. Schooling requires the active participation of many, including students, families, public officials, local organizations, and the larger community.

As every educator knows, families are children's first teachers. On the very first day of school, there are wide differences in children's readiness to learn. Some children have educated parents, some do not. Some come from homes with books, newspapers, magazines, and other reading materials, some do not. Some parents encourage their children to do their schoolwork and set aside a place and a time for them to study, some do not. Some parents take their children to the library, zoo, museum, and other places of learning, while some do not. As a result of different experiences in early childhood, some children begin school with a large vocabulary, while others do not.

Researchers Betty Hart and Todd R. Risley studied the language development of young children and found a huge disparity between children from impoverished families and children from professional families. Before the age of three, children from the advantaged families had vastly more exposure to words and encouragement than children who grew up in poor households.[12] Their study implies the need for early intervention, even before the age of three, as well as intensive adult education for parents.

Families must do their part to get children ready for school. Families implant basic attitudes and values about learning, as well as the self-discipline and good manners necessary for learning in a group. Families must remain involved with their children, encourage them, monitor their schoolwork, limit the time they spend with electronic devices, meet with their teachers, and see that they have a regular place to study. They must encourage them to take their schooling seriously, respect their teachers, and behave appropriately in school.

Children from families that provide a literate environment are likely to be more successful in school than children who lack this initial advantage. And what of the children whose families, for whatever reason, are unable to provide support for learning at home? They too must be educated, and schools must go to extra lengths to be sure that they learn the social behaviors and skills that make learning possible. One of the reasons that so-called no-excuses schools, such as KIPP, have achieved good results is that they unabashedly teach the behaviors and attitudes that students need for success in school. Students are taught to sit up straight; dress neatly; look at the teacher; shake hands firmly; make eye contact with the person who is talking; don't speak out in class unless called upon by the teacher; be nice; work hard. Many parents like the idea that the school will teach these behaviors and attitudes, because they want to protect their children from what they perceive as the chaos of the streets, the destructive behavior of gangs, and the bullying of other students. The no-excuses schools are a response to the weakening of social norms that once supported parents; now even the best efforts of families are often contradicted by what children see on television, in the movies, and in their interactions with peers.

What is surprising is that the public schools ever *stopped* expecting children to act with civility in relations with their classmates and teachers. When I was a student in public schools in Houston many years ago, every teacher told the class to sit up straight, speak only when called upon, stop talking out of turn, and listen to your neighbor when he or she was speaking. We were constantly reminded to "be nice" and "work hard," though in somewhat different language. Those who did not behave appropriately were sent to the principal's office, not to face corporal punishment (although the big boys did), but to bear the shame and humiliation of having been sent there.

Schools must enforce standards of civility and teach students to respect themselves and others, or they cannot provide a safe, orderly environment, which is necessary for learning. The regular public schools must learn this lesson from the no-excuses schools and restore the historic tradition of public schools as places where students learn good behavior, good citizenship, and the habits of mind that promote thoughtfulness and learning.

Our nation's commitment to provide universal, free public education has been a crucial element in the successful assimilation of millions of immigrants and in the ability of generations of Americans to improve their lives. It is unlikely that the United States would have emerged as a world leader had it left the development of education to the whim and will of the free market. The market has been a wonderful mechanism for the development of small and large business enterprises; it has certainly been far more successful in producing and distributing a wide range of high-quality goods and services than any command-and-control economy. But the market, with its great strengths, is not the appropriate mechanism to supply services that should be distributed equally to people in every neighborhood in every city and town in the nation without regard to their ability to pay or their political power. The market is not the right mechanism to supply police protection or fire protection, nor is it the right mechanism to supply public education.

To be sure, we must respect and value the diversity made possible by private and religious schools. We should see the coexistence of these different kinds of schools as an ecosystem of educational institutions that has developed over many years and has served our nation well. None seeks to destroy or replace the other, and each serves different populations and sometimes the same populations at different times.

As a nation, we need a strong and vibrant public education system. As we seek to reform our schools, we must take care to do no harm. In fact, we must take care to make our public schools once again the pride of our nation. Our public education system is a fundamental element of our democratic society. Our public schools have been the pathway to opportunity and a better life for generations of

Americans, giving them the tools to fashion their own life and to improve the commonweal. To the extent that we strengthen them, we strengthen our democracy.

At the present time, public education is in peril. Efforts to reform public education are, ironically, diminishing its quality and endangering its very survival. We must turn our attention to improving the schools, infusing them with the substance of genuine learning and reviving the conditions that make learning possible.

School and Society

WHEN I COMPLETED THE FINAL DRAFT of this book on November 10, 2009, I hit the "send" button with a mixture of joy and sadness. Joy to be finished, sadness because I couldn't keep revising, polishing phrases, adding new material to reflect the latest events. I had no idea what was in store for the book or for me. Would it be reviewed or even noticed? Would it find its intended audience? And what would happen if the powerful figures criticized in the book did notice and react? I thought about the Monty Python comedy series, in which a giant shoe comes out of nowhere to squash a character, and wondered whether that would happen to me. For months, I worried and waited.

When the book finally was published in March 2010, it got attention, mainly because I had changed my views. News stories claimed I had made a U-turn, that I had recanted everything I once believed. This was not true. I had changed my mind about means, not ends. My basic educational philosophy remained the same. I have always wished that every child might have the same high-quality education I wanted for my children and now want for my grandchildren. Over half a dozen years, I had been thinking out loud, in print and on blogs, reevaluating my views in public and sorting out the evidence as it accumulated. Eventually, I came to the realization that free markets coupled with test-based accountability would not solve our education ills and actually risked making them worse. It is, I suppose, a commentary on our polarized political culture that changing one's mind should be so extraordinary. It is even more unusual, I

243

have discovered, to say, "I was wrong." That's a shame. How can we learn if we never change our views and never admit error?

The book did find its intended audience. It became a best seller. I received more than a thousand incredibly moving e-mails and letters from teachers, parents, administrators, and other citizens. Many are published on my Web site; some writers requested anonymity, and others asked that I not post their letter, fearful that they might be identified by their supervisor. So far the giant shoe has not managed to squash me, although I've taken my share of criticism, some fair, some not, on the air and in print.

In this added chapter, I examine some of the significant events that have occurred since the book's completion and review recent research about the major trends in American education. I also address the changes needed to bring about the improvement in education that everyone desires.

In the book, I described something new that was happening in public education, something that called itself reform but looked like a wave of deliberate destruction, sweeping away schools and educators and dispersing children to untried destinations. It began with No Child Left Behind, which established a regime of annual testing for all students in grades three through eight and mandated a utopian goal that all students would achieve proficiency in reading and mathematics by 2014. If any group in a school was not on track to meet that target, the entire school would be stigmatized as failing and face escalating sanctions. NCLB set up the nation's public schools to fail, and as the magical year drew closer, more and more of them did fail. By 2011, Secretary of Education Arne Duncan had warned that the proportion of "failing schools" would rise to 82 percent during the year.[1] By 2014, if the law remained unchanged, very few public schools would be left standing, untouched by state intervention and punishment.

In retrospect, NCLB was the worst education legislation ever passed by Congress. Its remaining supporters are few. It was presumptuous, intrusive, and harmful. It presumed that Congress knows how to reform schools, which it does not. It empowered the federal government to extend its mandates into every public school classroom in the nation, negating the role of states and localities in directing their public schools. It assumed that scores on standardized, multiple-choice tests are the end goal of education, which they are not. The law's rigid prescriptions and humiliating, destructive sanctions demoralized educators across the nation, substituting the judgment of Congress for that of professionals. As I predicted in the book, this narrow-minded definition of success served mainly to encourage narrowing the curriculum, gaming the system, teaching to bad tests, and cheating. In the nearly two years since the book was published, cheating scandals have been uncovered in various districts and cities, most notably in Washington, D.C., and Atlanta, Georgia. Properly designed and used, tests can provide helpful information, but in the era of NCLB, test scores became the sole measure of student and school achievement.

NCLB created a national education policy that neglected the central purpose of education: to shape good human beings, good citizens, people of good character with the knowledge and skills to make their way in the world and to join with others to sustain and improve our democracy. Children learn many things in the home and in their community. But they go to school to learn to read, write, study great literature, do mathematics, understand science, learn about history and civics, acquire a second language, and engage in the arts, while learning to work together, play together, and think for themselves. The broad and humanistic goals of education ought not be reduced to scores on multiple-choice tests of basic skills. Doing so narrows the purposes of education and diminishes the professional responsibilities of teachers and principals.

NCLB had other undesirable effects. As its prescriptions failed more schools, public confidence in public education and in the education profession declined. Consequently, political pressure for privately managed schools grew, as did proposals to deprofessionalize education so that inexperienced individuals could assume the roles of teacher, principal, and superintendent. Schools that had once been the heart and soul of their communities closed their doors, to be replaced by small schools, charter schools, and privately managed schools. Some very troubled inner-city schools, plagued by violence and disorder, closed their doors and spread their unaddressed problems to other schools. Some schools were subjected to a process called transformation, which meant that the principal was fired, along with half or all of the staff. Business-minded reformers envisioned a market system where parents chose schools like they shopped for shoes, schools advertised their services, and school boards acted as though they were managing a stock portfolio. The market would determine which schools would live and which would die.

The grim reaper, sent by Congress, was swinging his scythe, and as time on the NCLB clock ran out, many schools had to die. No appeal to emotion, to tradition, to justice, or to any definition of success other than test scores could stay the fatal blow.

After a decade of NCLB, the process Congress set in motion in 2001 was finally reaching its intended destination. No matter the cause or reason, schools with low test scores would pay the price; in the eyes of the self-proclaimed reformers, there could be no excuse for low scores. So, fire the teachers, fire the principals, padlock the doors, try something new, and see what happens. Any school that could not raise students' scores year after year had to go. The law assumed, for reasons no one could recall, that whatever took the place of the school with low scores was bound to be an improvement. Almost overnight, consultants and new organizations appeared like flowers in spring, ready to give advice (for a steep price) on how to raise test scores, how to turn around a school, how to evaluate teachers, how to start a new school, how to train noneducators to become principals, how to do whatever the law required. Education entrepreneurship became an emerging growth industry (some wag referred to NCLB as "no consultant left behind"). And all the while, the testing industry saw a dramatic escalation in demand for its products.

In time, many of the new schools also fell into the cycle of failure, unless they managed to avoid enrolling the students who dragged their scores down: students with profound disabilities, students who were homeless, students who couldn't read English, students recently released from the juvenile justice system.

For the first time in American history, a *federal* law required local public schools to close their doors, convert to private management, or fire the staff. Throughout our history, the federal government had observed the principle of federalism in relation to education; states and localities paid the lion's share of education costs, and education was considered to be largely, if not entirely, a state and local function. (Currently the federal government pays about 10 percent of the cost of K–12 education, while states and localities pay for 90 percent.) That's how constitutional scholars interpret the Tenth Amendment, which reserved for the states those powers not assigned to the federal government. At least since 1965, when the Elementary and Secondary Education Act was passed, the federal government's role had been to subsidize the education of the neediest students, enforce civil rights, conduct research, gather information, and subsidize college costs. That was a significant role, but it did not involve telling local public schools what they must do to be successful or what would happen if they were not successful. All this changed with No Child Left Behind, followed by Race to the Top: Congress and two successive administrations—those of George W. Bush and Barack Obama—felt no compunction about telling districts how to reform their schools and imposing harsh punishments for failure to comply or to succeed.

In its first few years, NCLB didn't seem to be such a bad thing, and 2014 was a long way off. Teachers were paying more attention to poorly performing students and were helping some of them reach whatever the state called proficiency. That seemed sensible. But making improvement every year was not enough to satisfy the law, which demanded 100 percent proficiency. As the date grew closer, the number of schools likely to meet this goal (attained by no other nation) grew smaller. The consequences unfolded so gradually, garnering so much bipartisan support and media accolades, that the draconian nature of these measures was not immediately apparent to the public. The closings, one after another, bothered almost no one except the educators, parents, and students affected. Neither Congress nor the Bush or Obama administrations listened to them.

Not only were they ignored, but their cries were muffled by a well-publicized, heavily subsidized campaign to close more schools and fire more teachers, and to do it more energetically than even NCLB demanded.

THE FIRST SALVO OF THE NEW GET-TOUGH CAMPAIGN occurred in February 2010, when Frances Gallo, the school superintendent of Central Falls, Rhode Island—the state's smallest and poorest district—announced her intention to fire every staff member of the city's only high school because of its low test scores. She had the strong support of state Education Commissioner Deborah Gist. If the staff did not agree to longer working hours, everyone would be fired—not only seventy-four teachers, but also reading specialists, guidance counselors, physical education teachers, the school psychologist, the principal, and three assistant principals. Students and parents defended the teachers, saying that "they treat us with respect" and "they stay when we need help," but to no avail.[2]

Secretary of Education Arne Duncan endorsed the proposed mass firings of the teachers (none of whom had been individually evaluated) and applauded state and local officials for "showing courage and doing the right thing for kids." Duncan said, "This is hard work and these are tough decisions, but students only have one chance for an education, and when schools continue to struggle, we have a collective obligation to take action." Speaking to the U.S. Chamber of Commerce a few days later, President Obama supported the firing of the Central Falls staff and made a point of acknowledging former Secretary of Education Margaret Spellings, one of the architects of NCLB, because "she helped to lead a lot of the improvement that's been taking place and we're building on."[3]

Eventually the local teachers' union settled with the Central Falls school district, and the immediate crisis passed. But its effects lingered and reached an audience far beyond Rhode Island. For the first time, teachers across the nation understood that the long-established rules of their chosen career had changed. They awakened to the possibility that *their* school and *their* career might be subject to the inexorable ticking of the NCLB clock. They began to realize, as John Donne had written, "Never send to know for whom the bell tolls; it tolls for thee."

For Central Falls High School, the experience was unsettling and painful. After the détente between district officials and teachers, staff morale plummeted. Within a year, twenty-six teachers had left or had been fired. New leadership at the school hired enthusiastic new teachers, but absenteeism by both teachers and students became a chronic problem, and student discipline deteriorated. The number of in-school suspensions soared. The events of the previous year seemed to convince students that their teachers were incompetent and to blame for their own poor performance or lack of effort. In May 2011, the teachers in the tiny district passed a resolution of no-confidence in Superintendent Frances Gallo by a vote of 244–8. Claudio Sanchez of National Public Radio concluded that the district's "transformation" plan was "in shambles." The high school had become, he said, "a cautionary tale about the complexities of school reform and whether the federal government should be dictating what those reforms should be." In this district, where reform had been bluntly imposed, trust among administrators, teachers, students, and parents was broken. There were no winners.[4]

The events in Central Falls provided a perfect backdrop for the cover of *Newsweek* on March 15, 2010. The cover said enticingly, "The Key to Saving American Education." Behind the bold headline, on an image of a blackboard, was written again and again: "We must fire bad teachers. We must fire bad teachers." Inside the magazine, the story by Evan Thomas and Pat Wingert began like a fairy tale. It said, "Once upon a time, American students tested better than any other students in the world." But now they had declined and ranked only in the middle among nations, about the same as Lithuania. *Newsweek* described the performance of the schools as "a national embarrassment as well as a threat to the nation's future."[5] The story was indeed a fairy tale, because there was no time in the past when American schools were first in the world on international tests. When the first international assessments were administered in the mid-1960s, our students ranked at or near the bottom of those nations tested. In the 1970s, 1980s, and 1990s, American students were often in the bottom quartile or near the international average, never first in the international rankings.[6] But the story of decline was hard to resist, and the *Newsweek* writers chose not to resist it.

Thomas and Wingert's story introduced a narrative of failure and redemption that would soon become familiar as the script for the new "reform movement." Unlike dissident school reform movements in the past, this one had the support of the nation's wealthiest foundations, corporate executives, Wall Street hedge fund managers, leaders of the technology sector, and the top elected officials of both major political parties. Its ranks included few working teachers, but its extraordinary wealth and political power more than compensated for the lack of support within the profession. The movement asserted that American education was failing and that this failure was due to the large numbers of "bad teachers," who were protected from accountability by their unions and by the nefarious practice of tenure. The reformers, who were strongly committed to free-market principles and competition, sought to replace big-city public school systems with a marketplace of choices, featuring privately managed charter schools, and to break free of union contracts. The new charter schools were staffed by a regular infusion of young, enthusiastic, and inexperienced teachers, most of whom left within two or three years; these schools relied heavily on standardized test scores to measure the quality of teachers and schools.

Certain themes were central to the reform movement: first, that the nation's public schools were failing; second, that students who have three or four or five extraordinary teachers in a row will excel, no matter the students' background, while students who have even two weak teachers in a row fall so far behind that they can never recover; third, that firing a teacher is almost impossible because of union rules; fourth, that the failure of the schools was rationalized by those with a "defeatist mindset," who defended the status quo and wrongly blamed poverty or families or students for low scores instead of blaming bad teachers.[7]

Nowhere had these ideas moved faster than in New Orleans. There, in 2005, Hurricane Katrina had flooded large parts of the city, killed over 1,000 people, destroyed thousands of homes, and caused a dramatic exodus of residents from the city. Many public schools were severely damaged. After the hurricane, the state closed most of the public school system. Every teacher, every staff member of the public schools was fired, and many students moved away permanently. This turned out to be, in *Newsweek*'s view, a lucky break, because it gave New Orleans the chance to start over. Secretary of Education Duncan later declared that Hurricane Katrina was "the best thing that happened to the education system in New Orleans."[8] The writers in *Newsweek* agreed. With the floundering public school system gone, the state leaders invited private managers to open charter schools, and in a few short years, New Orleans became a paradigm for the corporate style of education reform: no public school system, no union, a competitive environment, great results. Researchers disagreed about the real effects of the new paradigm, whether the students were the same pre-Katrina and post-Katrina, whether the state's standards were consistent, whether the successful charters excluded students with disabilities, and whether the new charters used the few remaining public schools as dumping grounds for low-performing students. Whatever the ultimate judgment about the changes in New Orleans, closing the nation's public schools and staffing them with inexperienced young college graduates hardly seems to be a successful recipe for national school reform.

Absent a physical catastrophe like Hurricane Katrina, how could the American public system "regain" what *Newsweek* described as "its lost crown as the envy of the world"? *Newsweek* pointed to

Central Falls, where a brave local superintendent threatened to fire every last teacher unless her demands were met. Here, the narrative concluded, was a "notable breakthrough." Here was the solution to a national quagmire in which incompetent and lazy teachers retained their jobs for life, while the public schools continued their ceaseless decline.

The *Newsweek* story marked the beginning of a massive media blitz for the corporate reform movement. I call it the corporate reform movement not because everyone who supports it is interested in profit but because its ideas derive from business concepts about competition and targets, rewards and punishments, and "return on investment." In contrast, educators talk about curriculum and instruction, child development, pedagogy, conditions of learning (such as class size), resources, conditions of students' lives that affect their health and motivation, and relations with families and communities. To many leaders of the reform movement, such issues are either trivial or distractions. They insist that every child can learn (which is true, even though children learn at different rates and in different ways) and that anything less than a goal of 100 percent proficiency signifies someone making excuses for bad teachers.

At this point the ideology of the corporate reform movement becomes indistinguishable from that of No Child Left Behind, with its utopian claim that 100 percent of all children must be proficient, regardless of their language difficulties, special-education status, or conditions over which teachers have no control (such as poverty and homelessness). In their own eyes, the reformers think of themselves as leaders of a new civil rights movement, which is vaguely comical considering that many of its leaders come from Wall Street and corporate suites and stand at the apex of wealth and power, a sector not usually found at the forefront of egalitarian social movements. They speak grandiosely of working toward a day when all children will get an excellent education, but their methods rely so heavily on testing and accountability that the prospect of an excellent education for all diminishes as the power of their movement grows. What they have engendered is not an excellent education for all, but a nation dedicated to test preparation and testing, where children are drilled ad nauseam in the narrow skill of picking the right answer from multiple-choice questions. No matter whether test scores go up or down, this is not the quintessence of an excellent education. It is not even a worthy goal.

Nonetheless, the corporate reform movement acquired national attention for its agenda in September 2010, with the release of the film *Waiting for "Superman."* Never has a documentary about education been so munificently promoted. Not only were there anticipatory news articles many months before its release, but it was featured on the cover of *Time* magazine; it was highlighted twice on Oprah Winfrey's popular television show; NBC devoted a week of programming called "Education Nation" to showcasing its themes and heroes. Bill Gates gave the producers $2 million to publicize the film, and it was shown to state legislatures and other influential audiences. President Obama even invited the five children featured in the film to visit him in the White House.

Like the corporate reform movement, the film presents itself as a plea for liberal, enlightened political views but is in fact deeply reliant on free-market principles. The strong underlying message, like that of the *Newsweek* story, is that American public schools are a disaster, in both urban and suburban districts. According to the film, the only hope for the future lies with privately managed charter schools, which can fire teachers at will. The film follows five children as they seek to escape assignment to a public school and gain entry into a charter school. The film has heroes—charter school founders, billionaire philanthropist Bill Gates, and Michelle Rhee, then chancellor of the District of Columbia Public Schools, whose trademark was her enthusiasm for firing teachers and principals. And it has villains—principally the teachers' unions, which protect "bad" teachers. Since 1971, the film says, spending has more than doubled but test scores have remained flat. The viewer is told that 70 percent of eighth-grade students are "below grade level" in reading, and a map shows the small proportion of students—between 20 percent and 30 percent—in each state who are "proficient." A chart shows how poorly American students score on international tests, and Stanford University economist Eric Hanushek claims the United States would rise to the top of the international standings if 5–10 percent of teachers were fired every year, based on their students' test scores. The charter schools shown in the film are cheerful places. Not a single successful public school is portrayed. The public school is clearly a dreadful and sclerotic institution, one that will certainly doom a generation of children, with dire implications for our nation's future. Inevitably, the audience becomes emotionally involved with the adorable children, hoping they win the lottery admitting them to a charter school.

This was certainly an appalling and alarming story. But like the *Newsweek* story, *Waiting for "Superman"* was a fairy tale, based on half-truths, exaggerations, and misrepresentations.

Is American education in free fall, declining from a time of glory half a century earlier (as *Newsweek* said) or forty years earlier (as *Waiting for "Superman"* claimed)? No. On the National Assessment of Educational Progress (NAEP), the only longitudinal measure of student achievement, American students in fourth grade and eighth grade have made significant test-score gains in reading and mathematics since 1978, when the tests were first administered. Richard Rothstein wrote, "On these exams, American students have improved substantially, in some cases phenomenally. In general, the improvements have been greatest for African-American students, and among these, for the most disadvantaged." Furthermore, there has been major progress in reducing the achievement gap between black and white students; however, most of that progress occurred in the 1970s and 1980s, probably in response to desegregation, increased economic opportunity for African-American families, federal investment in early childhood education, and class size reduction.[9]

Critics of American public schools hark back to a supposed golden age of public schooling forty or fifty years ago. Very likely, they don't recall the three major changes that have occurred since the 1960s: First, legally sanctioned racial segregation ended. The active intervention of the courts and the federal government broke down a system that was unjust and oppressive. But the gains for desegregation prompted white flight and black middle-class flight from urban schools, producing districts with concentrated racial isolation and poverty. Second, the courts and Congress required the public schools to open their doors to students with disabilities, a move that was necessary, expensive, and challenging for the schools, especially when students with severe behavioral problems were mainstreamed with motivated students. Third, changes in federal immigration policy brought millions of non-English-speaking students into the nation's public schools. This was also an era that saw the weakening of two-parent families and the rise of digital technology, with its power for both education and distraction.

Those who claim our schools have deteriorated refer to a long-lost time when public schools were segregated, excluded most students with disabilities, and had relatively few non-English-speaking students. It was also a time when teachers had near-complete authority in their classrooms. Anyone with a sense of history should admire the resilience of this engine of democracy, which has surmounted a political obstacle course over the past half-century. One could reasonably argue that the curricula in history and English have been watered down over the years, that standards of behavior have been relaxed in ways that impair teaching and learning, and that teachers' authority has been whittled away. But at the same time, the curricula in science and mathematics are far more demanding than what was generally available half a century ago. A vigorous debate about curriculum, pedagogy, and discipline should give rise to a curriculum reform movement and to efforts to restore teachers' autonomy and authority, not to a movement to privatize and deprofessionalize American public education. Today's "reformers" ought to know that even in the 1950s, the schools were considered to be in crisis, with critics such as Rudolf Flesch warning that Johnny couldn't read, and others such as Admiral Hyman Rickover warning that the schools' lack of rigor was causing the nation to fall behind the international competition.[10]

Reformers assume that American students lost ground compared to students in other nations and that the United States lost its position as first in the world, but this is not accurate. The first international assessment was administered in mathematics in the mid-1960s, and our seniors scored last among twelve nations. In the international tests of mathematics and science that students in many different nations have taken over the past four decades, American students have consistently performed poorly. A federal report in 1992 said the only consistent message of the international tests over the previous three decades was that "students from the United States, regardless of grade level, generally lag behind many of their counterparts from other developed countries in both mathematics and science achievement." Scholar Yong Zhao found it "puzzling" to hear President Obama react with alarm in his 2011 State of the Union address to the most recent international test scores and yet go on to say we should ignore "the naysayers predicting our decline," because the United States "still has the largest, most prosperous economy in the world. No workers—no workers are more productive than ours. No country has more successful companies or grants more patents to inventors and entrepreneurs. We're the home to the world's best colleges and universities, where more students come to study than any place on Earth." Zhao wrote that this great economic success must have been created by the same generation that ranked at the bottom of the international tests. The lesson: We can learn from the tests, we certainly should improve our students' knowledge and skills, but we should not assume that they predict national prosperity or decline.[11]

The claim made in *Waiting for "Superman"* that 70 percent of our eighth-grade students read "below grade level" is inaccurate. The only source for national reading scores is the federal NAEP, which does not report scores by grade level. NAEP has four achievement levels: advanced, which is very high performance, equivalent to an A+ (in 2009, only 3 percent of our eighth-grade students scored at the advanced level in reading); proficient, which is defined by NAEP's governing board as "solid academic performance," equivalent to an A or a strong B (32 percent of eighth-grade students scored at or above proficient); and basic, defined as partial mastery of the knowledge and skills needed for the grade tested, which would be equivalent to a C (75 percent of students were at or above basic). So, instead of 70 percent of eighth-grade students reading "below grade level," NAEP shows that 25 percent of students in this grade are "below basic." That 25 percent includes students who are learning English and students with various disabilities. It is hard to understand why so many reformers—including Davis Guggenheim, the director of *Waiting for "Superman"*—got such a basic fact wrong.

Is it true that teachers can almost never be fired? No. About 50 percent of those who enter teaching leave within five years.[12] Virtually no other profession, certainly not law or medicine, has comparable attrition rates. This high turnover is problematic because teachers in their first year are just learning how to teach. In their first three or four years of teaching, teachers can be (and are) fired without any reason at all. Due process rights, also known as tenure, are not a guarantee of lifetime employment; they simply mean that a teacher has the right to a hearing before he or she may be terminated. If too many "bad teachers" are getting due process rights, then we have a problem with weak administrators who award tenure without evaluating teacher performance. If the process of removing incompetent teachers is too prolonged, then district officials should insist on shortening it.

Do teachers' unions cause low performance by protecting "bad teachers"? I argue in Chapter 9 that unions do not cause high performance or low performance; they give teachers a collective voice in negotiations about working conditions and compensation and protect teachers against arbitrary or abusive decisions. If unions were a primary cause of low performance, we would expect to find particularly high academic performance in states that do not allow teachers to negotiate binding contracts, such as Texas, Virginia, Nevada, Arizona, and Tennessee. But these states rank in the middle or near the bottom of the NAEP distribution, not at the top. The highest-ranking states are Massachusetts, Connecticut, and New Jersey, which have long had strong teachers' unions. If unions were a primary cause of low performance, charter schools, most of which are non-union, would perform consistently better than comparable neighborhood schools; they don't. And finally, the highest-scoring nation in the most recent international assessment was Finland, which is 100 percent unionized. Getting rid of collective bargaining is no cure for low performance. It might just clear the way for budget-conscious governors to slash education spending and privatize public schools without any organized opposition.

Has education spending soared over the past four decades? Yes, but more than a third of the new spending has gone to pay for special education services for students with disabilities.[13] Forty years ago, these students did not have the right to a free and appropriate public education. As a result of federal legislation and court orders, such services are now mandated, and they are usually very costly. When Congress passed the Education for All Handicapped Children Act in 1975, only one in five children with disabilities was enrolled in a public school. Many states routinely failed to provide a free education for children who were blind, deaf, mentally retarded, or who had other disabilities. When the law was reauthorized by Congress as the Individuals with Disabilities in Education Act (IDEA) in 1990, it guaranteed a free and appropriate education for these students. Though Congress promised to pay for 40 percent of the cost, it has never met that promise and has thus placed an enormous fiscal burden on school districts. If Congress kept its promise, it would provide immediate fiscal relief to every district in the nation.

Reformers like to say that poverty does not affect students' academic performance, but this is their wish, not reality. It is certainly true that children who live in poverty can learn and excel. But the odds are against them. Papering over that fact with slogans makes for bad policy. When children begin school, there is already an achievement gap. Children from affluent, even ordinary middle-class, homes have multiple advantages (more access to medical care, better nutrition, better educated parents, more books in the home), while children who live in poverty have multiple disadvantages (including ill health, poor nutrition, deteriorated housing, frequent moves, and economic insecurity, even homelessness). Poverty is a fact, not an excuse. It harms children and families. Why is it so politically controversial to acknowledge that poverty limits one's life chances? More than 20 percent of American children live in poverty. This is higher than in any other advanced nation. It should be considered a national scandal. But the corporate reform movement blames teachers for low test scores, ignoring the underlying social conditions that stack the deck against children who grow up in poverty. There is no question that schools in poor neighborhoods must be improved, but school reform will not be enough to end unemployment and poverty.

Reformers often say that three great teachers in a row—or four or five—can close the achievement gap. This widely repeated claim is based on a rough estimation by economists, who say that if a teacher can generate a ten-point gain in one year, then multiply the gain times three or four or five, and the gap will close. Beyond a vague idea that teachers are important, this claim has almost no policy relevance. No district has come anywhere near closing the achievement gap by lining up "great" teachers for consecutive years, because it is impossible to know in advance who the "great" teachers are or how to fill an entire school or district with them. Measuring teachers' ability to produce the same large gains year after year is monumentally imprecise; the teacher who is "great" one year may not be "great" the next. If we cannot identify who these "great" teachers are—to say nothing of how to find more of them and entice them into a low-paying profession that is constantly under attack—then the "three consecutive teachers" argument is really just a talking point, and a misleading one at that.

Reformers often say that the teacher is the single most important factor in raising student test scores. This is not quite right. Researchers have consistently concluded that the teacher is the single most important factor that affects student learning *inside the school*, but non-school factors matter a great deal more.[14] This does not diminish teachers' importance. Teachers can have a profound influence on their students, but on average, what families do or don't do influences academic outcomes even more. It is bewildering that so many of today's reformers ignore this basic fact and deride anyone who brings it up as "making excuses." With their money and influence, they are in a position to promote effective antipoverty programs, such as prenatal care for poor women and early childhood education, both of which are proven reforms. Perhaps they will do so in the future.

Geoffrey Canada's Harlem Children's Zone is held up as a model by reformers, but it actually proves that poverty and resources matter a great deal. Canada's HCZ is an antipoverty program in Harlem that provides a broad array of medical and social services to children and families, such as health programs, preschool, after-school tutoring, and parenting classes. Its three charter schools are far better funded than nearby regular public schools. Its small high school has classes of fewer than fifteen students with two licensed teachers in each classroom. Because it has a very wealthy board of trustees, HCZ has an endowment of $200 million. Even with the ample resources available to HCZ, its charters had many students in 2010 who did not meet state standards for proficiency in reading: 62 percent in one school, and 38 percent in the other. In the sixth grade, where students were in their second year, only 15 percent met state standards. When Geoffrey Canada first recruited students to his charter middle school, they entered with low scores; after three years, when their scores remained low, he kicked out the entire class. The neighborhood public schools can't do this.[15]

The Harlem Children's Zone demonstrates that resources matter and so does poverty. If pregnant women have good medical care and nutrition, their children have a better chance of being born healthy. If they are born healthy, they are less likely to have learning disabilities. If children are healthy and well nourished, they have a better chance of doing well in school. If children have access to high-quality early childhood education, they are likely to start school ready to learn. HCZ recognizes the necessity of addressing the conditions of children's lives and of helping their families. It would be wonderful if all children had the same advantages of medical and social services now available to children and families enrolled in HCZ programs. It would improve their chances of succeeding in school and in life. No matter how many charters are opened, no matter how often children are tested, their basic needs still must be met. Schools are very important, and good education is crucial, but schools alone can't create equality, especially if our nation's leaders in the financial sector, the foundation world, and government belittle the corrosive effects of poverty.

PRESIDENT OBAMA AND SECRETARY DUNCAN launched Race to the Top as their signature school reform program in 2009. The program dangled $4.3 billion in federal stimulus funds before cash-strapped states to induce them to adopt charter schools and merit pay, to judge teachers by students' test scores, and to turn around low-performing schools by NCLB-style punitive strategies (firing the principal, firing the teachers, closing the school, turning the school into a charter school, or handing it over to private management).

All of these are carrot-and-stick strategies, based on the view that humans must be incentivized by rewards and punishments or they won't do their best. Far from being twenty-first-century ideas, these strategies are firmly rooted in the early twentieth-century factory-model approach of Frederick Winslow Taylor, the father of "scientific management." Taylor believed that work could be carefully measured, and that workers would be more productive if employers identified the right combination of incentives and sanctions. Contemporary writers and scholars such as Edward Deci, Dan Ariely, and Daniel Pink have stressed that modern motivational theory recognizes the primacy of intrinsic motivation, not rewards and punishments. Those who are motivated by idealism, autonomy, and a sense of purpose actually perform better and work harder than those who hope for a bonus or fear being fired. Relying on extrinsic motivation, they concur, may actually hinder improvement, because people will work to make the target yet will lose sight of their goals as professionals. The essence of professionalism is autonomy, the freedom to make decisions based on one's knowledge and experience. Professionals act in relation to the goals of their profession, not in response to rewards and punishments for meeting targets. Professionals don't require a whip or a bonus to do the right thing for their students or clients or patients. Carrots and sticks are for donkeys, not for professionals.[16]

Like NCLB, Race to the Top was grounded in Taylorism, a century-old set of assumptions about how to motivate people and bring about change. It too assumes that change occurs by incentivizing educators with rewards and punishments. Like NCLB, Race to the Top relied on testing and accountability as its lever of change. If schools couldn't raise their scores enough, then it was necessary to apply punitive strategies, euphemistically described as "reconstitution" or "transformation." Eager to win federal funds, many states applied; eleven were chosen, plus the District of Columbia. Many states hastily revised their laws to improve their chances of winning. They agreed to open more privately managed charter schools; to evaluate teachers by their students' test scores; to shut down or "transform" low-performing schools; and to offer merit pay to teachers who raised test scores. None of these strategies had strong evidence or research to support it. In many cases, the laws imposed poorly designed, ill-conceived policies enacted solely to be eligible to receive federal funding during a budget crisis, not because of evidence they might improve education.

Some of these strategies had already been put into place in Chicago when Arne Duncan was superintendent. His program, called Renaissance 2010, relied on closing low-performing schools and opening new schools, especially charter schools. When 2010 arrived, nearly one hundred new schools had been opened to replace or transform low-performing schools. Chicago's independent education journal, *Catalyst*, faulted the program on many grounds: Three of every four students in Chicago public schools still attended a low-performing school; the district had opened no new schools in nearly half of the neighborhoods with the highest needs; the new charters received significantly more private funding than regular public schools, yet many were imperiled by a deficit; teacher turnover in the charters rivaled that of the city's lowest-performing regular schools; and only sixteen of the city's ninety-two new schools met the state average in test scores. Journalists at *Catalyst* complained about the charters' lack of transparency; although they received substantial public funding, they refused to open their financial records and employment lists for inspection, claiming they were not public entities. A 2009 study by the independent Consortium on Chicago School Research determined that most students from closing schools had been shifted to other low-performing schools. There were surely some bright spots, some good new schools, and the possibility of future improvement. But it was hard to understand why Renaissance 2010—with its unimpressive results—should serve as a national model.[17]

Despite the flaws of Race to the Top, the media loved the idea of a race, with states competing to adopt the reforms identified as transformative by the U.S. Department of Education. There was high drama, with winners and losers. The reform movement combined the federal government's vast financial resources and bully pulpit with the sizable financial power of some of the nation's biggest philanthropies. Matters such as research, evidence, and experience took a backseat to public relations as the corporate reform movement shifted into high gear. It presented its favored ideas as the very definition of school reform. Anyone who questioned the charter movement was "against reform," regardless of research on charters' overall middling results or revelations of financial self-dealing at some. Anyone who challenged the idea of using test scores to evaluate teachers, close schools, and hand out bonuses was denounced as a defender of the status quo. The reform movement gave Democratic endorsement to traditional Republican ideas of accountability and choice, and the result was called bipartisan. Secretary Duncan even said there was zero opposition to his agenda.[18]

Yet despite the magical combination of federal spending, foundation backing, and Hollywood glamour, the corporate reform movement experienced unexpected setbacks.

Eloquent and principled opposition came from an unexpected quarter. On July 26, 2010, seven civil rights groups released a joint statement excoriating the Obama administration's Race to the Top and its Blueprint, a proposal that would rename NCLB and reauthorize the Elementary and Secondary Education Act.[19]

The statement, called the "Framework for Providing All Students an Opportunity to Learn Through Reauthorization of the Elementary and Secondary Education Act," was endorsed by the Lawyers Committee for Civil Rights Under Law, the National Association for the Advancement of Colored People (NAACP), the NAACP Legal Defense and Educational Fund Inc., the National Council for Educating Black Children, the National Urban League, the Rainbow PUSH Coalition, and the Schott Foundation for Public Education.

The groups lambasted the administration for relying on competitive grants instead of distributing federal dollars on the basis of need and reform plans. "If education is a civil right," they said, "children in 'winning' states should not be the only ones who have the opportunity to learn in high-quality environments. Such an approach reinstates the antiquated and highly politicized frame for distributing federal support to states that civil rights organizations fought to remove in 1965." They said that "the civil right to a high-quality education is connected to individuals, not the states." A "market-based" competition for federal funding would favor the "better-resourced states and communities" and leave many children behind.[20]

The civil rights groups opposed closing schools, except as a last resort; they pointed to Renaissance 2010 in Chicago as evidence that closing schools and firing school staffs disrupt communities without necessarily improving student achievement. No school should be closed, they maintained, without collaboration with parents, the local community, and teachers, and without first providing the support to help the school improve. They also questioned the administration's "extensive reliance on charter schools" as a turnaround strategy: "While charters can serve as laboratories for innovation, we are concerned about the overrepresentation of charter schools in low-income and predominantly minority communities. There is no evidence that charter operators are systematically more effective in creating higher student outcomes nationwide." And they expressed concern that charters were less willing to enroll English-language learners, students in need of special education, and poor children than regular public schools in high-minority districts; they feared that this might contribute to "education-driven gentrification through the disproportionate exclusion of students with the greatest needs."

Most current reform proposals, they said, were "'stop gap' quick fixes that may look new on the surface but offer no real long-term strategy for effective systemic change. The absence of these 'stop gap' programs in affluent communities speaks to the marginal nature of this approach."

The civil rights groups made a plea for equitable funding and for evidence-based reforms, including high-quality early childhood education and "a stable supply of expert, experienced educators for all communities," instead of "a revolving door of untrained and under-supported novice teachers who cannot create or sustain a high-quality educational program." They urged the federal government to discourage the use of test data "as the sole or primary measure of teacher effectiveness. Rather, effectiveness should be defined by teachers' experience, knowledge, skills, and classroom performance, as well as their individual contributions to student learning and their joint efforts to improve learning within the school."

THERE WAS MORE TROUBLE FOR the corporate reform narrative in 2010. Even as the movement began to enjoy the flush of publicity and media admiration, some of its stars lost their luster.

A central feature of the corporate reform narrative was the New York City miracle. After Mayor Michael Bloomberg took control of the schools and installed tough accountability measures, the city's proficiency rates went up and up, and the achievement gap between students of different racial groups seemed to be closing.

But in July 2010, the miracle disappeared when the New York State Education Department announced that the state's proficiency rates had been vastly inflated. State education leaders knew that the dramatic leaps in state scores over the years were not matched by equivalent rises on NAEP. After many complaints, the state commissioned Daniel Koretz of Harvard University and Jennifer Jennings of New York University to conduct an independent evaluation of the state tests. The researchers found that the state's exams had become easier over time. According to a summary of their findings, "Students who received the minimum score to pass the state math tests in 2007 were in the 36th percentile of all students nationally, but in 2009 they had dropped to the 19th percentile."[21]

When the state recalibrated the scores for 2010, pass rates dropped across the state. Nowhere was the drop in proficiency rates more shocking than in New York City. In 2007, based on its rapidly rising state scores and the apparent narrowing of the achievement gap, New York City won the Broad Prize as the most improved urban district in the nation. In 2009, the mayor persuaded the city council to reverse a term-limits law so he could run for a third term in office, and his victory was based in part on the city's soaring test scores. But when the state readjusted the scores, the proportion of New York City public schools students reaching proficiency on state tests in reading dropped from 69 percent to 42 percent, and in mathematics from 82 percent to 54 percent. One school in the Bronx saw its third-grade pass rate drop from 81 percent to 18 percent. Principals, teachers, parents, and students were dismayed.[22]

Mayor Bloomberg had testified to Congress in 2008 that his reforms had substantially narrowed the black-white achievement gap, in some cases reducing it by half. But with the new scores in mathematics and reading, the New York Times reported, "the proficiency gap between minority and white students has returned to about the same level as when the mayor arrived."[23]

A few months after the scores plummeted, Mayor Bloomberg made a surprise announcement: Chancellor Joel Klein was stepping down and would be replaced by publishing executive Cathie Black. Klein departed to work for Rupert Murdoch's News Corporation, where he would sell educational technology to the schools (News Corporation paid $360 million to purchase an educational technology company, Wireless Generation, that had worked for Klein's Department of Education); he soon became chief adviser to Murdoch and News Corporation in a lurid phone-hacking scandal in the United Kingdom.

Black had no experience in education, but the mayor said reassuringly that she was a "superstar manager." Black lasted only three months. Shortly after an opinion poll showed that only 17 percent of the public approved of her job performance—and that the mayor's approval ratings were also falling—the mayor replaced her with a trusted deputy mayor, Dennis Walcott.[24]

Under Mayor Bloomberg and Chancellor Klein, New York City had become the acme of the data-driven corporate style of education reform. But the data themselves were no good. By relying so heavily on NCLB-style testing and accountability, the city system had downgraded everything in the curriculum other than reading and mathematics. They mattered most, because they determined whether a school was successful. By 2011, the graduation rate had risen to 61 percent, but remediation rates in basic skills for the city's graduates who entered the City University of New York remained stubbornly high: 49 percent of those who entered any CUNY college, and 75 percent of freshmen at community colleges. The State Education Department developed new measures showing that only 41 percent of high school graduates in the state were ready for college or a good career; in New York City, the figure was only 23 percent, not counting special-education students. Despite these discouraging returns, despite years of continually testing, test-prepping, grading, evaluating, and issuing letter grades and school report cards, school officials did not reconsider their inordinate reliance on test-based accountability. They planned to collect more data.[25]

The 2010 mayoral election in the District of Columbia was another setback for the corporate reform movement. When Adrian Fenty was elected mayor in 2006, he decided to model his school reform plans on New York City because of its impressive (and later discredited) test score gains. Like Mayor Bloomberg, he won control of the public schools and promised a major overhaul. With the advice of Joel Klein, Fenty selected Michelle Rhee to lead the D.C. school system. Rhee, an alumna of Teach for America and founder of a similar organization, the New Teacher Project, quickly took charge. She closed underutilized buildings, fired principals and teachers, battled the teachers' union, launched a performance pay plan, and become known nationwide for her brash, confrontational style.

When Mayor Fenty ran for reelection in the Democratic primary against city council president Vincent Gray in September 2010, Rhee's controversial reforms were a major issue in the election. Gray beat Fenty by a margin of 54 to 44. Fenty won an overwhelming majority of votes in predominantly white wards; Gray won an overwhelming majority of votes in predominantly black wards. Because white students account for about 5 percent of the public school enrollment in the district, it seems plain that black parents ousted Fenty. Rhee resigned a month after the election. She created an organization, StudentsFirst, whose main objectives were to end teacher tenure and seniority and to curb public-sector collective bargaining rights. She worked closely with conservative Republican governors in Florida, New Jersey, Indiana, Ohio, and other states, helping to devise their education agendas.

D.C. test scores came under scrutiny when *USA Today* revealed a major cheating scandal in the D.C. public schools as part of a national investigation. Electronic scanners detected statistically improbable erasure rates—answers changed from wrong to right—at more than half the public schools in the district. The investigation found a striking number of erasures at the Crosby S. Noyes Educational Campus. Students in one seventh-grade classroom at Noyes in 2009 averaged 12.7 wrong-to-right erasures on their answer sheets, whereas the average for students in that grade in all D.C. schools was less than 1. According to statisticians consulted by *USA Today*, "The odds are better for winning the Powerball grand prize than having that many erasures by chance."[26]

Michelle Rhee had repeatedly lauded Noyes and its principal because of the school's amazing test score gains. The proportion of students who were rated proficient in mathematics rose from 10 percent in 2006 to 58 percent in 2008; similar gains were recorded on reading tests. Rhee twice awarded bonuses to its principal and teachers. In 2009, the U.S. Department of Education recognized the school with a National Blue Ribbon award. The principal, Wayne

Ryan, was featured in recruitment advertisements for the district, with his picture and the question "Are you the next Wayne Ryan?" In 2010, Rhee promoted Ryan to instructional superintendent, where he supervised other principals. Ryan resigned three months after the USA Today story appeared. Rhee's successor, her former deputy Kaya Henderson, promised a full investigation. In 2011, under heightened test security, scores at the Noyes school dropped sharply in both reading and mathematics.[27]

A cheating scandal in Atlanta was even more momentous than the one in D.C., because it was thoroughly documented by independent investigators. After numerous allegations of cheating, Governor Sonny Perdue commissioned the investigation, which was released in 2011 by his successor, Governor Nathan Deal.[28] Investigators concluded that cheating was widespread and had occurred in response to the district administration's pressure to meet unrealistic targets. Numerous principals and teachers confessed to changing answers on state tests, and state officials promised criminal prosecutions for those who had cheated.

Superintendent Beverly Hall was "the belle of the business community" in Atlanta.[29] She spoke their language, the language of data-driven decision making, targets, metrics, and return on investment. Business leaders defended her in 2008, 2009, and 2010 when the Atlanta Journal-Constitution raised questions about the validity of gains on state tests. The pressure to get results backfired, encouraging the corrosive, criminal behavior that critics of high-stakes testing had warned about for years.

In the original printing of this book, I lauded Beverly Hall's accomplishments in Atlanta. I was impressed that the district made steady, significant gains on both NAEP and state tests. When Hall was recognized by her peers in the American Association of School Administrators as Superintendent of the Year in 2009, it seemed to confirm her success. But they were fooled and so was I.

What have we learned? First, everyone should view the results of high-stakes testing with a measure of skepticism. When teachers and principals are told they will lose their jobs if they don't get higher scores, they may get higher scores by any means necessary, including cheating. When the federal government and district officials set an impossible goal—100 percent proficiency—and link it to harsh sanctions, they too are complicit in the consequences. There have been many cheating scandals since Congress passed NCLB.[30]

Cheating is a choice, and it is inexcusable. But when the system demands impossible results, when whistle-blowers are punished, then the system itself incentivizes unethical behavior.

SINCE THE PUBLICATION OF THIS BOOK, new research on the corporate reform agenda offered little support for its favorite remedies.

Evaluations of charters continued to show that the charter sector on average does not outperform regular public schools. By their nature, charters vary widely. Some charters diligently serve children with high needs and are praiseworthy, regardless of their test scores. Some achieve consistently high test scores. But some are not good schools by any measure. In some states, charter expansion was encouraged by charter advocates' campaign contributions to governors and legislators.[31] Juan Gonzalez of the *New York Daily News* investigated and concluded that banks and equity investors were pouring money into charter construction to take advantage of a generous federal tax credit.[32]

Some charter school chains continued to get impressively high test scores. But charters in Detroit, Florida, Chicago, Los Angeles, and other districts did not outperform regular public schools.[33] Bruce Baker of Rutgers University studied New York City charter schools and found that the city's charters were serving fewer high-needs students than regular public schools, that some had substantial private funding, and that their academic outcomes on average were no better.[34] The U.S. Department of Education released a study in 2010 comparing middle school charters with regular public middle schools; it found no significant difference between the two sectors in either academic outcomes or behavior. The 2009 NAEP confirmed the same findings as in 2003, 2005, and 2007: There were few significant differences between charter students and students in regular public schools, whether the students were black, Hispanic, low-income, or in urban districts.[35]

Another favorite strategy of the corporate reformers was merit pay. Popular among business-minded reformers since the 1920s, merit pay was studied intensively at the National Center on Performance Incentives at Vanderbilt University, which released a major evaluation in September 2010. One group of middle-school teachers in Nashville was offered a bonus of $15,000 if they could raise test scores over a three-year period, while another group was not eligible for the bonus. At the end of three years, there was no difference overall between the test scores of students taught by the two groups of teachers. This was the most rigorous study ever conducted of merit pay, but it did not impress the U.S. Department of Education. Within days of the release of the Vanderbilt study, the department awarded nearly $500 million for merit pay programs and promised an additional $500 million in the near future.[36]

The New York City Department of Education tried a different approach to performance pay: It offered schoolwide bonuses to schools that raised their scores. After distributing $56 million over three years, the city ended the program in 2011. A study by the Rand Corporation found that the bonus program had no effect on student performance or on teachers' attitudes toward their jobs. Undeterred by the failure of its initiative, the city administration promised to find another merit pay plan that worked better. The city had previously tried a program that paid students to get higher test scores; that didn't work either.[37]

Although vouchers were not part of Obama and Duncan's Race to the Top strategy, many Republican governors supported them. For many years, vouchers seemed to be a dead issue, confined to Milwaukee, Cleveland, and D.C. But after the elections of 2010, when conservative Republicans won control in many states, vouchers were once again a viable option. In Indiana, Governor Mitch Daniels persuaded a Republican legislature to pass a sweeping, statewide voucher plan. Other governors, such as Rick Scott of Florida and Tom Corbett of Pennsylvania, hoped to do the same. They ignored the results of the nation's longest-running voucher program, in Milwaukee, where vouchers had been available for low-income students since 1990. When the Wisconsin test scores were released in 2011, students in the Milwaukee public schools had higher scores than those in voucher schools; the scores of low-income students in the two sectors were similar. Researchers at the University of Arkansas released the fourth of five annual reports on the Milwaukee voucher program and found no difference in test scores between students in the voucher program and those in the regular public schools.[38]

In 2009, Milwaukee participated for the first time in NAEP for urban districts. African-American students in the Milwaukee public schools had very low scores, no better (and sometimes worse) than their peers in Alabama, Georgia, Louisiana, and Mississippi.

Competition did not improve the public schools. It did not create a rising tide; no boats were lifted. Having spent $1 billion, supposedly to help low-income African-American children, the State of Wisconsin had developed a dual taxpayer-financed system that did not benefit the children in greatest need. Despite these dismal results, Governor Scott Walker proposed in 2011—and the state legislature agreed—to lift the income caps in Milwaukee and to expand the program to a larger geographical area. Voucher supporters in the state legislature no longer claimed they would produce higher test scores or better education, but rather that they would help to cut costs.[39]

RACE TO THE TOP ADDED ITS OWN TWIST to NCLB, and that was the idea of evaluating teachers by student test scores. States that didn't do so would lose points in the competition for federal money. Many states, including those that did not win federal funding, agreed to evaluate teachers in this manner. The theory, propounded by economists such as Eric Hanushek of the Hoover Institution and Robert Gordon (who became deputy director of the Office of Management and Budget in the Obama administration), was that teachers should be judged—paid and fired—to a large extent by "performance." In new state legislation, student test scores typically counted for 40–50 percent of the weight in a teacher's evaluation for tenure or promotion. Using value-added formulas, described in Chapter 9, states and districts were expected to rate teachers as "highly effective," "effective," "ineffective," and so forth. Such evaluations would serve to identify teachers who should be removed. As mentioned earlier, Hanushek recommended the removal of 5–10 percent of teachers whose value-added rating was lowest; he maintained that this "teacher deselection" would cause average achievement to rise dramatically, perhaps to the level of Finland, the world's highest-performing nation.[40]

Imagine the effect on morale among teachers if schools had a policy of firing 5–10 percent of their teachers routinely. Successful schools emphasize teamwork. But with regular purges, a culture of collaboration would be replaced by a culture of fear and anxiety, as teachers wondered, "Who will get the ax this year? Will I have a job next year?" There is something cruel as well as counterproductive about this data-driven scheme. It would pit teacher against teacher. It would certainly incentivize teachers to avoid students with the highest needs, where big test score gains are unlikely, and it would incentivize them to avoid teaching gifted students, whose scores are already near the ceiling. It would also have dismal consequences for high-poverty schools and districts, where teacher mobility rates are already intolerably high.

Let me be clear: No school should employ incompetent teachers. But it should be the job of the principal, working with a peer review team of teachers, to identify such teachers, offer them help, and remove those who can't be helped.

Putting so much emphasis on test scores produces other outcomes that harm the quality of education. It inevitably encourages schools to narrow the curriculum, reducing time for subjects that are not tested and therefore don't count, such as the arts, physical education, foreign languages, history, and civics. It ensures that district leaders will spend more and more resources on test preparation and that more valuable instructional time will be sacrificed to test prep and interim assessments. It increases the likelihood that teachers will teach to the test, even to bad tests. It promotes gaming the system, doing whatever it takes to raise scores by manipulating the tests or student assignments. It leads to cheating, as we have seen occur in many districts since the passage of No Child Left Behind, with its unrealistic mandates and severe punishments.

All of this collateral damage would be reason enough not to emphasize test scores when evaluating teachers. But a growing body of research shows that the measures themselves are inaccurate and unstable. A group of scholars (myself included) published a statement in mid-2010 summarizing the research and explaining the problems with using test scores to evaluate teachers. The group included some of the nation's leading experts on testing. Among many other cautions, the group warned that the use of value-added measurements would likely lead to the misidentification of effective and ineffective teachers, because the measures are statistically insufficient to the task and because so many factors that influence test scores would not be taken into account.[41]

No measure is perfect, but the estimates of value-added and other "growth models," which attempt to isolate the "true effect" of an individual teacher through his or her students' test scores, are alarmingly error-prone in any given year. Sean Corcoran, an economist at New York University, studied the teacher evaluation systems in New York City and Houston. He found that the average "margin of error" of a New York City teacher was plus or minus 28 points. So, a teacher who was ranked at the 43rd percentile compared to his or her peers might actually be anywhere between the 15th percentile and the 71st percentile. The value-added scores also fluctuate between years. A teacher who gets a particular ranking in year one is likely to get a different rating the next year. There will always be instability in these rankings, some of which will reflect "real" performance changes. But it is difficult to trust any performance rating if the odds of getting the same rating next year are no better than a coin toss.[42]

And there are other problems, Corcoran noted. If a different test were given, the rankings for teachers based on test scores would change. The same goes for changing the value-added model—one model might rate a teacher highly while another might rate him or her poorly using the same data. Missing and incorrect data plague the huge, complicated data sets used to generate these measures. Students are not randomly assigned, so a teacher who is assigned more difficult students would be penalized. It is hard to see why such an inaccurate measure, tied to state test scores that are known to be unreliable, should determine whether to terminate a teacher's career or to award a bonus.[43]

Michael Winerip of the *New York Times* reported a disturbing story that exemplifies some of the problems with value-added ratings in New York City. He examined the "teacher data reports" for one highly regarded seventh-grade teacher, Stacey Isaacson. Teaching in a school with selective admissions, Isaacson proved to be extremely successful: All but one of her sixty-six students reached proficiency on the state English test, and many were admitted to the city's most competitive high schools. Her colleagues, principal, and students think she is a terrific teacher. But according to the complex, thirty-two-variable model on which the teacher data report relies, Isaacson is one of the worst teachers in the school system. Her students entered with a score of 3.57 out of a possible four points from the previous year; the algorithm predicted that they should leave with a score of 3.69, but they averaged "only" 3.63. This landed Isaacson in the bottom 7th percentile of all teachers in the city (lower than 93 percent of all teachers) and guaranteed that she would not get tenure. So, despite her success, despite the rave reviews from her principal, despite her two Ivy League degrees, the teacher data report put her at the bottom of the heap; she missed the statistical target by six one-hundredths of a point on a test that is not a finely tuned scientific instrument. This is a surefire way to demoralize teachers and to elevate numbers above human judgment. This is a mindless way to evaluate teacher quality. As Winerip titled his article, "Evaluating New York Teachers, Perhaps the Numbers Do Lie."[44]

The biggest public controversy about value-added ratings occurred in the summer of 2010 when the *Los Angeles Times* created its own rating system for thousands of elementary teachers in the Los Angeles school district. It requested test score data over several years from the district, then hired a researcher from the Rand Corporation to apply a statistical model and rate teachers according to their effectiveness in raising test scores. When the ratings were complete, the *Times* published them for individual teachers online, including their names, for all to see. The series included the customary caveat that test scores do not tell you everything you need to know about a teacher or school and should not count for more than half of a teacher's evaluation.[45] But the series proceeded to rate teachers based solely on the scores, with no other variables included. The series began with a front-page photograph of a fifth-grade teacher who was rated ineffective by the *Times*. How humiliating for him. The same story named a third-grade teacher who was respected by her principal, her colleagues, and parents, and who was a National Board Certified Teacher. Despite her accolades, the *Times*' rating system placed her in the bottom 10 percent of all elementary teachers. When reporters confronted her with her scores, she promised to do better.[46]

Most testing experts, knowing the unreliability of these ratings, were appalled, especially by the naming of names. Even proponents of using these statistical models in high-stakes decisions came out against publishing individual names. William Sanders, one of the pioneers of the value-added methodology, said the analysis could identify those at either extreme, but "can you distinguish within the middle? No, you can't, not even with the most distinguished, value-added process that you can bring to the problem." Dan Goldhaber, an economist and proponent of the methodology, wrote an opinion piece in which he strongly opposed releasing the names of individual teachers. Aside from technical objections, he argued, "I cannot think of a profession in either the public or private sector where individual employee performance estimates are made public in a newspaper."[47]

Secretary of Education Arne Duncan was among the few who praised the *Los Angeles Times*.[48] Ironically, the U.S. Department of Education had just published a study about the degree of random error in these value-added ratings—error that is due in large part to student-level factors and to nonrandom assignment of students to classrooms and schools. The more years of data that are available, the study found, the less error there is likely to be in classifying teachers, but even if one used the best models with several years of data, the odds of misclassification were still 25–35 percent. The study recommended a combination of value-added assessment and principal assessment as being more accurate than either method alone.[49]

Many researchers, including Derek C. Briggs and Ben Domingue of the National Education Policy Center, challenged the methodology of the *Times'* ratings, but the reporters defended their methodology and even insisted that the Briggs-Domingue critique supported their original analysis.[50] The *Times* acted not as an impartial news organization, but as a protagonist in the debate. The reporters claimed their results showed a wide variation in teachers' value-added scores, which is to say that teacher quality matters. But, as Matthew Di Carlo of the Albert Shanker Institute noted, "The *Times'* claim that the [Briggs-Domingue] analysis confirmed their findings because they too found wide variation in teacher effects is kind of missing the point. . . . The real issue, both in this case and in the larger debate over value-added, is whether we can measure the effectiveness of *individual teachers*."[51] No one disputed that teachers are important and that there are better and worse ones. What was in dispute was the accuracy of the ratings for individual teachers and whether it was ethical, fair, or prudent to publish them.

Mathematician John Ewing was appalled when he read the *Los Angeles Times'* account of the third-grade teacher, long lauded for her excellent teaching, who promised to improve when journalists confronted her with their low ratings of her effectiveness. He thought the reporters were "browbeating" her in a way that was "reminiscent of the Cultural Revolution." Ewing described "value-added modeling" as an example of "mathematical intimidation," an effort to shape public policy by pretending that data are necessarily objective and accurate, despite multiple cautions by knowledgeable experts about their limitations. He complained that the public debate had been framed "as a battle between teacher unions and the public." Ewing warned that data were being used to foreclose public questioning of a flawed methodology. He wrote:

> Of course we should hold teachers accountable, but this does not mean we have to pretend that mathematical models can do something they cannot. Of course we should rid our schools of incompetent teachers, but value-added models are an exceedingly blunt tool for this purpose. . . . Shouldn't we try to measure long-term student achievement, not merely short-term gains? Shouldn't we focus on how well students are prepared to learn in the future, not merely what they learned in the past year? Shouldn't we try to distinguish teachers who inspire their students, not merely the ones who are competent? When we accept value-added as an "imperfect" substitute for all these things because it is conveniently at hand, we are not raising our expectations of teachers, we are lowering them. And if we drive away the best teachers by using a flawed process, are we really putting our students first?[52]

Teacher evaluation was the most controversial issue in the education reform debate, because it was the most consequential. Corporate reformers treated it as a proxy for merit, the best way to identify who should be fired and who should get a bonus. Teachers, especially those in tested grades and subjects, were distrustful because they knew their ratings would depend in no small part on random error, as well as the composition of their classes and other factors beyond their control.

Arne Duncan and Bill Gates agreed that this was the most important of all reforms. States that wanted to compete for Race to the Top funding had to agree to tie teacher evaluations to student test scores. Having dropped his small-schools initiative, Bill Gates fastened onto teacher evaluation and teacher quality as the most crucial issue facing American education. His foundation spent millions of dollars to videotape thousands of teachers and to analyze the tapes, with the intention of devising a template for effective teaching. One wonders whether everyone could paint like Picasso if they spent hundreds of hours watching him paint or become a great conductor by observing hour after hour of great conductors. In 2010,

Gates advised the National Governors Association that states could save money by not paying extra for advanced degrees or experience and by increasing class size for the best teachers, the ones whose students get higher test scores. He stated that the "evidence" showed that seniority seemed to have no effect on student achievement after a teacher's first few years. He did not explain how American education would get better if teachers had less education, less experience, and larger classes.[53] There is copious evidence that teachers improve a great deal during their first few years of teaching, even by the narrow measure of test scores, and almost certainly improve in other, less measurable ways for many years after. I have yet to meet a single teacher who agrees that he or she stopped improving after a few years in the classroom. To teachers, it is a laughable, even insulting proposition.

With the federal government and foundations pouring so much money into teacher evaluation, districts are accumulating massive amounts of data. An educator in South America wrote me recently to say that American education has more data than any other education system in the world and more confusion about how to educate its students. There will no doubt be data about teacher "effectiveness"; the question is what to do with it. My strong belief is that the data should be placed in each teacher's personnel file as confidential information. It should not be made public, except when averaged across grades, schools, and districts. When the supervisor or principal is making a consequential decision, he or she should consider the data as part of a portfolio of evidence that includes regular observations, student work, peer reviews, and other direct interactions with the teacher. Any data should include raw scores, value-added scores, demographic information, and caveats about the valid and invalid uses of such data. Having a state legislature decide what proportion of a teacher's evaluation should depend on test scores makes no sense, especially given that they determined these proportions before having any idea what the other components would be. It is distinctly unprofessional and poor policymaking. Legislators are not competent to make such a determination.

IF EVIDENCE MATTERED, most of these issues would not be at the top of our nation's education agenda. But no matter how many research studies or evaluations were produced, the corporate school reform movement pressed forward, unfazed. It had much more than a Hollywood movie on its side. It had the unstinting support of the "billionaire boys' club," the powerful foundations that were pouring massive amounts of money into shaping education policy and that worked closely with the U.S. Department of Education. The Bill & Melinda Gates Foundation—or Bill Gates personally—leveraged his fortune to set the national policy agenda for school reform. The Broad Foundation's Superintendents Academy became a powerhouse, training dozens of superintendents in its data-driven, market-based philosophy, then sending them back to close low-performing public schools, open charter schools, and demand teacher evaluation by test scores. In 2011, there were Broad-trained superintendents in Los Angeles; Providence, Rhode Island; Charlotte-Mecklenburg, North Carolina; Chicago; Denver; New Orleans; Seattle; and many other districts, as well as Broad-trained state commissioners in New Jersey, Rhode Island, and Delaware. And wherever a Broad superintendent took over, other Broad graduates soon followed to cluster around him or her. Once in a while, a Broad superintendent resigned or was ousted, but there were always more prepared to step in. In a short ten years, thanks to the extraordinary wealth and vision of Eli Broad, the Broad Foundation managed to become the biggest training program in the country for urban superintendents, all of whom were grounded in the management philosophy of its founder.[54]

While the Broad Foundation trained leaders to run urban districts, the Gates Foundation invested in the policymaking apparatus of the nation's schools. Although Bill Gates had no experience in or expertise about public education, his immense wealth made him a cultural icon; when he spoke, governors, senators, and editorial boards paid close attention. In a time of severe budget shortfalls, his money was a siren song. He argued that achievement was flat, so everyone agreed it was flat; he declared that experience and education did not make teachers more effective, and state legislatures began changing their policies. He decided that the biggest problem in American education was teacher evaluation, and he dispensed almost $300 million to Tampa, Memphis, and Pittsburgh, as well as to charter schools in Los Angeles, to work on a new approach, so that teachers whose students got higher scores would be considered "effective," and those who did not would be terminated. Issues such as teaching to the test or narrowing the curriculum were of no concern to him. He wanted measurable results.[55]

Gates thought unions should become more flexible, more attuned to the modern workplace, and more committed to test-based evaluation, so he gave a few million to the two major teachers' unions, the National Education Association and the American Federation of Teachers, to give his ideas a try. But he gave even more millions to create new organizations of young teachers to urge state legislatures to weaken or eliminate seniority and due process rights. He was a strong supporter of charter schools, which are overwhelmingly nonunion. When a wave of conservative Republican governors—such as Chris Christie in New Jersey, Scott Walker in Wisconsin, Rick Snyder in Michigan, Tom Corbett in Pennsylvania, Rick Scott in Florida, and John Kasich in Ohio—came to office in 2010, they took the reform agenda launched by Gates and his ally Arne Duncan to the next level, cut the budget for public education, expanded the charter sector, encouraged privatization, attacked seniority and due process for teachers, and weakened or removed the unions' collective bargaining rights. Wisconsin Governor Walker's attack on the collective bargaining rights of public-sector workers spurred mass protests in the spring of 2011 but Walker, in full control of the legislature, was unmoved.

To advance its agenda, the Gates Foundation increased its spending on advocacy. From 2005 to 2009, the foundation quadrupled its annual spending on advocacy to $78 million. According to Sam Dillon in the *New York Times*, the foundation will pump an additional $100 million annually into advocacy over the next five to six years. That kind of money buys lots of advocacy and support. Gates funded the groups that wrote the Common Core standards, the groups that evaluated them, and the groups that advocated for them. Gates funded liberal groups such as Education Trust, centrist groups such as the Center for American Progress and the Center on Education Policy, and groups on the Right such as the American Enterprise Institute, the Thomas B. Fordham Foundation, Jeb Bush's Foundation for Educational Excellence, and the Media Bullpen. It funded groups that advocated for charter schools, such as the Education Equality Project, and groups that argued against seniority and tenure, such as TeachFirst, TeachPlus, and the New Teacher Project. Kenneth Libby, then a graduate student known for poring through tax filings of foundations and advocacy groups, commented,

"It's easier to name which groups Gates doesn't support than to list all of those they do, because it's just so overwhelming."[56] Gates's funding was not serendipitous. It focused on the ideas that were familiar to corporate leaders: a market-based approach to education, typified by common standards, pay for performance, data-driven decision making, and consumer choice.

But was this business approach good for education? Writing in *Dissent*, Joanne Barkan described the challenge that the aggressive venture philanthropists pose for American society:

> Can anything stop the foundation enablers? After five or ten more years, the mess they're making in public schooling might be so undeniable that they'll say, "Oops, that didn't work" and step aside. But the damage might be irreparable: thousands of closed schools, worse conditions in those left open, an extreme degree of "teaching to the test," demoralized teachers, rampant corruption by private management companies, thousands of failed charter schools, and more low-income kids without a good education. Who could possibly clean up the mess?[57]

Since I concluded my book in November 2009, I discovered that the billionaire boys' club extends far beyond the big three foundations that I wrote about in Chapter 10: Gates, Broad, and Walton. It includes super-rich individuals from Wall Street and the high-technology sector who have decided to have a go at reforming public education, which they view as a needy enterprise for poor children where they can perform good works. In these sectors, risk-taking produces fast change and large rewards. A hedge fund manager can make a bet and make millions overnight; an entrepreneur in the high-tech world can come up with a new idea that changes everything. Disruption works for them, but not so much for children. Children need a stable environment, a supportive family, and a dependable community of caring adults, not disruption.

The entrepreneurs from Wall Street are big players in school reform efforts. The hedge fund managers control billions of dollars in investments and can raise millions to subsidize their favorite charters and to support candidates who promise to advance the charter movement. When Andrew Cuomo wanted to raise Wall Street money for his gubernatorial campaign in 2010, he quickly learned that he needed the blessing of Democrats for Education Reform. DFER is the voice of the Wall Street hedge fund managers, the men who make eight-figure incomes (or more) and whose own children are unlikely ever to attend a public school. Members of DFER have contributed money to influential state and local politicians across the country, as well as key members of Congress, promoting charter schools, longer school days, an end to teacher seniority and tenure, and high-stakes testing. With strategic funding, DFER persuaded the New York legislature to raise the number of charters in the state from 200 to 460. Reporters from the *New York Times* noted that there was no Republican equivalent to DFER: "There does not have to be one: Many Republican officials readily embrace charter schools, whose ideological roots are in a free-market model of education." DFER's vast financial resources imported the Republican agenda into the Democratic Party. DFER's interests and strategies, even its membership, overlap with similar groups, such as Education Reform Now, the Education Equality Project, and Stand for Children.[58]

DESPITE THE BIPARTISAN SUPPORT and vast amounts of money promoting corporate reform, its prospects remain very much in doubt. After a decade or more in which its ideas have dominated national policy, it has experienced no successes. Research continues to demonstrate the invalidity of its strategies. Its narrative of decline and failure has no basis in historical reality. The districts that have applied its remedies most faithfully have little to show for their investment in terms of genuine educational improvement. And as teachers and parents understand its goals, they push back. In July 2011, several thousands gathered in Washington, D.C., to protest No Child Left Behind and Race to the Top and to demand thoughtful answers to the problems of today's students and schools. The SOS March on Washington, as it was called, was not organized by the teachers' unions but by a group of National Board Certified Teachers and Parents Across America. These grassroots organizations seek better education for children, more respect for teachers, and a vision of education that recognizes the worth of every child. The struggle between this vision and the goals of the corporate reform movement will not be soon resolved. History will indeed judge, as it always does. When historians write about this era some twenty or thirty years from now, my guess is that they will not view kindly those who sought to transform students into commodities, products and consumers, and to turn schooling into a marketplace.

DATA MAY BE USEFUL, if they are gathered honestly and reflect significant aspects of learning. Data may also be fraudulent and useless, if they are produced by cheating or gaming the system, or if they represent the results of intensive test preparation, which teaches students test-taking skills rather than the subjects themselves. In the years preceding the financial meltdown of 2008, several high-profile corporations boasted excellent data, right up to the day they went bankrupt. The media and the public must learn to view data with appropriate skepticism.

Testing too is important. Educators can glean from test results what students have and have not learned. But there is a risk in putting too much faith in tests and the data they generate. The biggest risk is in forgetting that test scores are an indicator, not the goal of education. When the indicator becomes the target, we lose sight of other, more important goals, such as the ability to understand and apply what is studied, to expand one's knowledge, and to develop good character and ethical ideals. A decade of NCLB has demonstrated that large investments in test preparation may raise scores without actually increasing students' knowledge and skills, and that many students who passed reading and math tests nonetheless needed remediation when they entered college. We have seen schools drop subjects not because they lack importance, but because they are not tested. We have seen cheating scandals. And when we reflect on why education matters, we think of virtues that are not and cannot be measured: character, curiosity, responsibility, persistence, generosity, integrity, kindness, initiative, ingenuity, compassion, creativity, moral courage. Even the subjects studied in school are not always easily quantifiable; a great history teacher, for example, inspires a passion for history, as great teachers in general inspire a love of learning. We don't know how to measure love of learning, but we do know that it matters more in the long run than any question that might be asked on a multiple-choice test.

We should also be concerned about the effects of years of dependence on multiple-choice testing. Some questions, such as in mathematics, have right answers. Simple factual questions (who was president of the United States during the Civil War?) have right answers. And it is important to know basic, essential facts about the world. However, a single-minded pursuit of the "right answer" is not likely to unleash creativity, imagination, and innovation. It would be far better to encourage students to think about the questions, to evaluate the validity of facts, to provide evidence for their assertions, to write essays, to conduct research, and to explain why and how they arrived at their solution to problems, even in mathematics and certainly in history.

It's good to have data to guide policy, but it is important not to confuse data with evidence. Data are representations of reality, not reality itself. Endless public wrangling over whether test scores are going up or going down obscures rather than edifies. If scores went up five points or twelve points or eighteen points, but students weren't prepared for postsecondary studies, hated learning, or had an exaggerated sense of their academic prowess, this is no victory. To make genuine improvement in our schools requires keen judgment and a broader view of education than test scores alone can provide.

The reformers often say they don't believe in relying solely on test scores, but their actions and policy preferences make clear that test-based measures are the cornerstone of their approach. They judge the failure and success of students, teachers, principals, schools, and districts based on test scores. They seek to alter long-standing policies, such as giving teachers a small salary increase for getting a master's degree, because these degrees are not always associated with teachers' ability to boost scores. And they insist that new evaluation or compensation systems include test-based measures of teacher effectiveness. They talk about using multiple measures, but it seems that only test scores really matter.

Two studies that reflect on our nation's current reform strategies are worthy of mention because they grapple not just with data, but with evidence, and by evidence I refer to thoughtful interpretation of data.

In 2011, the National Research Council of the National Academies of Science, our nation's most prestigious research organization, released a nine-year study called "Incentives and Test-Based Accountability." A seventeen-member panel of social scientists, including some of the foremost experts in the world, assessed the value of tying test scores to incentives: that is, to carrots and sticks, rewards and punishments. The panel concluded that test-based accountability led to score inflation, to gaming the system, and to behaviors that undermined the value of the scores. They also reviewed the evidence and found that test-based incentives have a decidedly meager track record in boosting student achievement. None of this is news to readers of this book. What we should know by now is that when incentives are tied to testing, the tests themselves may be rendered invalid. When students practice the test content day after day, they learn to take the test, but the scores may not truly indicate their skills or knowledge. We have adopted a national strategy designed to raise test scores without necessarily improving the quality of education.[59]

Marc Tucker of the National Center on Education and the Economy reviewed the practices of high-performing nations and concluded that we are on the wrong track. He wrote that "the education strategies now most popular in the United States are conspicuous by their absence in the countries with the most successful education systems." Charter schools, vouchers, annual grade-by-grade testing with multiple-choice standardized tests, closing schools with low scores, and evaluating teachers according to their students' scores: All of that, Tucker writes, is irrelevant. What the top nations in the world have done and we have not is recruited the best prospective teachers—not for a few years like Teach for America, but for a full and satisfying career as teachers and administrators. Teachers in these nations are highly respected professionals, with competitive compensation, high-quality professional training in elite institutions, and broad professional autonomy in the workplace. Each of these top nations has a broad national curriculum that includes the arts and music, social sciences, and other subjects. Teachers master the expectations of the national curriculum (it does not tell teachers how to teach, but describes in general terms what will be taught). This is a bold vision, but it suggests a very different way to understand school reform, one that is far from what our nation has attempted to do for the past decade or more.[60]

THE NEXT WAVE OF SCHOOL REFORM is bearing down on us. It will be packaged as the sine qua non of the twenty-first century: online learning. We will hear that lessons can be delivered at less cost and with greater efficiency through online instruction. We will hear that teachers cost too much, that their pensions and health care are a public burden. We will be told that virtual schools can accomplish more while permitting a reduction of 30 percent or more in the teaching force. Entrepreneurs will pitch visions of millions of children at their home or school computers, monitored by teachers they never meet, teachers who oversee one hundred or more screens. Think of the savings! Think of the profits! The United States currently spends over $600 billion a year on public education. Already, big corporations are jostling for position, amassing the content and technology to compete for student customers, all of whom have government funding strapped to their backs. When News Corporation bought the educational technology company Wireless Generation in 2010, Rupert Murdoch envisioned "a $500 billion sector in the US alone that is waiting desperately to be transformed by big breakthroughs that extend the reach of great teaching."[61]

To speak ill of technology and the marvels of our digitized world comes close to a sacrilege. And yet I must. Technology is a wonderful tool. It has many valuable uses in school, in the workplace, and at home. Students can use computers to do research, to write, to explore, to create, to invent. In no way do I dismiss the importance of technology inside or outside the classroom. Nor do I dismiss the value of self-education, which is the crux of lifelong learning and is mightily facilitated by new technologies. But for most purposes, students need teachers as well as one another. Students require a wise and experienced person who offers encouragement, who presents the subject in a compelling manner, who sets standards of personal conduct, who monitors more than a blinking screen. Minds develop in response to the social interaction of a lively classroom, where learners debate, discuss, and exchange ideas. Some things are best done alone, such as reading, writing, practicing an instrument, and reflecting. Others are best done in groups, such as singing in a chorus, performing in an orchestra, acting in a play, playing team sports, discussing a novel, or debating a historical controversy.

I have never forgotten an exchange I read in *Forbes* in 1984, regarding the coming revolution in education.[62] An article written by senior editor Kathleen K. Wiegner celebrated what technology would do to transform education. In the next issue, the magazine published a dissenting commentary written initially as an internal memo by its technology editor, Stephen Kindel. He wrote:

> What kind of transformation will computers generate in kids? It could well be a lot less than all the hype would indicate. Just as likely as producing far more intelligent kids is the possibility that you will create a group of kids fixated on screens—television, videogame, or computer. The notion of learning at your own speed is a hoary educational cliche beloved by computer ed folks. In theory it sounds wonderful. In fact, it eliminates the community of the classroom, turns the student into a lone figure engaged in a yearlong dialog with a disembodied voice. What would happen to class discussion—and, more important, the sense of rubbing against other minds?

Kindel observed that "the computer is a tool, like a hammer or a wrench, not a philosophers' stone" and that "education depends on the intimate contact between a good teacher—part performer, part dictator, part cajoler—and an inquiring student. The importance of the teacher is not necessarily as a conveyor of information but as a catalyst to interest students in learning for themselves." He predicted that when this revolution came to pass, the poor would get computers, and the rich would get teachers. Of course, that isn't quite right. The rich get both computers and teachers.

WHEN I WAS A GRADUATE STUDENT IN THE EARLY 1970S, I discovered a surprising secret about American education: In almost every decade of the twentieth century, there was a crisis. In the early decades, critics said the schools were too academic and were failing to prepare students for an industrial economy. Their loud complaints produced the first significant federal education legislation, the Smith-Lever Act of 1914 and the Smith-Hughes Act of 1917, to promote vocational education. In the 1930s, critics complained that the schools were failing to meet the needs of youth or of the economy; federal programs were created (the Civilian Conservation Corps and the National Youth Administration) to fill the gap. In the 1940s, critics complained that the schools were underfunded, overcrowded, and unprepared for the postwar economy and the atomic age. In the early 1950s, critics assailed the schools for their lack of academic rigor. Then, when the Soviets launched Sputnik in 1957, public figures and the media blamed the schools for losing the space race and jeopardizing the nation's security. In response, Congress passed the National Defense Education Act of 1958. In the 1960s, the nation "discovered" poverty, and the schools were again subject to searing criticism because they reflected the prejudices of the larger society. Congress reacted with the Civil Rights Act of 1964, banning racial discrimination in the schools and other public institutions. In the late 1960s and early 1970s, the schools were lambasted by critics who discerned, as author Charles Silberman put it, a "crisis in the classroom" due to "mindlessness" and the routinization of education. In response came a flurry of pedagogical experiments, such as open classrooms and student freedom to select their own curriculum. In 1983, a federal commission declared that the United States was "a nation at risk" because of the failings of our schools. Since the late 1990s, the crisis in education has centered on the achievement gap between children of different races. The gap is not new: It is the result of a long history of racial oppression and prejudice. Nonetheless, critics blame the schools and teachers for the existence of the gap and for the failure to close it.

This is what I have learned after many decades of studying American education: Education is a reflection of society. Education is integrally related to the society in which it is embedded. Education is intended to improve society by improving the knowledge and skills of the people, but education works incrementally over years, not overnight. The public schools have been one of the primary instrumentalities of American democracy, disseminating knowledge and skills widely and making social mobility possible.

But schools cannot by themselves solve the problems of poverty and inequality. As W. E. B. Du Bois said in 1935, speaking to an audience of African-American teachers in Georgia, the only way schools can improve society is to make men more intelligent by teaching them academic skills. If they fail to do that, he warned, the schools will fail in all other functions "because no school as such can organise industry, or settle the matter of wage and income, can found homes or furnish parents, can establish justice or make a civilised world."[63]

Although some school reformers of our own day believe that schools alone can create equality, Du Bois knew this was not possible. Schools can provide a route out of poverty for determined individuals, but schools by themselves—no matter how excellent—cannot cure the ills created by extreme social and economic inequality. They cannot create jobs or repair broken families or end neighborhood deterioration or stop crime. The achievement gap begins long before the first day of school.

School reform therefore must occur in tandem with social reform. A good place to start is investing in prenatal care, to ensure that every poor pregnant woman receives appropriate medical attention and nutrition, to avoid the risks of low birth weight and preventable disabilities. Next in an agenda of social reform would be an investment in early childhood education, from birth to five years. Children's intellectual, emotional, and social development is likely to be impaired if they lack the basic necessities of life during these crucial years, and it may be enhanced if children (and their families) receive appropriate social, medical, and economic support. The billions of public and private dollars devoted to testing and accountability over the past decade might have revolutionized our efforts to improve children's lives and might have enabled nearly all to arrive at school ready to learn.

When children grow up without the basic necessities, when they live in neighborhoods where violence and physical deterioration are ever-present, when they see incarceration as a normal fact of life, their chances to succeed in school are substantially diminished. Unfortunately, every testing program—be it the SAT, the ACT, NAEP, or state scores—shows a tight correlation between family income and scores: Children from affluent families have the highest scores, and children from poverty have the lowest scores. On the SAT for reading, students whose family income is in the lowest bracket (under $20,000) have an average score of 437, while students whose family income is in the highest bracket (over $200,000) have a mean score of 568; the gap is as large and as regular in mathematics.[64]

The same pattern is found on international assessments. When the results of the Program for International Student Assessment (PISA) were released in December 2010, American students placed in the middle of the pack of participating nations. Secretary Duncan and President Obama described the results as a devastating reflection on the quality of American education. Yet American schools with low poverty rates (fewer than 10 percent of students eligible for free or reduced-price lunch) had average reading scores of 551, higher than the average scores of the schools in Korea (539), Finland (536), and Japan (520). And those American schools where between 10 and 25 percent of students were poor had average scores (527) comparable to those of schools in Korea, Finland, and Japan.[65]

Poverty matters. An exceptional school here or there may break the pattern for a tiny number of students—usually with the benefit of extra private funding and extended time—but the pattern will persist so long as social conditions remain unchanged, so long as there are districts and schools with intense concentrations of students who are both racially segregated and impoverished.

Schools too must certainly improve. The status quo today is intolerable. After many years in which the nation has placed its highest priority on test-based accountability, we have little to show for it other than small increments in test scores, billions squandered on testing and test preparation, and vast numbers of teachers and administrators demoralized by utopian goals and harsh sanctions.

We must, as President Obama said in his 2011 State of the Union address, pursue educational strategies that encourage innovation, creativity, and imagination. Every student should have a full curriculum that includes not only the basic skills but also the arts, history, civics, geography, literature, the sciences, mathematics, and foreign languages. Students should have access to strong career and technical programs. Every school should have up-to-date technology for teaching and learning. Students should be encouraged to read and write, to discuss and debate, to experiment and explore, to think differently, to work in groups, and to work alone. Assessment should rely primarily on students' demonstrations of their knowledge and skills. Standardized tests should be used sparingly, not more than once or twice a year, and then only for diagnostic purposes. Class sizes, especially for students with the highest needs, must be small enough so they receive individual attention.

The teaching profession must become more professional, with higher standards for entry into the profession and for achieving due process rights. Our goal as a society must be to turn teaching into a valued and respected career, as befits its importance. Universities must recruit top-notch students into teaching and provide the education and training they need to be successful. The federal government should create a loan-forgiveness program to pay off the student debt of those who enter teaching and remain for at least five years. In time, the attrition rate for teachers should decline from its present scandalous level of 50 percent in the first five years to single digits.

If we strengthen the teaching profession, recognize the importance of experienced leaders, improve the conditions of teaching and learning, enrich the curriculum, and rely on assessments that ask students to demonstrate their knowledge and skills, our schools will surely change for the better. If we simultaneously take concrete steps to reduce poverty and to increase the life chances of children born into poverty, their readiness for learning will improve, and so will their academic prowess.

And finally, we need to reorient our social and educational vision to see each and every child as a precious human being, a person of endless potential. Not rated by his or her test scores. Not defined by his or her family demographics. But as a person who is growing, developing, in need of adult guidance, in need of a challenging and liberating education, an education of possibilities and passion.

We need a strong and vibrant public education system. We need to give our children a good start in life. None of this is outside our reach or grasp, although such ideas are far from our present rhetoric and strategies for education reform. Our future as a nation depends on our actions today.

Notes

CHAPTER ONE

1. Alfred L. Malabre Jr., *Lost Prophets: An Insider's History of the Modern Economists* (Boston: Harvard Business School Press, 1994), 220.

2. Diane Ravitch, "Tot Sociology: Or What Happened to History in the Grade Schools," *American Scholar* 56, no. 3 (Summer 1987): 343–354; Ravitch, "Bring Literature and History Back to Elementary Schools," in *The Schools We Deserve: Reflections on the Educational Crises of Our Time* (New York: Basic Books, 1985), 75–79; Ravitch, *Left Back: A Century of Failed School Reforms* (New York: Simon & Schuster, 2000).

3. William Chandler Bagley, *Classroom Management: Its Principles and Technique* (New York: Macmillan, 1907), 3; William Henry Maxwell, "On a Certain Arrogance in Educational Theorists," *Educational Review* 47 (February 1914): 165–182, esp. 165–167, 171.

4. Diane Ravitch, "Programs, Placebos, Panaceas," *Urban Review*, April 1968, 8–11; Ravitch, "Foundations: Playing God in the Ghetto," *Center Forum* 3 (May 15, 1969): 24–27.

5. Diane Ravitch, *The Great School Wars: New York City, 1805–1973* (New York: Basic Books, 1974).

6. Diane Ravitch, *The Revisionists Revised: A Critique of the Radical Attack on the Schools* (New York: Basic Books, 1978).

7. Diane Ravitch, *The Troubled Crusade: American Education, 1945–1980* (New York: Basic Books, 1983).

8. Diane Ravitch and Chester E. Finn Jr., *What Do Our 17-Year-Olds Know? A Report on the First National Assessment of History and Literature* (New York: Harper & Row, 1987), 10–11.

9. *History–Social Science Framework for California Public Schools, Kindergarten Through Grade Twelve* (Sacramento: California State Department

of Education, 1988); see also Diane Ravitch, "Where Have All the Classics Gone? You Won't Find Them in Primers," *New York Times Book Review*, May 17, 1987; Ravitch, "Tot Sociology."

10. David Osborne and Ted Gaebler, *Reinventing Government: How the Entrepreneurial Spirit Is Transforming the Public Sector* (Reading, MA: Addison-Wesley, 1992).

11. Jason Peckenpaugh, "Reinvention Remembered: A Look Back at Seven Years of Reform," GovernmentExecutive.com, January 19, 2001, www.gov exec.com/dailyfed/0101/011901p1.htm.

12. James C. Scott, *Seeing Like a State: How Certain Schemes to Improve the Human Condition Have Failed* (New Haven, CT: Yale University Press, 1998).

13. Sol Stern, "School Choice Isn't Enough," *City Journal*, Winter 2008.

CHAPTER TWO

1. The National Council of Teachers of Mathematics had already written mathematics standards.

2. Lynne V. Cheney, "The End of History," *Wall Street Journal*, October 20, 1994.

3. Karen Diegmueller, "Panel Unveils Standards for U.S. History," *Education Week*, November 2, 1994.

4. *Los Angeles Times*, "Now a History for the Rest of Us," October 27, 1994; Gary B. Nash, Charlotte Crabtree, and Ross E. Dunn, *History on Trial: Culture Wars and the Teaching of the Past* (New York: Knopf, 1997).

5. U.S. Congress, Senate, *Congressional Record* (January 18, 1995), S1026–S1040.

6. Diegmueller, "Panel Unveils Standards"; Diane Ravitch, "Standards in U.S. History: An Assessment," *Education Week*, December 7, 1994; Ravitch, letter to the editor, *New York Times*, February 14, 1995.

7. Diane Ravitch, "Revise, but Don't Abandon, the History Standards," *Chronicle of Higher Education,* February 17, 1995.

8. Bill Clinton and Al Gore, *Putting People First: How We Can All Change America* (New York: Times Books, 1992), 85–86.

9. Diane Ravitch, "Social Studies Standards: Time for a Decisive Change," in *Reforming Education in Arkansas: Recommendations from the Koret Task Force, 2005* (Stanford, CA: Hoover Press, 2005), 69–74. The standards cited here are similar to those in most other states.

10. Diane Ravitch, *The Language Police: How Pressure Groups Restrict What Students Learn* (New York: Knopf, 2003), 124–125. For this book, I read the standards in English language arts and history/social studies in every state in the nation.

11. The law said that the state plans must include challenging academic standards, and that state plans had to win the approval of the U.S. secretary of education. However, by June 2003 every state plan was approved, even though many did not have challenging academic standards. Lynn Olson, "All States Get Federal Nod on Key Plans," *Education Week*, June 18, 2003.

12. Josh Patashnik, "Reform School: The Education (On Education) of Barack Obama," *New Republic*, March 26, 2008, 12–13.

13. David Brooks, "Who Will He Choose?" *New York Times*, December 5, 2008; *Washington Post*, "A Job for a Reformer," December 5, 2008; *Chicago Tribune*, "Obama and Schoolkids," December 9, 2008. Republicans recognized that President Obama was embracing some of the GOP's core beliefs, including school choice, merit pay, and accountability. Richard N. Bond, Bill McInturff, and Alex Bratty, "A Chance to Say Yes: The GOP and Obama Can Agree on School Reform," *Washington Post*, August 2, 2009.

14. Diane Ravitch, *The Troubled Crusade: American Education, 1945–1980* (New York: Basic Books, 1983), 228–266.

15. Edward B. Fiske, "College Entry Test Scores Drop Sharply," *New York Times*, September 7, 1975.

16. College Entrance Examination Board, *On Further Examination: Report of the Advisory Panel on the Scholastic Aptitude Test Score Decline* (New York: College Entrance Examination Board, 1977), 26–31.

17. President's Commission on Foreign Language and International Studies, *Strength Through Wisdom: A Critique of U.S. Capability* (Washington, D.C.: U.S. Government Printing Office, 1979); National Science Foundation and U.S. Department of Education, *Science and Engineering Education for the 1980s and Beyond* (Washington, D.C.: U.S. Government Printing Office, 1980).

18. For his perspective on *A Nation at Risk*, see Terrel H. Bell, *The Thirteenth Man: A Reagan Cabinet Memoir* (New York: Free Press, 1988), 114–143.

19. National Commission on Excellence in Education, *A Nation at Risk: The Imperative for Educational Reform* (Washington, D.C.: U.S. Government Printing Office, 1983), 5–6.

20. Ibid., 8.

21. Ibid., 8–9.

22. Ibid., 18–22.

23. Ibid., 24–27.

24. Ibid., 25.

25. Ibid., 30.

26. Ibid., 7.

27. David C. Berliner and Bruce J. Biddle, *The Manufactured Crisis: Myths, Fraud, and the Attack on America's Public Schools* (Reading, MA: Addison-Wesley, 1995), 3–5, 139–140, 184.

28. See, for example, Richard Rothstein, "'A Nation at Risk' Twenty-five Years Later," Cato Unbound, April 7, 2008, www.cato-unbound.org/2008/04/07/richard-rothstein/a-nation-at-risk-twenty-five-years-later/.

CHAPTER THREE

1. Marshall S. Smith and Jennifer O'Day, "Systemic School Reform," in *The Politics of Curriculum and Testing: The 1990 Yearbook of the Politics of Education Association*, ed. Susan H. Fuhrman and Betty Malen (London: Falmer, 1991), 233–267. See also Maris A. Vinovskis, "An Analysis of the Concept

and Uses of Systemic Educational Reform," *American Educational Research Journal* 33, no. 1 (Spring 1996): 53–85.

2. Diane Ravitch, "National Standards and Curriculum Reform: A View from the Department of Education," *NASSP Bulletin*, December 1992.

3. The Bloomberg administration dissolved the administrative structures of the community school districts after the mayor won control of the public schools in 2002. The district lines remained on paper, but the districts were no longer functioning administrative entities.

4. Joyce Purnick, "Alvarado Resigns as Schools Chief, Offering Apology," *New York Times*, May 12, 1984. See also Paul Teske et al., "Public School Choice: A Status Report," in *City Schools: Lessons from New York*, ed. Diane Ravitch and Joseph P. Viteritti (Baltimore: Johns Hopkins University Press, 2000), 313–338.

5. Kenneth Goodman, *What's Whole in Whole Language?* (Portsmouth, NH: Heinemann, 1986), 25, 37–38.

6. Jeanne S. Chall, *Learning to Read: The Great Debate* (New York: McGraw-Hill, 1967). See also Diane Ravitch, *Left Back: A Century of Failed School Reforms* (New York: Simon & Schuster, 2000), 353–361, 443–448.

7. National Academy of Education, *Becoming a Nation of Readers: The Report of the Commission on Reading* (Washington, D.C.: U.S. Department of Education, 1985), 37.

8. See Catherine E. Snow, M. Susan Burns, and Peg Griffin, eds., *Preventing Reading Difficulties in Young Children* (Washington, D.C.: National Academy Press, 1998); National Reading Panel, *Teaching Children to Read: An Evidence-Based Assessment of the Scientific Research Literature on Reading and Its Implications for Reading Instruction* (Washington, D.C.: U.S. Department of Health and Human Services, 2000); G. Reid Lyon and Louisa C. Moats, "Critical Conceptual and Methodological Considerations in Reading Intervention Research," *Journal of Learning Disabilities* 30, no. 6 (November–December 1997): 578–588; Louisa C. Moats, *Teaching Reading IS Rocket Science* (Washington, D.C.: American Federation of Teachers, 1999).

9. For examples of strategy instruction, see Stephanie Harvey and Anne Goudvis, *Strategies That Work: Teaching Comprehension to Enhance Understanding* (Portland, ME: Stenhouse, 2000). See also AUSSIE: Partners in Professional Development, "Literacy Resources," www.aussiepd.com/resources/literacy.

10. Lori Jamison Rog, *Guided Reading Basics: Organizing, Managing, and Implementing a Balanced Literacy Program in K–3* (Portland, ME: Stenhouse, 2003); Sewell Chan, "By the Script," *New York Times*, July 31, 2005; Meredith I. Honig, *New Directions in Education Policy Implementation: Confronting Complexity* (Albany: State University of New York Press, 2006), 38–44.

11. P. David Pearson and Janice A. Dole, "Explicit Comprehension Instruction: A Review of Research and a New Conceptualization of Instruction," *Elementary School Journal* 88, no. 2 (November 1987): 162.

12. Richard F. Elmore and Deanna Burney, "Investing in Teacher Learning: Staff Development and Instructional Improvement," in *Teaching as the*

Learning Profession: Handbook of Policy and Practice, ed. Linda Darling-Hammond and Gary Sykes (San Francisco: Jossey-Bass, 1999), 265.

13. The papers produced by this federally funded project can be found at www.lrdc.pitt.edu/hplc/hplc.html. The cost of the project was provided by Grover Whitehurst, director of the Institute of Education Sciences, in an e-mail to the author, May 15, 2007.

14. The figures vary for the amount of the district's budget dedicated to professional development, with some studies saying 3 percent, while Alvarado told Hedrick Smith on the PBS program *Making Schools Work* that the amount was "over 12 percent." See www.pbs.org/makingschoolswork/dwr/ny/alvarado.html.

15. New York City Department of Education, *Annual School Reports, 1987–1988*.

16. Lauren Resnick, Anthony J. Alvarado, and Richard F. Elmore, "Developing and Implementing High-Performance Learning Communities," *Solicitation Proposal RC-96–1370*, U.S. Department of Education, 1995, 1–2.

17. Elmore and Burney, "Continuous Improvement in Community District #2, New York City," High Performance Learning Communities Project, University of Pittsburgh, 1998, 1, www.lrdc.pitt.edu/hplc/Publications/ContinuousImprove.pdf.

18. Lauren Resnick and Michael Harwell, "High Performance Learning Communities District 2 Achievement," HPLC Project, 1998, 19, www.lrdc.pitt.edu/hplc/Publications/Achieve%20I%20Final.pdf.

19. Michael Harwell et al., "Professional Development and the Achievement Gap in Community School District #2," HPLC Project, 2000, 21–22, www.lrdc.pitt.edu/hplc/Publications/Achievement%20III.pdf.

20. Elmore and Burney, "School Variation and Systemic Instructional Improvement in Community School District #2, New York City," HPLC Project, 1997, 5–6, www.lrdc.pitt.edu/hplc/Publications/School%20Variation.pdf.

21. Ibid., 4, 12–13.

22. Ibid., 25–28.

23. High Performance Learning Communities Project, "Final Report," *Contract #RC-96–137002*, Office of Education Research and Improvement, U.S. Department of Education, 2001, 27–28, www.lrdc.pitt.edu/hplc/Publications/HPLC_FinalReport_Sept2001.pdf.

24. Louisa C. Spencer, "Progressivism's Hidden Failure," *Education Week*, February 28, 2001.

25. Lois Weiner, "Standardization's Stifling Impact," *Education Week*, February 28, 2001.

26. Anthony J. Alvarado and Elaine Fink, letter to the editor, "Critiques of District 2 Are Seen as Baseless," *Education Week*, March 28, 2001; Shelley Harwayne, letter to the editor, "District 2: 'Results Speak for Themselves,'" *Education Week*, April 4, 2001.

27. National Council of Teachers of Mathematics, "Exploring Krypto," http://illuminations.nctm.org/LessonDetail.aspx?id=L803.

28. Matthew Clavel, "How Not to Teach Math," *City Journal*, March 7, 2003; Barry Garelick, "Discovery Learning in Math: Exercises Versus

Problems," *Nonpartisan Education Review/Essays* 5, no. 2 (2009), www.npe .ednews.org/Review/Essays/v5n2.htm.

29. Ronald Drenger, "Math Profs Rail Against Dist. 2 Methods," *Tribeca Trib,* July/August 2001; the name of the group—NYC HOLD—is an acronym for "Honest Open Logical Decisions" on Mathematics Education Reform; see www.nychold.com.

30. Lois Weiner, "Construction of District 2's Exemplary Status: When Research and Public Policy Elide," paper, Annual Conference, American Educational Research Association, April 2002, www.nychold.com/weiner-aera-02. html; Weiner, "Research or 'Cheerleading'? Scholarship on Community School District 2, New York City," *Education Policy Analysis Archives* 11, no. 27 (August 7, 2003).

31. Lauren B. Resnick, "Reforms, Research and Variability: A Reply to Lois Weiner," *Education Policy Analysis Archives* 11, no. 28 (August 7, 2003); see Weiner's response to Resnick: Weiner, "Reply to Resnick's 'Reforms, Research and Variability,'" *Education Policy Analysis Archives* 11, no. 28c (February 2, 2004).

32. Public Broadcasting Service, *Making Schools Work*, with Hedrick Smith, www.pbs.org/makingschoolswork/.

33. Teske et al., "Public School Choice: A Status Report."

34. The source of the census data for 1990 and 2000 is an Internet tool called Social Explorer, created by demographer Andrew Beveridge at Queens College of the City University of New York. Social Explorer permits the user to identify specific census tracts and compare them along different demographic dimensions. Beveridge and Jordan Segall of Queens College analyzed District 2 and citywide census data for 1990 and 2000. Some of the data may also be found at NYC Department of City Planning, "New York City Public Schools: Demographic and Enrollment Trends, 1990–2002, Manhattan," 47, www.nyc .gov/html/dcp/pdf/pub/schlmanhattan.pdf.

35. Ibid.

36. According to New York State Education Department data, from 1988 to 1998 the proportion of white students increased from 26 percent to 31.2 percent (in the rest of the city, white enrollment declined from 21 percent to 16 percent). The proportion of Hispanic students declined from 24.5 percent to 21.1 percent (in the city system, it increased from 34 percent to 37 percent). Asian students remained constant at one-third (triple the proportion in the city schools). The proportion of African American students declined from 15.4 percent to 13.9 percent (in the city system, it dropped from 39 percent to 36 percent).

37. The source of the achievement data was the New York State Department of Education. Similar gaps existed on the city tests from 1995 to 1998.

38. District 26 in Queens in New York City was demographically and economically similar to District 2. These two affluent districts outperformed the rest of the city, though District 26 generally outperformed District 2 and had smaller achievement gaps. In District 26, 60 percent of African American and Hispanic students met state standards in reading in fourth grade in 1999,

compared to 78.5 percent of Asian students and 80.4 percent of white students; in fourth-grade mathematics, 69 percent of African American students and 76 percent of Hispanic students met standards, compared to 89 percent of whites and 91 percent of Asians. In eighth-grade reading, 81 percent of Asian students and 76 percent of white students met the standards, compared to 53 percent of African American students and 55 percent of Hispanic students; in eighth-grade mathematics, 79.5 percent of Asian students and 61.3 percent of white students met the standards, compared to 33 percent of African American and Hispanic students. Source: New York State Education Department, "Performance of Students Scoring in ELA and Math Grade 4 and 8 by Ethnicity," 1999.

CHAPTER FOUR

1. California Department of Education, Educational Demographics Unit—CBEDS; data available at Ed-Data: Education Data Partnership, www.ed-data.k12.ca.us.

2. Ann Bradley, "San Diego Teachers Strike in Dispute Over Pay," *Education Week*, February 7, 1996.

3. Maureen Magee, "Similar Dramas Play Out at S.D., L.A. Schools," *San Diego Union-Tribune*, June 5, 2000.

4. Salary schedule provided by Camille Zombro, chapter leader of the San Diego Education Association, in an e-mail to author, July 9, 2009.

5. Jane Hannaway and Maggie Stanislawski, "Flip-Flops in School Reform: An Evolutionary Theory of Decentralization," in *Urban School Reform: Lessons from San Diego*, ed. Frederick M. Hess (Cambridge, MA: Harvard Education Press, 2005), 54.

6. Ibid., 57.

7. Bess Keller, "Peer-Coaching Plan Approved in San Diego," *Education Week*, May 19, 1999.

8. Maureen Magee, "Former Principals Win Case Against District," *San Diego Union-Tribune*, November 6, 2004.

9. San Diego City Schools, "Blueprint for Student Success in a Standards-Based System: Supporting Student Achievement in an Integrated Learning Environment," March 14, 2000, 1, www.sandi.net/initiatives/ciia/000314blueprint.pdf.

10. Richard F. Elmore and Deanna Burney, "Investing in Teacher Learning: Staff Development and Instructional Improvement," in *Teaching as the Learning Profession: Handbook of Policy and Practice*, ed. Linda Darling-Hammond and Gary Sykes (San Francisco: Jossey-Bass, 1999), 285; see also 274–279.

11. Jeff Archer, "Wary Foundations Tie Grants to Leadership Stability," *Education Week*, February 12, 2003.

12. Maureen Magee, "Sweeping School Reform Is Approved: 3–2 Decision Made Despite Thousands of Protesters," *San Diego Union-Tribune*, March 15, 2000.

13. Micah Sachs, "The Hardest Job in America?" *San Diego Jewish Journal*, September 2003.

14. Lea Hubbard, Hugh Mehan, and Mary Kay Stein, *Reform As Learning: School Reform, Organizational Culture, and Community Politics in San Diego* (New York: Routledge, 2006), 173.

15. Hannaway and Stanislawski, "Flip-Flops in School Reform,"55–56.

16. Amy M. Hightower, *San Diego's Big Boom: District Bureaucracy Supports Culture of Learning* (Seattle: Center for the Study of Teaching and Policy, University of Washington, 2002), 8, 11.

17. Hannaway and Stanislawski, "Flip-Flops in School Reform," 64–65; see also Darling-Hammond and Sykes, *Teaching as the Learning Profession*.

18. Elmore and Burney, "Investing in Teacher Learning," 269.

19. Ibid., 270–271.

20. Matt Potter, "It Was the Biggest Mystery," *San Diego Reader*, October 24, 2002.

21. Joe Williams, "The Labor-Management Showdown," in *Urban School Reform*, 46.

22. Maureen Magee, "Bersin: Alvarado's Role to Be Curtailed," *San Diego Union-Tribune*, December 6, 2002; Chris Moran, "Chief S.D. School Reformer to Leave: Superintendent Calls Departure 'Mutual,'" *San Diego Union-Tribune*, February 5, 2003.

23. American Institutes for Research, *Evaluation of the Blueprint for Student Success in a Standards-based System* (Palo Alto, CA: AIR, 2002), II-10; AIR, *Evaluation of the Blueprint for Student Success in a Standards-Based System: Year 2 Interim Report* (Palo Alto, CA: AIR, 2003); Chris Moran, "Report Card on Reform Just So-So," *San Diego Union-Tribune*, May 13, 2003; Hugh Mehan, Lea Hubbard, and Mary Kay Stein, "When Reforms Travel: The Sequel," *Journal of Educational Change* 6, no. 4 (2005): 329–362.

24. AIR 2003 study, II-27, II-28, II-29.

25. Hightower, *San Diego's Big Boom*, 19.

26. Larry Cuban and Michael Usdan, "Fast and Top-Down: Systemic Reform and Student Achievement in San Diego City Schools," in *Powerful Reforms with Shallow Roots: Improving America's Urban Schools*, ed. Larry Cuban and Michael Usdan (New York: Teachers College Press, 2003), 78, 82, 88–89.

27. Daphna Bassok and Margaret E. Raymond, "Performance Trends and the Blueprint for Student Success," in *Urban School Reform*, 308–309, 314–315.

28. Ibid., 310–317.

29. Julian Betts, "San Diego City Schools: Evidence Suggests Bersin Reforms Working," *San Diego Union-Tribune*, October 14, 2005.

30. Maureen Magee and Helen Gao, "A Change in Plans," *San Diego Union-Tribune*, June 12, 2005. There is no single consistent measure for the Blueprint era because the state changed its tests during this time. However, Magee and Gao note that on the state's "academic performance index," San Diego's gains from 2002 to 2004 were smaller than those recorded by school districts in Santa Ana, Fresno, San Bernardino, Long Beach, Los Angeles, Garden Grove, San Francisco, Oakland, and Sacramento. San Diego had higher scores than most of these districts, but the other districts made greater gains.

31. Sheila Byrd, "San Diego City Schools: Creating a Standards-Based Curriculum for English Language Arts," unpublished manuscript, San Diego Review, 2004, http://old.sandi.net/events/sdreview/eng_math_sci_cirricula.pdf.

32. Byrd, e-mail to author, June 14, 2006.

33. San Diego Education Association, "Vote of Confidence Survey Results," June 20, 2001. A copy of the survey was provided to the author by Camille Zombro of the SDEA.

34. Author's conversation with Marty Batcheler, LCSW, Kaiser Permanente, January 31, 2007.

35. Carl A. Cohn, "Empowering Those at the Bottom Beats Punishing Them from the Top," *Education Week*, April 25, 2007.

36. Anthony S. Bryk and Barbara Schneider, *Trust in Schools: A Core Resource for Improvement* (New York: Russell Sage Foundation, 2002), 123.

CHAPTER FIVE

1. Michael Bloomberg, "Our Children Deserve Better," campaign document, June 11, 2001 (downloaded June 29, 2003, from a Web site [mikefor mayor.org] that has since been closed).

2. Diane Ravitch, "A History of Public School Governance in New York City," in *When Mayors Take Charge: School Governance in the City*, ed. Joseph P. Viteritti (Washington, D.C.: Brookings Institution Press, 2009), 171–186.

3. Javier C. Hernandez, "In Debate Over Schools, Panel Is No Threat to the Mayor's Grip," *New York Times*, April 23, 2009.

4. Diane Ravitch, *The Great School Wars: New York City, 1805–1973* (New York: Basic Books, 1974), 92–99.

5. Abby Goodnough, "Schools Chief Is Soaking Up Advice in San Diego," *New York Times*, August 14, 2002.

6. Mike France, "Can Business Save New York Schools?" *BusinessWeek*, June 9, 2003; Elissa Gootman and David M. Herszenhorn, "Consultants Draw Fire in Bus Woes," *New York Times*, February 3, 2007.

7. James Traub, "New York's New Approach," *New York Times*, August 3, 2003; Deidre McFadyen, "Educators in Region 4: Don't Stop Us from Teaching Our Kids," *New York Teacher*, January 18, 2005.

8. As leader of General Electric, Welch was known for his tough, uncompromising attitude toward employees. See Thomas F. O'Boyle, *At Any Cost: Jack Welch, General Electric, and the Pursuit of Profit* (New York: Knopf, 1998), 72–76; Mary Hoffman, "Jack Welch Is My Daddy," ICE-UFT, March 8, 2005, http://ice-uft.org/daddy.htm; Geoff Colvin, "The CEO Educator," *Fortune*, October 1, 2009 (online version).

9. David M. Herszenhorn, "Not So Long Out of School, Yet Running the System," *New York Times*, March 25, 2004.

10. Deidre McFadyen, "Trouble in the Workshop," *New York Teacher*, February 17, 2005; Catherine Gewertz, "Grading the Mayor," *Education Week*, October 26, 2005; Sol Stern, "A Negative Assessment: An Education Revolution That Never Was," *Education Next* 5, no. 4 (Fall 2005): 12–16.

11. National Right to Read Foundation, "Selection of a Systematic Phonics Program for NYC Students," February 4, 2003, www.nrrf.org/phonics_nyc -2-4-03.htm; Sol Stern, "Bloomberg and Klein Rush In," *City Journal*, Spring 2003; Stern, "Tragedy Looms for Gotham's School Reform," *City Journal*, Autumn 2003; Open letter from "Education Faculty from Colleges and Universities across the New York City Area" to Michael Bloomberg, Joel Klein, and Diana Lam, re: " The New System-Wide Instructional Approach to Literacy and the Restructuring of Districts into Regions," February 10, 2003.

12. Carrie Melago and Erin Einhorn, "Bus Fiasco Hell on Wheels from Day 1," *New York Daily News*, February 2, 2007; Gootman and Herszenhorn, "Consultants Draw Fire in Bus Woes."

13. Erin Einhorn, "Education Job Titles Stump Parents," *New York Daily News*, December 26, 2007.

14. National Center for Education Statistics, *The Nation's Report Card: Trial Urban District Assessment, Science 2005* (Washington, D.C.: U.S. Department of Education, 2006); Jennifer Medina, "City Schools Fail to Comply with State Rule on Arts Classes," *New York Times*, March 7, 2008; Richard Kessler, Center for Arts Education, "Testimony to the Joint Meeting of the Committees (Senate Committee on Cultural Affairs, Tourism, Parks, and Recreation; Assembly Committee on Tourism, Arts, and Sports Development) re: The Impact of Potential Budget Cuts to the Arts Industry, Tourism, and Living Museums," February 3, 2009, www.cae-nyc.org/potential_budget_cuts.

15. Diane Ravitch and Randi Weingarten, "Public Schools, Minus the Public," *New York Times*, March 18, 2004.

16. Jennifer Medina, "Albany Panel Signals It Won't Give the Mayor Carte Blanche on Schools," *New York Times*, May 6, 2009.

17. David M. Herszenhorn, "Bloomberg Wins on School Tests After Firing Foes," *New York Times*, March 16, 2004; *New York Sun*, "Bloomberg's Finest Hour," March 17, 2004.

18. Clara Hemphill et al., *The New Marketplace: How Small-School Reforms and School Choice Have Reshaped New York City's High Schools* (New York: Center for New York City Affairs, The New School, 2009), 15.

19. New York City Department of Education, "NYC Results on the New York State 2006–2009 English Language Arts (ELA) Test (Grades 3–8)," http://schools.nyc.gov/accountability/Reports/Data/TestResults/2009/ELA/2006-2009_ELA_Citywide_ALL_Tested_web.xls; New York City Department of Education, "NYC Results on the New York State 2006–2009 Mathematics Test (Grades 3–8)," http://schools.nyc.gov/accountability/Reports/Data/TestResults/2009/Math/2006-2009_Math_ALL_TESTED_CITYWIDE.xls.

20. Meredith Kolodner, "City Students Are Passing Standardized Tests Just by Guessing," *New York Daily News*, August 11, 2009; Diana Senechal, "Guessing My Way to Promotion," *GothamSchools*, August 17, 2009, http://gothamschools.org/2009/08/17/guessing-my-way-to-promotion/; Javier C. Hernandez, "Botched Most Answers on New York State Math Test? You Still Pass," *New York Times*, September 14, 2009. For the conversion charts for the New York state tests in English and mathematics, see New York State Education

Department, "English Language Arts (ELA) and Mathematic [sic] Assessment Results," www.emsc.nysed.gov/irts/ela-math/.

21. NYC Public School Parents, http://nycpublicschoolparents.blogspot.com.

22. Carl Campanile, "Gates' $4 Mil Lesson," *New York Post*, August 18, 2009.

23. United Federation of Teachers, "Teachers Want Chancellor Klein to Do a Better Job," press release, June 26, 2008, www.uft.org/news/better_job/; Elissa Gootman, "Bloomberg Unveils Performance Pay for Teachers," *New York Times*, October 17, 2007; Randi Weingarten, address to the UFT Delegate Assembly, June 24, 2009, www.uft.org/news/issues/speeches/resignation_address/.

24. David M. Herszenhorn, "Charter School Will Not Go Into School for the Gifted," *New York Times*, June 24, 2006.

25. New York City Department of Education, "Mayor Bloomberg and Chancellor Klein Announce Achievement of Major Milestone in the Creation of 100 Charter Schools," press release, February 10, 2009.

26. Vanessa Witenko, "Most Vulnerable Students Shut Out of Charter Schools," InsideSchools.org, May 19, 2009, http://insideschools.org/blog/2009/05/19/most-vulnerable-students-shut-out-of-charter-schools/.

27. Jennifer L. Jennings, "School Choice or Schools' Choice? Managing in an Era of Accountability," paper, Annual Meeting, American Sociological Association, New York City, August 2007.

28. Hemphill et al., *The New Marketplace*, 1–7.

29. Ibid., 58.

30. David M. Herszenhorn, "In Push for Small Schools, Other Schools Suffer," *New York Times*, January 14, 2005; Samuel G. Freedman, "Failings of One Brooklyn High School May Threaten a Neighbor's Success," *New York Times*, May 7, 2008; Hemphill et al., *The New Marketplace*, 35–38.

31. Gootman, "Bloomberg Unveils Performance Pay for Teachers"; Gootman, "Teachers Agree to Bonus Pay Tied to Scores," *New York Times*, October 18, 2007; United Federation of Teachers, "55/25 Update," www.uft.org/member/money/financial/5525/.

32. Erin Einhorn, "Only in N.Y. Schools Can Get an 'A' and 'F,'" *New York Daily News*, December 12, 2007; Leonie Haimson, "Testimony Before the City Council Education Committee on the DOE School Grades," December 10, 2007, http://nycpublicschoolparents.googlegroups.com/web/testimony%20school%20grades%2012%2007.doc; Jennifer Jennings, "In NYC, More F Schools than A Schools in Good Standing with NCLB," Eduwonkette blog, September 16, 2008, http://blogs.edweek.org/edweek/eduwonkette/2008/09/in_nyc_more_f_schools_than_a_s_1.html.

33. New York City Department of Education, "Chancellor Klein Releases 2009 Progress Reports on Elementary, Middle, and K–8 Schools," press release, September 2, 2009; *New York Post*, "An Avalanche of A's," September 4, 2009; *New York Daily News*, "Stupid Card Trick," September 4, 2009; Jennifer Medina, "As Many Schools Earn A's and B's, City Plans to Raise Standards," *New York Times*, September 4, 2009.

34. Jennifer Medina, "Teacher Bonuses Total $27 Million, Nearly Double Last Year's," *New York Times*, September 5, 2009; Diane Ravitch, "Bloomberg's Bogus School Report Cards Destroy Real Progress," *New York Daily News*, September 9, 2009.

35. Hemphill et al., *The New Marketplace*, 2, 11–12; Meredith Kolodner and Rachel Monahan, "Four Schools in Bottom 10 in State Tests Were Newly Opened," *New York Daily News*, July 13, 2009 (the headline said four, but the story identified five new schools in the bottom ten).

36. New York State Education Department, "English Language Arts (ELA) and Mathematic [sic] Assessment Results," www.emsc.nysed.gov/irts/ela-math/; for New York state and New York city scores from 1999–2006, see www.emsc.nysed.gov/irts/ela-math/2006/ela-06/Grade3-8ELA-2006.ppt and www.emsc.nysed.gov/irts/ela-math/2006/math-06/Grade3-8Math.ppt. After the first two years of mayoral control, the Department of Education began adding the score gains of the year 2002–2003 to its own total, although these tests were administered before the mayor's reforms were implemented. When the 2002–2003 scores were released, department officials did not treat them as their own. See David M. Herszenhorn, "City English Scores in Statewide Testing Show Marked Gain," *New York Times*, May 21, 2003; Elissa Gootman, "Math Scores Rise Sharply Across State," *New York Times*, October 22, 2003. After 2007, the city's scores on state tests continued to rise, with the most extraordinary gains occurring in 2008–2009. Gains from 2006 to 2009 should be viewed with caution in light of the state education department's purposeful lowering of expectations during that period. The New York State Education Department changed the tests in 2006 when it extended them to grades 3–8 (previously only grades 4 and 8 were tested). Test scores from 1999–2005 are discontinuous with those from 2006 onward and should not be compared, but education officials regularly made comparisons across the years.

37. National Center for Education Statistics, *The Nation's Report Card: Trial Urban District Assessment, Mathematics 2007* (Washington, D.C.: U.S. Department of Education, 2007), 50–51; National Center for Education Statistics, *The Nation's Report Card: Trial Urban District Assessment, Reading 2007* (Washington, D.C.: U.S. Department of Education, 2007), 50–51; Jennifer Medina, "Little Progress for City Schools on National Test," *New York Times*, November 16, 2007. Some experts questioned the fourth-grade math gains, because 25 percent of test takers were given accommodations (such as extra time), a proportion far larger than in any other city tested and double the proportion that received accommodations in New York City in 2003. Elizabeth Green, "N.Y. Gave the Most Breaks for School Exam," *New York Sun*, November 21, 2007.

38. New York City Department of Education, "New York City Public School Students Make Gains on 2007 National Assessment of Educational Progress (NAEP) Tests," press release, November 15, 2007; Medina, "Little Progress for City Schools on National Test."

39. Elissa Gootman and Sharona Coutts, "Lacking the Credits to Graduate, Some Students Learn a Shortcut," *New York Times*, April 11, 2008; Javier C.

Hernandez, "Students Still Sliding By, Critics Say," *New York Times*, July 13, 2009; Jennifer L. Jennings and Leonie Haimson, "Discharge and Graduation Rates," in *NYC Schools Under Bloomberg and Klein: What Parents, Teachers, and Policymakers Need to Know*, ed. Leonie Haimson and Ann Kjellberg (New York: Lulu, 2009), 77–85, www.lulu.com/content/paperback-book/nyc-schools-under-bloomberg -klein-what-parents-teachers-and-policymakers-need-to-know/7214189.

40. Javier C. Hernandez, "A New High School, with College Mixed In," *New York Times*, March 19, 2009.

41. Elissa Gootman and Robert Gebeloff, "With New City Policy, Gifted Programs Shrink," *New York Times*, October 30, 2008.

42. *New York Times*, "New York State Test Scores," August 4, 2009, http:// projects.nytimes.com/new-york-schools-test-scores/about.

43. David M. Herszenhorn, "A Gold Star for Schools: Overview," *New York Times*, May 19, 2005; Sol Stern, "Gotham's Telltale Reading Tests," *City Journal*, Autumn 2006.

44. Quoted in Michael Winerip, "Test Scores Up? Cheer (Don't Analyze)," *New York Times*, June 29, 2005.

45. James F. Brennan, "New York City Public School Improvement Before and After Mayoral Control," in *NYC Schools Under Bloomberg and Klein: What Parents, Teachers, and Policymakers Need to Know*, ed. Leonie Haimson and Ann Kjellberg, 105–113; Joel Klein, "Chancellor's Testimony Before City Council Education Committee on DOE's Preliminary Expense Budget," March 26, 2009, http://print.nycenet.edu/Offices/mediarelations/News andSpeeches/2008–2009/20090326_budget_testimony.htm; Nicole Gelinas, "NYC's Fiscal Future," *New York Post*, October 27, 2009.

CHAPTER SIX

1. *Ebony*, "5 Questions for Marian Wright Edelman," January 2004.

2. Frederick M. Hess and Michael J. Petrilli, "The Politics of No Child Left Behind: Will the Coalition Hold?" *Journal of Education* 185, no. 3 (2004): 13–25.

3. Walt Haney, "The Myth of the Texas Miracle in Education," *Education Policy Analysis Archives* 8, no. 41 (August 19, 2000); Stephen P. Klein et al., "What Do Test Scores in Texas Tell Us?" *RAND Issue Paper IP-202*, RAND, Santa Monica, CA, 2000, 2, 9–13.

4. For an excellent overview of the law, see Frederick M. Hess and Michael J. Petrilli, *No Child Left Behind Primer* (New York: Peter Lang, 2006).

5. Frederick M. Hess and Chester E. Finn Jr., eds., *No Remedy Left Behind: Lessons from a Half-Decade of NCLB* (Washington, D.C.: AEI Press, 2007); for Betts's reference to choice in California, see 148–152.

6. Julian Betts, "California: Does the Golden State Deserve a Gold Star?" in *No Remedy Left Behind*, 130.

7. Elissa Gootman, "Report Assails Tutoring Firms in City Schools," *New York Times*, March 8, 2006.

8. The chief executive Officer of Kaplan (a major supplier of tests and test prep materials) said on a PBS program that his business had grown from

annual revenues of $70 million in 1991 to $2 billion in 2007 "on the back of testing growth of all kinds." The other major testing companies—McGraw-Hill's CTB division, Pearson's Harcourt Assessment, and Houghton Mifflin's Riverside unit—would not disclose their revenues. The same program said that tutoring was a $4 billion industry, whose growth was propelled by NCLB. "The New Business of Education," *Nightly Business Report*, February 18, 2008, www.pbs.org/nbr/site/onair/transcripts/080218i/. See also Thomas Toch, *Margins of Error: The Education Testing Industry in the No Child Left Behind Era* (Washington, D.C.: Education Sector, 2006); Karla Scoon Reid, "Federal Law Spurs Private Companies to Market Tutoring," *Education Week*, December 8, 2004.

9. National Center for Education Statistics, *The Nation's Report Card: Reading 2007* (Washington, D.C.: U.S. Department of Education, 2007), 9, 27.

10. Margaret A. Spellings, editorial, Forbes.com, January 23, 2008, www.forbes.com/2008/01/22/solutions-education-spellings-oped-cx _dor_0123spellings.html; Andrew Dean Ho, "The Problem with 'Proficiency': Limitations of Statistics and Policy Under No Child Left Behind," *Educational Researcher* 37, no. 6 (2008): 351–360.

11. Hess and Finn, *No Remedy Left Behind*, 327–328.

12. Ibid.

13. David J. Hoff, "Schools Struggling to Meet Key Goal on Accountability," *Education Week*, January 7, 2009.

14. National Center for Education Evaluation and Regional Assistance, *Turning Around Chronically Low-Performing Schools* (Washington, D.C.: U.S. Department of Education, 2008).

15. Linda Jacobson, "NCLB Restructuring Found Ineffectual in California," *Education Week*, February 20, 2008; Caitlin Scott, *Managing More than A Thousand Remodeling Projects: School Restructuring in California* (Washington, D.C.: Center on Education Policy, 2008).

16. Caitlin Scott, *A Call to Restructure Restructuring: Lessons from the No Child Left Behind Act in Five States* (Washington, D.C.: Center on Education Policy, 2008), 1–3.

17. Sam Dillon, "Under 'No Child' Law, Even Solid Schools Falter," *New York Times*, October 13, 2008.

18. National Science Foundation, "All Students Proficient on State Tests by 2014?" press release, September 25, 2008, www.nsf.gov/news/news_summ. jsp?cntn_id=112312; M. J. Bryant et al., "School Performance Will Fail to Meet Legislated Benchmarks," *Science* 321, no. 5897 (September 26, 2008): 1781–1782.

19. Sam Dillon, "Students Ace State Tests, but Earn D's from U.S.," *New York Times*, November 26, 2005; National Center for Education Statistics, *The Nation's Report Card: Reading 2007* (Washington, D.C.: U.S. Department of Education, 2007). See also Kevin Carey, "Hot Air: How States Inflate Their Educational Progress Under NCLB" (Washington, D.C.: Education Sector, 2006).

20. Chester E. Finn Jr. and Michael J. Petrilli, foreword to *The Proficiency Illusion*, by John Cronin et al. (Washington: D.C.: Thomas B. Fordham Institute and Northwest Evaluation Association, 2007), 3.

21. Ibid.

22. Angela Montefinise, "Lost Lessons in Test-Prep Craze," *New York Post*, January 28, 2007.

23. Laurie Fox and Holly K. Hacker, "Dallas–Fort Worth Students Struggle with TAKS' Short-response Written Test," *Dallas Morning News*, July 20, 2008.

24. Jennifer McMurrer, *Choices, Changes, and Challenges: Curriculum and Instruction in the NCLB Era* (Washington, D.C.: Center on Education Policy, 2007), 1; McMurrer, *Instructional Time in Elementary Schools: A Closer Look at Changes for Specific Subjects* (Washington, D.C.: Center on Education Policy, 2008), 2.

25. Linda Perlstein, *Tested: One American School Struggles to Make the Grade* (New York: Henry Holt, 2007).

26. *The Nation's Report Card: Reading 2007*, 8, 28; National Center for Education Statistics, *The Nation's Report Card: Mathematics 2007* (Washington, D.C.: U.S. Department of Education, 2007), 8, 24. See also Bruce Fuller et al., "Gauging Growth: How to Judge No Child Left Behind?" *Educational Researcher* 36, no. 5 (2007): 268–278.

27. National Center for Education Statistics, *Achievement Gaps: How Black and White Students in Public Schools Perform in Mathematics and Reading on the National Assessment of Educational Progress* (Washington, D.C.: U.S. Department of Education, 2009), 7, 29.

28. *The Nation's Report Card: Reading 2007*, 9, 27; *The Nation's Report Card: Mathematics 2007*, 9, 25.

CHAPTER SEVEN

1. Milton Friedman, "The Role of Government in Education," in *Economics and the Public Interest*, ed. Robert A. Solo (New Brunswick, NJ: Rutgers University Press, 1955), 123–144.

2. Diane Ravitch, *The Troubled Crusade: American Education, 1945–1980* (New York: Basic Books, 1983), 27–41; Paul Blanshard, *American Freedom and Catholic Power* (Boston: Beacon Press, 1949).

3. In 1985, in *Aguilar v. Felton*, the Supreme Court prohibited the provision of federally funded services to religious schools; in 1997, in *Agostini v. Felton*, the Court reversed its 1985 ruling.

4. See Terrel H. Bell, *The Thirteenth Man: A Reagan Cabinet Memoir* (New York: Free Press, 1988), 89–98, 128–131.

5. The John M. Olin Foundation supported my research projects at Teachers College, Columbia University, and New York University. With its financial assistance, I wrote *Left Back: A Century of Failed School Reforms* in 2000. With the Olin Foundation's aid, Joseph Viteritti and I edited collections of essays about school reform in New York City, civic education, and the effects of commercial mass culture on children.

6. John E. Chubb and Terry M. Moe, *Politics, Markets, and America's Schools* (Washington, D.C.: Brookings Institution Press, 1990), 2, 12.

7. Ibid., 217.

8. Ibid., 217–225.

9. A good overview of the Milwaukee and Cleveland cases is available in Joseph P. Viteritti, *Choosing Equality: School Choice, the Constitution, and Civil Society* (Washington, D.C.: Brookings Institution Press, 1999), 98–108.

10. Ray Budde, *Education by Charter: Restructuring School Districts; Key to Long-Term Continuing Improvement in American Education* (Andover, MA: Regional Laboratory for Educational Improvement of the Northeast and Islands, 1988), www.eric.ed.gov/ERICDocs/data/ericdocs2sql/content _storage_01/0000019b/80/1d/96/8c.pdf.

11. Albert Shanker, National Press Club Speech, Washington, D.C., March 31, 1988, 6, www.reuther.wayne.edu/files/64.43.pdf.

12. Ibid., 12, 14, 15–17, 20–21.

13. Albert Shanker, "State of Our Union," speech, 70th Convention of the American Federation of Teachers, San Francisco, California, July 2, 1988, www.reuther.wayne.edu/files/64.50.pdf; Albert Shanker, "A Charter For Change," *New York Times*, July 10, 1988.

14. Albert Shanker, "Goals Not Gimmicks," *New York Times*, November 7, 1993.

15. Joseph Lieberman, "Schools Where Kids Succeed," *Reader's Digest*, January 1999,145–151.

16. National Charter School Alliance, "Top 10 Charter Communities by Market Share," 2008, www.publiccharters.org/files/publications/2008 Market Share Report.pdf.

17. Diane Ravitch and William A. Galston, "Scholarships for Inner-City School Kids," *Washington Post*, December 17, 1996.

18. Scott W. Hamilton, ed., *Who Will Save America's Urban Catholic Schools?* (Washington, D.C.: Thomas B. Fordham Institute, 2008), 6.

19. See, for example, John F. Witte, Troy D. Sterr, and Christopher A. Thorn, *Fifth-Year Report: Milwaukee Parental Choice Program* (Madison, WI: Robert LaFollette Institute of Public Affairs, University of Wisconsin-Madison, 1995); Paul E. Peterson, "A Critique of the Witte Evaluation of Milwaukee's School Choice Program," *Occasional Paper 95–2*, Harvard University Center for American Political Studies, 1995.

20. Cecelia Elena Rouse and Lisa Barrow, "School Vouchers and Student Achievement: Recent Evidence and Remaining Questions," *Annual Review of Economics* 1 (2009), 17–42. A study of the Florida voucher program in 2009 found that the 23,259 students using publicly funded vouchers to attend private schools did no better or worse than similar students in public schools. The study, commissioned by the state legislature, was conducted by economist David Figlio; Ron Matus, "Study Finds Vouchers Don't Make Difference," *St. Petersburg Times*, June 30, 2009.

21. Patrick J. Wolf, *The Comprehensive Longitudinal Evaluation of the Milwaukee Parental Choice Program: Summary of Baseline Reports*, SCDP

Milwaukee Evaluation Report #1 (Fayetteville: University of Arkansas, 2008), 9; Alan J. Borsuk, "Voucher Study Finds Parity," *Milwaukee Journal Sentinel*, February 26, 2008.

22. Patrick J. Wolf, *The Comprehensive Longitudinal Evaluation of the Milwaukee Parental Choice Program: Summary of Second Year Reports*, SCDP Milwaukee Evaluation Report #6 (Fayetteville: University of Arkansas, 2009), 11; Alan J. Borsuk, "Study Finds Results of MPS and Voucher School Students Are Similar," *Milwaukee Journal Sentinel*, March 26, 2009.

23. Patrick J. Wolf et al., *Evaluation of the D.C. Opportunity Scholarship Program: Impacts After Two Years; Executive Summary* (Washington, D.C.: U.S. Department of Education, June 2008), xiii–xiv; Wolf et al., *Evaluation of the D.C. Opportunity Scholarship Program: Impacts After Three Years; Executive Summary* (Washington, D.C.: U.S. Department of Education, 2009), v.

24. Wolf et al., *Evaluation of the D.C. Opportunity Scholarship Program: Impacts After Three Years; Executive Summary*, v–vi, xiv–xviii.

25. Alan J. Borsuk, Sarah Carr, and Leonard Sykes Jr., "Inside Choice Schools: 15 Years of Vouchers," *Milwaukee Journal Sentinel*, June 12–18, 2005; Carr, "Teachers Paid from Sale of Mercedes," *Milwaukee Journal Sentinel*, December 17, 2005.

26. Borsuk, Carr, and Sykes, "Inside Choice Schools: 15 Years of Vouchers"; Martin Carnoy, Frank Adamson, and Amita Chudgar, *Vouchers and Public School Performance: A Case Study of the Milwaukee Parental Choice Program* (Washington, D.C.: Economic Policy Institute, 2007), 2; Borsuk, "20,000 Students Now Use Vouchers," *Milwaukee Journal Sentinel*, November 9, 2008.

27. Bill Turque, "37,000 to Start D.C. Public School Year, Well Below Budgeted Figure," *Washington Post*, August 24, 2009; Jessica Gresko, "D.C. Public Schools to Fire 388, Cites Budget Cuts," *Washington Times*, October 3, 2009. See also Jack Buckley and Mark Schneider, *Charter Schools: Hope or Hype?* (Princeton, NJ: Princeton University Press, 2007), 25.

28. National Center for Education Statistics, *The Nation's Report Card: Reading 2007* (Washington, D.C.: U.S. Department of Education, 2007), 54, 62; *The Nation's Report Card: Mathematics 2007* (Washington, D.C.: U.S. Department of Education, 2007), 50, 58.

29. Sam Dillon, "Collapse of 60 Charter Schools Leaves Californians Scrambling," *New York Times*, September 17, 2004.

30. Kristen A. Graham, "SRC Told Firms Need New Role," *Philadelphia Inquirer*, June 11, 2009; Brian Gill et al., *State Takeover, School Restructuring, Private Management, and Student Achievement in Philadelphia* (Santa Monica, CA: RAND Corporation, 2007), 39–41; Ron Zimmer et al., "Evaluating the Performance of Philadelphia's Charter Schools," Working Paper, RAND Education, Mathematica Policy Research, and Research for Action, 2008, iii. See also Kristen A. Graham, "Study: District-Run Phila. Schools Top Manager-Run Ones," *Philadelphia Inquirer*, April 9, 2009.

31. Martha Woodall, "Charter Schools' Problems Surfacing," *Philadelphia Inquirer*, December 29, 2008; Dan Hardy, "Charter School Appeals to Block Release of Records," *Philadelphia Inquirer*, June 11, 2009.

32. Buckley and Schneider, *Charter Schools: Hope or Hype?*, 81–88.

33. Jeanne Russell and Jenny LaCoste-Caputo, "Just How Well Have Charter Schools Worked?" *San Antonio Express-News*, January 28, 2007.

34. KIPP Web site, www.kipp.org/01/; see Jay Mathews, *Work Hard. Be Nice.: How Two Inspired Teachers Created the Most Promising Schools in America* (Chapel Hill, NC: Algonquin Books, 2009).

35. James Vaznis, "Charter Schools Lag in Serving the Neediest," *Boston Globe*, August 12, 2009.

36. Jeffrey R. Henig, *What Do We Know About the Outcomes of KIPP Schools?* (Boulder, CO, and Tempe, AZ: Education and the Public Interest Center & Education Policy Research Unit, 2008), 13; Katrina R. Woodworth et al., *San Francisco Bay Area KIPP Schools: A Study of Early Implementation and Achievement, Final Report* (Menlo Park, CA: SRI International, 2008), ix, 26–29, 33–34, 63.

37. F. Howard Nelson, Bella Rosenberg, and Nancy Van Meter, *Charter School Achievement on the 2003 National Assessment of Educational Progress* (Washington, D.C.: American Federation of Teachers, August 2004); Diana Jean Schemo, "Charter Schools Trail in Results, U.S. Data Reveals," *New York Times*, August 17, 2004; National Center for Education Statistics, *America's Charter Schools: Results from the NAEP 2003 Pilot Study* (Washington, D.C.: U.S. Department of Education, 2004), 1.

38. "Charter School Evaluation Reported by *The New York Times* Fails to Meet Professional Standards," display advertisement, *New York Times*, August 25, 2004; Caroline M. Hoxby, *Achievement in Charter Schools and Regular Public Schools in the United States: Understanding the Differences* (Cambridge, MA: Harvard University and National Bureau of Economic Research, 2004).

39. Chester E. Finn Jr., "No August Break in Charter-land," *Education Gadfly*, August 19, 2004, www.edexcellence.net/gadfly/index.cfm?issue=159#a1941.

40. Martin Carnoy, Rebecca Jacobsen, Lawrence Mishel, and Richard Rothstein, *The Charter School Dust-Up: Examining the Evidence on Enrollment and Achievement* (Washington, D.C.: Economic Policy Institute and Teachers College Press, 2005), 122–123.

41. Schemo, "Public Schools Perform Near Private Ones in Study," *New York Times*, July 15, 2006; Henry Braun, Frank Jenkins, and Wendy Grigg, *Comparing Private Schools and Public Schools Using Hierarchical Linear Modeling* (Washington, D.C.: U.S. Department of Education, National Center for Education Statistics, 2006), iii–v.

42. Christopher Lubienski and Sarah Theule Lubienski, *Charter, Private, Public Schools and Academic Achievement: New Evidence from NAEP Mathematics Data* (New York: National Center for the Study of Privatization in Education, Teachers College, Columbia University, 2006), 2–5, 40. See also Ron Zimmer et al., *Charter Schools in Eight States: Effects on Achievement, Attainment, Integration, and Competition* (Santa Monica, CA: RAND Corporation, 2009).

43. Erik W. Robelen, "NAEP Gap Continuing for Charters: Sector's Scores Lag in Three Out of Four Main Categories," *Education Week*, May 21, 2008, 1, 14.

44. Atila Abdulkadiroglu, Thomas Kane, et al., *Informing the Debate: Comparing Boston's Charter, Pilot and Traditional Schools* (Boston: The Boston Foundation, 2009), 39; *Boston Globe*, "Top-Scoring Schools on the 10th Grade MCAS," 2008, www.boston.com/news/special/education/mcas/scores08/10th_top_schools.htm; Jennifer Jennings, "The Boston Pilot/Charter School Study: Some Good News, and Some Cautions," Eduwonkette blog, January 7, 2009, http://blogs.edweek.org/edweek/eduwonkette/2009/01/the_boston_pilotcharter_school.html.

45. Vaznis, "Charter Schools Lag in Serving the Neediest."

46. Center for Research on Education Outcomes (CREDO), *Multiple Choice: Charter School Performance in 16 States* (Stanford, CA: Stanford University, 2009); Lesli A. Maxwell, "Study Casts Doubt on Charter School Results," *Education Week*, June 15, 2009.

47. Caroline M. Hoxby, Sonali Murarka, and Jenny Kang, *How New York City's Charter Schools Affect Achievement* (Cambridge, MA: New York City Charter Schools Evaluation Project, 2009); Jennifer Medina, "Study Shows Better Scores for Charter School Students," *New York Times*, September 22, 2009; *Wall Street Journal*, "Do Charters 'Cream' the Best?" September 24, 2009; *Washington Post*, "Charter Success," September 27, 2009.

48. Tom Loveless and Katharyn Field, "Perspectives on Charter Schools," in *Handbook of Research on School Choice*, ed. Mark Berends, Matthew G. Springer, Dale Ballou, and Herbert J. Walberg (New York: Routledge, 2009), 111–112.

49. Buckley and Schneider, *Charter Schools: Hope or Hype?*, 267.

50. Barack Obama, "President Obama's Remarks to the Hispanic Chamber of Commerce," *New York Times*, March 10, 2009; *USA Today*, "Obama Wants 5K Closed Schools to Rebound," May 11, 2009; Michele McNeil, "Racing for an Early Edge," *Education Week*, July 15, 2009.

CHAPTER EIGHT

1. Scoring errors are not uncommon. In March 2006, the College Board confirmed that scoring errors on the SAT affected over 4,600 students; in the same month, the Educational Testing Service settled a case for $11 million involving scoring errors on tests used for teacher certification, which affected 27,000 test takers. Karen W. Arenson, "Testing Errors Prompt Calls for Oversight," *New York Times*, March 18, 2006; for an analysis of testing errors and their causes, see Kathleen Rhoades and George Madaus, *Errors in Standardized Tests: A Systemic Problem* (Chestnut Hill, MA: National Board on Educational Testing and Public Policy, Lynch School of Education, Boston College, 2003).

2. College Board, "Score Range," www.collegeboard.com/student/testing/sat/scores/understanding/scorerange.html; College Board, "Effects of Coaching

on SAT Scores," www.collegeboard.com/prod_downloads/highered/ra/sat/coaching.pdf.

3. National Research Council, *High Stakes: Testing for Tracking, Promotion, and Graduation*, ed. Jay P. Heubert and Robert M. Hauser (Washington, D.C.: National Academy Press, 1999), 275–276.

4. Robert L. Linn, "The Concept of Validity in the Context of NCLB," in *The Concept of Validity: Revisions, New Directions, and Applications*, ed. Robert W. Lissitz (Charlotte, NC: Information Age Publishing, 2009), 195–212.

5. Ibid., 200.

6. Joshua Benton and Holly K. Hacker, "Analysis Shows TAKS Cheating Rampant," *Dallas Morning News*, June 3, 2007.

7. Jennifer L. Jennings, "School Choice or Schools' Choice? Managing in an Era of Accountability," paper, Annual Meeting, American Sociological Association, New York City, August 2007; two principals of small high schools of choice told Jennings that careful selection of students was "a matter of organizational survival" in the age of accountability (31); Maria Sacchetti and Tracy Jan, "Pilot Schools Setting More Hurdles," *Boston Globe*, July 8, 2007.

8. Martin Carnoy, Rebecca Jacobsen, Lawrence Mishel, and Richard Rothstein, *The Charter School Dust-Up: Examining the Evidence on Enrollment and Achievement* (New York: Economic Policy Institute and Teachers College Press, 2005), 29–65; Richard Rothstein, "Holding Accountability to Account: How Scholarship and Experience in Other Fields Inform Exploration of Performance Incentives in Education," Working Paper 2008–04, National Center on Performance Incentives, Vanderbilt University, Nashville, Tenn., 2008, 40–41.

9. Jennings, "School Choice or Schools' Choice?" 34–36.

10. David N. Figlio and Lawrence S. Getzler, "Accountability, Ability and Disability: Gaming the System," *Working Paper 9307*, National Bureau of Economic Research, Cambridge, MA, 2002; Richard Rothstein, Rebecca Jacobsen, and Tamara Wilder, *Grading Education: Getting Accountability Right* (Washington, D.C.: Economic Policy Institute and Teachers College Press, 2008), 67–70; Laurel Rosenhall and Phillip Reese, "Schools Reclassify Students, Pass Test Under Federal Law," *Sacramento Bee*, April 27, 2008. See also Linda McSpadden McNeil et al., "Avoidable Losses: High-Stakes Accountability and the Dropout Crisis," *Education Policy Analysis Archives* 16, no. 3 (January 31, 2008).

11. Meredith Kolodner and Rachel Monahan, "Can You Do These Math Tests? With Easier Exams This Year, *News* Puts You to the Challenge," *New York Daily News*, June 7, 2009.

12. Rothstein et al., *Grading Education*, 69; New York State Education Department, "Testing Accommodations for Former Limited English Proficient/English Language Learners," Albany, New York, October 2008, 1, www.emsc.nysed.gov/sar/accommodations10–08.pdf.

13. Edith Starzyk, Scott Stephens, and Thomas Ott, "Districts 'Scrubbing' Away Thousands of Students' Test Scores," *Cleveland Plain Dealer*, September 8, 2008.

14. New York State Education Department, "Grade 3–8 Math Results 2009," slide 42, www.emsc.nysed.gov/irts/ela-math/2009/math/2009Math -FINAL-5-29-09.ppt; Meredith Kolodner and Rachel Monahan, "Low Test Standards Are a Form of Social Promotion, Say Experts," *New York Daily News*, July 15, 2009; New York State Education Department, "English Language Arts (ELA) and Mathematic [sic] Assessment Results," www.emsc.nysed.gov/ irts/ela-math/; New York City Department of Education, "NYC Results on the New York State 2006–2009 English Language Arts (ELA) Test (Grades 3–8)," http://schools.nyc.gov/accountability/Reports/Data/TestResults/2009/ ELA/2006–2009_ELA_Citywide_ALL_Tested_web.xls.

15. New York State Education Department, "Regents Examination in Integrated Algebra, June 2009: Chart for Converting Total Test Raw Scores to Final Examination Scores (Scale Scores)," www.emsc.nysed.gov/osa/concht/june09/ ia-cc-609.pdf; New York State Education Department, "Regents Examination in Living Environment, June 2009: Chart for Converting Total Test Raw Scores to Final Examination Scores (Scale Scores)," www.emsc.nysed.gov/osa/ concht/june09/livenvcc-609.pdf.

16. Civic Committee of the Commercial Club of Chicago, *Still Left Behind: Student Learning in Chicago's Public Schools* (Chicago: Commercial Club, 2009), 2, 6–11; Greg Toppo, "Chicago Schools Report Contradicts Obama and Duncan," *USA Today*, July 12, 2009.

17. Steve Koss, "Test Score Inflation: Campbell's Law at Work," in *NYC Schools Under Bloomberg and Klein: What Parents, Teachers, and Policymakers Need to Know*, ed. Leonie Haimson and Ann Kjellberg (New York: Lulu, 2009), 87–94, www.lulu.com/content/paperback-book/nyc-schools-under-bloomberg -klein-what-parents-teachers-and-policymakers-need-to-know/7214189.

18. National Research Council, *High Stakes*, 279.

19. Daniel Koretz, *Measuring Up: What Educational Testing Really Tells Us* (Cambridge, MA: Harvard University Press, 2008), 253–255.

20. Ibid., 242–247.

21. Donald T. Campbell, "Assessing the Impact of Planned Social Change," in *Social Research and Public Policies: The Dartmouth/OECD Conference*, ed. G. M. Lyons (Hanover, NH: Public Affairs Center, Dartmouth College, 1975), 35.

22. Koretz, *Measuring Up*, 237–239.

23. Rothstein et al., *Grading Education*, 45–52.

24. *Education Week*, "Two Lenses: Academic Achievement," in *Quality Counts 2009*, January 8, 2009, 39.

25. T. Keung Hui, "Too Much School Testing, Panel Says," *News & Observer* (Raleigh, NC), November 19, 2007.

26. For a historical discussion of the tendency to excuse students from responsibility for their learning, see Paul A. Zoch, *Doomed to Fail: The Built-in Defects of American Education* (Chicago: Ivan R. Dee, 2004).

27. Jason Snipes, Fred Doolittle, and Corinne Herlihy, *Foundations for Success: Case Studies of How Urban School Systems Improve Student Achievement* (Washington, D.C.: Council of the Great City Schools, 2002), 169–176;

Deinya Phenix, Dorothy Siegel, Ariel Zaltsman, and Norm Fruchter, "Virtual District, Real Improvement: A Retrospective Evaluation of the Chancellor's District, 1996–2003" (New York: Institute for Education and Social Policy, New York University, 2004).

28. Cecilia Elena Rouse, Jane Hannaway, Dan Goldhaber, and David Figlio, "Feeling the Florida Heat? How Low-Performing Schools Respond to Voucher and Accountability Pressure," Working Paper #13, CALDER, Urban Institute, Washington, D.C., 2007, 5–7, 22; Dan Goldhaber and Jane Hannaway, "Accountability with a Kicker: Preliminary Observations on the Florida A+ Accountability Plan," *Phi Delta Kappan* 85, no. 8 (2004): 598–605.

29. Kim Severson, "Systematic Cheating Is Found in Atlanta's School System," *New York Times*, July 5, 2011 (http://www.nytimes.com/2011/07/06 /education/06atlanta.html?scp=1&sq=Systematic%20Cheating%20Is%20 Found%20In%20Atlanta%27s%20School%20System%20&st=cse); Michael Winerip, "Cracking a System in Which Test Scores Were for Changing," *New York Times*, July 17, 2011 (http://www.nytimes.com/2011/07/18/education /18oneducation.html?scp=1&sq=Michael%20Winerip%20Atlanta&st=cse).

30. "Special Investigation into CRCT Cheating at APS: Overview, Interviews, School Summaries," *Atlanta Journal-Constitution*, July 5, 2011 (http:// www.ajc.com/news/volume-1-of-special-1000798.html), p. 350. See also, Aaron Pallas, "Why Organizational Misconduct Happens: A Look at the Atlanta Cheating Scandal, *A Sociological Eye on Education*, July 14, 2011 (http://eyeoned.org/content/why-organizational-misconduct-happens-a -look-at-the-atlanta-cheating-scandal_255/?utm_source=feedburner&utm _medium=feed&utm_campaign=Feed:+HechingerReport+%28Hechinger+ Report%29).

31. Robert Glaser, "Commentary by the National Academy of Education," in *The Nation's Report Card: Improving the Assessment of Student Achievement*, chairmen, Lamar Alexander and H. Thomas James (Washington, D.C.: National Academy of Education, 1987), 51.

CHAPTER NINE

1. David Nakamura, "Fenty to Oust Janey Today," *Washington Post*, June 12, 2007; critics were not persuaded by her claims because of the lack of independent evidence. See www.dailyhowler.com/dh071107.shtml.

2. Evan Thomas, Eve Conant, and Pat Wingert, "An Unlikely Gambler," *Newsweek*, September 1, 2008. The online version of the article was titled "Can Michelle Rhee Save D.C.'s Schools?" and dated August 23, 2008.

3. Nakamura, "Fenty to Oust Janey Today."

4. Thomas et al., "An Unlikely Gambler"; Sam Dillon, "A School Chief Takes On Tenure, Stirring a Fight," *New York Times*, November 13, 2008.

5. Bill Turque, "Rhee Says Consultant's Report Shows Pay Plan is Sustainable," *Washington Post*, March 3, 2009.

6. *Wall Street Journal*, "Rhee-Forming D.C. Schools: A Democrat Shakes Up Washington's Failed Public Schools," November 22, 2008.

7. Amanda Ripley, "Can She Save Our Schools?" *Time*, December 8, 2008, 36–44.

8. Thomas R. Brooks, *Towards Dignity: A Brief History of the United Federation of Teachers* (New York: United Federation of Teachers, 1967), p. 12.

9. Terry M. Moe, "No Teacher Left Behind," *Wall Street Journal*, January 13, 2005.

10. See Joan Baratz-Snowden, *Fixing Tenure: A Proposal for Assuring Teacher Effectiveness and Due Process* (Washington, D.C.: Center for American Progress, 2009).

11. National Commission on Teaching & America's Future, *What Matters Most: Teaching for America's Future* (New York: NCTAF, 1996), 10–11, 95–96.

12. S. Paul Wright, Sandra P. Horn, and William L. Sanders, "Teacher and Classroom Context Effects on Student Achievement: Implications for Teacher Evaluation," *Journal of Personnel Evaluation in Education* 11, no. 1 (April 1997): 57–67. See also William L. Sanders and June C. Rivers, "Cumulative and Residual Effects of Teachers on Future Student Academic Achievement," research progress report, University of Tennessee Value-Added Research and Assessment Center, Knoxville, Tenn., 1996.

13. William L. Sanders, "Value-Added Assessment from Student Achievement Data: Opportunities and Hurdles," *Journal of Personnel Evaluation in Education* 14, no. 4 (December 2000): 329–339, esp. 330. A scholarly debate erupted when William Sanders's methods and value-added assessment were criticized by Audrey Amrein-Beardsley, "Methodological Concerns About the Education Value-Added Assessment System," *Educational Researcher* 37, no. 2 (2008): 65–75. Sanders responded in an interview: Debra Viadero, "'Value-Added' Pioneer Says Stinging Critique of Method is Off-Base," *Education Week*, May 7, 2008.

14. Eric A. Hanushek and Steven G. Rivkin, "How to Improve the Supply of High-Quality Teachers," *Brookings Papers on Education Policy*, ed. Diane Ravitch (Washington, D.C.: Brookings Institution Press, 2004), 14, 16, 19, 21–23.

15. Richard Rothstein, "Comment," *Brookings Papers on Education Policy* (2004), 26–27.

16. Robert Gordon, Thomas J. Kane, and Douglas O Staiger, "Identifying Effective Teachers Using Performance on the Job," Discussion Paper 2006–01, Brookings Institution, Washington, D.C., 5–6.

17. Ibid., 8.

18. Some educators created personality profiles to screen potential teachers, but economists ignored them; www.ed.gov/news/newsletters/innovator/2004/0223.html.

19. Dale Ballou, "Sizing Up Test Scores," *Education Next*, Summer 2002, 12–13, 15.

20. Dan Goldhaber and Michael Hansen, *Assessing the Potential of Using Value-Added Estimates of Teacher Job Performance for Making Tenure Decisions* (Washington, D.C.: CALDER, Urban Institute, 2008), 1, 5–6.

21. Cory Koedel and Julian R. Betts, "Re-examining the Role of Teacher Quality in the Educational Production Function," Working Paper #2007–03, National Center on Performance Incentives, Vanderbilt University, Nashville, TN, 2007; Helen F. Ladd, "Teacher Effects: What Do We Know?" 2008, www.sesp.northwestern.edu/docs/Ladd_Northwestern_paper_042108.pdf.

22. Brian A. Jacob, Lars Lefgren, and David Sims, "The Persistence of Teacher-Induced Learning Gains," NBER Working Paper 14065, National Bureau of Economic Research, Cambridge, MA, 2008, 30, 33.

23. Jesse Rothstein, "Teacher Quality in Educational Production: Tracking, Decay, and Student Achievement," Princeton University and NBER, Cambridge, MA, 2009, www.princeton.edu/~jrothst/published/rothstein_vam _may152009.pdf; Debra Viadero, "'Value-Added' Gauge of Teaching Probed," *Education Week*, July 15, 2009.

24. Malcolm Gladwell, "Most Likely to Succeed: How Do We Hire When We Can't Tell Who's Right for the Job?" *New Yorker*, December 15, 2008.

25. Nicholas D. Kristof, "Our Greatest National Shame," *New York Times*, February 15, 2009.

26. Teach for America Web site, www.teachforamerica.org/about/our_ history.htm; see also Donna Foote, *Relentless Pursuit: A Year in the Trenches with Teach for America* (New York: Knopf, 2008).

27. Ildiko Laczko-Kerr and David C. Berliner, "The Effectiveness of 'Teach for America' and Other Under-Certified Teachers on Student Academic Achievement: A Case of Harmful Public Policy," *Education Policy Analysis Archives* 10, no. 37 (September 6, 2002).

28. Paul T. Decker, Daniel P. Mayer, and Steven Glazerman, *The Effects of Teach for America on Students: Findings from a National Evaluation* (Princeton, NJ: Mathematica Policy Research, 2004).

29. Linda Darling-Hammond et al., "Does Teacher Preparation Matter? Evidence About Teacher Certification, Teach for America, and Teacher Effectiveness," *Education Policy Analysis Archives* 13, no. 42 (October 12, 2005).

30. Zeyu Xu, Jane Hannaway, and Colin Taylor, *Making a Difference? The Effects of Teach for America in High School* (Washington, D.C.: CALDER, Urban Institute, 2009), 3; Charles T. Clotfelter, Helen F. Ladd, and Jacob L. Vigdor, "Teacher Credentials and Student Achievement in High School: A Cross-Subject Analysis with Student Fixed Effects," NBER Working Paper 13617, National Bureau of Economic Research, Cambridge, MA, 2007.

31. Thomas J. Kane, Jonah E. Rockoff, and Douglas O. Staiger, "Photo Finish: Teacher Certification Doesn't Guarantee a Winner," *Education Next* 7, no. 1 (Winter 2007): 64. See also Kane, Rockoff, and Staiger, "What Does Certification Tell Us About Teacher Effectiveness? Evidence from New York City," NBER Working Paper 12155, National Bureau of Economic Research, Cambridge, MA, 2006.

32. Linda Darling-Hammond et al., "Does Teacher Preparation Matter?" 14; Kane, Rockoff, and Staiger, "What Does Certification Tell Us About Teacher Effectiveness? Evidence from New York City," 34; Donald Boyd et al., "How Changes in Entry Requirements Alter the Teacher Workforce and Affect Student Achievement," *Education Finance and Policy* 1, no. 2 (Spring 2006): 207.

33. Phil Gonring, Paul Teske, and Brad Jupp, *Pay-for-Performance Teacher Compensation: An Inside View of Denver's ProComp Plan* (Cambridge, MA: Harvard Education Press, 2007).

34. Susan Sclafani and Marc S. Tucker, *Teacher and Principal Compensation: An International Review* (Washington, D.C.: Center for American Progress, 2006), 19–21, 42.

CHAPTER TEN

1. In the mid-1960s, the Black Power movement became a political force, demanding black control of institutions located in black communities.

2. For a description of the clash between the Ocean Hill–Brownsville district and the United Federation of Teachers, see Diane Ravitch, *The Great School Wars: New York City, 1805–1973* (New York: Basic Books, 1974), 352–378.

3. Historians continue to debate whether the concerted efforts of Northern philanthropists on behalf of African American children in the South were helpful. Some contend that they colluded with the white leadership to close down private and sectarian black schools and to push black children into public school systems that were controlled by unsympathetic, racist whites. Eric Anderson and Alfred A. Moss Jr., *Dangerous Donations: Northern Philanthropy and Southern Black Education, 1902–1930* (Columbia: University of Missouri Press, 1999).

4. David Halberstam, "The Very Expensive Education of McGeorge Bundy," *Harper's*, July 1969, 21–41; Ravitch, "Foundations: Playing God in the Ghetto," *Center Forum* 3 (May 15, 1969): 24–27.

5. See, for example, Raymond Domanico, Carol Innerst, and Alexander Russo, *Can Philanthropy Fix Our Schools? Appraising Walter Annenberg's $500 Million Gift to Public Education* (Washington, D.C.: Thomas B. Fordham Foundation, 2000), for case studies of New York City, Chicago, and Philadelphia.

6. Domanico et al., *Can Philanthropy Fix Our Schools?*, 28–29; Alyson Klein, "Bush Calls for Resolve on NCLB Renewal," *Education Week*, January 8, 2009.

7. Frederick M. Hess, introduction to *With the Best of Intentions: How Philanthropy Is Reshaping K–12 Education,* ed. Frederick M. Hess (Cambridge, MA: Harvard Education Press, 2005), 4–5.

8. Ibid., 5–6.

9. Ibid., 9–11.

10. The Web site of the Walton Family Foundation, www.waltonfamily foundation.org/aboutus/2007grants.asp.

11. Donald G. McNeil Jr., "Gates Foundation's Influence Criticized," *New York Times*, February 16, 2008.

12. Bill & Melinda Gates Foundation, "All Students Ready for College, Career and Life: Reflections on the Foundation's Education Investments, 2000–2008," September 2008, 3–4, www.gatesfoundation.org/learning/Documents/reflections-foundations-education-investments.pdf.

13. Bill Gates, Prepared Remarks, National Governors Association/Achieve Summit, February 26, 2005, www.nga.org/Files/pdf/es05gates.pdf. See also TED, "Bill Gates on Mosquitos, Malaria and Education," www.ted.com/talks/bill_gates_unplugged.html.

14. American Institutes for Research, *Executive Summary: Evaluation of the Bill & Melinda Gates Foundation's High School Grants, 2001–2004* (Washington, D.C.: AIR, 2005), 8; AIR, *Rigor, Relevance, and Results: The Quality of Teacher Assignments and Student Work in New and Conventional High Schools; Evaluation of the Bill & Melinda Gates Foundation's High School Grants* (Washington, D.C.: American Institutes for Research, 2005), 43, 56; Erik W. Robelen, "Gates High Schools Get Mixed Review in Study," *Education Week*, November 16, 2005.

15. Allison Sherry, "Manual's Slow Death," *Denver Post*, May 7, 2006; Catherine Gewertz, "Failed Breakup of H.S. in Denver Offering Lessons," *Education Week*, March 15, 2006; Colorado Children's Campaign, "Breaking Up is Hard to Do: Lessons Learned from the Experiences of Manual High School," 2005, www.coloradokids.org/includes/downloads/ngupishardtodo. pdf; Jay Greene and William C. Symonds, "Bill Gates Gets Schooled," *BusinessWeek*, June 26, 2006.

16. Gary Lichtenstein, "What Went Wrong at Manual High?" *Education Week*, May 17, 2006.

17. Bob Geballe, "Bill Gates' Guinea Pigs," *Seattle Weekly*, July 20, 2005.

18. Geballe, "Bill Gates' Guinea Pigs"; Mountlake Terrace High School, "Mountlake Terrace High School Profile 2008–2009," www.edmonds.wednet. edu/MTHS/Profile_0809.pdf.

19. Valerie E. Lee and Julia B. Smith, "High School Size: Which Works Best and For Whom?" *Educational Evaluation and Policy Analysis* 19, no. 3 (1997) 205–227.

20. Linda Shaw, "Foundation's Small-Schools Experiment Has Yet to Yield Big Results," *Seattle Times*, November 5, 2006.

21. Valerie E. Lee and Douglas D. Ready, *Schools Within Schools: Possibilities and Pitfalls of High School Reform* (New York: Teachers College Press, 2007), 153–156.

22. Kate N. Grossman, "Small Schools Gain, but Test Scores Don't Show It," *Chicago Sun-Times*, August 3, 2006; Joseph E. Kahne et al., *Small Schools on a Larger Scale: The First Three Years of the Chicago High School Redesign Initiative* (Chicago: Consortium on Chicago School Research, University of Chicago, 2006); Sarah Karp, "Chicago High School Test Scores Stall, Including Those at Transformation Schools," *Catalyst Chicago*, September 15, 2009, www.catalyst-chicago.org/notebook/index.php/entry/379. For a scathing critique of the corporate takeover of the small school movement, see Michael Klonsky and Susan Klonsky, *Small Schools: Public School Reform Meets the Ownership Society* (New York: Routledge, 2008).

23. Greene and Symonds, "Bill Gates Gets Schooled"; New Visions for Public Schools, "New Century High Schools: Evidence of Progress," www.newvisions.org/schools/nchs/evidence.asp.

24. Jennifer L. Jennings and Aaron Pallas, "Who Attends New York City's New Small Schools?" paper, Annual Meeting of the American Educational Research Association, San Diego, California, April 2009. Chicago's Renaissance 2010 plan closed low-performing high schools and replaced them with

new ones, but only 2 percent of the students who had been enrolled in the low-performing schools enrolled in the new ones. See Sarah Karp and John Myers, "Duncan's Track Record," *Catalyst Chicago*, December 15, 2008; see also Marisa de la Torre and Julia Gwynne, *When Schools Close: Effects on Displaced Students in Chicago Public Schools* (Chicago: Consortium on Chicago School Research, University of Chicago, 2009).

25. Clara Hemphill et al., *The New Marketplace: How Small-School Reforms and School Choice Have Reshaped New York City's High Schools* (New York: Center for New York City Affairs, The New School, 2009).

26. Debra Viadero, "Foundation Shifts Tack on Studies: Scholars Say Gates Risks Losing Valuable Findings," *Education Week*, October 25, 2006.

27. Erik W. Robelen, "Gates Learns to Think Big," *Education Week*, October 11, 2006. I was a trustee of the Thomas B. Fordham Foundation and Thomas B. Fordham Institute for many years (I resigned in April 2009); I opposed the foundation's decision to accept Gates's funding for its programs, not because of any doubts about the Gates Foundation, but because I wanted Fordham to remain independent and free to be a critic.

28. Ibid.

29. Ibid.

30. Elizabeth Green, "Gates Foundation Will Steer Its Education Giving in a New Direction, But How Much Impact Will the Billions Have?" *GothamSchools*, November 12, 2008, http://gothamschools.org/2008/11/12/gates-foundation-will-steer-its-education-giving-in-a-new-direction-but-how-much-impact-will-the-billions-have/; AIR, *Evaluation of the Bill & Melinda Gates Foundation's High School Grants Initiative: 2001–2005 Final Report* (Washington, D.C., AIR: 2006), 9; Bill & Melinda Gates Foundation, "All Students Ready for College, Career and Life."

31. Bill Gates, "School Reform That Works," *Washington Post*, January 28, 2009.

32. Philissa Cramer, "Eli Broad Describes Close Ties to Klein, Weingarten, Duncan," *GothamSchools*, March 11, 2009, http://gothamschools.org/2009/03/11/eli-broad-describes-close-ties-to-klein-weingarten-duncan/.

33. Abby Goodnough, "Klein is Said to Be Planning a Strategic Map for Change," *New York Times*, October 3, 2002.

34. Jeanne Allen, foreword to *National Model or Temporary Opportunity? The Oakland Education Reform Story*, by Joe Williams (Washington, D.C.: Center for Education Reform, 2007).

35. Williams, *National Model or Temporary Opportunity?*, 3–4.

36. Ibid., 6–7.

37. Katy Murphy, "Report: Oakland Charters Outshine District Schools," Education Report blog, February 10, 2009, www.ibabuzz.com/education/2009/02/10/report-charter-schools-outshine-district-schools-in-oakland/; California Charter Schools Association, *A Longitudinal Analysis of Charter School Performance in Oakland Unified School District: A District and Neighborhood Matched Comparison Analysis*, January 2009, 9, 28, www.ibabuzz.com/education/wp-content/uploads/2009/02/charter-report-0209.pdf; Oakland Unified

School District, "School Portfolio Management: Comparing Oakland Charter Schools to OUSD District Schools," August 17, 2007, 28, www.weebly.com/uploads/4/1/6/1/41611/spm_charter_schools_08.17.07_v2.pdf; Murphy, "Report: Oakland Charters Outshine District Schools," comment #6.

38. Dan Katzir, "Ten Years of K–12 Lessons Learned and Reform Opportunities in 2009," remarks as prepared for delivery, Democrats for Education Reform event, Denver, Colorado, March 11, 2009.

39. Grants by the Eli and Edythe L. Broad Foundation are listed on the foundation's Form 990, which is filed annually with the Internal Revenue Service. These forms can be found on GuideStar.org. When I had trouble locating the 990 for 2007, the latest available, the foundation generously sent it to me. The Eduwonkette blog at *Education Week* posted the 990 forms for several foundations, including the Broad Foundation, from 2003 to 2005, at http://blogs.edweek.org/edweek/eduwonkette/2008/02/funding_frenzy_1.html.

40. Ibid.

41. David M. Herszenhorn, "Billionaires Start $60 Million Schools Effort," *New York Times*, April 25, 2007.

42. NewSchools Venture Fund, http://newschools.org/.

43. Michael Petrilli, "The Race to the Top: The Carrot That Feels Like a Stick," Flypaper blog, July 23, 2009, www.edexcellence.net/flypaper/index.php/2009/07/the-race-to-the-top-the-carrot-that-feels-like-a-stick/.

44. Fred Hiatt, "How Bill Gates Would Repair Our Schools," *Washington Post*, March 30, 2009; Gates, Speech to the National Conference of State Legislatures, July 21, 2009, www.gatesfoundation.org/speeches-commentary/Pages/bill-gates-2009-conference-state-legislatures.aspx.

45. Andrew J. Rotherham and Richard Whitmire, "Close Underperforming Charter Schools, Reward Those That Work," *U.S. News & World Report*, June 17, 2009.

CHAPTER ELEVEN

1. Ina V. S. Mullis and Michael O. Martin, "TIMSS in Perspective: Lessons Learned from IEA's Four Decades of International Mathematics Assessments," in *Lessons Learned: What International Assessments Tell Us About Math Achievement*, ed. Tom Loveless (Washington, D.C.: Brookings Institution Press, 2007), 35.

2. Deborah Meier, "'Data Informed,' not 'Data Driven,'" Bridging Differences blog, March 5, 2009, http://blogs.edweek.org/edweek/Bridging-Differences/.

3. Common Core, *Why We're Behind: What Top Nations Teach Their Students But We Don't* (Washington, D.C.: Common Core, 2009), www.commoncore.org/_docs/CCreport_whybehind.pdf. Tom Loveless of the Brookings Institution tells me that many low-performing nations also have a balanced curriculum. If so, it is unclear why the United States should be one of the few nations that focuses only on reading and mathematics, showing no concern for other important studies.

4. Jeanne S. Chall, *Learning to Read: The Great Debate* (New York: McGraw-Hill, 1967); Chall, *The Academic Achievement Challenge: What Really Works in the Classroom?* (New York: Guilford Press, 2000). For a concise description of

the parts of speech and their relationship to writing, see University of Ottawa, "Parts of Speech," www.arts.uottawa.ca/writcent/hypergrammar/partsp.html.

5. Carol Jago, *With Rigor for All: Teaching the Classics to Contemporary Students* (Portland, MN: Calendar Islands Publishers, 2000); in *The Language Police*, I compiled (with the help of Rodney Atkinson, an expert elementary school teacher and specialist in children's literature) a list of classics for children. Diane Ravitch, *The Language Police: How Pressure Groups Restrict What Students Learn* (New York: Knopf, 2003), 203–234.

6. Ravitch, *The Language Police*, 162.

7. National Center for Education Statistics, *The Nation's Report Card: U.S. History 2006* (Washington, D.C.: U.S. Department of Education, 2007).

8. See E. D. Hirsch Jr., *The Making of Americans: Democracy and Our Schools* (New Haven, CT: Yale University Press, 2009); Core Knowledge Foundation, *Core Knowledge Sequence: Content Guidelines for Grades K–8* (Charlottesville, VA: Core Knowledge Foundation, 1999), 1–4.

9. To understand how textbooks are shaped by pressure groups in these two key states, see Ravitch, *The Language Police*.

10. Massachusetts Department of Elementary and Secondary Education, "TIMSS Results Place Massachusetts Among World Leaders in Math and Science," press release, December 9, 2008, www.doe.mass.edu/news/news.asp?id=4457.

11. William H. Schmidt, statement for U.S. TIMSS, Michigan State University, College of Education, December 2008, http://ustimss.msu.edu/mnpresre.html.

12. Betty Hart and Todd R. Risley, "The Early Catastrophe: The 30 Million Word Gap by Age 3," *American Educator*, Spring 2003. See also Hart and Risley, *Meaningful Differences in the Everyday Experience of Young American Children* (Baltimore: Brookes, 1995).

EPILOGUE

1. U.S. Department of Education, "Duncan Says 82 Percent of America's Schools Could 'Fail' Under NCLB This Year," March 9, 2011, www.ed.gov/news/press-releases/duncan-says-82-percent-americas-schools-could-fail-under-nclb-year.

2. Jennifer D. Jordan and Linda Borg, "Central Falls to Fire Every High School Teacher," *Providence Journal*, February 13, 2010.

3. Jennifer D. Jordan, "Every Central Falls Teacher Fired, Labor Outraged," *Providence Journal*, February 24, 2010; Diane Ravitch, "First, Let's Fire All the Teachers!" *Huffington Post*, March 2, 2010.

4. Stephen Beale, "Central Falls Teachers Vote No Confidence in Gallo," *Providence Journal*, May 24, 2011; Dana Goldstein, "Report from Central Falls, RI: How Do You Change a School's 'Culture'"? www.danagoldstein.net/dana_goldstein/2011/03/report-from-central-falls-ri-how-do-you-change-a-schools-culture.html; Claudio Sanchez, "Changes at R.I. School Fail to Produce Results," National Public Radio, June 13, 2011, www.npr.org/2011/06/13/137116333/central-falls.

5. Evan Thomas and Pat Wingert, "Why We Must Fire Bad Teachers," *Newsweek*, March 6, 2010.

6. Diane Ravitch, *National Standards in American Education: A Citizen's Guide* (Washington, DC: Brookings Institution Press, 1995), pp. 84–86.

7. Thomas and Wingert, "Why We Must Fire Bad Teachers."

8. Nick Anderson, "Education Secretary Duncan Calls Hurricane Katrina Good for New Orleans Schools," *Washington Post*, January 30, 2010.

9. Richard Rothstein, "Fact-Challenged Policy," Economic Policy Institute, March 8, 2011; Paul E. Barton and Richard J. Coley, *The Black-White Achievement Gap: When Progress Stopped* (Princeton, NJ: Educational Testing Service, 2010).

10. For more on the crisis of the 1950s, see Diane Ravitch, *The Troubled Crusade: American Education, 1945–1980* (New York: Basic Books, 1983); and *Left Back: A Century of Battles Over School Reform* (New York: Simon & Schuster, 2000).

11. Elliott A. Medrich, *International Mathematics and Science Assessment: What Have We Learned?* (Washington, DC: National Center for Education Statistics, 1992), p. 29, http://nces.ed.gov/pubs92/92011.pdf. See also Yong Zhao, "'It Makes No Sense': Puzzling Over Obama's State of the Union Speech," January 30, 2011, http://zhaolearning.com/2011/01/30/"it-makes-no-sense"-puzzling-over-obama's-state-of-the-union-speech.

12. Lisa Lambert, "Half of Teachers Quit in Five Years," *Washington Post*, May 9, 2006.

13. Juan Diego Alonso and Richard Rothstein, "Where Has the Money Been Going? A Preliminary Update," Economic Policy Institute Briefing Paper #281, October 28, 2010, Table XI, p. 9.

14. Matthew Di Carlo, "Teachers Matter, but So Do Words," Shanker Blog, July 14, 2010; Matthew Di Carlo, "Teacher Quality on the Red Carpet; Accuracy Swept Under the Rug," Shanker Blog, September 16, 2010; Richard Rothstein, "How to Fix Our Schools," Economic Policy Institute, issue brief #286, October 14, 2010.

15. Sharon Otterman, "Lauded Harlem Schools Have Their Own Problems," *New York Times*, October 12, 2010; Paul Tough, *Whatever It Takes: Geoffrey Canada's Quest to Change Harlem and America* (New York: Houghton Mifflin: 2008), pp. 236–246. See also Diane Ravitch, "The Myth of Charter Schools," *New York Review of Books*, November 11, 2010.

16. Edward L. Deci and Richard Flaste, *Why We Do What We Do: Understanding Self-Motivation* (New York: Penguin, 1996); Dan Ariely, *Predictably Irrational: The Hidden Forces That Shape Our Decisions* (New York: Harper Perennial, 2010); Daniel H. Pink, *Drive: The Surprising Truth About What Motivates Us* (New York: Penguin, 2009).

17. "Searching for Equity," *Catalyst*, Summer 2010; Marisa de la Torre and Julia Gwynne, *When Schools Close: Effects on Displaced Students in Chicago Public Schools* (Chicago: Consortium on Chicago School Research, 2009); Nick Anderson, "Stronger Measures Applied to Struggling Schools; To Get Federal Funds, Reform Efforts Include Replacing Principal, Staff," *Washington Post*, December 28, 2009; "Test Data Help Cloud Duncan's Legacy as

Chicago's Schools Chief," *Washington Post*, December 29, 2010. The national media paid little attention to Renaissance 2010 in Chicago (Nick Anderson of the *Washington Post* being an honorable exception).

18. Sam Dillon and Tamar Lewin, "Education Chief Vies to Expand U.S. Role as Partner on Local Schools," *New York Times*, May 3, 2010.

19. Valerie Strauss, "Civil Rights Groups Skewer Obama Education Policy," The Answer Sheet, *Washington Post*, July 26, 2010.

20. "Framework for Providing All Students an Opportunity to Learn Through Reauthorization of the Elementary and Secondary Education Act," July 26, 2010, http://naacpldf.org/files/case_issue/Framework%20for%20Providing%20All%20Students%20an%20Opportunity%20to%20Learn%202.pdf.

21. Jennifer Medina, "State's Exams Became Easier to Pass, Education Officials Say," *New York Times*, July 19, 2010.

22. Sharon Otterman and Robert Gebeloff, "When 81% Passing Suddenly Becomes 18%," *New York Times*, August 1, 2010.

23. Sharon Otterman and Robert Gebeloff, "Triumph Fades on Racial Gap in City Schools," *New York Times*, August 15, 2010.

24. Michael Goodwin, "Bad Sign for Fading Black," *New York Post*, March 20, 2011, www.nypost.com/p/news/local/bad_sign_for_fading_black_aD28186AEWtKRBA4POft2H#ixzz1H9Yt9RCR; Diane Ravitch, "The Education of Lord Bloomberg," *New York Review of Books*, April 11, 2011.

25. Anna M. Phillips and Robert Gebeloff, "In Data, 'A' Schools Leave Many Not Ready for CUNY," *New York Times*, June 22, 2011; Sharon Otterman, "Most New York Students Are Not College-Ready," *New York Times*, February 7, 2011.

26. Jack Gillum and Marisol Bello, "When Standardized Test Scores Soared in DC, Were the Gains Real?" *USA Today*, March 30, 2011.

27. Bill Turque, "Ex-Noyes Principal Wayne Ryan Resigns," *Washington Post*, June 20, 2011; Nick Anderson, "Scores Fall for Some D.C. Schools amid Test Security Questions," *Washington Post*, August 2, 2011.

28. Kim Severson, "Systematic Cheating Is Found in Atlanta's School System," *New York Times*, July 5, 2011; Michael Winerip, "Cracking a System in Which Test Scores Were for Changing," *New York Times*, July 17, 2011.

29. Alan Judd, "Major Execs Invested in Hall," *Atlanta Journal-Constitution*, July 17, 2011; Maureen Downey, "Following 'Pass or Perish' Path in Education, We've Lost Our Way," *Atlanta Journal-Constitution*, July 13, 2011.

30. Yong Zhao, "Ditch Testing: Lessons from the Cheating Scandal in Atlanta," July 14, 2011. See all four parts of this series of posts.

31. Aaron Marshall, "House-Senate Budget Committee Faces Major Questions on Charter Schools," *Cleveland Plain Dealer*, June 20, 2011. Tracie Mauriello, "Corbett's Team Jingles with Donors," *Pittsburgh Post-Gazette*, December 10, 2010.

32. Juan Gonzalez, "Albany Charter Cash Cow: Big Banks Making a Bundle on New Construction as Schools Bear the Cost," *New York Daily News*, May 7, 2010.

33. Joy Resmovits, "Detroit Charter High Schools Underperform Public Counterparts, Analysis Shows," Huffington Post, July 8, 2011; Rebecca Vevea, "Tests Raise Questions About Extending Days," New York Times, July 1, 2011; "FCAT Results: Charter Schools Have High Failure Rates," CBS Local News, Miami, July 5, 2011, http://miami.cbslocal .com/2011/07/05/fcat-results-show-charter-schools-failure-rate-much-worse -than-public-schools; Howard Blume and Sandra Poindexter, "L.A. Unified Bests Reform Groups in Most Cases," Los Angeles Times, August 18, 2011.

34. Bruce Baker and Richard Ferris, Adding Up the Spending: Fiscal Disparities and Philanthropy Among New York City Charter Schools (Boulder, CO: National Education Policy Center, 2011).

35. Philip Gleason et al., The Evaluation of Charter School Impacts (Washington, DC: U.S. Department of Education, 2010), www.mathematica-mpr .com/publications/pdfs/education/charter_school_impacts.pdf; Diane Ravitch, "Obama and Duncan Are Wrong About Charters," Bridging Differences blog, Education Week, November 16, 2009.

36. Matthew G. Springer, Dale Ballou, et al., Teacher Pay for Performance: Experimental Evidence from the Project on Incentives in Teaching (Nashville, TN: National Center on Performance Incentives, 2010), www.performance incentives.org/data/files/gallery/ContentGallery/POINT_Report_Executive _Summary.pdf.

37. Sharon Otterman, "New York City Abandons Teacher Bonus Program," New York Times, July 17, 2011; Jennifer Medina, "Cash Offers Not Enough to Improve Student Test Scores," New York Times, April 8, 2010.

38. Erin Richards and Amy Hetzner, "Choice Schools Not Outperforming MPS: Latest Tests Show Voucher Scores About Same or Worse in Math and Reading," Milwaukee Journal Sentinel, March 29, 2011; Erin Richards, "Voucher Testing Data Takes a New Twist: Voucher, MPS Kids on Par, Study Finds," Milwaukee Journal Sentinel, March 30, 2011.

39. National Center for Education Statistics, The Nation's Report Card: Trial Urban District Assessment: Reading 2009 (NCES 2010–459), Institute of Education Sciences, U.S. Department of Education, Washington, D.C., pp. 64–65; National Center for Education Statistics, The Nation's Report Card: Trial Urban District Assessment: Mathematics 2009 (NCES 2010–452), Institute of Education Sciences, U.S. Department of Education, Washington, D.C., pp. 60–61; National Center for Education Statistics, The Nation's Report Card: Reading 2009 (NCES 2010–458), pp. 52, 64; National Center for Education Statistics, The Nation's Report Card: Mathematics 2009 (NCES 2010–451), pp. 51, 60. "School Vouchers Under the Microscope: Do They Really Improve Student Achievement?" Huffington Post, April 1, 2011, www.huffingtonpost .com/2011/04/01/school-vouchers-education-reform_n_843861.html; "Fix the Flaw First," Milwaukee Journal Sentinel, March 7, 2011; Matthew DeFour, "DPI: Students in Milwaukee Voucher Program Didn't Perform Better in State Tests," Wisconsin State Journal, March 29, 2011.

40. Eric A. Hanushek, "Teacher Deselection," in Creating a New Teaching Profession, ed. Dan Goldhaber and Jane Hannaway (Washington, DC: Urban Institute, 2009), www.stanfordalumni.org/leadingmatters/san_francisco/

documents/Teacher_Deselection-Hanushek.pdf; see also Matthew Di Carlo, "Will Firing 5–10 Percent of Teachers Make Us Finland?" Answer Sheet blog, *Washington Post*, December 18, 2010.

41. Eva L. Baker, Paul E. Barton, Linda Darling-Hammond, Edward Haertel, Helen F. Ladd, Robert L. Linn, Diane Ravitch, Richard Rothstein, Richard J. Shavelson, and Lorrie A. Shepard, *Problems with the Use of Student Test Scores to Evaluate Teachers* (Washington, DC: Economic Policy Institute, 2010).

42. Sean Corcoran, *Can Teachers Be Evaluated by Their Students' Test Scores? Should They Be? The Use of Value-Added Measures in Policy and Practice* (New York City: Annenberg Institute for School Reform, 2010).

43. Ibid.

44. Michael Winerip, "Evaluating New York Teachers, Perhaps the Numbers Do Lie," *New York Times*, March 7, 2011.

45. "Los Angeles Teacher Ratings: FAQ & About," *Los Angeles Times*, http://projects.latimes.com/value-added/faq.

46. Jason Felch, Jason Song, and Doug Smith, "Who's Teaching L.A.'s Kids?" *Los Angeles Times*, August 14, 2010.

47. Larry Abramson, "'L.A. Times' Teacher Ratings Database Stirs Debate," National Public Radio, August 27, 2010, www.npr.org/templates/story/story.php?storyId=129456212; Dan Goldhaber, "Getting Ahead of the Teacher-Accountability Curve," *Seattle Times*, August 29, 2010. After this book was completed, I received an e-mail on August 26, 2011, from economist Thomas Kane, who advises the Gates Foundation. He told me he opposes public release of individual value-added ratings, "to preserve some minimal level of privacy in the supervisor-employee relationship, to maintain some space for teachers to brainstorm with their peers and their supervisors about ways to improve." Quoted with permission.

48. Jason Felch and Jason Song, "U.S. Schools Chief Endorses Release of Teacher Data," *Los Angeles Times*, August 16, 2010.

49. Peter Z. Schochet and Hanley S. Chiang, *Error Rates in Measuring Teacher and School Performance Based on Student Test Score Gains* (Washington, DC: Institute of Education Sciences, National Center on Education Evaluation and Regional Assistance, 2010), http://ies.ed.gov/ncee/pubs/20104004/pdf/20104004.pdf, pp. 35–36.

50. Derek C. Briggs and Ben Domingue, Due Diligence and the Evaluation of Teachers (Boulder, CO: National Education Policy Center, 2010); "*Times* Responds to Criticism of Teacher Analysis," *Los Angeles Times*, February 14, 2011; Nick Anderson, "Researchers Fault *L.A. Times* Methods in Analysis of California Teachers," *Washington Post*, February 8, 2011; Frederick Hess, "LAT on Teacher Value-Added: A Disheartening Replay," Frederick Hess, Straight Up, *Education Week*, August 17, 2010; Frederick Hess, "My Take on the *LA Times* Reanalysis," *Education Next*, February 11, 2011.

51. Matthew Di Carlo, "Value-Added: Theory Vs. Practice," Shanker Blog, February 18, 2011, http://shankerblog.org/?p=1928.

52. John Ewing, "Mathematical Intimidation: Driven by the Data," *Notices of the American Mathematical Society* 58, no. 5 (May 2011): 671.

53. Bill Gates, "How Teacher Development Could Revolutionize Our Schools," *Washington Post*, February 28, 2011; Arne Duncan, "The New Normal: Doing More With Less," American Enterprise Institute, November 17, 2010, www.aei.org/docLib/20101117-Arne-Duncan-Remarks.pdf.

54. Christina A. Samuels, "Critics Target Growing Army of Broad Leaders," *Education Week*, June 8, 2011. See also Parents Across America, "A Guide to the Broad Foundation's Training Programs and Policies."

55. Daniel Golden, "Bill Gates' School Crusade," *Bloomberg Business Week*, July 15, 2010.

56. Sam Dillon, "Behind Grass-Roots School Advocacy, Bill Gates," *New York Times*, May 21, 2011.

57. Joanne Barkan, "Got Dough? How Billionaires Rule Our Schools," *Dissent*, Winter 2011.

58. Nancy Hass, "Scholarly Investments," *New York Times*, December 4, 2009; Trip Gabriel and Jennifer Medina, "Charter Schools' New Cheerleaders: Financiers," *New York Times*, May 9, 2010. For origins of DFER, see Steven Brill, *Class Warfare: Inside the Fight to Fix America's Schools* (New York: Simon & Schuster, 2011).

59. Michael Hout and Stuart W. Elliott, eds., *Incentives and Test-Based Accountability* (Washington, DC: National Academies Press, 2011).

60. Marc S. Tucker, *Standing on the Shoulders of Giants: An American Agenda for Education Reform* (Washington, DC: National Center on Education and the Economy, 2011), pp. 3, 7–8.

61. Anna Phillips, "Murdoch Buys Education Tech Company Wireless Generation," Gotham Schools, November 22, 2010.

62. Kathleen K. Wiegner, "Stumbling into the Computer Age," *Forbes*, August 13, 1984, pp. 35–40; James W. Michaels, "The Stories Behind the Story," *Forbes*, August 27, 1984, pp. 4, 156.

63. W. E. B. Du Bois, "Curriculum Revision," address to Georgia State Teachers Convention, April 12, 1935, Du Bois Papers, Park Johnson Archives, Fisk University, quoted in Kenneth James King, *Pan-Africanism and Education: A Study of Race Philanthropy and Education in the Southern States of America and East Africa* (New York: Oxford University Press, 1971), p. 257.

64. *2010 College-Bound Seniors: Total Group Profile Report* (New York: College Board, 2010), http://professionals.collegeboard.com/profdownload/2010-total-group-profile-report-cbs.pdf, table 11, p. 4.

65. H. L. Fleischman, P. J. Hopstock, M. P. Pelczar, and B. E. Shelley, *Highlights from PISA 2009: Performance of U.S. 15-Year-Old Students in Reading, Mathematics, and Science Literacy in an International Context* (Washington, DC: National Center for Education Statistics, 2010), pp. 9, 16.

Index

DIANE RAVITCH is Research Professor of Education at New York University. From 1991 to 1993, she was Assistant Secretary of Education and Counselor to Secretary of Education Lamar Alexander in the administration of President George H.W. Bush. President Clinton appointed her to the National Assessment Governing Board, which oversees federal testing. She is the author or editor of over twenty books, including *The Language Police* and *Left Back*, and her articles have appeared in numerous newspapers and magazines. In 2011, she was awarded the Daniel Patrick Moynihan Prize by the American Academy of Political and Social Sciences for her careful use of social science research to advance the public good. A native of Houston, Ravitch graduated from the Houston public schools, Wellesley College, and Columbia University. She lives in Brooklyn, New York.

AWARDS
The National Education Association's Friend of Education Award

The Charles W. Eliot Award from the
New England Association of Schools and Colleges

The Outstanding Friend of Education Award from the Horace Mann League

The American Education Award from the
American Association of School Administrators

The Distinguished Service Award from the
National Association of Secondary School Principals

The Distinguished Alumni Award from
Teachers College at Columbia University

The Daniel Patrick Moynihan Prize of the
American Academy of Political and Social Science

Outstanding Book in Education from the
American Association for Teaching and Curriculum